THE MINHAGIM

מנהגים

THE MINHAGIM

The Customs and Ceremonies of Judaism, Their Origins and Rationale

by

ABRAHAM CHILL

SEPHER-HERMON PRESS
New York

THE MINHAGIM

Published by Sepher-Hermon Press, Inc.

LC No. 78-62153
ISBN 0-87203-076-8 (hardcover)
ISBN 0-87203-077-6 (paperback)

5th Printing, 1989

In the everlasting memory
of my beloved parents

משה חיים ב״ר צבי עקיבא ז״ל
נפ׳ תשעה באב, תשכ״ב

August 9, 1962

רות בת ישראל משה ז״ל
נפ׳ י״ט באב, תשל״ג

August 17, 1973

הנאהבים והנעימים בחייהם
ובמותם לא נפרדו
תנצב״ה

FOREWORD

Jewish practice is an intricately woven texture of law and custom. While the law tends to be fixed in such way that local variations are minimal, patterns of custom are rich in their diversity. The exact legal status of *minhag*, i.e. custom, is not always clear. In some cases it is treated as no more than popular practice, which should be respected, but is not authoritative and binding. In other cases local custom has been hallowed by long usage and is viewed as essential to proper Jewish religious observance. There are even the extreme cases in which custom overrides and supersedes the law itself. The popular Yiddish epigram to the effect that *minhag* nullifies law is based (knowingly or unknowingly) on a statement exactly to that effect in the Palestinian Talmud (cf., *Baba Mezia*, Ch. VII, Halacha 1).

While the official instances in which the law bows to local custom are relatively few and are restricted to rather specifically defined areas, respect for custom is deeply rooted in Jewish religious life. *Minhag* is folkway, but it is more than just folkway. Established custom is seen, in some instances, as a source of law embodied in the practice of the people. If the original legal basis of the practice has been lost to us, the *minhag* still preserves a correct pattern of practice. Even when we are dealing with pure custom, the practices of established Jewish communities express deeply felt and authentic Jewish values. This is implied in the rabbinic recommendation that when we are uncertain about the law we should seek guidance from the established practice of the people, "*Puk ḥazi mai amma devar.*"

While variations of local *minhag* can be discerned, to some extent, in various areas of Jewish practice (including matters involving commercial transactions), it is most prominent in *rites du passage.* In every culture, including our own, such critical occasions as birth, puberty, marriage and death evoke from the people elaborate patterns of fixed and ritualized customary behavior. In Judaism, these often involve a complex combination of universally recognized law and widely varying local *minhag*. No Jew can approach such occasions with the pure law as his only guide. The ways in which we celebrate a birth or a *berit milah*, the manner in which we arrange the details of a wedding, are incomplete and unsatisfying without the rich and expressive motifs which local customs introduce. Knowledge and understanding of these customs is indispensable for those who want to live a full and satisfying Jewish life.

As Jewish communities have disintegrated over the centuries in various places, their customs have been totally lost or else survive only as historical memories. Scholars may continue to study and investigate them; but their original power which lent striking color and special meaning to great Jewish occasions no longer functions effectively in our lives. Even among those Jewish communities whose history has not been interrupted, we have the growing phenomenon of generations that have lost their direct connection with the ways of their ancestors. All too often Jewish ceremonies today are planned with the advice of a standard book of contemporary etiquette rather than in accordance with the customs and traditions of our fathers. Even when they satisfy the standards of pure Jewish legal propriety, they are impoverished by the absence of the atmosphere and tonal quality of a true Jewish ceremony. This melancholy fact characterizes much of contemporary Jewish practice, especially in America and Western Europe.

Rabbi Abraham Chill has done a great service to all who seek an introduction to the range and richness of *minhagim* in the major areas of Jewish life. In his book he has explored with great care the customs of the various communities, and he has set them forth in a form which will be readily understood by every intelligent reader. His work is a contribution to all who seek a basic understanding of the varieties of Jewish *minhagim*. It is equally valuable for the important practical guidance that it offers to sincere Jews who would like to include in their ceremonial life not only the spare purity of the law, but also the beautiful poetry and art of ancestral Jewish custom.

Marvin Fox
Brandeis University
Waltham, Massachusetts

PREFACE

Endless hours of mental and physical effort were exacted from the author before this volume could be put into the hands of the publisher. The vast amount of research, thinking, planning and re-thinking of the subject matter was taxing.

However, the author acknowledges the fact that without the assistance of others this project would have been more difficult to accomplish.

I wish to record gratefully the literary help that I received from Rabbi Leonard Oschry whose gift for lucid and succinct phraseology immeasurably helped in the styling; to Rabbi Aaron Rakefet for his part in checking out all the sources and references; to Mr. Samuel Gross, the publisher, who has insisted that this volume be as all-inclusive as possible and whose personal interest, devotion and dedication to the progress and development of this book were a source of inspiration to the author.

Above all, I acknowledge the inestimable assistance that I received from my very talented wife, Libbie, who over a long period of time exhibited the greatest of patience and indulgence in taking dictation in longhand, typing, correcting and retyping the manuscript. This assistance may have been of a mechanical nature but to the author it was of prime value.

Unbeknown to them, my children and grandchildren served as a driving force that did not permit me to rest until the book was completed.

To all, I am humbly and truly grateful.

Abraham Chill

8 Ellul, 5738
September 10, 1978

CONTENTS

the New Moon in the synagogue/*Erev Rosh Ḥodesh* as *Yom Kippur Katan*/*Rosh Ḥodesh* as women's holiday—the reasons/Half-*Hallel*, Torah reading and *Musaf* on *Rosh Ḥodesh*/Why half-*Hallel*/*Hallel* on *Rosh Ḥodesh* mitzvah or *minhag*/Allusion to the extra month in a leap year/Reappearance of the moon as sign of atonement/*Kiddush Levannah*, its symbolism/Concluding with the *Alenu* prayer—the reason.

forming the mitzvah/The ritual of waving of the Four Species and its reasons/*Simhat Bet ha-Sho'evah* and *Nisukh ha-Mayim/Hosha'na Rabba*, the name and the importance/The ritual of circling the *Bimah* seven times—the reasons/Why we flail the *aravot/Shemini Atzeret*, a separate holiday, in the Torah and the Midrash/*Simhat Torah* and its highlights/*Hakafot/Aliyah* for every man/*Kol ha-ne'arim*/Completion of the Torah and beginning it anew/*Hatan Torah* and *Hatan Bereshit*.

the *ḥuppah* first—the source/Why the bride circles the groom/The
Tenaim prior to the wedding/The Benediction of Betrothal (*Birkhat
Erusin*)/The act of betrothal/The witnesses/Betrothal by ring—the
reasons/Reading of the *Ketubah*/The Seven Benedictions of Marriage
(*Birkhat Nissuin*)/Breaking of a glass—the reasons/Why the groom
wears a *kittel* under the *ḥuppah*/Some yemenite marriage customs/
Seven days of marriage celebration—Biblical precedents/The *Sheva
Berakhot*—difference between Ashkenazim and Sephardim/Some unique
wedding customs/Why the bride presents the groom with a *tallit*/ Why a
benediction is not recited over the mitzvah of getting married.

of putting on *tefillin* and being called up to the Torah/The *Barukh shepetarani* blessing and its origin/The tradition of delivering a Talmudic discourse in conjunction with a festive meal/Reading of the Haftorah and acting as *sheliaḥ tzibbur*/Practicing the mitzvah of *tefillin* before becoming *bar mitzvah.*

27. DEATH AND MOURNING 319

Fundamental principles of Judaism concerning death/Why cremation and burial in a vault are not permitted/*Lo'eg la-rash*/Sanctity of the soul/Washing hands upon leaving a cemetery/Closing the eyes of the deceased/The dead body is covered and placed on the ground—the reasons/Why candles are lit beside the body/The custom of pouring out water in front of the house of the deceased—the reasons/The *Ḥevrah Kadisha*—its function and name/Why we dress the dead in white linen shrouds/The custom of wrapping the body of a man in a *tallit*/The ritual of *keriah*—its source and procedure/Burying the dead on the day of death—Biblical sources and mystical reasons/Interring the body in the ground—the Biblical source/Burial in a casket or without/Why jewelry is removed from the dead before burial/Why we stop seven times when carrying the body to the grave/Placing the body in the grave with the head towards the west and the feet toward the east—the reason/Filling in the grave—its customs and their reasons/Placing the hands on the casket—its symbolism/The *Shurah*/The custom of tearing up grass and throwing it over the shoulder when leaving the cemetery—the reasons/Why we don't dry our hands after washing them when leaving the cemetery/In Jerusalem sons don't follow the father's bier to the cemetery—the kabbalistic reason/What happens when the parent of a bride or bridegroom dies on the day of the wedding/The *Seudat Havra'ah*—why the first meal of the mourner is provided by neighbors/Eggs as a symbol of mourning/The four periods of mourning: *Aninut*, *Shiv'ah*, *Sheloshim*, the Twelve Months—their sources and prohibitions/Why the mirrors are covered during the *Shiv'ah*/Why the major holidays abrogate the mourning periods/When is a widow or widower permitted to remarry/The *Kaddish*—its source and purpose/Why the Kaddish is recited for eleven months only/Why the *Kaddish* is in Aramaic/Oriental mourning customs/Erecting a monument—its source and purpose/The *Yahrzeit*—its observances/The *Yahrzeit* in the Kabbalah: the *Hillula*/ *Yizkor*/Why those whose parents are living leave the synagogue during *Yizkor*/Immortality of the soul, resurrection of the dead and the future redemption of Israel.

INTRODUCTION

To live Jewishly is to weave an elaborate and intricate pattern for which the main guidelines are drawn by the Torah. The observance of the mitzvot is predicated on the Jew's recognition that above him is One God, Who, while transcending all human experience, is nevertheless concerned with man's actions and Who has ordained an ideal life-style for His people.

In themselves, however, these main guidelines are not enough. They are, after all, laws imposed upon the Jewish people, albeit for their own benefit, by an uncompromising Authority— God. The people had no voice in framing them. Though they may have adopted the code voluntarily by exclaiming: *"Na'aseh ve nishma"*[1] "We will do and obey," our Rabbis are quick to add that God inverted the mountain and held it above their heads like an upturned bowl, from beneath which, unless they agreed to accept His laws, they would never emerge alive.[2] However this may be, the pattern of Jewish life is completed by a fascinating network of *minhagim*, which have evolved throughout the ages, often varying from place to place, but which are all inspired by faith and devotion and, as will presently be seen, can have the force of law.

The word *minhag* is derived from the root *nahog*, meaning "to lead." By means of these practices the spiritual leaders of former times, in various communities throughout the world, aimed to preserve the folk-thinking, conscience and character of the community. The people for their part were willingly led to adopt such practices, which expressed their instinctive urge and symbolized their individual feelings of devotion and loyalty to the traditional Jewish way of life. The *minhag* was the vehicle by which the Jew demonstrated his devotion to God in a manner wholly spontaneous and embracing something of his own personality. It follows that the English language has no exact equivalent for the word *minhag*, which denotes a time-hallowed, authorized practice, often based demonstrably on biblical or Rabbinic law but nowhere expressly enacted as such. For the purposes of translation "custom," though inadequate, must suffice. "*Minhag* can supersede halakhah," says a well-known passage in the Jerusalem Talmud,[3] while Tosafot to the Babylonian Talmud[4] put the same idea in a slightly different form—"the *minhag* of our fathers is Torah" (i.e., as valid and binding as

Torah). From this R. Moses Isserles draws the practical conclusion: "No man may deviate from the *minhag* of his city."[5]

The *Sefer ha-Mat'amim*,[6] quoting *Ḥomot Yesharim*, distinguishes between three types of *minhagim*, viz. (1) those which serve as a "fence around the law"[7]—a safeguard against inadvertent violation of the Torah; (2) those which stimulate the awareness of the Jew, who, without them, might become submerged in materialism, lethargy or indifference, and (3) those which express the Jew's love of the *mitzvot* by embellishing them with additional observances (*hiddur mitzvah*). Decorating the basket of *bikkurim* (first fruits) and gilding the horns of the sacrificial ox in ancient times are typical examples of this last category. Modern instances might be the singing of *zemirot* (table hymns) on Shabbat, covering the *ḥallot* with a handsomely embroidered *mappah* instead of a plain white cloth, and attaching a silver *atarah* to the border of one's *tallit*.

Jewish communities in the Diaspora, exposed to alien influences and conscious of their minority status, reacted to their environment in one of two ways. Either they adapted themselves to the gentile majority and borrowed some of its social mores: rabbis and cantors wore clerical robes in imitation of the Christian clergy (photographs show even some leaders of the nineteenth-century German orthodoxy wearing the white linen bands (*Beffchen*) which characterized the Lutheran pastorate); a bride was accompanied by bridesmaids in the synagogue, as in the church; after circumcision, as after baptism, the infant might be presented by his "godfather" with a silver chalice. Or else there was a deliberate, conscious reaction against the prevailing custom, such as the Jewish tendency to cover the head during prayer and religious study and hence to avoid "*gillui rosh*" (bareheadedness) at all times: non-Jews, when entering their houses of worship, remove their hats as a mark of respect and solemnity; for this very reason the Jew keeps his hat on. It is not quite certain in which category we should place the long caftan and fur-trimmed hat (*shtreimel*) which have long been the traditional garb of East-European Jews. Formerly worn by the upper classes of gentile society, they were later adopted by the Jews as their Sabbath and festival dress.[8]

It is an inevitable consequence of the dispersion of Jewry that there should be vast local diversity in *minhagim*. The impact of the favorable or unfavorable relations between Jew and gentile and between synagogue and church resulted in the formulation of certain *minhagim*; often, if a community adopted a *minhag* which the local rabbi viewed as reflecting Christian thought or practice, he invoked the injunction of "*uve-ḥukotehem lo telekhu*," "and you shall not walk in their statutes."[9]

In order to fully evaluate the importance of *minhag* in Jewish life one must consider also the role of the *ḥumra*. A *ḥumra* is a rule whereby the Jew's life, already disciplined within the confines of the *halakhah*, is yet further restricted. In such matters as these the Sefardim follow the rules laid down by the Bet Yoseph (R. Joseph Caro, compiler of the Shulḥan Arukh), while the Ashkenazim follow the ReMA (R. Moses Isserles). A *minhag* which has been adopted and approved by the local rabbinate has the force of a *neder* (vow), i.e., the residents who are subject to the jurisdiction of that rabbinate must observe it as if they had personally and voluntarily undertaken to do so.

Problems can arise when the Jews of different local origins settle in the same city. In a famous Talmudical passage[10] the Scriptural words *lo titgodedu*,[11] originally translated "you shall not cut yourselves," are interpreted as if derived from *gedud* (a group, party), to mean "you shall not make separate groups," forbidding the establishment of separate lawcourts in the same city, one deciding cases according to Bet Hillel and the other according to Bet Shammai. Maimonides[12] lays down this principle as an absolute prohibition. To quote R. Yehiel Michel Tukatzinsky, the Jewish people should be "one nation having one place of prayer, one heart and one way of fearing God."[13]

An exception to this principle are the edicts (*gezerot*) promulgated by spiritual leaders of former times. These decrees once adopted, become obligatory only upon those Jews for whom they were originally intended—for example, some are binding only upon Ashkenazim, others only upon Sefardim. There is an important difference between such an "official" *gezerah* and a *ḥumra* associated with a particular community, the former being more stringent in its application. Examples are: (1) the prohibition of eating legumes on Passover, which is binding only upon Ashkenazim; (2) the prohibition of polygamy, a *gezerah* of Rabbenu Gershom, who proclaimed for the Ashkenazim a *ḥerem* (ban) on anyone who should disobey it; this ban was due to expire at the end of the year 5000, but was prolonged indefintely; (3) the prohibition under all circumstances of the levirate marriage (*yibbum*)[14] in apparent contravention of the law of the Torah, thus making the alternative of *ḥalitzah* mandatory; this rule, too, is observed only by the Ashkenazim but has not been adopted by the Sefardim.

The widespread custom of "knocking" every time Haman's name is pronounced during the public reading of the Megillah on Purim is based on the Scriptural injunction to "blot out the remembrance of Amalek."[15] R. Abraham Isaac Sperling, the author of *Ta'amei ha-Minhagim*,[15] warns against discontinuing or even ridiculing this practice, although one may find it unbecoming to the dignity of the synagogue or contrary to the spirit of the modern age.

This same authority, in discussing the concept of "*minhag* supersedes *halakhah*," qualifies it by stating that it applies only to ancient, well-founded *minhagim*, not to such as have arisen through some error and lack any basis of authority.

In compiling this volume no attempt has been made to include such local customs as are either inexplicable or can be clearly traced to non-Jewish origins.

In addition to the self-imposed limitations, this book will no doubt be found to suffer also from inadvertant omissions and errors. Nevertheless it is, within its scope, a pioneering effort in the English language designed to fill, however inadequately, a regrettable gap in our religious literature. The author of *Ḥayyei Avraham*,[17] quoting from Mishnah *Avot*,[18] "You are not obliged to complete the work, but neither are you free to desist from it," writes: "Whoever acts from compulsion is neither to be praised nor blamed. You are commanded to perform a Divinely ordained task. Whether your contribution be great or small, your intention must be to carry out your Heaven-imposed task: put forth your hand and write. Do not refrain from acting while you have the strength nor delay until 'evil days'[19] (old age) come upon you." Impelled by such thoughts as these, I have compiled this volume. I do not pretend to have written the last, or even penultimate word on the *minhagim*. It is, however, my hope and prayer that this work may serve to spread an understanding and appreciation of our precious heritage and thus promote the spiritual regeneration of our people in English-speaking lands.

SOURCES

1. Exodus 24:7
2. B. Shabbat 88a: This teaches us that the Holy One, blessed be He, overturned the mountain like a bowl and told them: "If you accept the Torah, well and good; but if not, here shall be your burial place."
3. Bava Metzia VII, 1.
4. Menaḥot 20b, s.v. Nifsal.
5. Oraḥ Ḥayyim 425, 1.
6. Introduction, p. 3.
7. Mishnah Avot I, 1.
8. See article 'Dress' in *Encyclopedia Judaica*.
9. Leviticus 18:3.
10. Yevamot 14a.
11. Deuteronomy 14:1.
12. *Yad*, Hilkhot Avodah Zarah, 12:14.
13. *Sefer Eretz Yisrael*, Introduction.
14. See Deuteronomy 25:5-10.
15. Ibid. 25:19.
16. *Ta'amei ha-Minhagim* pp. 376-377.
17. *Ḥayyei Avraham*, Introduction.
18. II, 16.
19. Ecclesiastes 12:1.

ANNOTATED LIST OF SOURCES

ABUDRAHAM (first published in 1541)—a comprehensive code and exposition of synagogue ritual—the blessings and the prayers —by R. David b. Joseph Abudraham. He is reputed to have been a pupil of R. Jacob b. Asher, author of the *Tur*, but there is evidence to the contrary. The work is popular in nature, written for the masses who, in the author's opinion lacked familiarity with the relevant laws and customs. He accordingly included expository comments on the prayers and most popular *piyyutim*. (For this work the photographic reprint published in Israel in 1973 has been used.)

ARUKH HA-SHULḤAN, a comprehensive code of Jewish law arranged in the order of the Shulḥan Arukh, chapter by chapter —by R. Yeḥiel Michel Halevi Epstein (1835-1905). In this work the author has brought the Shulḥan Arukh up to date by presenting the final summations of the Halakhic rulings up to his time. He takes the reader through the labyrinth of the various opinions and rulings and then states the Halakhic decision to be followed in practice. In the view of the author of this book, the Arukh Hashulḥan is the final authority on the various laws and customs mentioned herein, and so the work is referred to extensively.

BAYIT ḤADASH (abbr. BaḤ) by R. Joel Jafeh Sirkis (1570-1641), a commentary on R. Jacob b. Asher's *Tur*. His immediate motive in writing this commentary was to reestablish the authority of the *Tur*, which had been challenged in many instances by R. Joseph Karo's commentary, *Bet Joseph*, and his code, the *Shulḥan Arukh*. He elucidates and analyzes each *halakhah* in depth. His work is quoted and referred to constantly in the standard commentaries on the *Shulḥan Arukh*.

BEN ISH ḤAI by R. Joseph Ḥayyim b. R. Elijah al-Ḥakam, the last of the great rabbis of modern times in Baghdad where he officiated for fifty years (1859-1909). The work is a compilation of aggadic and halakhic homilies blended with kabbalistic comments, and arranged to follow the order of the Sidrah of the Week. First published in Jerusalem in 1898, the work has become popular among Oriental communities and has been republished several times.

DARKHE MOSHEH by R. Moses Isserles (1520-1572) of Cracow. His first major Halakhic work, it is a running commentary on the *Tur* and the *Bet Joseph* in which the author laid the foundation of his later glosses on the *Shulḥan Arukh*, and in which he is at pains to defend the decisions of the German halakhic authorities against the Spanish. Known by his initials as the RaMA, R. Moses Isserles became acknowledged as the greatest halakhic authority of Ashkenazi Jewry.

DERISHAH U-PERISHAH, a dual commentary on the *Tur* by R. Joshua Falk Katz (mid-16th century) and printed in the standard editions of that code, consisting of (a) *Perishah*, an elucidation of the text and giving various interpretations thereof, and (b) *Derishah* which adduces the sources and additional glosses to those of the *Darkhe Mosheh*. The author defends the position of the *Tur* against that of the *Bet Joseph*, where the latter differs with him.

DOVER MESHARIM an exposition and defense of the attitude adopted in Eretz Israel towards determining the time of nightfall by R. Ḥanokh Zundel Grosberg (Jerusalem, 1956).

HALIKHOT TEMAN by R. Joseph Kappaḥ (third edition, Jerusalem 1969), an account of the Jewish life in the city of San'a, Yemen, holiday observances, method of education, family and home life; arts and crafts, occupations; various customs, practices and beliefs.

ḤAYYE AVRAHAM by R. Abraham b. Raphael Kalfon—a miscellany culled from previous works on all customs connected with prayer ritual, and Sabbath and holiday services (reprinted Leghorn, 1863).

ḤUPPAT ḤATANIM by R. Raphael b. Ḥezekiah Meldola of Venice. It covers the entire range of laws, rites and customs pertaining to marriage from *shiddukhin* (betrothal preliminaries), through the *ḥuppah*, to the laws and customs pertaining to *niddah*, the menstrual cycle, including the *halakhot* pertaining to *Mikva'ot*.

MASSA BAVEL, an account by R. David Sassoon of Bombay of his journey undertaken to Baghdad in 1910, the birthplace of his parents, and of his researches into the past of this ancient community. The book contains a chapter on the prayer ritual of this community. Originally published in English, the work was translated into Hebrew (the third Hebrew edition edited and annotated by Meir Benayahu, was used by the author of this work.)

MEḤOLAT HA-MAḤANAYIM by R. Israel David Margaliot-Yafeh is an exposition of liturgical customs with their rabbinic sources arranged in the form of questions and answers. Pressburg, 1859.

MEKOR HA-HALIKHOT VEHA-DINIM by R. Abraham b. Joshua Heshel Efron (Vilna 1901, reprinted in Israel, 1972) in which the laws and customs scattered through the Babylonian and Jerusalem Talmud, Siphra, Siphre, Tosefta, Mekhilta and Midrashim are traced back to explicit source references in the Scriptures or to Scriptural expositions of the Rabbis of the Talmud.

MINHAGE ERETZ ISRAEL by R. Jacob Gelis (Jerusalem, 1968), deals with the practices, laws and customs observed by the Jews of Eretz Israel in all generations to the present day, arranged to follow the order of the Shulḥan Arukh, with explanatory notes, source references and comparisons.

MINHAGE MAHARIL. A compendium of the *minhagim* of the entire year as established by Rabbi Jacob Halevi of Moellin (c.1360-1427), a leading authority on Ashkenazi customs, especially on liturgy. First published in Sabionette, 1616.

OTZAR KOL MINHAGE YESHURUN by Rabbi Abraham Eliezer Hirshowitz of Pittsburg, a compilation of Jewish customs and their origin as drawn from the works of the earlier and later authorities (fourth edition, Israel 1970).

OTZAR YISRAEL, a popular Hebrew encyclopedia in 10 volumes edited by Judah David Eisenstein (New York, 1907-1913).

SEFER ERETZ ISRAEL by R. Yeḥiel Michel Tukatzinsky. The authoritative guide for present practice in the Eretz Israel Ashkenazi community. It is divided into two parts: I—a systematic codification of laws and customs observed in Eretz Israel today where these differ with current practice in the diaspora; II—a survey of the mitzvot that depend upon Eretz Israel for their fulfillment. (Reprinted, Jerusalem, 1955.)

SEFER HA-MAT'AMIM (acronym for *Mekorim Tovim 'Al Minhage Yisrael Mekudashim*, lit. "Worthy Sources for Hallowed Jewish Customs"), by Isaac Lipi of Siedlce. The work has as its purpose to demonstrate that every Jewish custom has its origin in some worthy spiritual source, for "if Israel are not prophets, they are nevertheless the sons of prophets." (Reprinted, Jerusalem, 1968).

SEFER HA-MANHIG by R. Abraham ben Nathan Ha-Yarḥi (i.e. of Lunel. ca. 1155-ca. 1215), one of the earliest works describing the customs of various Jewish communities with their sources and reasons. First published in Constantinople, 1519. An annotated critical edition was published by Dr. Yitzḥak Raphael, Jerusalem, 1978.

SEFER HA-MINHAGIM comprising all customs observed during the entire year, by R. Isaac of Tyrnau, a disciple of R. Shalom of Vienna (end of fourteenth century). The work is quoted and referred to extensively in R. Moses Isserles' glosses on the *Shulḥan Arukh*, R. Mordecai Jaffe's *Levush* and in the works of many other authorities. An expanded version in Yiddish was published with many woodcut illustrations. Enjoying great popularity, it has appeared in many editions, notably in Venice, 1590 and Amsterdam, 1645. A number of illustrations appearing in this book are reproductions of the woodcuts of this *Minhagim Bukh*.

SEFER HA-TODA'AH by Eliahu KiTov (Mokatovski), a popular and poetic elucidation of the laws and precepts, the festivals and appointed seasons of Israel, arranged in the sequence of the months of the year. Both aggadic and halakhic material are included. A very popular contemporary work, it has been published in several editions. It has also appeared in an English translation under the title of *The Book of Our Heritage.*

SEFER KIDDUSHIN VE-NISSUIN by R. Abraham Ḥayyim Freiman (Jerusalem, 1964) a historical survey of Jewish marriage laws from the time of the redaction of the Talmud—containing the main sources, the decisions and responsa of the rabbinic courts and great authorities—through the various enactments and *haskamot* of the subsequent generations.

SHA'AR HA-MIFKAD by R. Raphael b. Aaron ibn Shim'on, rabbi of Egypt and its environs, listing and elucidating the customs observed in the holy city of Jerusalem and its environs, and including those practises which have been omitted from previous works or have not been properly expounded before, with supplementary remarks by R. Jacob Kafiluto (reprinted, Israel 1968).

SHULḤAN ARUKH by R. Joseph Karo, the code of Jewish law par excellence. With the additions of R. Moses Isserles and with its numerous commentaries it is the universally accepted guide in matters of Jewish law and ritual.

TA'AME HA-MINHAGIM U-MEKORE HA-DINIM by R. Abraham Isaac Sperling (first published in 1890), the most popular compendium of Jewish ritual, its customs and traditions. It contains anecdotes and parables of the rabbis and hasidic Rebbes. The expanded Jerusalem edition was used by the author of this work. A selection from this book has been translated into English and published under the title, *Reasons for Jewish Customs and Traditions.*

TUR by R. Jacob b. Asher (b. Germany c. 1270, from where he emigrated together with his father to Spain in 1305, finally settled in Toledo, d. 1340). This major code, his *magnum opus*, is a summary of all the laws in effect in his time, and is arranged in four *turim* (lit. "rows," actually sections). It incorporates all the additional legal decisions that had accumulated since the time of Maimonides. The views of the various authorities are given as well as the sources, and where these differ, R. Jacob generally follows the view of his illustrious father, R. Asher, "the Rosh."

Synagogue

Today the synagogue is the most sacred institution in Jewish life; and so it has been for centuries. It has been the spiritual fortress of the Jew in the most hostile environment to which he was banished; the fathomless source from which he drew inspiration and consolation even in times when his very existence was threatened. Here the Jew communed with his God and found peace and solace even when his body was racked with suffering. In its persistent attempt to convert Jews to Christianity, the medieval Church, fully aware of the vital role the synagogue played in the social and religious life of the Jew, made frequent attempts in collusion with secular governments to deny the Jews the right to build or to worship in a synagogue.[1]

Yet, the origin of the synagogue is not clear and is the subject of dispute among the scholars. All agree that it is a successor to the *Beth Hamikdash*, the Temple which in turn was a successor of the *Mishkan*—the Tabernacle in the desert. In these two institutions, however, the service took the form of sacrifice rather than of prayer. Yet there are indications that simple prayer without the attending sacrifice was already prevalent in the very early periods of Jewish history. Hannah, for instance, as is related in the Book of Samuel (1:1) *prayed* to God for a child. There is no mention made that she brought a sacrifice. Similarly, when Solomon dedicated the first Temple he offered a lengthy prayer and, again, no mention is made of any accompanying sacrifices. Soon after the return from the Babylonian exile, the Men of the Great Assembly composed and instituted some of the basic prayers which are recited to this very day, such as the *Amidah*, the Eighteen Benedictions. The Talmud also relates that a great synagogue existed in Alexandria, Egypt, even before the destruction of the Temple where the service consisted exclusively of prayer and the reading of the Torah. This edifice was so large that those who sat far away from the congregational reader could not hear him recite the prayer. A flag had to be raised at the appropriate times to signal when "Amen" was to be said.

Also, the Mishnah mentions the existence of *Mishmarot* and *Ma'amadot.* The Priests and Levites were divided into twenty-four divisions or "guards" (*Mishmarot*), each of which would spend a week in rotation conducting the Temple service. Similarly, the entire people of Israel was divided into 24 districts, each district attached to a particular *Mishmar.* When the time arrived for the *Mishmar* to take over the service, a *Ma'amad* (lit. "station")—a group of the district would accompany them to the Temple to act as representatives of the entire population, while the rest of the district would gather in their towns during that week and spend the period in prayer.

The synagogue as we know it today, received its final form in the first century C.E. immediately after the destruction of the Second Commonwealth. The Temple was razed and the inhabitants driven into exile. Sacrifices could no longer be offered. The houses of prayer from that time were no longer limited to secondary role in Jewish worship. They were elevated to a level of sanctity not far below that of the Temple. In fact, several features of the Temple were incorporated in the physical architecture and furnishings of the synagogue.

Because the synagogue is in effect the substitute for the Temple, the worshipper, during the *Amidah*, should stand facing the Temple site, irrespective of where he sits in the synagogue. It is for this reason that the Temple is often called *Talpiot.* This word is comprised of two parts: *Tel* means a mound, and *piot* means mouths. That is to say, the place to which all words of the mouth in supplication were directed.[2] The word "synagogue" is Greek in origin. It is a translation of the Hebrew *bet knesset* and the Aramaic *be kenishta*—a house of assembly. In Yiddish and colloquial English it is known as *Shule*, from the German "Schule" meaning school. The synagogue was originally used for prayers as well as study, and to accentuate the dominance of study over prayer, the synagogue was called *Shule.* Another reason: *shibbeḥu ve-hodu li-shemo*, "they praised and gave thanks to His Name." The first letters of the three Hebrew words make up the word *Shul.* The implication is that the synagogue is the place where the Jew offers his praise and thanksgiving to God.[3]

A *mezuzah* is not affixed to the doorpost of a synagogue's entrance because only a dwelling—a place where one eats, sleeps and drinks—is subject to the obligation of *mezuzah.* Since it is forbidden to engage in these functions in a synagogue a *mezuzah* is unnecessary.[4]

On the other hand, a *mezuzah* must be attached to a *bet ha-midrash*, a house of study, because the scholars who study there are accustomed to take their meals there in order to save time. Nowadays, the synagogue is regarded as a *bet ha-midrash*, since many mundane functions, including the serving of refreshments, take place there and it is no longer devoted exclusively to prayer. Our synagogues must have *mezuzot.*

It is customary for the worshipper entering the synagogue to recite the verse "How goodly are thy tents O Jacob, thy dwelling places O Israel" (Numbers 24:5), and then sit down for a few moments to meditate. Before leaving the synagogue he must again sit down and meditate for a short while. As the source and authority for this custom two verses are cited: "Happy are they who dwell in Your house—they will be continually praising You" (Ps. 84:5) which is taken to refer to the meditation before the service; and "Surely the righteous will give thanks unto Your Name, the upright shall dwell before Your presence; (Ps. 104:14), which refers to the moments of meditation before leaving the synagogue.[5]

Naturally, the sanctity of the synagogue requires that we treat it with respect and awe. To enter a synagogue indifferently or casually borders on sacrilege. A certain measure of psychological attunement and spiritual affinity is needed to prepare us for the inspiration the synagogue has in store for us.

To insure the proper atmosphere, the following rules of conduct, among others, must be observed in the synagogue:

(a) Eating, drinking and sleeping in the synagogue are proscribed. Sauntering aimlessly or using the synagogue as a shortcut is also forbidden. Nor may one use the synagogue to take shelter from the heat or rain. Based on these restrictions the reader can now judge for himself what modes of behavior would be considered disrespectful in a synagogue.[6]

(b) It is forbidden to enter the synagogue with the head uncovered.[7] On numerous occasions, the Rabbis of the Talmud took the position that the characteristic Jewish way of showing respect is to cover one's head. Contrary to other ethnic groups and religions which consider the removal of one's headgear as a sign of respect, the Jew shows his deference to God by keeping his head covered. Since God is present everywhere it is customary of the Jew to wear some head covering at all times, either a hat or a skull cap. To be sure, the non-observance of this custom is not as severe as the transgression of more fundamental precepts, such as the Sabbath and the dietary laws. Yet, entering a synagogue with a bared head is considered a blatant and arrogant defiance of Jewish mores and religious committment. Worshipping God in the *Mikdash Me'at*, the miniature Temple, warrants that we manifest our respect in the Jewish manner.

(c) In certain Oriental Jewish communities it is customary for the congregant to remove his shoes before entering the synagogue. Western Jews consider this unbecoming and improper as a mere imitation of the Islamic custom.[8]

(d) The bearing of weapons, such as exposed swords, daggers or guns in a synagogue is forbidden because it is contrary to the sanctity and function of the synagogue. The synagogue should bring peace, happiness and contentment; weapons cause death.[9]

(e) The synagogue should be erected on the highest ground of the town so that, literally speaking, the Jew may look up to his house of worship. A Biblical source for this rule is the verse in Proverbs (1:21), "At the top of the busy places will she call forth."

In other words, the *Shekhinah*, the immanence of God, will call forth from a place high above the busy home.[10]

(f) The stringent rules based on the profound awe with which the Jew must relate to the synagogue do not apply to makeshift or temporary houses of worship. Rented premises used for holding services must be treated with some degree of respect but are not to be accorded the same degree of sanctity as an established synagogue.[11]

When one enters a traditional synagogue he will most likely find some or all of the following architectural features, ritual objects and appurtenances:

Ezrat Nashim—a separate section or gallery set aside for women. The setting aside of an *Ezrat Nashim* in the synagogue, our *Mikdash Me'at*, is patterned on the *Ezrat Nashim* of the *Bet Ha-Mikdash* of ancient days. As the Talmud (Sukkah 51a) relates, during certain celebrations in the Temple in Jerusalem vast throngs congregated to witness the festivities. The Sages, concerned lest a co-mingling of the sexes give rise to frivolous behavior contrary to the dignity and sanctity of the Temple, therefore decreed that a special gallery be erected for the women. Since that time, in every traditional Jewish House of Worship a separate section is set aside for women.

After all, entering the synagogue has a specific purpose —to commune with God. This is no easy task and not always are we successful in attaining this closeness to God. Yet, we must at least remove, as far as possible, the distractions that might divert our attention from our communing with God. Jewish law, tåking due account of the frailties of human nature, recognizes how likely to attract a worshipper's attention the proximity of members of the opposite sex may be.

For this reason throughout the millenia every authority has recognized the importance of an *Ezrat Nashim* in a synagogue. Mixed seating, by contrast, is definitely of Christian origin.

Bimah— Upon entering a traditional synagogue one immediately notices an elevated platform or *Bimah* from where the

Torah is read during services. One of the basic specifications with respect to the *Bimah* is that it be erected in the center of the synagogue. Several reasons have been proposed:

(a) Since the Temple had been destroyed, the Bimah supplants the altar that stood in the center of the Temple courtyard. It was that altar that the processions with the *Lulavim* would circle during the Sukkot festival. In the synagogue, too, the worshippers carrying their *Lulavim* march around the *Bimah* which stands in the center of the synagogue.

(b) The *Bimah* is primarily used for the reading of the Torah. Therefore it is appropriate that is should stand in the center of the synagogue to make the Torah reading equally audible in all sections of the synagogue. In Sephardic synagogues both the reader of the Torah and the *Ḥazan* who leads the prayer service perform their functions from this center *Bimah*. In Ashkenazi synagogues the Torah is read from the *Bimah* while the leader of the prayer service stands at a lectern placed in front, or on the right hand side of the Ark.[12]

(c) According to Jewish tradition the Temple stood in the very center of the universe so as to diffuse its spiritual light throughout the world. Hence the *Bimah* where the Torah is read stands in the center to convey that its teachings should radiate to the entire world.

(d) The *Bimah* in the center of the synagogue is to remind us of the encampment of the Children of Israel in the desert during their sojourn from Egypt to the Promised Land. The Twelve Tribes were arranged to form a square with the Tabernacle at the center over which hovered the Divine Presence, the *Shekhinah*.[13]

Aron Kodesh—Holy Ark. While the entire synagogue is holy, an even higher degree of sanctity attaches to the Ark, the repository of the Scrolls of the Law. It is placed against or within that wall of the synagogue which faces the direction of the location of the Temple. As mentioned, our prayers are to be directed towards Jerusalem and the worshipper accordingly faces both the Ark and the Temple when praying. Since most European and all American communities lie west of *Eretz Yisrael*, the worshipper entering the synagogue from the west will face the Ark in the east.[14]

The unique sanctity of the Torah scroll warrants that the Ark in which it reposes should be designated from the very start as an *Aron Kodesh*, a Holy Ark. If, however, some enclosed area in the eastern wall of the synagogue had originally been set aside as a receptacle for valuable articles, and then a Torah was placed in it, it would not be considered an *Aron Kodesh*. Nevertheless, if an encasement large enough to hold a *Sefer Torah* is put together and then placed in a niche in the wall, it does assume the sanctity of an *Aron Kodesh*.[15]

If the *Sefer Torah* represents the apex of holiness in the synagogue, it should follow that the Congregation remain standing during the entire Torah reading as a sign of respect. There are indeed many worshippers who do so. Most people however, remain seated because the *Bimah* on which the Torah rests and is unrolled is elevated and, therefore, considered *Reshut Bifne Atzmo*, an independent domain. Not being confined within the same area as the Torah, the worshipper is not regarded as being in its presence and is, therefore, not obligated to endure the hardship of standing throughout the reading of the Torah portion.[16]

Parokhet—Curtain. A special decorative curtain, called the *parokhet*, hangs in front of the Ark. The prototype of this appurtenance of the synagogue was the *parokhet* that hung in the Temple separating the Holy of Holies from the rest of the Temple. As in almost every feature of the synagogue we attempt to simulate the characteristics of the ancient Temple, so the Ark with the Torah in it corresponds to the Holy of Holies and the *parokhet* is meant to divide that area from the rest of the synagogue.

Windows. Every synagogue should have its windows cut out from the upper part of the walls. There are two reasons for this:

a. If the windows were to be at eye level the worshipper could easily be temped to gaze through them and thus become distracted from his prayers.

b. In the Middle Ages non-Jews would deliberately pass by the Jewish House of Worship during the prayer service and look through the windows. The Jewish mode of worship would appear strange and outlandish to them and they would mock and ridicule it, thus disrupting the service.

According to the Kabbalists every synagogue should be provided with twelve windows. According to them, originally there was no uniform mode and content in prayer. Each one of the Twelve Tribes had its own, specific manner of worship symbolized by the twelve windows.[17]

Menorah—Candelabrum. Our synagogues being replicas of the ancient Temple, one will find a Menorah placed in the vicinity of the altar or the lectern. However, while the features of the synagogue were intended to remind us of similar features of the ancient Temple, they may not be exact replicas. This is derived from the admonition in Exodus (20:20), "You shall not make unto you" which the Rabbis interpreted to mean that we are not permitted to duplicate exactly the articles of the Temple. Therefore, while we retain a candelabrum in our synagogues to commemorate the Menorah in the Temple, some variation must be introduced so that it will not be an exact replica. In many congregations this is accomplished by fashioning a candelabrum consisting of six branches as contrasted with the seven branched candelabrum in the Temple. Others retain the seven branches but never light more than five so as to differentiate from the one in the Temple where all seven branches were lit. In modern times, the electric candelabrum is regarded as sufficiently dissimilar to its Temple counterpart to be acceptable.[18]

Ner Tamid—Perpetual Light. In every synagogue, generally in front of the Ark, there burns a light at all times. This is known as the *Ner Tamid.* As was stated in reference to the Menorah, each day in the ancient Temple the receptacles were cleaned and the wicks and the oil were changed. The *Ner Ma'aravi*, the westernmost branch of the candelabrum burned continually. When the cleansing of the other six branches was finished, a taper lighted from the western branch was used to rekindle the remaining branches. The early authorities, such as Naḥmanides, identify the *Ner Ma'Aravi* as the *Ner Tamid* or Perpetual Light. The purpose of this *Ner Ma'aravi* was to remind the Jew of the everlasting presence of God's *Shekhina* within the confines of the Temple. Similarly, the *Ner Tamid* in our synagogues symbolizes God's presence in the Synagogue.[19]

SOURCES

1. See Solomon Grayzel, *The Church and the Jews in the 13th Century*, Rev. ed., Hermon Press 1966.
2. *Ben Ish Ḥai*, p. 74, 75.
3. *Sefer ha-Mat'amim* p. 12.
4. *Sefer ha-Mat'amim* Section 2 p. 7. See below p. 98.
5. *Tur Oraḥ Ḥayyim, Baḥ* Chapter 151.
6. *Tur Oraḥ Ḥayyim* 151.
7. *Tur Oraḥ Ḥayyim, Bet Yoseph* 151.
8. *Arukh ha-Shulḥan* 151 par. 9.
9. *Arukh ha-Shulḥan* 151 par. 10.
10. *Arukh ha-Shulḥan* 150 par. 3.
11. *Tur Oraḥ Ḥayyim, Bet Yoseph* 154.
12. *Sefer M'Ḥolat ha-Maḥanaim* p. 298.
13. *Tur Oraḥ Ḥayyim* 150; *Arukh ha-Shulḥan* 150 par. 9; *Sefer ha-Mat'amim* p. 13; *Mikdash Me'at* by Rabbi Zalman Druck, Jerusalem 1973 p. 42.
14. *Arukh ha-Shulḥan, Oraḥ Ḥayyim* 150 par. 8.
15. *Arukh ha-Shulḥan, Oraḥ Ḥayyim* 154, par. 6.
16. *Rama, Yoreh Deah* 242 par. 18; *Ta'amei ha-Minhagim* p. 70.
17. *Sefer ha-Mat'amim* p.12; *Ta'amei ha-Minhagim* p. 70.
18. *Mikdash Me'at* pp. 49, 55, 56.
19. See clue in *Kli Yakar*, Exodus 27:20.

Tallit and Tzitzit

All the laws of *tallit* and *tzitzit* stem from the Biblical pronouncement, "And the Lord spoke unto Moses saying, 'Speak unto the children of Israel, and order them to make fringes for themselves in the *corners* of their garments throughout their generations and they should put on the fringe of each corner a *thread of blue.* And it shall be to you as a fringe, that you may *look at it*, and *remember* all the commandments of the Lord, and do them; so that you go not astray after your own heart and your own eyes, after which you go astray; that you may remember and do all My commandments, and be holy unto your God. I am the Lord your God, who brought you out of the land of Egypt, to be your God; I am the Lord your God" (Numbers 15:37-41). There is also the verse, "You shall make yourself *twisted cords (gedilim)* upon the four corners of your covering, with which you cover yourself"(Deut. 22:12).

In order to fully understand these quotations, it is necessary to underscore the phrases: "that they make"; "in the corners of their garments"; "a thread of blue"; "so that you may look upon it"; "and remember all the commandments of the Lord"; "twisted cords"; "with which you cover yourself."

The component parts of the *tzitzit* are:

(a) *Tallit (*pl. *taleitim):* a garment having four distinct corners.

(b) *Kanaf (*pl. *knafot):* the corner where a hole is made three fingerbreadths from the edge, and through which the threads are drawn.

(c) *Anaf:* that part of the Tzitzit which is tied, wound and knotted.

(d) *Gedil* (pl. *gedilim*): the parts of the fringes that hang loose.

(e) *Petil* (pl. *petilim*). the twisted strands which make up the fringe.

The last three components comprise the *tzitzit*; all five components comprise what is commonly known as the *tallit*.

Since a *tallit*, a common article of clothing, receives its sanctity only when the tzitziot are properly attached, and since *tzitziot* command our reverence only when they are part of a *tallit*, we will use these words *tzitzit* and *tallit* interchangeably, because each one is dependent upon the other.

In ancient days, the Jews wore their *taleitim* all day long. Under those circumstances they could fulfill the mitzvah of *tzitzit* in its entirety as they could see the fringes constantly. When the Jews were driven into exile, and were forced to live within different cultures, they would have made themselves a butt of ridicule had they worn their *taleitim* in public. In order to overcome this handicap the custom was instituted to wear a *tallit katan*, the *tallit* of a small boy, with the appropriate *tzitziot* worn under the outer garments. Even today, one may observe the *tzitziot* of this *tallit katan* protruding from the outer garments of observant Jews, either completely exposed or tucked into a side pocket and only partially visible, in order to be in keeping with the injunction: "that you may *look* at them."[1] Those who tuck their *tzitziot* into their trousers feel that the rule, "You shall *see* and *remember*," is fulfilled when they get dressed. So a Jew should have two *taleitim*:

(a) A *tallit gadol* for the complete fulfillment of the mitzvah of *tzitziot*. (This will be clarified in a later paragraph.)

(b) A *tallit katan* for the purpose of looking and remembering all day long. Incidently, the term "small boy," referred to above is very indefinite. What the Rabbis seem to have had in mind was an average-sized boy of nine—the age at which a boy begins to develop physically. To have chosen a younger and smaller child would have been absurd. By about the age of nine, a boy enters the first phase of physical maturity.[2].

What type of garments require the attachment of *tzitziot*? Here we find a difference of opinion (Menaḥot 39b). Since the identical word *beged* (garment) used in connection with *tzitzit* is also mentioned in another context in the Torah related to the symptoms of leprosy and, and since there we are given specific details as to the material of the garment—wool or flax—some are of the opinion that the mitzvah of *tzitzit* too, applies only to garments made of wool or flax. Other authorities hold that since *beged* in the context of *tzitzit* is mentioned without any qualification (The Torah generalizes: "to make fringes for themselves in the corners of their *garments* throughout their generations" [Numbers 15:38]), here the word "garment" is not restricted to those fabrics, but includes garments of other materials as well.

Mention has been made of several key phrases used in the Scriptural passage dealing with the mitzvah of *tzitzit*. One was, "And they shall make." This implies a prescribed sequence in the attachment of the *tzitzit*, a procedure which may not be changed. Thus, a *tallit* would be disqualified if a person cut out a garment with three corners, threaded these with *tzitziot* and then decided to cut another corner and thread that one as well. The reason for this is "*Ta'aseh Velo Min Ha-Asui. . .*": "You shall make (initially) and not complete as an afterthought." In other words, a *tallit* only needs *tzitzit* when it is a proper *tallit*, i.e., it already has four corners to which the *tzitziot* are to be attached.[3] Another example: a person decides that he would like a new *tallit* although he still keeps his old one. He then proceeds to buy some expensive cloth and cuts it into a garment with four corners. He thinks that instead of the tedious chore of threading the new garment with *tzitziot*, it would be easier for him to cut out the four corners of his old *tallit*, together with their fringes and sew them on to the four corners of his new *tallit*. This too, would not work because of the same principle. The first step must be the preparation of the *tallit*; only afterwards may one proceed to attach the *tzitziot*. In the above instance, the *tzitziot* had already been knotted before their attachment to the new *tallit*.[4]

The Sages defined precisely what constitutes a garment in

which *tzitzit* need to be threaded. They describe it as one that is used to cover the entire body and not merely specific parts. For example, would a four cornered hat require *tzitziot*? Would a four cornered silk scarf require *tzitziot*? The answer is: no. These items are worn either for beauty or for the benefit of the head and neck alone.[5]

If a non-Jew ties the *tzitziot* into the *tallit*, it is disqualified. In this area the consensus is that only a member of the Jewish faith may validly perform the act because the Torah explicitly states "Speak unto the *children of Israel* and order them to make" (Numbers 15:38). This implies that only the children of Israel can fulfill this requirement. On the question whether a woman is qualified to make and insert *tzitziot*, we find a difference of opinion. Those that think that a woman may, base their position on the point that "children of Israel" excludes only non-Jews. The phrase as such includes men, women and children of the Jewish faith. Those that rule a woman may not participate in this religious function pinpoint the word "bene," meaning "the sons" (rather than "the childen") [of Israel], which would exclude women. The prevailing opinion is that technically, women are not disqualified. However, somehow they have never shown any great desire to become involved in the making of *tzitziot*.[6]

One who borrows an unfringed garment is exempt for thirty days from threading its corners with *tzitziot*. The basis for this is the verse: "You shall make the twisted cords on the four corners of *your* covering"(Deut. 22:12). This implies that the garment must belong to him. Use of the garment for less than thirty days does not indicate ownership. However, after thirty days, or if the borrower intended to keep it longer than for thirty days, he must insert the *tzitziot* immediately.

All this applies as long as the owner is fully aware that his garment has been borrowed and has no objections. It is permissible, however, to help oneself to the *tallit* of someone else without the knowledge of the owner, because we assume that the latter would not object to his *tallit* being used for a religious purpose for a short period of time. On the other hand, if it is known that the owner does object on the ground that the garment may become soiled or creased, the *tallit* may not be borrowed.[7]

What is the technical procedure of threading the *tzitziot* into a *tallit*. As noted previously, the first step is to secure a four cornered piece of cloth woven of wool or flax, preferably large enough to cover most of the body. This, of course, disqualifies those *taleitim*, wool or silk, which merely cover the neck and hang down to the sides. The next step is to obtain threads long enough that, when the process is over, these will still be a length of twelve fingers placed horizontally side by side. In view of the fact that the *tzitziot* perform a specific function in the daily life of the Jew, and are not intended simply for ornamental purposes, it is imperative that both when one weaves them and when they are being inserted in to the *tallit*, one should declare aloud one's intention in preparing the *tzitziot* for the sake of the mitzvah. So important is this aspect of the procedure that, if omitted, the *tallit* and *tzitzit* are disqualified.

The next step is to take sets of four threads—one set for each corner—three of which are of the same length and one considerably longer. The four are then drawn through one of the holes so that the maker finds himself holding eight threads, seven of equal length and one much longer. He then takes four in one hand and four in the other and ties the two sets together in a double knot. The longer thread is then wound around the others seven times. Then, once again he makes a double knot and proceeds to wind the long thread eight times round the rest. Again he makes a double knot and he then winds the longer thread around the others eleven times; again he makes a double knot followed by a winding of thirteen times. He finishes the procedure with a final double knot. A number of reasons are advanced for this procedure:

(a) The numerical value of *tzitzit* is six hundred; there are five knots and eight threads. Added together, the figures total six hundred and thirteen, which corresponds to the number of the six hundred and thirteen *mitzvot*.

(b) There are thirty nine thread windings (7, 8, 11, 13). This corresponds to the numerical value of *HaShem Eḥad* ("The Lord is One"), using the letters of the Ineffable Name.[8]

(c) Even if one would like to increase the number of the windings beyond the number thirteen, it is not allowed because, according to the Kabbalah, there are seven Heavens and six spaces between them leading to the Divine seat of God.[9]

(d) Why must there be eight threads? These are intended to represent the eight organs of the body with which man sins most; the eye, ear, nose, mouth, hand, foot, heart, and the sexual organ. Hence, the eight threads comprising the *tzitzit* must act as a constant reminder to man to be aware of his susceptibility to sin through these members of his body.[10]

What happens if on examining the threads it is discovered that one will not be long enough to leave twelve fingerbreadths after being threaded and knotted? In that case he may join on another piece to that thread in order to meet the requirements. However, if he became aware of its inadequacy after he threaded, wound and knotted it, he may not add any appendage because of the principle of *Ta'aseh Velo Min Ha'asui.*[11]

In ancient times one of the four threads was blue. In those days a marine animal was known with either blue blood or a blue secretion of some sort which was used to dye the thread. At some point in history Jews became unable to identify the species from which the dye originated. Subsequently only white threads were used, despite the fact that the Torah enjoins us to include one of blue. About the year 1885, Rabbi Gerson Henokh Leiner of the city of Radzin in Poland claimed that he had discovered the breeding area of this *Ḥilazon* (the blue blooded animal) somewhere off the coast of Italy. Both he and his many disciples immediately started to dye one thread of each set blue, using the blood of this fish. A furor ensued in the entire Rabbinic world at the time. While the Ḥassidim of Radzin until this day wear a thread of blue in their *Tzitziot*, the vast majority of Rabbinic authorities have rejected Rabbi Leiner's claim of identification.[12]

The Torah instructs us to include a thread of blue to remind us to keep God's laws. But how does looking at the *tzitziot* move us to remember? The Talmud (Menahot 43b; Sotah 17a) answers:

The blue thread reminds us of the blue waters of the Mediterranean; the blue water is a reflection of the blue sky; the blue sky, in turn, is a reflection of the sapphire seat of God. Thus, by a chain reaction the blue thread reminds us of God's commandments.

It is very important to remember, in threading the *tzitziot*, to attach fringes of wool only to a woolen garment and fringes of flax only to a linen garment. To use flax in a woolen garment or vice versa would violate the prohibition against *Sha'atnez* (Deut. 22:11).

After the *tzitziot* have been tied into the *tallit*, it is customary to sew on an *atarah*, an additional strip of cloth as a neckband for the upper part of the *tallit*. Two reasons are offered:

(a) There is a tradition that any religious act performed for the first time in a particular way should be performed the same way afterwards. For example, during their journey from Egypt through the desert to the Promised Land, the children of Israel were obliged to dismantle and reassemble the *Mishkan*, the Tabernacle, for each stage of their journey. They numbered each plank and curtain, so that every time they put the Tabernacle together they placed each part in its original position. Similarly, once a person decides which side of the *tallit* should lie upon his head and shoulders he must try to place it in the same position every time he wraps himself in the *tallit*. The *atarah* shows him which side of the *tallit* is to be placed upon the head and shoulders.

(b) The weight of the *atarah* helps to keep the *tallit* in place and prevents the rest of the *tallit* from sliding down.[13] In time, people began to sew on very elaborate and ornamental *atarot*, beautifully embroidered in silver or gold. However, the majority of Sephardi and many Ashkenazi Jews refrain from using these ornamental *atarot* on the ground that they place too much emphasis on the upper part of the *tallit* when, in fact the really important part of the *tallit* is that which covers the rest of the body.[14]

One of the sharpest differences of opinion among the Sages concerning the laws of the *tzitzit* is in Menaḥot 42b. There the question is raised whether *tzitzit* is a *ḥovat gavra* (a duty devolving upon the person) that is, that every man is obliged to have *tzitziot* in his garment only when he wears it; or a *ḥovat beged* (an obligation applying to the garment) that is, that every four-cornered garment a person possesses must have *tzitziot* even though it may lie in a trunk. The prevailing opinion is that *tzitzit* is *ḥovat gavra.*

So, every Jew who wears this type of *tallit* must first tie *tzitziot* to it. The question then arises: What about women? Here the well known principle applies that women are exempt from *mitzvat aseh sheha-zeman grama*, any positive commandment which has to be performed at a definite time. From the verse:"And it shall be to you for a fringe so that you may look at it"(Numbers 15:39), we infer that the *Tallit* has to be worn only during the daytime when we can look at the *tzitziot.* At night, when we cannot see the *tzitziot* we are accordingly exempt from this mitzvah. Hence, there is a set time for this mitzvah and therefore women are exempted. What if a woman insists that she does not wish to be exempt, but would like to wear a *tallit*? Technically, she cannot be stopped from doing so, yet all the authorities have condemned this attitude as a form of presumptuousness on her part.[15]

The Rabbis of the Talmud (Menaḥot 43a) deal with the case of a blind man. If, as we have noted, *tzitziot* are intended to be seen, should a blind man who wears a four cornered cloak be obliged to have *tzitziot* inserted in them. After all, he cannot see them. The final ruling is that a blind man is obligated to fulfill the same duty as any normal person. The basis for this decision is that although the Torah prescribes that the *tzitziot* are to be seen, it also qualifies this statement by saying, "You shall make yourself twisted cords on the four corners of your covering when you cover yourself." Therefore, the fact that he covers himself with the garment obliges him to "make twisted cords upon the four corners." He many not see it but he *is* wrapped in a four cornered garment and so must provide it with *tzitziot.*[16]

The Rabbis declare that *lailah lav zeman tzitzit* (one is exempt from the mitzvah of *tzitzit* at night). A very interesting clash of opinion occured between two medieval Rabbinic "giants" concerning the word "night." According to Maimonides the *time* of wearing is the important factor. In other words, both day and night garments require *tzitziot* when worn by day. According to Rabbi Asher the emphasis is placed upon the *garment*, i.e. a day garment always requires *tzitziot*; but a night garment never needs to have *tzitziot* even when worn during the daytime. Most authorities concur with Maimondes. As a consequence of this decision one is exempt from inserting *tzitziot* in shrouds although a living person might conceivably wear one, because it is considered a garment for the night (death).[17]

The Torah does not define the clause "so that you may look at it." How clearly must it be visible? Is a blurred image sufficient? The Rabbis ruled that the time for one to wrap himself in a *tallit* is the moment one can distinguish between blue and white. However, even this criterion is not definitive. The Sephardi authorities maintain that an hour before sunrise would be in keeping with the thinking of the Rabbis. This practice is followed in Israel and in most Jewish communities throughout the world.[18]

Again, although the Torah instructs us to attach the *tzitziot* to a four cornered garment, it does not tell us how this garment is to be worn. It was only during the *Geonic* period (600-1038 C.E.) that the authorities decreed that the *tallit* must be worn *ke'atifat ishmaelim* i.e., in the Arabs' way of wearing clothes which cover their heads and bodies. Some authorities rule that the *tallit* must be worn from the shoulders down. All this revolves around the verse in Deuteronomy (22:12) previously mentioned.

For this reason, before wrapping oneself in a *tallit* the worshipper recites the benediction: "Blessed are You O Lord our God, King of the Universe who did command us to *enwrap* ourselves with *tzitzit.*" Here the word to *enwrap* is crucial: it indicates that most of the body must be covered. What of a *tallit katan* which is far too small to cover most of the body? Because a *tallit katan* has as its purpose only to serve as a reminder when we are not wearing a *tallit gadol*, we recite the prayer: "Blessed are You, O Lord our God, King of the Universe who commanded us concerning the law of *tzitzit.*" Here we do not say, "to enwrap ourselves with *tzitzit.*" However, the custom is to wrap the *tallit katan* around the head and shoulders for a moment so as to create the appearance of enwrapping.[19] This is to satisfy all opinions.

When one puts on his *tallit* he takes hold of the *tzitziot* by all four corners, raises them to the level of his neck and envelopes his entire head, while throwing the *tzitziot* behind his left shoulder. He remains for a few moments in this position and then releases the ends allowing them to fall down over his body. The background for this practice is an *aggadah:* When the Children of Israel were ready to cross the Red Sea, the waters became enraged. Whereupon, the Angel Gabriel called out, "You waters to the right of the Children of Israel had better subside because this people is soon to receive the Torah from the right hand of God. You waters to the left of the Children of Israel had better subside because this people is soon to set their phylacteries on their left hands. You waters in the rear had better become still because this people will wear their *talleitim* and *tzitziot* on their backs." This admonition caused the raging waters to become calm and to separate so as to form twelve passages, one for each tribe. In remembrance of this event, the Jew throws his *tzitziot* and the larger part of the *tallit* onto his back.[20]

While some, particularly Sephardi Jews, wear all white *talleitim*, others may wear theirs with blue or black stripes running down the length of the garment.

Those that prefer the blue stripes want to have the blue color to remind them of the now unobtainable blue thread which used to be a part of the *tzitzit*.

Those who choose black stripes do so for practically the same reason, but with a slight difference. They too, wish to remind themselves of the blue thread (*tekhelet*). However, to prevent the blue stripe being considered a real substitute for the blue thread, they choose black.

Those who opt for an all white *tallit* do so for the following reasons:

(a) White represents atonement and forgiveness.

(b) The purity of white represents the Divine virtue of compassion and mercy.[21]

(c) There may be a play on words in the verse: *Vehayah ha' atufim leLavan* (Genesis 30:42), the plain meaning of which is "So the feebler were Laban's." However, *atufim* may be an allusion to *lehitatef*, to enwrap; *Lavan* also means white. Hence, the basis for donning a white *Tallit.*[22]

When does one begin to wear a *tallit?* Customs differ. In many communities every young boy begins to wear a *tallit* regularly upon becoming Bar Mitzvah. This custom is based upon the admonition of the Sages: "When a young boy understands the significance of *tallit*, his father should buy one for him"(Sukkah 42a). The underlying thought is the educational value of such a practice. In most communities throughout the Jewish world, however, the custom is that one begins wearing a *tallit* regularly only upon getting married. This dates back to the custom prevailing in the days of the Talmud (Kidushin 29b) when a married man was recognizable by the garment which he wore over his head and body. Two reasons are suggested for this practice:

(a) In the Torah (Deut. 22:12, 13) we find the mitzvah of *tzitzit* followed immediately by a pronouncement concerning the taking of a wife.

(b) Looking at the *tzitziot* is a reminder of all God's laws and commandments. Even more, wrapping oneself in the *tallit* is a physical enveloping of oneself in the all embracing radiation emanating from God. This should afford the Jew the overpowering spiritual joy to carry out God's will. However, in societal thinking, a man cannot truly enjoy life without a wife. Hence, the happiness that one experiences through religious performance is conditioned upon the happiness the husband is granted through having a wife. Therefore one begins to wear a *tallit* only once he is married.[23]

Every morning and evening, the Jew should recite the *Keriat Shema*, the last passage of which deals with the mitzvah of *tzitzit*. It is customary to hold the two front *tzitziot* in the left hand during the morning recitation of this prayer. Why? The following reasons are given:

(a) These two *tzitziot* have sixteen strands and ten knots, a total of twenty-six. The numerical value of the Hebrew letters of the Ineffable Name also add up to twenty-six. These *tzitziot* are held in the left hand opposite the heart to demonstrate our profound devotion and heartfelt attachment to all the commandments that God gave us.[24]

(b) We have already noted that a basic aspect of the *tzitzit* is that by looking at them we remind ourselves of our duties as Jews. By holding the *tzitzit* in our hand we see them more easily.

(c) The Psalmist proclaims: "All my bones will say, 'Lord, who is like unto Thee?'"(Psalms 35:10). The Aggadah explains that King David took pride in the fact that the actions of all his limbs were directed to the service of God. He placed the *tefillin* on his left hand and with his fingers grasped the *tzitziot* of his *tallit.*[25]

It is also customary to hold the *tzitziot* during the recital of *Barukh She'Amar* ("Blessed be He that spoke and the world came into being") in the morning service. Eleven times we recite, "Blessed be He" without mentioning the name of God. We therefore hold the *tzitzit* in our hand as if to say that the "Blessed be He" refers to the Ineffable Name the numerical value of the letters of which corresponds to that of *tzitzit.*[26]

It is also customary, at the conclusion of these paragraphs, to pass the *tzitziot* over one's eyes and then kiss them. There are three reasons for this:

(a) According to the *Kabbalah* the passing of the *tzitziot* over the eyes is a remedy against blindness.

(b) When one passes the *tzitziot* over his eyes he cannot avoid seeing them, thus fulfilling the Biblical injunction, "And you shall look at them." *Tzitz* means to see.[27]

(c) We kiss the *tzitziot* to demonstrate our love for this mitzvah.

Finally, the *Zohar* makes a poignant statement about the mitzvah of *tzitzit.* "He who recites the *Keriat Shema* without wearing the *tzitziot* bears false witness against himself." This is not speaking about one who has either flung off all religious observance or who has never been educated to appreciate its value. Certainly, one who never prays has no need of a *tallit*, which for him, possesses no meaningful significance. The person referred to here is the one who is formally observant while being insensitive to genuine religious commitment. He sees no cardinal sin in reciting the *Shema* without wearing a *tallit*. This is dishonest behavior according to the *Zohar*. At the very moment when this worshipper says, "and these *tzitziot* shall be to you a reminder," he stands before God without *tzitziot*.[28]

SOURCES

1. *Arukh ha-Shulḥan* 14, par. 9 and 8, par. 17.
2. *Tur Oraḥ Ḥayyim* 16; *Arukh ha-Shulḥan* 16, par. 1.
3. *Arukh ha-Shulḥan* 10, par. 10.
4. *Arukh ha-Shulḥan* 15, par. 5.
5. *Arukh ha-Shulḥan* 10, par. 22.
6. *Tur Oraḥ Ḥayyim*; *Bet Yoseph*; *Darkei Moshe* 14.
7. Ibid; *Arukh ha-Shulḥan* 14, pars. 10, 11, 12.
8. *Tur Oraḥ Ḥayyim* 11; *Arukh ha-Shulḥan* 11, par. 18.
9. *Perishah* 11, par. 22.
10. *Ḥayye Avraham* p. 3b.
11. *Arukh ha-Shulḥan* 15, par. 2.
12. *Arukh ha-Shulḥan* 9, par. 12
13. *Sefer ha-Mat'amim* p. 45.
14. *Arukh ha-Shulḥan* 8, par. 10.
15. *Arukh ha-Shulḥan* 17, pars. 1, 2, 3.
16. *Tur Oraḥ Ḥayyim* 17.
17. *Tur Oraḥ Ḥayyim*, *Bet Yoseph* 18; *Arukh ha-Shulḥan* 19, pars. 1, 3.
18. *Sefer Eretz Yisrael* p. 18, 19.
19. *Tur Oraḥ Ḥayyim*; *Bet Yoseph*; *Darke Moshe* 8; *Arukh ha-Shulḥan* 8, pars. 3, 5, 7, 8.
20. *Da'at Zekenim Mi-Ba'ale Tosafot*, Exodus 14:29.
21. *Ḥayye Avraham* 3b; *Sefer ha-Mat'amim* p. 45.
22. *Ben Ish Ḥai* p. 13.
23. *Sefer ha-Mat'amim* p. 44, 45.
24. *Arukh ha-Shulḥan* 24, par. 4.
25. *Ḥayye Avraham* 4a.
26. *Otzar Minhage Yeshurun* p. 157
27. *Sefer ha-Mat'amim* p. 46.
28. *Arukh ha-Shulḥan* 8, par. 1.

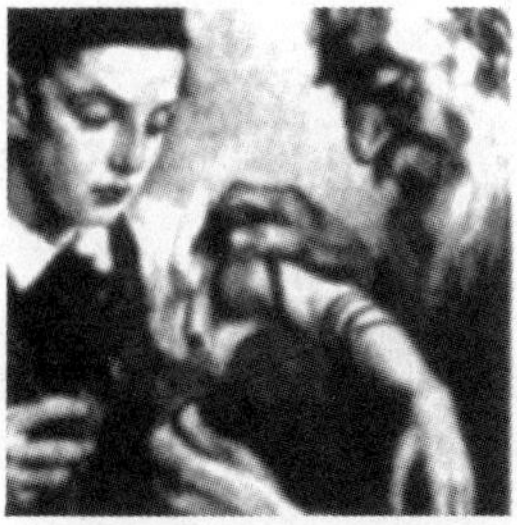

Tefillin

The commandment to wear *tefillin*, which is so centrally a part of Jewish life, goes back to four specific source-texts in the Torah:

(a) "And it shall be for a sign to you upon your hand, and for a memorial between your eyes, that the law of the Lord may be in your mouth" (Ex. 13:9).

(b) "And it shall be for a sign upon your hand, and for frontlets between your eyes" (Ex. 13:16).

(c) "And you shall bind them for a sign upon your hand and they shall be as frontlets between your eyes" (Deut. 6:8).

(d) "Therefore shall you place these My words in your heart and in your soul: and you shall bind them for a sign upon your hand and they shall be as frontlets between your eyes" (Deut. 11:18).

Except for these few brief references to *tefillin* in the Bible almost all the laws connected with it were conveyed orally to Moses on Mt. Sinai *(halakha le-Moshe mi-Sinai)*. In other words, the Torah itself does not tell how *tefillin* are to be made nor does it give precise instructions on how they are to be worn. Apparently *tefillin* was so taken for granted as a mitzvah which everybody kept that the traditions passed down by word of mouth were sufficient to assure its continuity. Even the Mishna did not find it necessary to go into the subject at any length, because when it was compiled the mitzvah of *tefillin* was universally observed. Later, however, as identification with this mitzvah weakened its hold, the Rabbis of the Talmud began a systematic and detailed description and analysis of *tefillin*.[1]

Basically *tefillin* is a compound mitzvah, including two separate and distinct *mitzvot*—the *tefillah shel yad*, the *tefillah* of the arm, being independent of the *tefillah shel rosh*, that of the head. Unlike a *tallit* with its four separate sets of *tzitziot* tied to the four corners of the garment, all of which consitute one single mitzvah, the two *tefillin* are considered two separate *mitzvot*. It is for this reason that, if one possesses a single *tefillah*, either of the hand or of the head, or if one is physically unable to wear both *tefillin*, the wearing of one still counts.[2]

How are *tefillin* made? A piece of the hide of a kosher animal is fashioned into a cubicle through the use of a mold. The hide must have come from a kosher animal only, as derived from the Scriptural verse "that the law of the Lord may be in your mouth" (Ex. 13:9), which appears in connection with the commandment of *tefillin* (see above). The Sages accordingly regard it as a requirement for the fulfillment of the mitzvah that *tefillin* should be made from the hide of a kosher animal, whose meat is permitted to be "taken into the mouth."[3]

During the process of molding the *tefillah* of the head, the letter *Shin* is embossed on the left and right side of the cubicle. One *Shin* has three prongs or strokes and the other four. There are several reasons for the variation in the number of prongs:

(a) The three strokes correspond to the threefold recitation of *kadosh, kadosh, kadosh* during our prayers. The four strokes correspond to the four occasions during the service when the *Kaddish* is recited.

(b) The three strokes remind us of the three days during the week when we read the Torah, and the four strokes are a reminder of the four days in the week when the Torah is not read.

(c) The three strokes correspond to the three Patriarchs: Abraham, Isaac and Jacob; the four strokes correspond to the four Matriarchs: Sarah, Rebecca, Rachel and Leah.[4]

(d) The combined numerical value of the two *Shins* is six hundred. The meaning of the word *shesh* which is composed of two *Shins*, is six. The seven strokes of the two *Shins* added to the number six hundred and the six for the word *shesh* together total six hundred and thirteen, corresponding to the number of mitzvot in the Torah.[5]

Through Kabbalistic influence "*Shaddai*," one of the names of God, is fashioned into the construction and the binding of the *tefillin*.[6] As we will see later, the letters of *Shaddai* are formed in the binding of both *tefillin*. In the construction, however, the "*Shin*" on the *tefillah shel rosh* is the only visible clue to God's Name. Another reason for the "*Shin*" being exposed is, as we noted, that the numerical value of the *Shin* is three hundred. This represents the three hundred days in the year on which *tefillin* are put on.[7]

Because of the prominence of the *Shin*, the *tefillah shel rosh* is accorded a higher sanctity than that of the *tefillah shel yad*.

The *tefillin* cubicles are each called *bayit* in Hebrew. Both cubicles are hollow. The *bayit* of the *tefillah shel yad* is undivided and it contains a single strip of parchment on which the following four Biblical passages are inscribed:

Exodus 13: 1-10.
Exodus 13: 11-16
Deuteronomy 6: 4-9.
Deuteronomy 11: 13-21.

The open end of the *bayit* is then covered with another piece of parchment called the *titura* (Aramaic for *bridge*).

The cubicle of the *tefillah* of the head is divided into four compartments. The same four Biblical passages are written on four separate pieces of parchment, each tied with a strand of calf's hair and placed in a separate compartment. This *bayit*, too is covered with a *titura*.

The reason for the difference in the number of parchments placed inside the *tefillah shel rosh* and the *tefillah shel yad* is the same as the reason for all the phsyical features of the *tefillin*: *Halakhah le-Moshe mi-Sinai*, an oral tradition handed down from the days of Sinai. Certain rationalizations have, however, been attempted such as that, while the hand has one function, that of action, the head has four functions—seeing, hearing, speaking and smelling all of which must be attuned to God's will.

Calf's hair is used to remind us that the cardinal sin committed by the Children of Israel in the desert was their worshipping of the Golden Calf. So, we are warned always to be alert to the pitfalls of worshipping strange gods.[8]

Maimonides ruled that the *titura* should be sewn to the *bayit* with twelve stitches, three on each side. However, he does permit ten or fourteen stitches. One authority explains this as follows: the number twelve corresponds to the twelve tribes of Israel. Ten represents the ten tribes of the Israelites, not including the *Kohanim* and the *Levites* with their specific and unique duties in the service of the Temple. Fourteen reminds us that even in the early stages of Jewish history, two more tribes were added, Ephraim and Menasseh, the two sons of Joseph.[9]

Extending from the back of the *tefillin* is something that resembles a canal *(ma'abarta)* through which the straps *(retzu'ot)* are looped. The *retzu'ot* serve to fasten the *batim* to the arm and to the head. All components of the *tefillin* must be painted black, also as a *halakha le-Moshe mi-Sinai.* A possible reason for this choice of color is that black is completely devoid of any admixture of color and so it conveys the total uniqueness of God.[10]

Although the *retzu'ot* must be black on the outside, their interior can be any color but red. The Sages were afraid that people who did not know that it was paint, might mistakenly take the red for blood oozing from the wound of someone who had lost his hand and was still trying to lay *tefillin.*[11]

Two straps which extend from the *tefillah shel rosh* hang loosely in front of the wearer. One strap should stretch at least to the area of the heart (this will be discussed in a later paragraph); the other should reach at least to the navel. The reason advanced for this is that they show that God's power reaches to the depths as well as to the heights of the Universe.[12]

In France during the Middle Ages a sharp conflict of opinion arose between Rabbi Shlomo Yitzḥaki (Rashi) and his grandson Rabbi Ya'akov known as Rabbenu Tam, which shook the Jewish scholastic world at that time. What was seemingly an insignificant matter dealing with the order of placing the four pieces of parchment in the four compartments of the *tefillah shel rosh*, resulted in a storm that has its repercussions until this very day. According to Rashi, basing his view on the order in which these four passages appear in the Torah, and going from the wearer's left to right, Ex. 13:1-10 was to be inserted first; Ex. 13:11-16 second; Deut. 6:4-9 third; Deut. 11:13-21 last. Rabbenu Tam, on the other hand, while agreeing that Ex. 13:1-10 and 11-16 were to be inserted in the same compartments that Rashi had advocated, laid down that Deut. 11:13-21 was to be inserted before Deut. 6:4-9. His reasoning was that Exodus 13:11-16 begins with the word *Ve-hayah* and so does the passage of Deut. 11:13-21. According to Rabbenu Tam, therefore, we should place both *Ve-hayahs* side by side. The first word of Deut. 6:4-9 begins with the letter *Shin*. Placed in the last compartment, this *Shin* would be immediately behind the *Shin* embossed on the *bayit*. Both Rashi and Rabbenu Tam had their respective supporters. Those in Rashi's camp were fond of relating how a pair of ancient *tefillin* were found near the grave of the prophet Ezekiel with the passages in the order given by Rashi. Rabbenu Tam's supporters argued that, on the contrary, this archaeological find proved their view: the *tefillin* had been buried because they were invalid.

All later authorities have adopted Rashi's view. However, there are still a large number of pious Jews who, in their wish to satisfy both opinions, begin their morning prayers wearing the *tefillin* advocated by Rashi, but towards the end of the service remove these *tefillin* and put on another pair with the passages in the order advocated by Rabbenu Tam.[13]

The authoritative ruling in ancient and Medieval times was that there was no need to examine the script of the Biblical passages in the *tefillin* unless one had reason to believe that they had been damaged or become unfit for use by the erasure of a letter or the fading of the ink. However, since the quality of the ink has deteriorated in modern times, defects are likely to develop and so periodic exmination should be made.[14]

The word for Phylacteries used in the Bible is *totafot*, commonly translated as "frontlets." It is in the Aramaic translation for this word by Onkelos that we find the word *tefillin*. What is the origin of the word *tefillin*?[15]

(a) The root of this word is *palel* which denotes judgment. The idea is that with the *tefillin* we bear testimony to the world that we are God's chosen people.[16]

(b) The root of this word is *peli'ah*, "to be separated." Through the *tefillin* we become independent, separate, and apart from all peoples of the world.

(c) The singular for *tefillin* is *tefillah* which means prayer. In other words during the prayers of *Keriat Shema* and *Shemoneh Esreh* in the morning, we should wear *tefillin*.[17]

The wearing of the *tefillin* will bring the Jew into communion with God through his mind, symbolized by the *tefillah shel rosh*, and his actions, as represented by the *tefillah shel yad* which directly faces the heart. When we put on *tefillin* we should be physically pure and mentally alert. Physical cleanliness also means that there should be no emission of wind. If a person feels that, due to some physical disability or mental anxiety, he cannot fulfill one or both of these requirements, he should not put on *tefillin*. It is the common view, however, that few people are in such a bad physical or mental condition as not to be able to put on *tefillin* for the few minutes that it takes to recite the *Keriat Shema* and the *Shemoneh Esreh*.

The importance of putting on *tefillin* cannot be overemphasized. The Rabbis of the Talmud go out of their way to underscore the importance of this Mitzvah. For example, "One who is conscientious in accepting the yoke of the Kingdom of Heaven must wear his *tefillin* during prayers" (Berakhot 13b, 14a); "He who does not wear *tefillin* is classifed as a sinner" (Rosh Ha-Shanah 17a); "For every day that one fails to put on *tefillin*, he breaks eight commandments" (The reference is to the four Biblical passages inserted in the *tefillah* of the arm, and the four in the *tefillah* of the head); "He who does not wear *tefillin* perjures himself because, at the very moment when he says in his prayers that God commanded him to wear *tefillin*, he chooses not to wear them" (Berakhot 14b); "He who puts on *tefillin* is assured of his rightful place in Heaven." This last pronouncement is a play on the words of the Scriptural passage *Adonai Aleihem Yiḥyu*, usually translated as "Lord, by these things men will live" (Isaiah 38:16). In this context it is interpreted to mean: "Those who have the name of God *upon* them shall live forever."[18]

Which is more important, *tefillin* or *mezuzah*; *tefillin* or the wearing of a *tallit*?

What should one do if one is so poor that one is unable to afford both *tefillin* and a *mezuzah*, and must make a choice between the two? Then *tefillin* takes precedence because, while *mezuzah* applies only to a house, *tefillin* has to do with the person himself. One can do without a home if necessary, but one cannot do without a body.[19]

The Jew puts on his *tefillin* only after he has first wrapped himself in his *tallit*, although apparently it is the former that possesses greater sanctity. Why is this?

(a) The *tallit*, as we have noted has many features that recall the six hundred and thirteen *mitzvot*. Symbolically, when one wraps oneself in a *tallit*, it is as if he is enveloping himself in the six hundred and thirteen *mitzvot*. This feature is absent from the *tefillin*.

(b) *Ma'alin ba-kodesh*. In religious practice we adopt an ascending order. *Tefillin*, as we have noted, have a higher degree of sanctity than the *tallit*. We therefore begin with the *tallit* and raise ourselves to the state when we are able to put on *tefillin*.

(c) *Tadir veshe-eno tadir, tadir kodem:* the more frequent take precedence over the less frequent. The *tallit* is worn every day of the year; the *tefillin*, only on weekdays but not on Saturdays or Holidays.[20]

The procedure of putting on *tefillin* is as follows: The *tefillah shel yad* must be put on first. This is indicated by the verse "And *they* shall be as frontlets between your eyes." In other words, when we bind the *tefillah shel rosh* on our heads a condition must exist where the plural term "they" can apply. This can only be attained if the *tefillah shel yad* is already in place at the time that the worshipper attends to the *tefillah shel rosh.*[21]

The top of the strap of the *tefillah shel yad* is tied into a loop through which the left hand is passed allowing the *bayit* to be drawn up as far as the muscle on the upper part of the arm close to the shoulder. Several reasons are advanced for the *tefillin* being placed on the arm of the left hand:

(a) In the original Hebrew, "And it shall be for a sign upon your hands" (Ex. 13:16), the word "yadekha" is spelled irregularly, and so can be divided into two words: *Yad*—hand; *Kehah*—weak, i.e. the weak hand. Thus, the Rabbis inferred that, "It shall be for a sign upon your (weak, left) hand."

(b) "My *hand* also has laid the foundation of the earth and *My right hand* has spread out the heavens"(Isaiah 48:13). In the first example the Prophet generalizes, and in the second he goes into detail. Since the "right hand" is specifically mentioned, we can take it that the "hand," without any particular qualification, refers to the left.

(c) The benediction accompanying the placing of the *tefillah* upon the hand is, "Blessed are You O Lord. . . to put on the *tefillin.*" With the right hand, we put the *tefillin* onto our left hand.

(d) The *tefillah shel yad* must be placed tilted towards the heart. The left hand is the one closest to the heart.

(e) The "hand" should remind us of the "strong arm" with which God brought the children of Israel out of the Egyptian slavery. A straight line is the shortest distance between two points. So, if God used his strong right arm and, figuratively speaking, grasped the children of Israel, Israel's left hand was directly opposite God's right hand.[22]

We have already mentioned the blessing recited *before* attaching the *tefillin* to the arm. This involves the principle of *over la-asiatan*, that is, that the benediction must be said prior to the completion of the mitzvah.

There is a difference of opinion between the authorities as to whether we should recite one blessing or two before putting on *tefillin.* One view would have us only say one, on the grounds that, although the mitzvah may be composed of two parts—the *tefillah* of the head and the *tefillah* of the hand—it is still only one mitzvah. Another opinion is that, since the two are separate components of the mitzvah, each is entitled to its own distinct blessing. Sephardi Jews say only one blessing, and in some Jewish communities where two benedictions are recited, the verse, "Blessed forever be the Name of His glorious Kingdom," is added after the second blessing. This insertion denotes the status of the benediction as one subject to dispute, as its purpose is to nullify a *bracha le-vatala* (an unnecessary blessing in which God's Name is taken in vain).

Those that say a second benediction for the *tefillah* of the head do so not because of *over la-asiatan* but rather as an adoration of God who blessed us with this mitzvah.[23]

The technical aspect of reciting the prayer before a mitzvah requires the person who is putting on the *tefillin* to recite the benediction during those few moments that elapse between the time he places the *tefillin* on his arm and the time he finishes fastening the strap to his arm. The idea is that once the *tefillah* is fastened he has already performed the mitzvah and any blessing uttered at this point would violate the requirement of *over la-asiatan.*[24]

The remaining part of the strap that was used to fasten the *tefillah shel yad* is then wound around the forearm seven times. The seven Hebrew words of the verse in Psalms (145:16) gives us the basis for this ritual: "Thou openest thy hand and satisfiest the desire of every living thing."[25] Others are of the opinion that the seven rings around the forearm correspond to the seven benedictions recited at a wedding ceremony. The *tefillin* are part of the ritual of the marriage of God and Israel.[26] This procedure is concluded by tying the strap around the palm of the hand.

The next step calls for the placing of the *tefillah shel rosh.* The *tefillah* must be set within the area of the head bound by the hair line and ending at the cranium where the skull of a newborn baby is soft. Then, to complete the procedure, one unwinds the strap from the palm and binds three rings around the middle finger while reciting the words of Hosea (2:21-22) "And I will *betroth* you unto me forever; I will *betroth* you unto me in righteousness and in justice and in lovingkindness and in mercy; and I will *betroth* you unto me in faithfulness and you shall know the Lord." These three betrothals of the children of Israel to God are symbolized by the three rings around the finger.

Another reason for this arrangement: we have previously mentioned that God's name *Shaddai* plays a dominant role in the *tefillin.* When the straps are wound around the upper arm they are arranged so as to form a *Shin*; the top part of the three rings around the middle finger take the form of a *Daled.* The rings on the under part of the finger are tied to form a *Yud.*[27] Together they compose the word *Shaddai.* Also the embossed *Shin* on the *bayit* of the head *tefillah* and the *Daled* of the knot at the nape of the neck, plus the *Yud* of the knot of the loop around the arm, all add up to *Shaddai.*

The *tefillah shel yad* must always be covered, because the Rabbis interpret the verse "And it shall be for a sign *unto you* upon your hand," (Ex. 13:9) to mean that it is a personal matter. Only "to you," privately, shall it be a sign, but not to others. The *tefillah shel rosh*, on the other hand, must always be exposed (Deut. 28:10).[28]

Furthermore, the *tefillah shel yad* is directed towards the heart. The thoughts of the heart are always hidden and internal. The other *tefillah* is on the head which includes the eyes. The eyes always see what is exposed.[29]

All this of course, applies only to the right-handed person. A left-handed individual binds his *tefillin* on his right, his weaker arm.[30]

The procedure of removing the *tefillin* is the reverse of putting them on. First, the *tefillah shel rosh* is taken off and then the *tefillah shel yad*. Two reasons are suggested for this:

(a) We have previously indicated that because the Torah says,

"They shall be as frontlets between your eyes," in referring to the *tefillah shel rosh*, the plural "they" implies that the *tefillah shel yad* must already be in its place by the time the *tefillah shel rosh* is placed on the head. Should we remove the *tefillah shel yad* first, the *tefillah shel rosh* would remain without the "they" being operable.

(b) In referring to the *tefillah shel yad*, the Torah describes it as an *ot*, a sign; when speaking of the *tefillah shel rosh* the Torah states, "It shall be for a remembrance." We are to remember the meaning of the sign indicating that God took us out of Egypt. So, if we remove the *tefillah shel yad* first, while the remembrance of the *tefillah shel rosh* remains, we are at a loss as to *what* we are supposed to remember (the "sign" itself having already been removed).[30]

Now the question arises: as to the correct time for putting on *tefillin* in the morning; when does the day actually begin? Here, too, the authorities base their views on the Torah: "And all the nations of the earth shall *see* that you are called by the name of the Lord" (Deut. 28:10). We have already noted that the *Shin* on the *tefillah shel rosh* represents the Name of God. So, *tefillin* must be worn when "all the nations of the earth shall see the *Shin*." The Rabbis deduced that we can put on *tefillin* when there is enough light for two acqaintances to recognize each other.[31]

There are occasions when one is not allowed to put on *tefillin*. For instance, one is not supposed to lay *tefillin* at night because the Torah (Ex. 13:10) tells us to fulfill this mitzvah "*mi-yamim yamimah*." This is commonly translated from "year to year." However, the root of these two words is *yom*, daytime. Thus, the Rabbis have interpreted the phrase to mean that the mitzvah of *tefillin* is to be carried out only during the daytime.[32]

As already noted, the Sabbath and Holidays are occasions when the Jew is not supposed to put on *tefillin*. This is because the Torah refers to the Sabbath, *tefillin*, and Circumcision as *ot*, a unique sign, the Sabbath being the sign of Israel's awareness that God created the world in six days and rested on the seventh,

Circumcision being a stamp on the body of the Jew affirming a sign by means of which the Jew confirms that it was God's power (lit., hand) that brought the Jewish people out of Egypt.

In Jewish jurisprudence testimony must be substantiated by two witnesses. Therefore, during the weekday, the Jew's submission to God is attested to by two witnesses—the sign of the *tefillin* and the sign of circumcision. On *Shabbat*, the day itself is a sign and corroborates the testimony of the circumcision, hence *tefillin* are unnecessary. If *tefillin* were to be put on on the Sabbath, the whole concept of testimony would be overdone and lose its importance. Holidays, like the Sabbath, also constitute such signs.[33]

The question whether *tefillin* should be worn during the intermediary days of a Festival *(ḥolo shel moed)* brought into focus a sharp difference of opinion. Are these days considered an integral part of the Festival and so exempt from *tefillin* or are they regarded as ordinary weekdays? Some of the authorities who are opposed to the putting on of *tefillin* base their decision on the Zohar where we are told that laying *tefillin* during the *holo shel moed* would be an affront to God, who, figuratively speaking, wears *tefillin* as a sign of joy that His people are celebrating a holiday on earth. By himself putting on *tefillin*, however, during this part of the holiday (as if they were ordinary weekdays) the Jew, as it were, cuts short the joy of God. Those that are in favor of putting on *tefillin* hold the view that days when one is permitted to work should be treated as weekdays.[34] Sephardim and Ḥassidim do not wear *tefillin* on intermediary days because their ritual is very much influenced by *Kabbalah*. Most Ashkenazi Jews, however, do wear them, except in Israel where the Sephardic practice has gained unanimous acceptance.

During the day when a close relative has passed away, the mourner should not wear *tefillin*. A verse in Amos (8:10) is the basis for this view: "And its end shall be a day of bitterness." The idea is that the day when a close relative dies is a sad one for all who care for him. In Ezekiel (24:17) the Prophet encourages the people by saying that there will be an end to mourning, that in the future "you shall place your diadem upon you," which the Rabbis interpret to mean *tefillin.* On the other hand, when one is experiencing the trauma of bereavement, one is not expected to wear the "diadem of joy," the *tefillin.*[35]

Originally, the Sages had no hesitation in exempting a bridegroom from putting on *tefillin* on the morning after his wedding, arguing realistically that at such a time he could not possibly concentrate all his thoughts on them. This concentration, as we have previously noted, as well as a clean body, were the preconditions necessary for putting on *tefillin.* It is a later, and perhaps even more realistic view that, in fact, *no one* can avoid letting his thoughts wander while wearing *tefillin,* and that, as the bridegroom is in this no exception, he should wear them.[36]

Because *Tishah Be'Av* is a national day of mourning, the wearing of *tefillin* is postponed from the morning till the afternoon *(Mincha)* prayer.[37]

When visiting a cemetery or in the immediate vicinity of the dead, the wearing of *tefillin* is also forbidden. The idea underlying this is inferred from the passage in Proverbs (17:6), "Whoever mocks the poor, blasphemes his Maker." In this case the dead person is regarded as "poor," that is, utterly lacking in the capacity for performing *mitzvoth.* Anyone who puts on his *tefillin* near the dead is therefore showing little consideration for the latter's state of deprivation and is, in effect, saying: "See! You are inferior to me because I can wear *tefillin* while you cannot." However, he many remain in the vicinity of the dead if he removes the *tefillah shel rosh,* which is the exposed and visible *tefillah,* and remains only with the *shel yad,* which, as we have seen, always remains covered. The Rabbis' consideration for the dead is such that they attribute to them the feelings a living person might have if deprived of this great mitzvah.[38]

SOURCES

1. *Otzar Yisrael* s.v.: Tefillin.
2. *Tur Oraḥ Ḥayyim*; *Arukh ha-Shulḥan* 26, par. 1, 2.
3. *Tur Oraḥ Ḥayyim* 32; *Arukh ha-Shulḥan* 32, par. 23.
4. *Ḥayye Avraham* p. 5b.
5. *Minhage Yeshurun* p. 208.
6. *Encyclopedia Judaica* Vol. 15, p. 900.
7. *Sefer ha-Mat'amim* p. 132.
8. *Minhage Yeshurun* p. 209.
9. *Ḥayye Avraham* p. 5b, 6a.
10. *Ḥayye Avraham* p. 6a.
11. *Arukh ha-Shulḥan* 35, par. 5.
12. *Minhage Yeshurun* 209.
13. *Tur Oraḥ Ḥayyim* 34; *Perishah* 34, par. 1.
14. *Tur Oraḥ Ḥayyim*; *Bet Yoseph* 39; *Arukh ha-Shulḥan* 39, par. 6.
15. *Tur Oraḥ Ḥayyim* 25; *Perishah*, par. 9; *Ḥayye Avraham* 5a; *Minhage Yeshurun* 212.
16. S.R. Hirsch, *Ḥoreb*, Ch. 38.
17. *Tur Oraḥ Ḥayyim* 37; *Bet Yoseph*; *Arukh ha-Shulḥan* 37, Pars. 3,4; 38, par. 2.
18. *Tur Oraḥ Ḥayyim* 37; *Perishah* 37, par. 1; *Ben Ish Ḥai* p. 19, par. 7.
19. *Tur Oraḥ Ḥayyim*; *Bet Yoseph* 38; *Arukh ha-Shulḥan* 38, par. 16.
20. *Tur Oraḥ Ḥayyim*; *Bet Yoseph* 25; *Perishah* 25, par. 1; *Arukh ha-Shulḥan* 25, par. 1.
21. *Arukh ha-Shulḥan* 25, par. 9.
22. *Avudraham* p. 130.
23. *Arukh ha-Shulḥan* 25, pars. 9, 10, 11, 12, 13.
24. *Arukh ha-Shulḥan* 25, par. 15.
25. *Minhage Yeshurun* p. 211.
26. *Sefer ha-Mat'amim* p. 133.
27. *Minhage Yeshurun* p.212.
28. *Arukh ha-Shulḥan* 27, par. 15.
29. *Arukh ha-Shulḥan* 25, par. 15.
30. *Ḥayye Avraham* p. 6b.
31. *Tur Oraḥ Ḥayyim*; *Bet Yoseph*; *Perishah* 30.
32. *Arukh ha-Shulḥan* 30, par. 2.
33. *Tur Oraḥ Ḥayyim* 31; *Arukh ha-Shulḥan* 31, par. 1; *Ḥayye Avraham* p. 6b; *Ben Ish Ḥai* p. 20; *Avudraham* p. 31.
34. *Tur Oraḥ Ḥayyim*; *Bet Yoseph* 31; *Ben Ish Ḥai* p. 20.
35. *Tur Oraḥ Ḥayyim* 38; *Arukh ha-Shulḥan* 38, par. 8.
36. *Tur Oraḥ Ḥayyim*; *Bet Yoseph* 38; *Arukh ha-Shulḥan* 38, par. 9.
37. *Tur Oraḥ Ḥayyim*; *Bet Yoseph* 45; *Arukh ha-Shulḥan* 45, par. 1.

Keriat Shema

The belief in the unity of God is the cornerstone of the entire superstructure of our religion. One may be meticulously observant of all the commandments and yet it is meaningless if he lacks belief in the oneness of God.

The affirmation of the oneness of God is declared in the Biblical verse "Hear O Israel, the Lord our God, the Lord is *One*" (Deuteronomy 6:4), which is a translation of "*Shema Yisrael Adonai Elohenu Adonai Eḥad.*" (Henceforth, we will refer to this pronouncement as the *Shema*.)

The *Shema* is recited four times each day; at the *Maariv* service, in bed before sleep overtakes us, in the morning before the recitation of chapters dealing with the sacrifices and finally, during the *Shaḥarit* prayers. The Kabbalists explain the reasons for these daily pronouncements of the *Shema* as follows: In the evening man has returned to a more sedate life than the one he has experienced all day in the marketplace. His mood and mentality change. In this state of transition he should immediately confirm his subimission to God by reciting the *Shema*.

The Talmud (Berakhot 60b) states that upon retiring to his bed for the night one should repeat the *Shema*. According to the Midrash (Psalm 4) this is a protection against demons. Other authorities, rather than associating the *Shema* with demons contend that this is a Rabbinic decree intended to affirm one's belief in the unity of God at a different phase of his daily life cycle.

The early recitation of the *Shema* in the course of the reading of the chapters dealing with the sacrifices is a continuation of this affirmation but at the beginning of the daily routine.

Finally, in the *Shaḥarit* service, man reaffirms his belief in One God prior to resuming his normal daily activities. Each of these four instances serves as an inspiration to permeate him after his communion with his God.[1]

Basically, the uttering of the *Shema* is limited to its repetition at the *Shaḥarit* and the *Maariv* services. The Torah commands us "You shall teach them diligently to your children, *speaking of them* when you sit in your house, and when you walk by the way, when you *lie down* and when you *rise up*" (Deuteronomy 6:7). The words "lie down" and "rise up" refer to the time of the day when people awaken, and when people retire. This means: you shall speak these words *during the day* and *during the evening.* Because the term "*these words*" is vague, many opinions resulted among the early scholars as to its meaning. They all agree that it is a Biblical injunction that the *Shema* must be recited at least twice daily; there is disagreement, however, as to what parts of the Scriptures are included in the Biblical commandment of, "you shall speak of them." Some authorities contend that the Biblical injunction refers to all three sections of the *Shema* (see below); others opine that only the recitation of the first chapter of the *Shema* is of Biblical origin. The majority opinion, however, is that the first verse, *Shema Yisrael*, etc. alone is the subject of "You shall *speak* of them."[2]

Yet the entire *Shema* consists of three portions of the Scriptures: Deuteronomy 6:4-9; Deuteronomy 11: 13-21; and Numbers 15: 37-41. Why were particularly these three portions of the Torah chosen? Two interesting explanations are proposed:

(a) First we recite the *Shema*, thus confirming our unshakeable belief in One God. This is followed by the second paragraph which gives evidence of our submission to God's law. Finally we read the third portion which deals with the fringes *(tzitziot)* of a garment which in turn reminds us of the Exodus from Egypt and the Omnipotence of God (Berakhot 13a). This paragraph is also the last one because whereas all other commandments incorporated in paragraph two are applicable all the time, the commandment of fringes applies only during the day but not during the night.

(b) The Jerusalem Talmud (Berakhot, Chapter 1) maintains that all the Ten Commandments could either directly or indirectly be inferred from the three chapters of the *Shema*. For example, "I am the Lord Your God" from "Hear O Israel"; "You shall have no other Gods" from "The Lord is One"; "You shall not take the name of the Lord in vain" from "You shall love the Lord", etc.[3]

It should be noted that a sentence is inserted between "Hear O Israel" and the beginning of the chapter, "And you shall love the Lord your God, etc." This sentence, "Blessed be His glorious and sovereign name forever and ever" which is recited inaudibly, is not to be found in the entire Scriptures. Yet it is incorporated into the most fundamental of all Scriptural readings. Why?

The Talmud relates that when Jacob lay on his deathbed he called to his children, "Gather yourselves together and hear, you sons of Jacob; and hearken to Israel your father." The Sages comment that Jacob was prepared to reveal to his twelve sons the time of the final redemption when suddenly he felt himself divested of the presence of the *Shekhinah*. Attributing this sudden lapse to the unworthiness of his sons, he anxiously inquired whether any one of them had been indiscreet or unfaithful to God, for which their father was being penalized by the departure of the *Shekhinah* from him. Whereupon, they all replied in unison, "Hear O Israel (addressing themselves to Jacob, whose name was also Israel) The Lord our God, the Lord is One." In other words, have no fears, none of us has strayed. Thereupon, Jacob joyously answered, "Blessed be His glorious and sovereign name for ever and ever." Therefore, when we recite the "Hear O Israel" (addressing ourselves to the people of Israel) we, too, recite the verse "Blessed be, etc."[4]

Why is this verse recited inaudibly? Two explanations are advanced:

(a) According to the Mystics the Angels offer their prayer of adoration to God in the words, "Blessed be His Glorious and Sovereign Name forever and ever." When Moses scaled the heavens to receive the Law from the hands of God, he heard this verse repeated by the Angels time and again. When he returned to his people with the Tablets he boldly confessed that while the Tablets were given to him by God, he surreptitiously appropriated the benediction of the Angels and brought it down to earth. Since this smacked of mischief we recite it silently out of humility.[5]

(b) There is a strict injunction that we are not permitted to add nor subtract even one word from the full text of the Torah. When reciting the *Shema* we are reading portions that are found in the Torah proper. However, we have already noted that the sentence "Blessed be He, etc." is not to be found in the Torah. Including this sentence in the *Shema* might be construed as an addition of an unauthorized verse. We therefore recite this sentence in a whisper to indicate that it is not a Scriptural verse.[6]

It should be clear by now that the first verse "Hear O Israel, etc." is the foundation of the entire Jewish religion. As such, its reciting requires the deepest concentration and profound dedication. The *Shema* cannot be repeated in a perfunctory, casual manner which would diminish its significance. The *Shema* must be recited passionately in a genuine outpouring of emotion and in an ecstatic voice.

It is customary to close one's eyes and cover them with the palm of the hand when reciting the *Shema*. One reason is to avoid any distraction whatsoever from complete concentration. Another reason: In Rabbinic literature a blind man is equated with the dead; neither can see the wondrous works of God. Just as a dying person yields his soul up to God so does one reciting the *Shema* by covering his eyes, thus blinding himself temporarily, submit himself to total trust in the omnipotence of God.[7]

An early authority, citing a Midrash in the beginning of Deuteronomy points out that the entire *Shema* consists of two hundred and forty five words. According to the Talmud the human body consists of two hundred and forty eight members. Were we to assign each word to one member, we would be short three words. Hence, the custom of adding *El Melekh Ne'eman*—"God is the Faithful King"—prior to the recitation of the *Shema*; or *Adonai Elohekhem Emet*—"I am the Lord your God, true"—at the conclusion of the *Shema*. *El Melekh Ne'eman* was chosen because the first letters of these three words comprise the word *Amen*. One authority condemns the practice of preceding the *Shema* with three words on the grounds that it is an unnecessary interruption in the sequence of the prayers. He advocates the second method of completing the two hundred and forty eight words.[8]

Still, the question arises: why is it necessary to have two hundred forty eight words corresponding to the two hundred forty eight members of the body? The following explanations have been advanced:

(a) The Hebrew letters whose numerical value totals two hundred forty eight comprise the word RaMaḤ. The Hebrew word for spear is *Romaḥ* which, too, totals two hundred forty eight. The inference is that the two hundred forty five words of the *Shema* plus the three added words totalling two hundred forty eight serve as a spear in the hands of the Jew to overpower the temptations of Satan.[9]

(b) According to another opinion, the reason why the Torah proper did not prolong the *Shema* with three additional words to correspond to the two hundred forty eight members of the body is based on the premise that man is able to control any function of his body with the exception of those of three organs: the heart, the eye and the ear. Oftimes one's heart may be misled by idle thoughts entering his mind unwittingly. Similarly, one may hear frivolous talk without forewarning, and one may also find himself gazing and lusting without prior thought. Hence, it may be assumed not to include these three organs of the body among the two hundred forty eight. The authorities, therefore, added these three extra words to the *Shema* to cover the virtually uncontrollable actions of the heart, the eyes and the ears.[10]

The Sages of the Talmud were inclined to allow the *Shema* to be read in any language intelligible to the reader. They took their cue from the first word, *Shema* which they interpreted to mean that one may recite the *Shema* in the language which he is accustomed to hearing and understanding. In due time, however, when Jews were dispersed throughout the world and they spoke the native language of the country in which they lived, it was discovered that the translation of key words in the *Shema* were being distorted and the meaning of certain phrases in one country was not identical with the meaning of these same phrases in another country. It was then decreed that in order to preserve the unanimity of the Jewish people the *Shema* should be recited in Hebrew only.[11]

We have already noted that *Keriat Shema*—the recitation of the *Shema*—is a commandment of Biblical origin. If so, why is it not required to recite a benediction before proclaiming the *Shema*? The answer is that one of the benedictions that one utters upon arising in the morning is: "Blessed are You, Our God, King of the Universe who hath sanctified us with these commandments and bidden us to devote ourselves to the study of the Torah." Since the *Shema* is composed of portions of the Torah, the early benediction of "devote ourselves to the study of the Torah" serves also as a preceding benediction for the recitation of the *Shema*.[12]

SOURCES

1. *Ben Ish Ḥai* p. 61.
2. *Arukh ha-Shulḥan* 58 par. 15.
3. *Avudraham* p. 46.
4. *Tur Oraḥ Ḥayyim* 61; *Perisha* ad locum.
5. *Ḥayye Avraham* p. 11a.
6. Ibid.
7. *Tur Oraḥ Ḥayyim* 61; *Arukh ha-Shulḥan* 61 pars. 1, 3; 63 par. 6; *Ta'amei ha-Minhagim* p. 33-34.
8. *Avudraham* p. 45.
9. *Ben Ish Ḥai* p. 160.
10. *Ḥayyei Avraham* p. 11a.
11. *Arukh ha-Shulḥan* 62 par. 3, 4.
12. *Ta'amei ha-Minhagim* p. 38.

Shemoneh Esreh

Although to the layman *Tefillah* denotes prayer in general, in Rabbinic literature it refers specifically to the eighteen benedictions known as the *Shemoneh Esreh* (also called the *Amidah*—Hebrew for standing, as they are recited when standing up).

Maimonides *(Hilkhot Tefillah)* says that it is a positive Biblical commandment to pray to God every day. This he deduces from the verse: "And you shall serve the Lord your God" (Ex. 23:25). The word "serve" is interpreted by the Rabbis to mean prayer. Here lies the classic difference between Maimonides and Naḥmanides. According to the former, while the nature, time and number of prayers to be recited during the day are not laid down in the Torah, the basic obligation to pray is. Since there is no set time for the fulfillment of this duty, women also are obliged to pray and are not exempt from doing so on the grounds that it is a mitzvah involving a time element. According to Naḥmanides, however, prayer is a Rabbinic decree, and not a Biblical one. So, according to him, while prayer is obligatory, omissions in this repect are not so serious as the neglect of a command from the Torah itself.

A Jew should pray as soon as he gets up in the morning. He should not attend to his own affairs or start on a journey or even taste any food or drink before praying because, by doing so he would be showing that his world was centered around himself rather than around his Creator. Rather, he should first express his gratitude to God for granting him another day.[1] There is a view that drinking water before prayer is not a sign of arrogance. Maimonides went a step further by putting forward the opinion that, if one is hungry or thirsty, like a sick person, he should be permitted to eat or drink before praying.[2]

As it was noted above, the most important of all our prayers—what we call *Tefillah*—are the "eighteen benedictions." However, there are other expressions of worshipping God, taken for the most part from the Psalms, that we recite before the *Tefillah.*[3]

How many blessings are there in the *Tefillah* or *Amidah*; when were they composed, and why?

As the term *Shemoneh Esreh* indicates, originally there were eighteen benedictions. In a subsequent period, however, a nineteenth blessing was added, one which condemned slanderers and traitors *(Vela-malshinim).* However, although there are nineteen at present we still refer to the *Amidah* as the "Eighteen Benedictions."

When were they composed? Who compiled them and why? According to tradition, the prayers of the *Amidah* existed from the earliest history of the Jewish people. With each new historical event another blessing was added: when Abraham was rescued from the burning furnace in Ur of the Chaldees, the benediction of *Magen Avraham* was composed. When Isaac was a hair-breadth away from being slaughtered, the prayer of *Meḥayye ha-metim* was instituted. When Jacob had his vision of the ladder spanning Heaven and earth, the prayer of *Ha-El ha-kadosh* was formulated. When Pharaoh appointed Joseph as his vice-regent, according to tradition, Joseph was instructed by an angel in seventy languages to enable him to cope with all the peoples that came to Egypt, and from this we get the prayer *Ḥonen ha-da'at.* When Reuben slept with his father's concubine Bilhah, his life became forfeit. However, he repented and was spared. Thus we have the *Ha-rotzeh bi-teshuvah.* When Yehudah acknowledged his guilt for having slept with his daughter-in-law, Tamar, disguised as a prostitute, he was forgiven. This occasioned the prayer of *Ḥanun ha-marbeh li-sloaḥ.* When the Egyptians oppressed our forefathers and God decided to redeem them, the prayer of *Go'el Yisrael* was instituted. When Abraham circumcised himself, he was healed, according to tradition, by the angel Raphael; hence the prayer *Rofe ḥole ammo Yisrael.* When, during his travels, Isaac was blessed with such abundance that his fields produced a hundred-fold, this evoked the prayer of *Mevarekh ha-shanim.* When in the days of Joseph, Jacob and all his sons gathered in Egypt, the entire Jewish community was gathered together for the first time. Thus evolved the prayer *Mekabbetz nideḥe ammo Yisrael.* When the Torah was presented to the children of Israel, the prayer *Ohev tzedakah u-mishpat* was added. When the Egyptians were drowned in the Red Sea, the prayer of *Shover oyevim* was instituted. When God kept the promise to Jacob that Joseph would be present at his death, the prayer of *Mish'an u-mivtaḥ la-tzaddikim* was adopted. When Solomon built the Temple the prayer of *Boneh Yerushalayim* was instituted. When the children of Israel emerged unscathed from the Red Sea, the prayer of *Matzmiaḥ keren yeshua* was composed. When the children of Israel in Egypt sighed under the yoke of slavery and their cries were answered by God, the prayer of *Shome'a tefillah* was introduced. When the Children of Israel erected a Tabernacle in the desert and the Shekhinah rested upon it, the prayer *Ha-maḥazir shekhinato le-Tzion* was formulated. When Solomon brought the Ark into the Temple and offered his Thanksgiving to God, the prayer of *Ha-tov shimmekha ulekha na'eh le-hodot* was recited. When the Children of Israel entered the Promised Land and were finally allowed to live in peace the prayer of *Oseh ha-shalom* was formulated.[4] Thus we see that the original *Amidah* was already in existence by the time of Ezra and Nehemiah. It was during this period, 428 B.C.E. onwards, that the *Anshe Knesset Ha-Gedolah*, the men of the Great Assembly, arranged these benedictions in their proper order. However, during the Hasmonean era several of the blessings were omitted by people who felt that in their homeland, they had become obsolete. It was during the days of Rabban Gamliel in Yavneh (70-100 C.E.) that the Sages reinstituted and regrouped the nineteen prayers of the *Amidah* in the order that is extant to this day.[5]

Why were these prayers of the *Amidah* arranged precisely in the sequence we know today? The following explanation is given: First, we recognize that, in our supplication to God, we ourselves are inadequate and we need the assistance of our forefathers, Abraham, Isaac and Jacob. Only then can we proceed to extoll the greatness of God. The third benediction speaks of man's awe before the holiness of God. This is followed by the prayer for understanding, without which, prayer and everything else are scarcely meaningful. Once we have been blessed with knowledge, we then acquire the motivation for *Teshuvah*, repentance. If there is repentence, there must be *Seliḥa*, God's forgiveness. Once we are assured of forgiveness, we can anticipate *Ge'ulah*, redemption. The eighth prayer of *Refa'enu*, "Heal us O Lord," was inserted here because circumcision takes place on the eighth day of a child's life and we pray to God for complete recovery. We then revert to the logical sequence and, after our request for spiritual redemption, we ask God to provide our physical and economic needs as well in the benediction of *Mevarekh ha-shanim*. However, to look after one's own material, and even spiritual needs is not enough for a Jew must also think of *Kelal Yisrael*—the entire Jewish community. Therefore, the tenth benediction *Teka be-shofar* ends with "Blessed are You O Lord Who gathers the dispersed of Israel." The final ingathering of Israel will be heralded by the blast of the Shofar. Once we have resettled in our own country we ask God—*Hashivah shoftenu*—to restore our judges and legal institutions and let the new society be organized on just lines. The twelfth blessing, which deals with slanderers and traitors follows closely on this plea for justice. Then, once we are rid of evil in society, righteousness will come into its own; hence the prayer of *Al hatzaddikim*. Following this comes the one of *Boneh Yerushalayim*, for the one place where true righteousness should be possible is the Holy City. When the centrality of Jerusalem is fully recognized, then the appearance of the Messiah—as represented by the prayer *Et tzemaḥ David*—would seem to be the natural next step. In this Messianic era, with the people of Israel living in the land of Israel, we can be quite certain that our prayers will be completely accepted and answered by God. Hence the prayer of *Shome'a tefillah.* If a people is moved to pray, they will want to worship the God who answers their prayers. This, of course, refers to the various sacrifices which are referred to in the prayer of *Retzeh.* The eighteenth benediction, *Modim*, is the one in which we thank God for accepting our prayers and look forward to receiving further kindness from Him. The concluding benediction *Sim shalom*, expresses the deepest hope for the most prized blessing of all—that of Peace.[6]

Maimonides tells us that there are the following requirements for the correct recital of the *Amidah:*

(a) A person must stand erect because, in Temple Days, the priest stood while he performed the ritual. Another reason is so as to differentiate between the lower forms of animals and the human being who is able to stand upright.[7] When standing erect, the worshipper should have his feet together, as if he had only one foot. There is a difference of opinion why this must be so. One authority traces back the reason for this to the Scriptural passage (Ezekiel 1:7) where the angels are described as having their legs appear as one. Since the whole idea of reciting the *Amidah* with the appropriate concentration is that we should appear before God as angels, our feet must be held in a position similar to theirs. Another view holds that while there is no resemblance whatsoever between us and the angels, we could more reasonably be compared to the Priests in the Temple while we are saying the *Amidah.* The latter used to ascend the ramp to offer their sacrifices on the altar with very short steps, setting the toe of one foot immediately behind the heel of the other. This kind of walk also gave them the appearance of only having one foot.[8]

(b) When reciting the *Amidah*, we must face the City of Jerusalem and the *Har ha-Bayit* where the Temple once stood. This implies that in all places west of Jerusalem we must face eastward. However, there is an opinion that one must face southeast because by facing due east, it might appear as if we were worshipping the sun.[9]

(c) One's bodily functions must be attended to before the *Amidah.* A sudden urge for bodily relief would definitely interfere with one's concentration on prayer. Furthermore, the Rabbis base this requirement on the verse "Prepare yourself to meet your God" (Amos 4:12).

(d) Proper dress is a prerequisite for acceptable prayer. This, too, is based on the above verse in Amos. In ancient times men wore one-piece robes with no undergarments. Dressed in this manner the lower parts of the body were visible when glancing down. This was considered inappropriate for the *Amidah*, and so trousers were worn. Until this day some Hassidic Jews use a *gartel* (belt) to separate the upper (spiritual) and lower (instinctual) parts of the body.

(e) The proper place for the *Amidah*, too, is important. There must be no partition in front of the worshipper during the *Amidah.* No obstruction must intervene between him and the eastern wall of the Synagogue. However, this does not apply to something that is fixed, such as a bench. All these considerations are based on the verse where we find Hezekiah turned his face to the wall and prayed to God (II Kings 20:2).[10]

(f) In what tone of voice must the *Amidah* be recited? The cue is taken from the verse, "Only her lips moved but her voice was not heard" (I Samuel 1:13). In the moment of her deepest communion with God, Hannah merely moved her lips but did not raise her voice. It has been suggested that raising the voice could imply that God does not hear what goes on in the heart.[11] Thus, during this deep emotional experience, we too are required to recite the *Amidah* in silence and only to move our lips while forming the words of the prayer. Another reason for silence is that it represents the manner in which angels are said to praise God.

(g) During the *Amidah*, the Rabbis have instituted that we should bend our knees and then bow on four different occasions: first, at the start of the *Amidah*; second, at the benediction which includes the name of Abraham; third, at *Modim*, and last, at the benediction that precedes the priestly blessing. On each occasion we bend our knees at the word *Barukh* and bow at the word *Attah*, resuming our erect posture at the word *Adonai*—all to demonstrate that God can raise up those who are bent.[12]

Maimonides adopts the Talmudic division of the *Amidah* into three separate sets of blessings. The first set, consisting of three blessings, are praises offered by a subject to his king before proceeding with any other business. The second set is composed of the next thirteen benedictions which belong in the category of *Bakashah*—"request." Having extolled his King, man feels secure in seeking God's favor. The last three benedictions form the *Hodayah*—prayers of gratitude. As we make ready to take leave of the King and are quite sure that our request will be given a serious hearing, we thank Him for His kindness.

Whether while reciting the *Amidah*, we are comparable to angels or to priests, the immediate vicinity of the place where somebody says the *Amidah* is considered to have a special sanctity. It is for this reason that one should avoid sitting or standing within the four cubits of a worshipper who is in the middle of the *Amidah*. With this in mind, Sephardi Jews make beckoning gestures to those who are close by to make them realize that the *Amidah* is ready to begin. Some say that the reason for these gestures lies in the Prophet's description of the angels' manner of worship: "*Mekabbelim ol malkhut shamayim zeh mi-zeh*," (they accept the yoke of God's kingdom one from the other).[13]

After all the preliminaries to the *Amidah* have been completed, the worshipper first takes three steps backward to make sure that his four cubits are unoccupied and then retraces those three steps forward and starts his *Amidah*. There are several reasons offered to account for this procedure:

(a) In keeping with the analogy with the king and his subject, no servant approaches royalty with an excess of confidence. He takes short hesitant steps to display his respect.

(b) According to the Aggadah, the children of Israel retreated three miles from Mt. Sinai and then retraced their steps back to the foot of the mountain. They did so out of their deep feelings of awe before the imminent event, the proclamation of the Ten

Commandments. Obviously, one cannot retreat as far as that before beginning the *Amidah.* Instead we take three steps backward, as a symbolic gesture.

(c) In the Bible we find three men, confronted by specific challenges, constructing their respective strategic lines of approach to those who had the power to change things: "And Abraham *approached* and said, 'Will You destroy the righteous along with the wicked?'" (Genesis 18:23); "And Judah *approached* (Joseph) and said, 'You are to me as Pharaoh'"(Genesis 44:18); "And Elijah *approached* the people and said to them: 'How long will you straddle the fence?'"(I Kings 18:21).

(d) When Moses went up to Mt. Sinai, according to the Aggadah, he passed through three separate degrees of darkness, *Ḥoshekh* (cloudiness); *Anan* (mist); *Arafel* (thick darkness).

(e) As we shall see shortly, the *Amidah* corresponds to the sacrifices. There was a ramp that led to the edge of the altar. Between the ramp and the altar proper stood three slabs of stone on three gratings. Thus, when the priest was ready to mount the altar with the sacrifice, it was necessary for him to take three steps on the three slabs of stone.[14]

Upon the conclusion of the *Amidah*, one must bow to the left and to the right and once again take three steps backward for reasons (a), (b), (c), (d), and (e) above.[15]

The many comparisons that have been made between the *Amidah* and the sacrifices in Temple time is due to the idea suggested by the Sages and accepted by Maimonides *(Yad Hilkhot Tefillah* Chap. 1) that we say the *Amidah* three times a day as substitutes for the daily communal sacrifices that were brought into the Temple:

Shaḥarit, the morning service, corresponds to *Korban Tamid shel Shaḥar*—the morning sacrifice.

Minḥah, the afternoon service, corresponds to *Korban Tamid shel Bein Ha-Arbayim*—the afternoon sacrifice.

Maariv, the evening service, corresponds to the process of burning the fat of the sacrifice during the night.

There was also an idea, endorsed by Maimonides, that Abraham was the first to pray in the morning; Isaac, in the afternoon; and Jacob, in the evening.

After having stepped back three paces, we remain where we are at least until the *Ḥazzan* begins his repetition of the *Amidah*. One who returns immediately to his original position is compared to a *kelev sheshav al ki'o*—a "dog who returns to his vomit." In other words, one moment the worshipper stands spiritually uplifted and close to his Maker, after which he steps back three paces, and immediately returns to his original position, thus giving the impression that he has no appreciation at all of the experience he has been granted.

Although the nineteen benedictions of the *Amidah* have been concluded, there is an epilogue, the devotion, *Elokai Netzor*. Towards the end of this piece, it is a custom to recite a verse from the Scriptures the first and last letter of which correspond to the first and last letter of one's name. Some think that this custom is in preparation for the time when one passes on and has to face the heavenly Court where he will be asked his name; the daily recital of the appropriate verse will aid him to remember it.[16] However, it is difficult to find any source for this idea. A more authentic reason is given by Rashi in his commentary on the verse "And your name shall witness salvation"(Micah 6:9). He makes the following observation: "From this we derive that one who each day recites a verse which begins and ends with the same letters as his name will be saved from *Gehenna* (hell)." [17]

SOURCES

1. *Tur Oraḥ Ḥayyim* 89.
2. *Bet Yoseph*, Ibid.
3. The Sephardi Jews always referred to the *Shemoneh Esreh* as the *Amidah*. Since this term is accepted today by practically every segment of the Jewish community, henceforth the *Shemoneh Esreh (Tefillah)* will from now on be referred to as the *Amidah* in this text. See Otzar Israel, s.v. *Shemoneh Esreh*.
4. *Levush*.

5. *Oraḥ Ḥayyim*, *Bet Yoseph* 112.
6. *Tur Oraḥ Ḥayyim* and *Bet Yoseph* 113-122.
7. *Ḥayyei Avraham* p. 17a.
8. *Arukh ha-Shulḥan* 95, par. 4.
9. *Tur Oraḥ Ḥayyim* 94.
10. *Tur Oraḥ Ḥayyim* 90.
11. *Ḥayyei Avraham* p. 11a.
12. *Tur Oraḥ Ḥayyim* p. 113.
13. *Ben Ish Ḥai* p. 70.
14. *Sefer ha-Mat'amim* p. 135.
15. Ibid.
16. Various editions of *Siddurim* attribute this practice and the reason for it to the holy SHELAH. However, it is not found in any of his works still extant.
17. I am indebted to Rabbi Abraham Kroll of Jerusalem who brought this Rashi in Micah to my attention. See also *Kitzur Shulḥan Arukh* Chap. 18, par. 15.

Birkhat Kohanim

When the reader, in his repetition of the *Amidah*, begins the *Birkhat Avodah (Retzeh)*, the first of the three concluding benedictions, the *Kohanim* present leave the rest of the congregation to take off their shoes and to have their hands washed by the Levites. (This custom follows the ritual of Temple times when the priests, at the conclusion of the sacrificial service, washed their hands and feet before pronouncing a blessing on the people). Then they return and take their stand in front of the Holy Ark on the so-called *dukhan*, the area designated for the Priestly Blessing.[1]

The origin of the Priestly Blessing is to be found in the Biblical verses: "So shall you bless the children of Israel: you shall say to them: the Lord bless you and keep you, the Lord make His face shine upon you, and be gracious to you; the Lord lift up his countenance upon you, and give you peace. So shall they put My name upon the children of Israel, and I will bless them" (Numbers 6:23-27). There are three distinct *Mitzvot* involved in the Priestly Blessing: "So shall you bless. . ."; "You shall say unto them. . ."; and "So shall they put My name upon the children of Israel. . ." This means that any *Kohen* who does not join in the pronunciation of the Blessings breaks three positive commands of the Torah. He cannot evade the responsibility with the pretext that he is not good enough or observant enough to give a blessing to his fellow-Jew, and that he would feel hypocritical in doing so. No matter how lax he may be as an individual in his religious observance, he is still duty-bound, unless he has ever killed anybody, to carry out his functions as a heriditary priest. Whatever his shortcomings as a Jew, he is still obliged to pronounce the Blessing. He, after all, is not the source of good but only God's chosen instrument through which blessing is invoked upon Israel.[2]

Since the Priestly Blessings culminate in the final word *Shalom* (peace), the natural place for them is immediately before the last benediction of the *Amidah*, which is itself a prayer for peace.

The priest must be totally involved in and concentrate completely on blessing the people with total goodwill and sincerity. The people for their part must concentrate their thoughts on the meaning and implication of the words. It is perhaps for this reason that the custom grew up during the Middle Ages that, while the *Kohanim* pronounced each word slowly and deliberately, the congregants would silently read or meditate upon an appropriate Scriptural verse beginning with, or at any rate containing, the particular word. A collection of such verses still appears, in small print, in many prayer books. Whether this *Minhag* is retained or discarded, every precaution must be taken to ensure that there is no distraction when the priests stand upon the *Dukhan* before the people. This is one of the reasons given for the requirement that the *Kohanim* remove their shoes. The Talmud (Sotah 40a) is afraid that, if a priest were to wear ordinary shoes, a shoelace might become untied and he would instinctively stoop to tie it to avoid embarrassment before the congregation. This would distract him and might even make him interrupt his blessing. To simplify matters, our Sages decided to ban the wearing of any shoes during the ceremony, even those which had no laces. Another reason why the *Kohanim* remove their shoes is that on several occasions those to whom the *Shekhinah* (Divine Presence) appeared were told to take off their shoes. This happened to Moses at the Burning Bush, and later to Joshua.[3] (The priests also carried out their duties in the Sanctuary barefoot). The aim of avoiding any distraction also underlies the rule that, while the people respond with Amen at the end of each of the three blessings, the person conducting the service remains silent so as to concentrate upon his specific function.

Any *Kohen* who has a visible physical defect or whose hands, face, or feet may be disfigured or bear some ineradicable mark is disqualifed from performing this ceremony, since this could serve to distract people's thoughts from concentration. This rule, however, only applies if the disfigurement is visible to the worshippers. In order to solve this problem and make it possible for a priest even with such a deformity to perform the mitzvah, the custom has been adopted that *all* the *Kohanim* cover their hands and faces with a *tallit*.[4] Some authorities question the need for this and maintain that the only essential requirement is that priests and congregation face each other with mutual respect and that the ritual be performed in a spirit of awe and reverence.[5] Perhaps for this reason the ending of the preceding blessing is (at any rate on festivals in the Diaspora) changed from "Who restores your divine presence to Zion" to "Whom alone we serve in awe."

In Temple days, the *Kohanim* used to bless the people every day of the year immediately after the conclusion of the morning offerings *(Korban Tamid shel Shaḥar)*. Later, when the Jewish people were dispersed all over the world, the ceremony of *Nesiat Kappayim* was restricted to the major festivals of the year. There are several reasons for this:

(a) Many Jews were so preoccupied with problems of material survival in a harsh and hostile world that they could not, on an ordinary weekday, spare the time which the ritual requires for its proper performance.

(b) As the last word *(be-ahavah)* of the priest's preparatory benediction indicates, he had to bestow his blessing on the people with love—that is, with whole-hearted goodwill and sympathy. But as long as Jews lived under conditions of rivalry, persecution and oppression, it was not easy for the *Kohanim* to overcome their antagonisms and concentrate their thoughts on love and goodwill, even towards their fellow-Jews. Only on the great festivals of the year, when even the atmosphere of the ghetto was permeated with joy and enthusiasm, could they be sure of attaining the state of mind which was the first prerequisite for carrying out this mitzvah.

(c) On the Sabbath Day, which might have seemed specially appropriate for this ceremony, the Rabbis in many parts of the world decided to dispense with it, for quite a different reason. So as to attain the necessary degree of purity, the priests would often immerse themselves in the *mikvah* before pronouncing the blessing. There was a risk that some *Kohanim*, ignorant of the laws of the Sabbath, might commit a breach of a Torah-prohibition by squeezing water from their hair or from a towel. The possiblity of such an occurance was so gravely regarded that, to guard against a breach of a negative mitzvah, a positive one was suspended on the Sabbath. (The *Lulav* and the *Shofar* are also not used on the Sabbath for similar reasons). In the Holy Land, however, this ruling was not applied; the Rabbis there were of the opinion that the positive mitzvah of the Priestly Blessing was more important than a possible infringement of Torah law.[6] Throughout Israel, therefore, the ceremony takes place daily throughout the year.

To return to our detailed description of the ritual, immediately after the reader's conclusion of the penultimate benediction of thanksgiving *(Modim)* and before the final prayer *(Sim shalom)*, the priests raise their hands to the height of their shoulders with the fingers pointing downward and the right hand held slightly higher than the left. This detail is traceable to the kabbalistic idea that the right hand represents *Ḥesed* (kindness) which should therefore prevail over the left hand, which embodies *Gevurah*, or strength. The two hands are brought together and the fingers arranged in such a way as to leave five openings between them. The number five is derived from a Midrashic interpretation of the verse "He peers through the lattice *(Metzitz min ha Ḥarakim)*" (Song of Songs 2:9). The particle *Heh*, with which the last word begins, was detached for homiletic purposes from the remainder of the word and given its numerical value of five. So, the Rabbis taught that while blessing the people the priests must peer through the five openings between the fingers.[7]

In Temple times one individual was appointed to call out

each word of the threefold Priestly Benediction, and this was then repeated aloud by the *Kohanim*. Nowadays in Israel the reader who is conducting the service does not perform this function so as to concentrate on his own particular job in hand. Instead another person from the congregation calls upon the *Kohanim* to begin the blessing which the reader then dictates to them word by word. He does not, however, as the congregation does, answer "Amen" at the end of each sentence of the Benediction since, if he were to do so, he might be distracted from his main function as representative of the congregation *(Sheliaḥ Tzibbur)*. Some authorities are of the opinion that the response "Amen" is not appropriate here, since it properly follows only a *Berakhah* beginning with the words *Barukh Attah* (Blessed art Thou . . .) and that the correct response is *Ken yehi ratzon* (So may it be His will) which normally follows a petition *(Bakkashah)*.[8]

If the reader himself is a *Kohen*, he does not take part in the *Dukhan* ceremony, which—quite apart from the question of distracting his attention from his duty as a reader—would involve his leaving his proper place; nor does he dictate the words for his fellow-priests to repeat, since by doing so he might give the impression that he is either not a priest or is in some way disqualified from acting as one. Instead he covers his face with his *Tallit* and waits in silence until the Priestly Benedictions are finished, whereupon he begins "*Sim shalom.*" But what if he is the only *Kohen* present? If that is so then the congregation will not be able to receive the Priestly Blessing if he does not give it to them. Basing their opinion on the *Mishnah* (Berakhot 34a) the majority of halakhic authorities tend to think that even in that case he should continue with the prayers and omit the Priestly Blessing altogether, on the grounds that the duties connected with *Nesiat Kappayim* might so preoccupy him that he would afterward have difficulty in resuming his recital of the *Tefillah*. If, however, he is confident that he can pronounce the Priestly Benediction without the risk of distraction, he may do so. In this case he must remove his shoes and have his hands washed before he begins the repetition of the *Amidah.*[9]

An interesting situation arises where a congregation consists entirely of *Kohanim.* Who is to bless and who is to be blessed? The rule is that, if there are more than ten adults present, a bare *minyan* remains to receive the blessing while the remainder ascend the *Dukhan* to pronounce it. If, however, there is exactly a *minyan*, they all ascend and pronounce the Blessing, even though there is apparently no congregation left in front of them to receive the Blessing. What they are in fact doing is invoking a blessing upon their fellow-Jews wherever they may be. The women and children who are present in the synagogue answer "*Amen.*" It is a positive *Mitzvah* in the Torah for the priests to bless the Jewish people, and therefore its importance cannot be overemphasized.[10]

The priests do not begin their blessing until they are invited to do so; the congregants do not answer "Amen" until the priests have finished pronouncing the last syllable of each verse; nor may the reader begin another verse until the last echo of the congregation's "Amen" has died away.[11] All this is in order that the words may be clearly heard, and that no extraneous sounds distract the attention of either the priests or the people.

The *Kohanim* must satisfy three essential conditions when they deliver the Blessing:

(a) It must be recited in the Hebrew language and no other, since the Torah prescribes: "So shall you bless the children of Israel" (Numbers 6:23). "So" means: "in this way only," viz. "in Hebrew."

(b) The *Kohanim* must stand while blessing the people. This is based on the verse "For the Lord your God has chosen him (the priest) out of all your tribes, to *stand* and serve. . . ." (Deuteronomy 18:5).

(c) The words must be pronounced clearly and audibly, since the Torah commands: "Say to them" (Numbers 6:23), i.e. "Say it so that the people can hear."

An ancient tradition which appears in the authoritative

codes forbids the congregation to look at the *Kohanim* while they recite the Blessing, and it is popularly believed that anyone who disobeys this rule is in danger of being blinded. This idea probably goes back to Temple times, when the Priestly Blessing was spoken exactly as it is written in the Torah, the Ineffable Name of God being pronounced three times. Although, since the Tetragrammaton has been replaced by another Name of lesser sanctity, this reasoning no longer applies today, the rule is still observed and is justified by the need for complete concentration. Instead of looking up at the priests, the people should either close their eyes or look down at their prayer-books; this, incidentally, is the behavior recommended to be followed during the silent *Amidah*.

It is usual to thank the *Kohanim* with the formula "*Yeyasher koḥakha!* (May you grow in strength)," when they return to their seats. Although in performing the *Dukhan* ceremony, the priests are merely obeying a positive command of the Torah and not doing any personal favor to their fellow congregants, since each priest could,as an individual, have attended some other service, we thank him for choosing to come to ours and so giving us the benefit of his services.[13]

SOURCES

1. *Yad, Hilkhot Temidim* 6:5.
2. *Tur Oraḥ Ḥayyim* 128.
3. *Sefer ha-Mat'amim*, p. 69.
4. *Bet Yoseph, Tur Oraḥ Ḥayyim* 128.
5. *Ta'ame ha-Minhagim*, p. 56.
6. *Sefer Eretz Yisrael*, p.21.
7. *Tur Oraḥ Ḥayyim*, 128.
8. *Ta'ame ha-Minhagim*, p. 55.
9. *Tur* and *Bet Yoseph, Oraḥ Ḥayyim*, p. 28.
10. *Arukh ha-Shulḥan*, 128.
11. Ibid. See also *Or Gadol* on Mishnah Megillah Chapter 4:10.
12. Ibid.
13. *Sefer ha-Mat'amim*, p. 69.

Taḥanun

Immediately after the weekday *amidah*, the congregation continues with the supplication (*taḥanun*), assuming the posture of *nefilat appayim* or "falling on one's face."[1] This is an appeal to God to forgive our sins and, while it is said, the head is inclined so as to rest upon the arm. The origin of this custom can be traced to the passage of the Torah (Deuteronomy 9:18-25) in which Moses, in his final address to the people, recalls how, during the forty days and nights he had spent upon the mountain, he had sat, stood, and fallen prostrate before God, pleading with Him not to destroy the people as a punishment for their idolatry. So here we are told that Moses, in imploring God's mercy, sat, stood and fell prostrate before Him. For this reason we sit during most of the introductory Psalms *pesuke de-zimrah* and the *shema*, stand for the *amidah* and fall upon our faces during the subsequent *taḥanun*.

The authorities are divided as to whether the head should be inclined right or left. Some hold that it should rest upon the left arm because the aristocracy of old used to recline on the left elbow when partaking of a banquet. This position—as we are reminded at the Passover Seder—was a sign of freedom and independence. Hence, according to this view, the Jew inclines his head to the left to show that, while he is independent of any need for human aid, he does rely upon God for forgiveness.[2] According to others, we should drop the head so that it rests on the right arm to remind us of the verse in the Song of Songs (2:6) "Let. . . his right hand embrace me." Other of our Sages prefer the right because of David's words: "The Lord is your shade upon your right hand"(Psalms 121:5); yet others who arrive at the same conclusion do so because *tefillin* are normally worn on the left arm, which cannot therefore be used for another purpose. The accepted halakhic decision is, however, that of the ReMA (Rabbi Moses Isserlis) in the *Shulḥan Arukh*, Chap. 131. He rules that, since the *taḥanun*-prayer forms part of both the *shaḥarit* (morning) and *minḥa* (afternoon) services, we should in the morning (when *tefillin* are worn) incline the head to the right, reversing the procedure in the afternoon when we do not wear *tefillin*. (Left-handed persons, who lay *tefillin* on the right arm, always incline the head to the left.)[3]

When lowering the head and the face onto the arm, one automatically covers them so as not to look at one's neighbor during this stage of his devotions. Two reasons are given for this. First, when the people prostrated themselves in the Temple, a space of four cubits was left between one person and the next so that nobody could listen to his neighbor's confession. For the same reason, we say *taḥanun* in an undertone and with our lips shielded by our arm. We do this also because our entreaties and expressions of penitence demand intense concentration, which would be disturbed by external sights or sounds. It is therefore helpful if we cover our head and eyes during this part of the service.[4]

We do not recite *taḥanun* in the evening service (*maariv)*, nor do we assume any prostrate position. The recital of this prayer is itself a somber and awesome experience, and would become exceedingly so at night.[5]

During the first week after the burial of a near relative a mourner is not allowed to leave his home. It is therefore usual for the three daily services to be held in the house of mourning throughout this period. At such services all *taḥanun*-prayers are omitted. In taking their loved ones from them, God has exercised His *middat ha-din* (His attribute of strict justice). Since we say *taḥanun* to plead with God to set aside this attribute and to treat us rather with mercy *(middat ha-raḥamim)*, we omit this prayer in a place where *middat ha-din* has lately been exercised.[6]

Conversely, on happy occasions, for example in the presence

of a bridegroom during the first seven days of his marriage, or at a circumcision, *taḥanun* is omitted for another reason. Looking forward to the future with optimism—whether it be for a happy and fruitful marriage or the joy of bringing up a Jewish child to study Torah and obey God's commandments—it is out of place even to mention *middat ha-din.*[7]

Taḥanun is not normally accompanied by *nefilat appayim* unless there is a *Sefer Torah* (Scroll of the Law) in the place where the prayers are held. This rule has its origin in the Biblical verse "Joshua. . .fell upon his face before the Ark of the Lord" (Joshua 7:6). In Jerusalem, however, *nefilat appayim* takes place even in the absence of a *Sefer Torah,* since the sanctity of Jerusalem is equated with that of the Holy Ark.[8]

On the Sabbath, and on all Festivals, *taḥanun* is omitted. The Sabbath is described (Exodus 31:13) as an *Ot*, a sign between God and Israel, indicating the relationship between them. At a time when the Jew rises to the level of attaining direct relationship with his Creator, *middat ha-din* would be out of place.[9] Nor is *taḥanun* recited on any of the lesser holidays such as Rosh Ḥodesh, the intermediate days (*ḥolo shel moed)* of Passover and Sukkot, the eight days of Ḥanukkah, two days of Purim, as well as the two days of Purim Katan in the first Adar of a leap year, Tu bi-Sh'vat, the three days preceding Shavuot *(shloshet yeme hagbalah)*, the day preceding every holiday *(erev yom-tov)*, the day following each of the three pilgrim festivals *(Shalosh Regalim)*, nor during the entire month of Nissan, nor during the days between Yom Kippur and Sukkot.

Also, under kabbalistic influence, it has become customary not to say *taḥanun* on *Lag ba-Omer* (the *yahrzeit* of Rabbi Shimeon ben Yoḥai, the author of the Zohar) which is observed with joyous festivities, especially in Eretz Yisrael.

Similarly, Hassidim omit *taḥanun* on the day of the *yahrzeit* of their revered Hassidic Masters, the rationale being the kabbalistic concept that the soul of the *tzaddik* (Hassidic Master) on the anniversary of his passing ascends to higher and higher spiritual levels in heaven, and so gives occasion for rejoicing to his followers on earth.

SOURCES

1. *Arukh ha-Shulḥan, Oraḥ Ḥayyim* 131 par. 1.
2. *Ḥayye Avraham* p.21a-b.
3. *Sefer ha-Mat'amim* p.97.
4. *Sefer Ha-Mat'amim* p.136.
5. *Arukh ha-Shulḥan, Oraḥ Ḥayyim* 131, par. 11.
6. *Arukh ha-Shulḥan* 131 par. 14.
7. *Arukh ha-Shulḥan* 131 par. 15.
8. *Sefer Eretz Yisrael*, p. 20.
9. *Ta'ame ha-Minhagim*, p. 59.

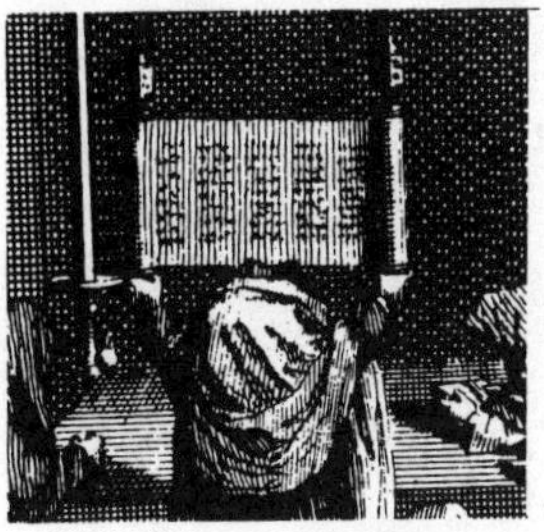

Torah Reading

A portion of the Torah is read four times a week: on Saturday morning, Saturday afternoon, Monday morning and Thursday morning, whether in the synagogue or at home, provided that a quorum of ten men is present. It is also read on holidays, festivals and fast days. Although the reading of the Torah is a very important part of the service on these days, it has no direct basis in the Torah proper. According to the Talmud (Bava Kamma 82a) and also according to a tradition cited by Maimonides (Yad Hilkhot Tefillah 12, par. 1), Moses decreed in the desert that the children of Israel should read the Torah on Saturdays, Mondays and Thursdays. A possible allusion to the reason for this decree is found in the Scriptural passage, "And they went three days in the wilderness and found no water"(Exodus 15:22). The Rabbis interpreted water as a poetic image for Torah, so that when, for instance, Isaiah cries out, "Ho, all you that thirst, come you for water!" (55:1). The inference is that, while wandering in the desert, the Children of Israel had become spiritually deprived, since they had gone three days without "water" or spiritual nourishment, and that this led to their becoming weary and quarrelsome. Moses therefore ordained that no three days were to pass without reading the Torah. To be spiritually healthy and alert, we are required to read the Torah on three days of every week.

Granted that three days must not pass without reading Torah, why should the choice fall on Monday, Thursday and Saturday only? Why were the other days not chosen? The Tosafists point out that Moses went up Mt. Sinai to receive the Tablets on a Thursday, and came down with them on a Monday

(Bava Kamma 82a). From this it seems that Monday and Thursday work together as an appropriate combination to win God's favor. This being the case, then Saturday is the only other day that could be included in the calculations of the three day cycle.[1] A hint of this may be inferred from Isaiah (55:6), "Seek the Lord while He may be found." The Hebrew word for "He may be found" is *Be-Himatz'o.* The numerical value of the *Bet* is two, that of the *Heh* is five; there remains the word *matz'o* "find Him." So, you can find Him on the second and fifth day of the week, by reading His Law.[2]

Support for the view that Moses also decreed the reading of the Torah on the various holidays lies in the verse: "And Moses proclaimed the Feasts of the Lord to the children of Israel" (Lev. 23:44). This means that he instructed them to read the passages in the Torah dealing with the various special occasions in the Jewish calendar.[3]

Later generations, however, had no clear idea of the procedure that Moses had established in the desert. They were in doubt as to whether only one man should read and that would be enough, or whether several should be called up to take part. It was Ezra the Scribe who finally decided that while seven were to be called to read from the Torah on Saturday mornings, only three were to be called up on Mondays and Thursdays. The reason for the reduced number on Mondays and Thursdays was that people should not be unnecessarily delayed from going to work. Also, the number three corresponds to the three divisions of the Bible: the Five Books of Moses, the Prophets, and the Hagiographa. Ezra also laid down the rule that the three men called up should read no less than a total of ten verses. Three reasons are given for this minimum:

(a) To remind the congregation of the Ten Commandments.

(b) To honor the ten *Batlanim.* These were pious people whose material needs were provided for by the community and who were in turn expected to sit in the synagogue and study Torah and be available to make up a *Minyan*, the quorum of ten adult males necessary for public worship.

(c) They represent the ten repetitions of the statement, "And God said" at the beginning of Genesis.[4]

Ezra also decreed that the Torah should be read on Saturday afternoons. A possible allusion to this is found in Psalms 69:13-14: "Those that sit in the gate talk against me. But as for me, I direct my prayer to You, O Lord." On Saturday afternoons when people were free from work, they used to gather at street corners to talk to one another. To eliminate a practice that might lead to malicious gossip, Ezra instituted that the Torah be read at this time. Although on the Sabbath afternoon, there is no problem of keeping people back from work, there were still only three men to be called up to read the Torah to allow sufficient time for preachers to give talks on Sabbath afternoon.[5]

Much later, while under foreign domination, the Jews were forbidden the reading of the Torah. The Jews obeyed the decree but instituted the reading of the Haftorah instead. The Haftorah was a portion from the Prophets which had some common theme with the portion of the Five Books of Moses that would normally have been assigned for that Shabbat. A minimum of 21 verses was to be read from the assigned section in the Prophets so as to parallel the seven men who would ordinarily have been called to read from the Five Books of Moses not less than three verses each. Although the decree forbidding the reading from the Five Books was later abolished, the custom of reading the Haftorah was retained, and continues till today. Another reason for reading the Haftorah: Rabbinic Law is emphatic on the point that during the reading of the Torah all talk must stop. Haftorah is derived from the same root as *patur*, "exempt." In other words, after *Keriat ha-Torah* the people are released from the ban against talking to one another. Understandably, during the recitation of the Portion of the Prophets, the prohibition against talking comes again into effect. A third reason: Haftorah can also mean "removal." The inference is that at the conclusion of *Keriat ha-Torah* we have "removed" ourselves from the period of *Shaharit*, the morning service and we are ready to commence the *Musaf*, the Additional Service.[6]

In ancient times, there were periods when people were very ignorant about this Jewish heritage. They spoke no Hebrew and therefore were unable to read the Torah. A translator had to be introduced into the service. After the Priest, or a Sage had read a verse of the Torah, the translator repeated it in Aramaic, the vernacular at the time. This was done in order to give the people the opportunity to understand what was being read. May we today appoint translators who would do the same for us in English, French or German? The answer is in the negative. Why should there be a difference between Aramaic and other languages? The answer given is that, since that was the vernacular used by all the Jewish people at that time, and since several section of the Scriptures were written in it, Aramaic had been accorded a measure of sanctity not ascribed to any other language.[7]

The letters of the Torah Scroll have no vowel points, but are read in a traditional way. A word made up of letters that are vowelled cannot be changed. Its pronunciation is precise and unalterable and lends itself to no alternative expression or interpretation. This rigidity is contrary to the Rabbinic capacity for variety and richness in the interpretation of Scriptures (See Talmud, end of Beraḳhot).[8]

To be fit for the obligatory Torah reading, a Torah Scroll must contain all the Five Books of Moses. It is not permitted to do the reading from one of the Books, even if all the other requirements relating to a *Sefer Torah* have been met. (These prerequisites include the use of parchment, the proper type of ink, the correct script, and the appropriate thread prepared from the sinews of a kosher animal for sewing the sheets together.) The Rabbis (Gittin 60a) felt that to read from a single book would not be in keeping with the dignity of the congregation, which comes to the Synagogue especially to hear from the Book of God—that is, from the entire Torah and not just one section. When a Jew recites the benediction over the reading of the Torah he means precisely that, the entire Torah and nothing less. What should a community that has no complete *Sefer Torah* do? In that case, they may read from what they have to prevent *Keriat ha-Torah* becoming forgotten, but no benedictions, before or after, may be recited.[9]

As we have already noted, Ezra established the custom of calling three men to the Torah Reading on Monday and Thursday mornings as well as on Saturday afternoons. These three were assigned a total of ten verses. The Sages, alert to human whims and sensibilities, realized that one of the three would be assigned four verses while the other two were allotted only three each; this would have led to resentment on the part of the other two. In ancient times, when each person who was called up read his portion to himself, it made no difference who read the four verses because each one considered his position superior to the others. The first would think his the greater honor since he had been called up first to the Torah; the second man called up would regard his as the most important *Aliyah* since the fourth branch of the seven branched candelabra in the Temple was regarded as the most important by virture of its central position; the third person called up would hold that his *Aliyah* was the most important because of the principal of *Ma'alin ba-Kodesh*—in Jewish ritual we follow an ascending order of sanctity. In later time, however, because people did not prepare themselves beforehand or did not know enough, many were incapable of reading from the Torah themselves and so the custom of having an official reader for the whole community was instituted. The ruling was then made that the four verses should be given either to the first or to the third person called up, and never to the middle person, since that would entail a certain measure of embarrassment to the person who had been given the first *Aliyah* by virtue of his being a *Kohen*.[10]

The study of Torah is open to all. No person is more entitled to learn than anyone else. Those that put their effort into learning become scholars; those that do not, remain ignorant. Logically, therefore, it should follow that the learned should be called up first to read from the Torah. However, the order for *Aliyoth* is first the *Kohen*, next the Levite, finally an ordinary Jew. There are three reasons for this sequence:

(a) In the Scriptures we find, "And Moses wrote down the law, and handed it over to the *Priests*, the sons of *Levi*. . . and to all the elders of *Israel*" (Deuteronomy 31:9). So, the Priests came first, the Levites second and the Israelites, third. It is irrelevant whether the *Kohen* is an outstanding scholar or barely literate. He is to be called up first.

(b) Also, in the Scriptures God instructs Moses about the priesthood: "You shall sanctify him, therefore, for he offers the bread of your God" (Lev. 21:8). The Rabbis interpret the words, "You shall sanctify him," to mean that one should honor him and give him his due respect by calling upon him first in the performance of any religious function.

(c) Other authorities suggest a more pragmatic reason. If the *Kohen*, whose elevated station in Jewish life is acknowledged, would not be called up first, the rest of the congregation might well clamor to be given that honor and altercations would erupt in the synagogue. Each person would claim to be more important than the next.[11] It is especially for this last reason that the authorities ruled that even if a *Kohen* should wish to forego the honor that is his due, and should say that he would not be offended if an ordinary Jew began the reading of the Torah, this may not be done.[12]

It is related that in a certain community it was a longstanding custom that once a year, and only once a year, a drive for funds for the upkeep of the synagogue would be launched, and the various honors associated with *Keriat ha-Torah* sold by auction. The *Kohen's Aliyah* would also be auctioned off, the *Kohen*, for his part, acquiescing either by foregoing the honor or by not being present at all. On one occasion, however, after his reading had been sold to someone else, a *Kohen* adamantly rejected either of the two options. The leaders of the congregation summoned the police and had the man forcibly evicted, a course of action which met with the approval of the Rabbinate. The basis for their approval was the importance of a time-honored custom in the Jewish community which could not be indifferently and callously set aside. Under normal circumstances, however, the *Kohen* must be called up first.[13]

When no *Kohen* is present at the commencement of the *Keriat ha-Torah*, however, an entirely new situation emerges; *Nitpardah ha-Havilah* (lit. "The package has become untied.") Anyone present may be called up to read first. Even if a Levite is present, he does not have to be called up first; we only pay deference to the Levite when a *Kohen* is present. In the absence of the latter, the Levite loses his position—"The package has become untied."

The situation becomes slightly more complicated when a *Kohen* and an Israelite are present, but not a Levite. Once again the *Kohen* assumes his primary importance and is called up first. He is then also assigned the *Aliyah* of the Levite, i.e. the same *Kohen* replaces the Levite. The reason for this procedure is the probability of a misunderstanding arising and producing serious consequences. For example, a latecomer might enter the synagogue while *Keriat ha-Torah* is in progress. He notices that the *Kohen* is about to conclude his reading. Then, he hears another *Kohen* being called up. He concludes that the first *Kohen* is a *Pagum* (i.e. his legitimacy as a *Kohen* is in doubt). The other person then spreads the rumor that the first *Kohen* is not a legitimate *Kohen* and as proof he submits the argument that another *Kohen* was called up immediately after him, instead of a Levite.

Two people who are close blood relations, such as a father and son or two brothers, may not be called up successively to read from the Torah. This rule has its basis in the Scriptures: "The *testimony* of the Lord is sure, making wise the simple" (Psalms 19:8). Reading from the Torah is the same as giving testimony. In Jewish jurisprudence, blood relatives may not testify as witnesses. Another reason: when the congregation observes two members of the same family being honored, they are likely to resent it, and may cast an evil eye *(Ayin ha-Ra)* upon the family.[14]

Let us now describe the procedure of *Keriat ha-Torah*. First, the Torah is removed from the Ark. The moment the Scroll becomes visible, the congregation must stand up as a sign of respect. Some say that when it is assumed that the Scroll has been removed from the Ark, everybody must get up even if they cannot see the Torah Scroll. It is due to this second opinion that miniature bells are suspended from many of the crowns used to adorn the *Sefer Torah.* The moment a Torah is taken out, the tinkling of the bells becomes audible, summoning the people to rise. This custom of attaching bells, however, was condemned by the vast majority of Rabbis because they would constitute musical instruments which are forbidden to be used on Sabbath. As the procession advances from the Ark to the center platform, the congregation should make an effort to approach as close as possible to the Torah and kiss it. Those a little further away stretch out their hand, touch the Torah with their fingers, and then kiss their fingers. By doing this, the worshippers demonstrate their deep love and respect for the Torah.[15] Some authorities restrict the kissing of the Torah to children: This is an effective way of inculcating the love of Torah in young people.[16]

Once the Torah has been placed upon the Table, that is, on the platform *(Bimah)*, the congregation may be seated. The reason: the platform is considered a separate domain, independent of the synagogue.[17]

Three men shall stand next to the Torah: a lay officer of the congregation, the reader, and the person called up to the Torah. Here are two basic reasons for this arrangement:

(a) When the Torah was given at Mt. Sinai the following were present: God, who gave it; Moses who transmitted it; and Israel who received it. On the *Bimah*, too, the official summons the person given an *Aliyah*; the reader *(Ba'al Kore)* actually does the reading, and the person called up listens to the law being read to him.[18]

(b). In essence, the Torah is an admonition to the Jew to avoid wrongdoing. In Jewish jurisprudence, when a warning is issued to anyone about to transgress, two witnesses must be present. This is substantiated in the Scriptures where God warns the children of Israel: "I call Heaven and Earth to witness against you this day" (Deuteronomy 4:26). Heaven and Earth were the witnesses.[19]

The representative of the congregation is now ready to call those honored with an *Aliyah* to the Torah. In doing so, he may not merely call out, "The *Kohen* is summoned to the Torah," because many *Kohanim* or Levites might be present and a great deal of confusion might ensue. Another reason proposed is a pragmatic one. Sometimes it is necessary to know a person's exact name. This is the case when a marriage contract is drawn up and even more important in the case of a Bill of Divorce. When the entire congregation hears a man's Hebrew name mentioned repeatedly, whenever he is called to the Torah, that name can be verified should any question arise concerning it.[20]

When the person being called up hears his name, he should walk to the *Bimah* by the shortest route and later return to his seat taking the longest route possible. This is to show his desire to come close to the Torah and his reluctance to leave it.[21]

Some authorities suggest that a basis for this is found in Ezekiel (46:9), "He that enters in the north gate to bow down, shall go out through the south gate.[22]

Although the congregation may remain seated, those who stand on the *Bimah* next to the Torah must remain standing. The origin for this is in Deuteronomy (5:28) where God is reported to have said to Moses, "But as for you, stand there beside Me, and I will tell you all the commandments which you will teach them."[23]

Communities differ in the way in which they observe the next procedure. In some localities the person called up unrolls the Scroll and recites the benediction. This is done because the Law specifically states that he must know the exact place in the Torah where the reading will begin, and over which he will recite his benediction. In other communities, however, he unrolls the Scroll, scrutinizes the passage to be read, and rolls the Scroll together, then intoning the blessing. The purpose of this method is to prevent the congregation suspecting that the benediction has been written into the Torah, and that the person called up *has* to read it from there. No suspicion can possibly arise if he rolls the Scroll together, before reciting the blessing.[24]

While the Torah is read, the person called up should grasp the stave that is nearest him around which the Scroll is rolled. There are three reasons given for this:

(a) In the Scriptures, Solomon, pointing to the Torah, exclaims: "A tree of life is she to those who *lay hold* on her, and everyone that *grasps* her firmly will be happy" (Proverbs 3:18).[25]

(b) In Joshua (1:8-9) we find God saying to Joshua, "This Book of the Law shall not depart out of your mouth." Since God used the word "this" he must have been pointing to a Scroll which Joshua apparently was holding in his hand.[26]

(c) The Talmud (Sukkah 41b) describes how, during the Festival of Sukkot, the people would go everywhere holding the *Lulav* in their hands. When they had a chance to read the Torah, they placed the *Lulav* on the ground. Why did they have to put down the *Lulav*? The Rabbis deduced from this that they had to put it down so as to hold something else, namely the stave of the Torah.[27]

We have already noted that on the Sabbath morning seven men are called up to the Torah. Each one recites a benediction before and after the reading. The same applies on occasions when fewer men are honored. It was different in ancient times. Then the first one called to the Torah recited the opening, and the last one the concluding, blessing. Those in between were exempt. Why was the law subsequently changed? Here, again, the authorities took the frailties of human nature into account. If the old way were still in force today, if someone were to walk into the synagogue during the Torah reading and not hear the person called up reciting the blessings, he would come to the conclusion that the community had abolished the opening and concluding benedictions completely. In ancient days this was no problem because each person called up read from the Torah himself, and it was common knowledge that only the first and last would recite the benedictions.[28]

After the first benediction is recited the reader responds aloud with "*Amen.*" Between the readings it is permitted to whisper. When a large congregation is present the low whispering of many individuals can add up to a great deal of noise. When the reader calls out "*Amen,*" it is the signal that he is ready to start the reading, and all talking must stop.[29]

We have already noted several times that the reason we have an official reader is due to the ignorance of the community and the inability on the part of many to read from the Torah by themselves. Nevertheless, it is the person called up who recites the benediction over the Torah and not the reader. The question arises: How can one recite a blessing for someone else performing the mitzvah? In order to avoid this difficulty the person called up is expected quietly to repeat the words when listening to the reader. If he is fluent enough actually to read the words himself, he should do so. In this way, he will avoid reciting a *Berakhah le-Vatalah*, "a blessing in vain."[30]

After the person called up has finished everything to do with his *Aliyah* he should not immediately come down from the platform, but instead should step aside and remain there until the next person to be called up has concluded his reading and benediction. The cause for this is the probability that, if he were to step down immediately just as the next person is coming up, he may miss hearing the latter's benediction, and not respond with the usual "Amen." When, however, the first person to be called up waits until the second concludes his reading, he has ample time to return to his seat and hear the benedictions of the third person to be called up.[31]

As he returns to his seat the congregants customarily greet him with, "*Yeya'asher Koḥakha* (May you grow in strength!)," or else, "*Ḥazak Barukh* (May you be strong and blessed)." The motive behind this custom is the Rabbinic saying that intense study of Torah weakens man's strength. The concentration required robs the man of his physical energies. Therefore, now that the person called up has just been engaged in studying Torah, we make a special prayer for him that he be strong despite this.[32]

We have already delineated the historical background for the reading of the Haftorah. It must be added that, before the section of the Prophets is read, the last few verses of the Torah reading are repeated. The Sages thought that, as important as the Prophets are, they must not be considered as sacred as the Five Books of Moses which were given by God Himself. Therefore, we read from the Torah first, and only then do we read from the Prophets.[33]

The final ritual is the *Hagbahah* and *Gelilah*. After the prescribed number of men have read, two additional men are called up: one lifts the Torah from the table *(Hagbahah)*; the other rolls the Scroll together and ties it, *(Gelilah)*. A Talmudic passage (Megillah 32a) indicates that the person who rolls the Scroll together should do so from the outside and tie it together from the inside while the one who raises the Torah remains seated holding it. To clarify the Rabbinic dictum, it is important to know that Sephardic Jews have their Torah Scrolls encased in a cylindrical capsule. This type of *Sefer Torah* is read while it stands upright. Therefore, it must first be taken out of its case and unrolled. It should be tied together, on the other hand, when the Scroll is in its encasement. The opinion of the Rabbis is that, by taking the Scroll out into the open, the congregation is in a better position to see the Script. Ashkenazic Jews place their Torah horizontally on a table. For them the Rabbinic ruling is that the man who rolls the Torah together should stand on the outside of the parchment with the script facing the person who is holding it. When tied together from the inside, the bow fastening the Scroll directly faces the cleavage to avoid having to place the *Sefer* face down the next time it is opened. In addition, when rolling up the Torah, the nearest seam should lie in the center of the cleavage to protect the parchment from tearing. Then, if the staves of the *Sefer* should accidentally be pulled in opposite directions, the seam would bear the brunt of the damage, and this can be more easily repaired.[34]

But why is it necessary to raise the Torah in the first place? Why can it not be tied while it is either standing on the table according to the Sephardic rite or lying horizontally in the Ashkenazic fashion? Nahmanides' commentary on the Torah (Deuteronomy 27:26), provides us with a clue: *Arur asher lo yakim et divre ha-Torah ha-zot*, "Cursed is he who does not confirm the word of this Law." *Yakim* is translated as "confirm." It may also mean to uphold. So, to satisfy both interpretations we publicly *affirm* the sanctity of the Torah by raising it aloft for all to see.[35]

SOURCES

1. *Perishah, Oraḥ Ḥayyim* 135.
2. *Avudraham* p. 71.
3. *Perishah, Oraḥ Ḥayyim* 135 par. 1; *Arukh ha-Shulḥan* ibid.
4. *Arukh ha-Shulḥan, Oraḥ Ḥayyim* 135, par. 3.
5. *Avudraham* p. 71.
6. *Avudraham* p. 93.
7. *Tur, Oraḥ Ḥayyim* 145; *Arukh ha-Shulḥan* 145 par. 1-2.
8. *Ḥayye Avraham* p. 22b.
9. *Tur, Oraḥ Ḥayyim, Bet Yoseph* 143. *Arukh ha-Shulḥan* 143, par. 2.
10. *Arukh ha-Shulḥan* 137, par. 2.
11. *Bet Yoseph, Oraḥ Ḥayyim* 135.
12. *Perishah, Oraḥ Ḥayyim* 135; *Arukh ha-Shulḥan* 135.
13. *Bet Yoseph, Perishah, Oraḥ Ḥayyim* 135; *Arukh ha-Shulḥan* 135, pars. 8, 9, 11, 13, 16, 24.
14. *Ḥayye Avraham* p. 25a.
15. *Ta'ame ha-Minhagim* p. 64.
16. *Darkhe Mosheh, Oraḥ Ḥayyim* 147, note 5.
17. *Ta'ame ha-Minhagim* p. 70.
18. *Sefer ha-Mat'amim* p. 95.
19. *Ta'ame ha-Minhagim* p. 153.
20. *Sefer ha-Mat'amim* p. 95
21. *Arukh ha-Shulḥan* 141 par. 9.
22. *Sefer ha-Mat'amim* p.94
23. *Arukh ha-Shulḥan* 141 par. 1.

24. *Tur, Bet Yoseph, Oraḥ Ḥayyim* 139.
25. *Sefer ha-Mat'amim* p. 94.
26. *Arukh ha-Shulḥan* 139 par. 15.
27. *Minhage Yeshurun* p. 159.
28. *Perishah, Oraḥ Ḥayyim* 139, par. 4.
29. *Minhage Yeshurun* p. 158.
30. *Tur, Oraḥ Ḥayyim* 141; *Arukh ha-Shulḥan* 141, par. 5.
31. *Arukh ha-Shulḥan* 141, par. 11.
32. *Ta'ame ha-Minhagim* p. 157.
33. *Ta'ame ha-Minhagim* p. 158-159.
34. *Arukh ha-Shulḥan* 147, pars. 13, 15.
35. *Ḥayye Avraham* p. 23a.

Ein K-Elokenu

In all Sephardic congregations—and by this we mean both those where Oriental Jews worship and Ashkenazic synagogues that follow the Sephardic ritual—the morning service ends with the popular verses of *Ein k-Elohenu*, followed by chapters from the Talmud, in particular the passage of *Pittum ha-ketoret* (Keritot 6a).

The first letter of the first three verses: *Ein k-Elohenu*, *Mi k-Elohenu*, *Nodeh l-Elohenu* are *Aleph*, *Mem* and *Nun*, which combine to form the word, *Amen*.

The Hebrew letters of the word *Amen* are also the first letters of *El Melekh Ne'eman*, O God, the trusted King.[1]

After proclaiming God as our trusted King, we continue with the verses *Baruch Elohenu* and *Attah Hu Elohenu* ("Blessed are you, our God," and "O, You are our God"). The final verse is "You are He before whom our ancestors offered the incense of spices."

Since we have mentioned incense, we immediately continue to study the relevant Talmudic passages (see above). However, the question arises as to why we should have to recite the *Ein k-Elohenu* before learning about the incense. According to the Talmud (Yoma 26a), the priests merited prosperity because of their incense offering. So, before studying the passages dealing with incense, the Jew should proclaim the *Ein k-Elohenu* declaring that his prosperity is not the result of his own efforts, but is rather the gift of God.[2]

In synagogues following the Ashkenazic ritual, *Pittum haketoret*, the order of compounding the incense is not recited.

Therefore the *Ein k-Elohenu* is also not recited during weekdays but only on Sabbaths and holidays. This is because the Talmud states that if one of the essential eleven ingredients of the incense was missing, the person guilty of this neglect was punishable by death. Since reciting the chapter describing the compounding of the incense is almost as if he were offering the incense himself, a person would incur this penalty if he inadvertently omitted even one of the necessary ingredients. On weekdays, this is a distinct possibility, since people are in a hurry to go to work. So, during the weekdays the service does not conclude with the *Ein k-Elohenu* followed by *Pittum ha-ketoret.* On the other hand, on Sabbaths and festivals when work stops and people can concentrate on their prayers, the service does end with the *Ein k-Elohenu* and *Pittum ha-ketoret.*[3]

In Israel, the vast majority of synagogues follow the Sephardic rite.

SOURCES

1. *Sefer ha-Minhagim* by Isaac Tirna. Introduction p. 1.
2. *Sha'are Teshuvah, Oraḥ Ḥayyim* 132 section 6.
3. *Tur Oraḥ Ḥayyim* 132.

Meals

This chapter will deal not with the casual snack, but with the regular meal which, in the Jewish view, involves the partaking of bread. Since bread is the staple food of man, its presence or absence is the determining factor as to whether all the rituals pertaining to a meal are to be observed. If one eats a piece of bread at least the size of an olive then he is eating a meal. On the other hand, if one should consume a far larger quantity of cake, it is not considered a meal. Therefore, in the ensuing chapter it is assumed that bread is included in the meal.

There are five distinct rituals involved in a meal:

(a) *Netilat yadayim* "Washing of the hands." This is referred to sometimes as *mayim rishonim* ("the first water"). Water is poured from a vessel onto each hand while the hand is raised upwards. This is indicated by the words *netilat yadayim* (lit. "raising of the hands") instead of, as might have been expected, *reḥitzat yadayim* ("washing the hands"). There is an opinion that the reason for doing this is the Biblical verse, "Then a spirit *took me up*" (Ezekiel 3:12) the Aramaic tanslation being *u-netalni* which has the same root as *netilat*. Another opinion is that the source is the verse (Psalms 134:2), "Lift up your hands toward the Sanctuary and bless the Lord."[1]

But why wash hands at all before the meal, particularly if they are not dirty? Three explanations are given for this:

1. A hygienic reason. Hands might become dirty or they might perspire and therefore become unfit to handle food. Although a few authorities accept this as the reason, most, however, reject it completely.[2]

2. Based on a Talmudic passage (Ḥullin 106a), many Rab-

binic scholars maintain that contemporary food habits should be governed by the laws of sacred food observed in Temple days. At that time the layman gave the priest the *terumah*—heave offering—from his produce. Since the priests were the recipients, the food itself became sanctified, and the layman, presenting the gift had to be careful not to defile his hands. Although we no longer have a Temple, and the laws of giving *terumah* do not apply, we wash, that is "purify," our hands before the meal so that when the Temple will be rebuilt and the laws of *terumah* reinstated, the Jew will already be accustomed to this ritual.[3]

3. The most accepted version is based on the verse "You shall therefore sanctify yourselves, and you shall be holy for I am holy" (Lev. 11:44). Before the priests approached to perform their duties in the Temple, they would wash their hands. Since the Rabbis have compared our homes to the Temple, our table to the altar, and our food to the sacrifices, we, the priests of our homes, must also sanctify our hands by washing them before we eat.[4] This is also why we should use a vessel for *netilat yadayim*, since that is how the ablutions of the priests were performed.[5]

(b) The second ritual is that of *ha-motzi*. As soon as possible after the washing and drying of the hands, we must recite the *ha-motzi* blessing: "Blessed are You, O Lord our God, King of the Universe Who will bring forth bread from the earth." However, before saying this, it is recommended that all ten fingers be placed over the bread. There are several reasons for this.

1. The Hebrew verse "The eyes of all wait hopefully upon You so that You should give them their food at the correct time" (Psalms 145:15) contains ten words.

2. Ten Biblical *mitzvot*, or commandments are involved in the process that takes place from the planting of a seed in the ground until it grows and finally is transformed into bread: (I) The prohibition against plowing a field with different types of animals, such as an ox and a donkey; (II) The prohibition against sowing the ground with mixed seeds; (III) The law of gleaning, i.e., that ears of corn which had been dropped by the reapers were to be left behind for the benefit of the poor. (IV) When

gathering his sheaves of corn the owner of a field forgot one and left it behind, he was to leave that too, for the poor *(shikḥah).* (V) When harvesting, the farmer had to leave the corner of his field to the poor *(pe'ah).* (VI) An offering *(terumah)* had to be made to the priest of at least two percent of the farmer's produce. (VII) The commandment of *ma'aser rishon* required that a tithe be given to the Levite; (VIII) *Ma'aser sheni* involved the transfer of ten percent of the produce to Jerusalem where it was to be consumed. (IX) *Ma'aser ani* was the tithe which every Jew donated to the poor on the third and sixth year of the *shemittah* (seven year) cycle. (X) *Ḥallah*, the piece of dough that is taken off before the rest is baked into bread and set aside to be given to the priest.[6]

3. There are ten stages from the time the soil is plowed until the bread is baked. These are: plowing, cutting the wheat, binding the sheaves, threshing, winnowing, selecting, grinding, sifting, kneading and baking.[7] We must realize, then, the vast amount of effort that went into making the bread we are eating, and that ultimately it all goes back to God's beneficence.

4. The prayer of *ha-motzi* consists of ten words.

As noted above, the blessing of *ha-motzi* is worded in the future tense. The most common explanation offered for why this is so is a Midrashic text that relates how in the days of the Messiah, when man will be totally free of sin, God *will* make actual loaves grow out of the ground, and man *will* then be spared the effort involved in the various processes we have mentioned. This is also why we describe God as making bread grow from the earth when in fact what He produces is only wheat. The description is of what will happen at some future time.[8]

(c) After the blessing of *ha-motzi* a little salt is sprinkled on the piece of bread before it is eaten. For this a number of reasons are offered:

1. We sprinkle salt on our bread to emphasize the similarity between the table at which we eat and the altar of Temple times, and between our food and the sacrifices. The Bible states: "And with all your meat-offerings you shall offer salt" (Leviticus 2:13).

2. Salt reminds us that the poor should be welcome guests at a Jewish table. According to the Midrash, the people of Sodom were severely punished for their inhospitality by being turned into blocks of salt.

3. Salt reminds us of the sin-offerings offered on the altar in the Temple. The Hebrew word *maḥal*, "to forgive" is composed of the same letters as *melaḥ*, salt.

4. Salt reveals the wonderful way in which God has created the world. The scientific fact that salt can change its state and, after being dissolved in water, be crystallised into salt once more, was known in Talmudic times and seemed to the Rabbis to highlight the wisdom of the Creator.

5. Salt is a common and inexpensive ingredient. When people are surrounded with plenty, they should give a thought to more austere ways of living and remember that food is a gift from God.

6. Salt and bread must go together because the letters comprising the word *melaḥ*—salt—are identical with the letters of *leḥem*—bread.

7. In the manufacture of salt, two opposite forces are at work: water and fire. Salt is crystallized from water boiled at high temperatures. Water irrigates the wheat fields while the fire of the sun dries and ripens the crops. Both join, at God's command, in the benevolent act of producing the fruit of the earth.[9]

(d) *Mayim Aḥaronim* ("Last Waters"). At the conclusion of the meal, the hands are again washed with special attention being paid to the rinsing of the three joints of the finger. Two suggestions have been made to explain this:

1. To remove the traces of food that we may have handled with our fingers.[10]

2. To avoid danger to health. The Talmud (Ḥullin 105a) explains that, in ancient times, people used a salt-extract from a bedrock to season their food. There was a danger that, after a meal, people might become drowsy and rub their eyes with their fingers. The *melaḥ sedomit* might have stuck to their fingers during the meal and rubbed into their eyes, blind them. Later

authorities (*Tosafot, Ibid.)* already mention that this type of salt was no longer used, and that the consequent danger to eyesight no longer existed. However, even if there is no longer any health risk, most authorities hold that *mayim aḥaronim* is a Rabbinic dictum, obligatory before the Grace after Meals.[11]

(e) *Kos* (Cup of Wine) and *Zimmun* (The Call to Grace). The Rabbis of the Talmud (Pesaḥim 105b) ruled that on several occasions blessings should be recited over a cup of wine. One of these occasions is the Grace after Meals. Indeed, when we have just enjoyed the gifts of God which keep us alive, we surely owe Him a deep-felt expression of gratitude and so recite the grace over a cup of wine. There is a difference of opinion, however, as to the circumstances which make this obligatory. Some authorities[12] hold that even if one eats by himself he should have a cup of wine on the table for the *Birkat ha-Mazon* (Grace). Others argue that the blessings after the meal are not so special that they should require a cup of wine. A third opinion calls for a cup of wine only in the case of *zimmun*, which will be explained shortly. The custom prevailing today is that a person dining alone does not need to have a cup of wine for the Grace. Where there is *zimmun*, the wine is obligatory as long as it is readily available and inexpensive.

Zimmun is a Hebrew word which means "invitation" or "summon." Where there are three or more individuals dining together, one invites the others to join in the recitation of the *birkat ha-mazon.*[13] There are several reasons for this procedure (Berakhot 45a):

1. In Psalms (34:4) we find, "O, magnify the Lord with me and let us exalt His name together." That is to say, one invites others to join him in offering praise to God, so that they can exalt His name together.

2. In Deuteronomy (32:3) we read, "When I proclaim the name of the Lord, give greatness to our God." One mentions the name of God, and the others are asked to respond.

In this ritual of *zimmun* one exclaims: "Come let us recite the benediction"—in Yiddish, the formula is: *Rabosai, mir velen benschen*,—whereupon, the rest respond: *yehi shem hashem mevorakh me attah ve'ad olam*, "May the name of the Lord be blessed from now and forever." What needs clarification is why this practice is at all necessary. The source for it is in the Zohar, (beginning of Deuteronomy) which speaks of the religious and psychological importance of preparations prior to the fulfillment of a mitzvah. The invitation of *zimmun* preceding the Grace itself is intended to create a mood of anticipation before the actual recitation of the *birkat ha-mazon.* [14]

In Sephardic and Hassidic communities, the custom is for the cup of wine to be handed to the one who will lead the *birkat ha-mazon.* In other communities, the person leading the Grace simply pours the wine into a cup, lifts it up from the table, and proceeds with the blessings.

The background for this difference lies in a subtle change of language between the Talmud and later authorities. Among the requirements for the "cup of blessing" that are enumerated in the Talmud (Berakhot, end of Chap. 7) the following expression is used: *notelo bi-shete yadav*, "he must *take* the cup of wine in his two hands." Thus, all he has to do is to raise the cup and he has fulfilled his obligation. The later ruling reads, however: *u-mekablo bi-shete yadav*, "and he *receives* the cup with his two hands." This implies that the cup is handed to him and he accepts it.[15]

Immediately before *birkat ha-mazon*, it is customary for all knives to be removed from the table. This is because, ever since the Destruction, the home has taken the place of the Temple, and our table is symbolic of the altar. The Bible says: "You shall not build it [the altar] of hewn stones for if you lift up your sword on it, you will have profaned it" (Exodus 20:22). By a sword, an instrument made of steel is meant, and a knife falls into that category. Furthermore, the Bible describes the work involved in the building of the Temple of King Solomon: "Neither hammer, nor axe, nor any tool of iron was heard in the house while it was being built" (I Kings 6:6). This objection to the presence of iron and steel during the construction of the Temple stems from the verse: "I have loved Jacob, and Esau I hated" (Malachi 1:3). Jewish sensibilities recoil from any association with Esau, who accepted his father's blessing: "And by the sword shall you live." So, when we praise God for the festive table, symbolic of the altar which promoted spiritual peace and emotional contentment, we cannot do so while the knife, the prototype of the sword which brings death and sadness in its wake, lies in front of us.[16]

A most unusual motive for removing the knife from the table before *birkat ha-mazon* is mentioned by a medieval sage.[17] He relates that once somebody, while reciting the Grace after meals, became so intensely depressed by reciting the paragraph about the rebuilding of Jerusalem that he took the knife lying on the table and stabbed himself with it. But this, of course, is not the commonly accepted reason why we do not have knives on the table.[18]

Another meaningful custom that is practiced in many communities throughout the world is that the bread must remain on the table during the *birkat ha-mazon.* There are a number of reasons given for this:

1. If we are soon going to ask God to continue providing us with food as He has done for this meal, there must be some outer manifestation of the good that we wish to continue. So, the bread is left on the table.

2. Food automatically reminds us of agricultural activities. One of the basic agricultural laws in Jewish society was that of *pe'ah*, leaving the corner of the field unharvested for the poor. To make us constantly conscious of the mitzvah of *pe'ah*, a piece of bread is left on the table.

3. Although we may have finished our meal and be ready to retire from the table, we must always be conscious of the possibility that at the very last moment a poor man may enter and ask to be fed. Let bread always be kept in readiness.

4. While people are perhaps prepared to thank God for food, they may overlook the fact that God provides for more than a bare minimum for survival. Therefore, we leave a piece of bread

on the table to show that we realize that God has given us more than we need, since, after we have had enough to eat, bread is still left over on the table.[19]

(f) *Birkat ha-Mazon—Grace After Meals.* While it might be natural for any religious person to thank God for providing him with the basic needs for survival, to the observant Jew, *birkat ha-mazon* is a positive commandment of the Torah. We are instructed: "And you shall eat and be satisfied and bless the Lord your God for the good land which He has given you" (Deut. 8:10). Commenting on this passage in Berakhot 7, the Rabbis of the Talmud say that "you shall bless" refers to *zimmun*; "the Lord your God" to the first of the four benedictions dealing with the plentiful amount of food granted by God to man; "on the land" refers to God's generosity in giving us the Holy Land; "the good," to Jerusalem; "that He has given you," refers to other forms of kindness that God shows the Jew. Because the *birkat ha-mazon* is of Biblical origin and is one of the highest expessions of man's indebtedness to God, the Rabbis decided that although, in general, prayers should be offered in their original Hebrew, these benedictions could be recited in any language that one understands. The Rabbis also ruled that even if one is not completely sober, that is no excuse for him not to say the *birkat ha-mazon.*[20]

The origin of these benedictions dates back to the earliest periods in Jewish history. The three-fold blessing of God's gift of food, God's gift of a national identity and God's gift of the sanctity of Jerusalem were originally conceived during three different periods. When God gave the manna, Moses immediately recognized the need for a prayer for food. When Joshua entered the Promised Land, he conceived the idea of a public expression of gratitude for national security and identity. When David prepared his plan to build a Temple in Jerusalem and when Solomon actually did build it, they realized that this aspect of religious commitment must be publicly recognized. However, the language and form of the *birkat ha-mazon*, as we know it today, was composed at a later date.

To sum up so far: The first three benedictions of *birkat ha-mazon*—food, national identity and the sanctity of Jerusalem—are of Biblical origin as interpreted by the Sages. The *birkat ha-mazon*, however, contains a fourth benediction which is Rabbinic in origin. It is the blessing, *Ha-tov, veha-metiv*, which extolls God who was good to us and will continue to do good to us. This was composed in the Academy of Yavneh and refers to God's beneficence after the downfall of Betar (135 C.E.). For twenty-five years the martyrs of Betar remained unburied. In fact, their bodies were used to fence in a vineyard. After lying exposed for a quarter of a century, the corpses were discovered, and miraculously they had not decomposed and were in a condition to be accorded a dignified burial. It is in commemoration of that event that this fourth blessing was inserted immediately after the benediction over Jerusalem.[21]

It is also for this reason that, upon concluding the blessing over Jerusalem, each individual utters the word, "Amen." Usually we answer "Amen" only after listening to a blessing uttered by someone else. However, here the "Amen" is intended to differentiate between the Biblical section of the benedictions and the one instituted by Rabbinic decree.

A difference of opinion arose over the question of whether one should recite the benedictions over forbidden foods. Maimonides (*Yad, Hilkhot Berakhot* Chap. 1) declares that this would be tantamount to mocking at God's word. Naḥmanides (*ibid*), on the other hand, is equally emphatic about his view that, as long as the person who ate the forbidden food was satisfied, he must recite the *birkat ha-mazon*. Both agree, however, that in a case where one has to eat forbidden food for health reasons, he is expected to say Grace.[22]

A sentence in the second of the four benedicitions reads as follows: "We thank You for Your covenant which you have sealed upon our bodies (circumcision), for the Torah You taught us, for the laws You made known to us . . ." The question arises as to what women, who are also obligated to recite *birkat ha-mazon*, should say in this context. Circumcision does not apply to them;

they are also exempt from obligatory study of the Torah; nor did they participate in the conquest of the Land. The answer is provided by some of our foremost Sages.[23] The *berit*, the sign on our bodies (circumcision) may also be translated as a covenant. At the time when Abraham circumcised himself and his household, God made a covenant with him that he would give him the Promised Land on condition that his descendants would fulfill their obligations as contained in the commandments of the Torah. This is the inference in the Scriptures: "And He gave them the land of nations so that they might observe His statutes and keep His laws" (Psalm 105: 44,45). Therefore, we find the covenant, the promise of the land, and the laws of the Torah grouped into one. This promise was not given to Abraham only but to all his descendants, including the women.

SOURCES

1. *Ta'ame ha-Minhagim* 74, 75; *Tur Oraḥ Ḥayyim* 162.
2. *Arukh ha-Shulḥan Oraḥ Ḥayyim* 158, par. 4.
3. *Tur Oraḥ Ḥayyim* 158; *Bet Yoseph* 168 and *Perishah* 158.
4. *Tur Oraḥ Ḥayyim* 158; *Arukh ha-Shulḥan* 158 par. 2; *Torah Temimah*, Leviticus 11:44.
5. *Tur Oraḥ Ḥayyim* and *Arukh ha-Shulḥan* 159; *Ben Ish Ḥai* p. 123.
6. *Tur Oraḥ Ḥayyim* 167; *Avudraham* p.170; *Ḥayye Avraham* p. 26a; *Arukh ha-Shulḥan* 167 par. 9.
7. *Avudraham* p. 170. It is not clear why this authority did not include sowing. In the listing of the thirty-nine major types of work forbidden on the Sabbath, sowing is included.
8. *Ḥayye Avraham* p. 26.
9. *Ḥayye Avraham* p. 25b; *Ben Ish Ḥai* 128.
10. *Avudraham* p. 172.
11. *Tur Oraḥ Ḥayyim, Bet Yoseph* 181; *Arukh ha-Shulḥan* 181, par. 2, 3, 5; *Ta'ame ha-Minhagim* p. 86.
12. *Tur Oraḥ Ḥayyim* 182.
13. *Arukh ha-Shulḥan* 192 par. 3.
14. *Tur Oraḥ Ḥayyim* 192; *Avudraham* p. 172; *Arukh ha-Shulḥan* 192 pars. 1, 2;*Ḥayye Avraham* p. 27b; *Sefer ha-Mat'amim* p. 9; *Ta'ame ha-Minhagim* p. 83-85.

15. *Tur Oraḥ Ḥayyim, Bet Yoseph, Perishah* 183; *Ben Ish Ḥai* p. 147 par. 16.
16. *Avudraham* p. 173; *Ta'ame ha-Minhagim* p. 82.
17. *Bet Yoseph, Oraḥ Ḥayyim* 180.
18. *Arukh ha-Shulḥan, Oraḥ Ḥayyim* 180 par. 5.
19. *Tur Oraḥ Ḥayyim, Perishah* 180; *Avudraham* p. 173; *Arukh ha-Shulḥan* 180 par. 3; *Sefer ha-Mat'amim* p. 9.
20. *Tur Oraḥ Ḥayyim* 185; *Arukh ha-Shulḥan* 185 pars. 1, 2, 12, 14.
21. *Tur Oraḥ Ḥayyim, Bet Yoseph* 187, 188, 189; *Arukh ha-Shulḥan* 187 pars.1, 2, 7, 8; 188 pars. 1, 3; 189 pars. 1, 2; *Ta'ame ha-Minhagim* p. 89.
22. *Arukh ha-Shulḥan* 196 pars. 1, 2, 3, 4.
23. *Bet Yoseph, Perishah, Oraḥ Ḥayyim* 187; *Arukh ha-Shulḥan* 187 par. 8.

Mezuzah

In two passages of the Torah (Deuteronomy 6:9 and 11:20), the Jew is commanded to write "these words" (the first two paragraphs of the *Shema*) and affix them to the doorpost of his house. The Hebrew word *mezuzah*, originally meaning a "doorpost," has come to be used also to designate the hand-written scroll which distinguishes the doors of a Jewish home.

Various reasons and explanations have been suggested for the practice of affixing the *mezuzah*. Some authorities lay stress on God's promise (Deut. 9:21) that observance of this commandment will be rewarded by length of life. Others see in the *mezuzah* a tangible symbol of the special relationship which exists between God and Israel. Whereas a human king sits in his palace while his soldiers stand guard outside to protect him, with Israel the position is reversed: the obedient Jew can stay at home secure in the protection of the Almighty who, by virtue of the *mezuzah*, keeps guard over his door. While our appreciation of the mitzvah is enriched by such explanations, our Rabbis are agreed that we need look no further than the twice-repeated precept of the Torah to prove the necessity for affixing a *mezuzah*.[1]

The *Sefer Torah* (Scroll of the Law), *tefillin* (phylacteries) and *mezuzah* must all be written by hand upon parchment prepared from the skin of a kosher animal. (This means that only skins of kosher species of animals—such as cattle, sheep or goats—may be used for this purpose. It does not mean that the particular animal from which the skin has been taken must necessarily have been ritually slaughtered.) The reason seems obvious: it would not seem quite right to use parchment made from the skin of a forbidden animal. In addition, the Scriptural expression "that the law of the Lord may be in your mouth" (Exodus 13:9), has been interpreted to mean that, for these kinds of ritual objects, only the skin of permitted animals may be used. The Torah specifically commands: "You shall *write* them," which implies that printing, or any such mechanical or photographic method of reproduction would render the scroll *pasul* (invalid). The last two letters of the Hebrew word *u-khetavtam* (and you shall write them) form the word *tam*, meaning "perfect," from which a number of typographical rules are derived. The expression, "you shall write *them*," is taken to convey that the passages in question must be written in their entirety, without any omission or imperfection. Even if only one letter is missing or wrongly written the whole *mezuzah* is invalidated.

There is a conflict of opinion as to whether or not the *mezuzah* must be written *li-shemah* (i.e. with the express intention that it be used for this purpose only). Arguing that *mezuzot* are purchased from many sources and that it would be impractical to have to trace the writer of each one in order to ascertain whether he had in fact written it *li-shemah*, Maimonides holds the view that such pure intentions are not a sine qua non. All authorities are agreed that the scribe must have the end purpose fully in mind when he transcribes a *Sefer Torah* or *tefillin*. The view that in this respect a *mezuzah* possesses lesser importance (so that in this case the scribe's intention is not an essential precondition) rests on the argument that, while a *Sefer Torah* and phylacteries are in the category of *ḥovat ha-guf*—a personal obligation incumbent upon the individual—the *mezuzah* is *ḥovat ha-bayit*, an obligation devolving upon the house. A Jew who has no house does not need a *mezuzah*. The generally accepted opinion is that a somewhat more lenient attitude may be adopted with regard to a *mezuzah* than is demanded for a *Sefer Torah* or *tefillin*. The conclusion is that, while the scribe's proper intention is required for a *mezuzah*, in an emergency, i.e., where insistence upon proving it might lead to undue delay or to the doorpost in question being left without any *mezuzah* altogether, this can be taken for granted.[2]

Before being put into its case the parchment is rolled up in such a way that, when it is unravelled, the words *Shema Yisrael* ("Hear O Israel") will be the first to appear. The affirmation of God's unit must be the first words to greet the Jew when he unwinds the *mezuzah.*

On the outside of the parchment as well as on the case the Hebrew word *Shaddai* (Almighty) is inscribed. Two reasons are given for this practice. According to the Kabbalists, this particular name of God serves as a protection against demons (*shedim).* Another explanation interprets the three letters separately: *Sh* stand for *shomer*—guardian; *D* stands for *delatot*—doors; *I* stands for Israel. Thus God stands as the guardian over the doors of the children of Israel.[3]

After the appropriate blessing has been recited, the *mezuzah* is affixed near the outer edge of the right-hand doorpost, (i.e. to the right of the person entering the house or room) more than two-thirds of the way up. The custom is to fix it diagonally upon the doorpost. This represents a compromise between two views which were current among the medieval scholars, some of whom held that it should lie horizontally while others insisted that it should be vertical.

Why particularly on the right doorpost? Because the word *beitekha* (your house) could be read as *biatekha* (your entering). Since a person is wont to step forward with his right foot first, it follows that, when approaching the door, he will encounter the right doorpost before the left.[4]

Maimonides specifies ten conditions which make the affixing of a *mezuzah* to a room or building obligatory:[5]

(a) The floor space must be at least four cubits square in area. A door leading to a closet of smaller dimensions is therefore exempt.

(b) The entrance must be framed by two proper doorposts.

(c) A lintel must be above them; the posts must be attached to the lintel and must stand firm.

(d) There must be a ceiling above the lintel.

(e) A door must be attached to the doorposts and must lead to a space enclosed by four regular walls and roofed over; this excludes a mere portico or colonnade.

(f) The entrance must be at last ten handbreadths in height.

(g) A *mezuzah* is required for regular everyday residence but not for a synagogue (unless someone lives there).

(h) It must be a place of human habitation, not—for example—a stable or cowshed.

(i) It must be a place in which the occupants behave with dignity and propriety; this excludes a bathhouse or a toilet.

(j) It must be a permanent abode, not a temporary shelter such as a *sukkah.* Anyone who moves into new quarters outside of Israel can, if he so desires, postpone affixing a *mezuzah* for the first thirty days since it may be regarded as a temporary abode for this length of time. In Israel, however, since any dwelling occupied by a Jew is considered a permanent home, one is obliged to affix a *mezuzah* immediately.

What should a person do if he is too poor to afford both a *mezuzah* for his home and *tefillin* for his prayers? Which should he rather buy? Whichever choice he makes, he is on sound halakhic ground. He may prefer to purchase *tefillin*, which, as *ḥovat ha-guf*, are his own personal obligation. If, on the other hand, he chooses to purchase a *mezuzah*, he may argue that, where necessary, one can usually borrow a pair of *tefillin*, whereas one could hardly borrow a *mezuzah* affixed to the door of a neighbor! The accepted view, however, is that, in such circumstances, one should buy *tefillin* rather than a *mezuzah.*[6]

Since the *mezuzah* is considered to have a somewhat lesser degree of sanctity than a *Sefer Torah* or *tefillin*, we are not permitted to take a sheet discarded from either of them and use it for a *mezuzah.* The rule invariably is: *ma'alin ba-kodesh ve-lo moridim*—in religious matters, we must always ascend to a higher level and never descend to a lower.[7]

Mezuzot attached to the home of a private individual must

be checked twice every seven years to ensure that no letter or word has faded or peeled off from the parchment. In the case of a public *mezuzah*, e.g., one affixed to a city gate, an inspection twice in fifty years is enough. The reason for this is that, if an examination had to be made more frequently, everyone in the city might plead that he had no time to attend to it and the *mezuzot* would not be checked at all.[8]

SOURCES

1. *Tur* and *Bet Yoseph, Yoreh De'ah* 285.
2. Ibid.
3. Ibid, also *Sefer ha-Ta'amim* p. 71.
4. *Tur, Yoreh De'ah* 289.
5. *Yad, Hilkhot Mezuzah*, beginning of 6.
6. *Shulḥan Arukh, Oraḥ Ḥayyim* 38.
7. *Tur, Yoreh De'ah* 290.
8. Ibid. See also *Perisha* ad loc.

Shabbat

The simple basis for the observance of the Sabbath Day is found in the biblical verses: "And the Children of Israel shall keep the Sabbath to observe the Sabbath throughout the generations, for a perpetual covenant. It is a sign between Me and the Children of Israel forever, for six days the Lord made Heaven and Earth, and on the seventh day He ceased from work and rested" (Ex. 31: 16-17). Thus, the cessation from work emanates from the fact that after six days of creation, God rested on the seventh. It is because of the objective to emulate God's pattern that the fourth of the Ten Commandments proclaims: "*Remember* the Sabbath Day to keep it holy. . . for six days the Lord made Heaven and Earth, and rested on the seventh day." This is a profound theological principle which not everyone is intellectually prepared to fathom. We, therefore, find that the Torah (Deut. 5:12-15), exhorts the Jew to *Observe* the Sabbath Day for "you shall remember that you were a servant in the Land of Egypt and the Lord brought you out of there; therefore, the Lord your God commanded you to keep the Sabbath Day." This is something that everyone can grasp. If God had not emancipated the Jew and had not taught the world a lesson in freedom, it is conceivable that today the major part of humanity would be toiling all seven days of the week. Therefore, in the Scriptures we find two different admonitions relating to the Sabbath: a. *Remember* the Sabbath (*Zakhor*); b. *Observe* the Sabbath (*Shamor*). Both point to the sanctification of the day.

The Torah makes specific reference to one aspect of the observance of the Shabbat only, the cessation from menial and constructive work. Yet, what may appear to be work for one may not be work for another. How do we determine whether an activity we are engaging in is to be considered work? The Sages of the Talmud deduced that the categories of labor forbidden on the Sabbath are those performed in the construction of the *Mishkan* (Tabernacle). By a thorough analysis of the forms, types and manners of these labors they arrived at a total of thirty-nine categories.

One cannot suddenly become transported from the profane into the sacred; from the drab, fatiguing life of an ordinary weekday to the tranquility and happiness of the Shabbat.

To make this transition possible, *hakhanah* (a preparatory period) is necessary. Getting into the mood and being fired with passionate anticipation of the arrival of the Shabbat can spell the difference between a day that is burdensome and one that is holy and joyful. With this in mind, one should choose to do one's shopping for the Shabbat on Friday, in order to indicate that he is not merely engaging in his routine shopping for food but is preparing to honor the Sabbath. The interest and enthusiasm involved in shopping for Shabbat are a significant and determining factor in the experience of the Sabbath day.[1] For the same reason one should not partake of a substantial repast on Friday so that he may sit down to the Sabbath meal eagerly and with greater appetite. The Sabbath meal will then become not only a routine function but the festive occasion that befits a sanctified day.[2] When on a journey on a Friday one should make sure to reach his destination or return to his home in sufficient time to prepare enough food for his Sabbath meals.[3]

In ancient times, when the Jew "dwelled under his vine and under his fig tree," every Friday afternoon a loud shofar blast would resound throughout the entire community. This was a signal to the farmers in the field that it was time to return to their houses to prepare for Shabbat. A little later in the day, the shofar would be blown a second time to remind the storekeepers to close their shops and go home. A third blast, close to sunset, was the final call to kindle the Sabbath lights and usher in the Sabbath.[4]

In modern times, with the Jews dispersed among gentiles it is inexpedient to call their attention to the imminence of the Shabbat by means of the shofar. But in some sections of Jerusalem the custom of sounding the shofar to announce the commencement of the Sabbath still prevails.

Although the lighting of the Sabbath candles is not Scriptural in origin, the custom is observed with the same solemnity as if it were biblically decreed. The time for kindling the candles is not universally uniform. In most Jewish communities throughout the world, candles are lit from eighteen to twenty minutes before sunset. In Jerusalem, it is an ancient custom to do it forty minutes before sunset. The basis for this discrepancy is in the interpretation of a Midrash (Genesis—end of Chapter 1). The Sages were curious to know why, at the close of each day of the creation, the Torah concludes with the words, "And it was evening and it was morning. . .first day, second day, third day, etc". On the last day, the Torah employs the word *ha-shishi, the* sixth day. The definite article *ha*, "the", is applied only in the proclamation of the sixth day. Why? One of the Sages explans that it was only at the last moment of the sixth day that the process of creation came to an end. But who except God, can pinpoint with certainty when the last moment of a day ends and when the first moment of the next day begins? To be sure then, the Sage argues, the seventh day, Shabbat, should begin "an hour" earlier on Friday afternoon to be certain that the exact moment of nightfall is included. Those who observe the eighteen to twenty minute period before sunset take the position that the "hour" spoken of by the Sage is not to be taken literally but to indicate some measure of time which would be a significant *tosefet*, "extension" of the Shabbat. The custom in Jerusalem is founded on the observance of the literal hour before nightfall that the Sage speaks about. Hence, if the interval between sunset and darkness is eighteen or twenty minutes, the remainder, completing the full hour, equals forty minutes.[5]

There is a difference of opinion as to why we have to light candles at all. Some authorities speculate that since the Prophet

(Isaiah 58:13) refers to the Shabbat as *oneg*, "delight", we make our sitting at the table a delight by adorning it with candlelight. Other opinions would have us understand the candles as a symbol honoring the sanctity of the day.[6] Yet another reason for the candlelighting: just as when one lights one candle from another, he does not diminish the light emanating from the original candle, so is it with the Shabbat. The Jew draws sufficient spiritual sustenance from the Shabbat to last him for the week, without detracting at all from the sanctity of the Shabbat.[7]

In any event, at least two candles must be kindled; one representing the commandment to "remember the Sabbath" (Ex. 20.8), the other representing "observe the Sabbath" (Deut. 5, 12). Some kindle seven lights to correspond to the seven days of the week or the seven lights of the Menorah in the Temple; others kindle ten candles in commemoration of the Ten Commandments. In many homes one candle is lit for each member of the family.[8]

The mistress of the house is charged with the duty of lighting the Sabbath candles. Two opposing views are set forth for entrusting her with the obligation:

(a) It was the woman who committed the first human transgression in the Garden of Eden and thereby caused the light of man's life to be extinguished. As an expiation she is to kindle the Sabbath candles in order to restore the brightness of that light.

(b) It is the woman who is responsible for bringing peace, serenity and happiness into the home. She should be given the honor of initiating the Sabbath by kindling the lights.

For the mistress of the house the Sabbath begins with the kindling of the candles; there is a difference of opinion, however, as to when the Sabbath starts for the male members of the household. Some authorities contend that at the same moment that the Sabbath begins for the woman, it begins for the man as well. In other words, when the woman of the house lights the candles in the home the whole household becomes obliged to observe the Sabbath. Others argue that the husband has yet another function to perform: attending services in the Synagogue. Therefore, for him the Shabbat begins with the evening prayers. The vast majority of Jewish homes follow the former view.[9]

After a woman lit the candles she covers her eyes with the palms of her hands and so recites the blessing. It has already been noted that the blessing should always be recited immediately prior to the performance of the mitzvah *over la-asiatan*. But by doing so she has already ushered in the *Shabbat* by her reciting the blessing after which she is forbidden to perform any work including lighting the candles. On the other hand, to kindle the lights and then recite the blessing over the candles, would violate the principle of *over la-asiatan*. To overcome this dilemma the woman first lights the candles and covers her eyes, thereby denying herself the enjoyment of the light of the Sabbath candles. Thus she fulfills all requirements; she did not enjoy the Sabbath candles until after making the blessing as to not to violate the principle of *over la-asiatan*.[10].

Care must be taken to put a tablecloth and the loaves of bread on the table on which the candles are placed before the kindling of the Sabbath lights. This is necessary because of the law of *tiltul*, i.e. it is forbidden on Shabbat to move objects that are not designated or unfit for use on this day. For example the candelabra which holds the candles may not be moved while they are burning—consequently it, too, may not be moved on Shabbat. For this reason one may not move the table either because it serves as the base for the candelabra. On the other hand, if bread is on the table in addition to the candelabra, the table becomes the base for an object, the bread, which is permitted on Shabbat. Hence, if one had to move the table he would be permitted to do so since it is now a base for a permissible object rather than for the forbidden object only.[11]

The Jew arrives at the Synagogue Friday evening to usher in the Shabbat with appropriate prayers. It is almost a universal custom, if time permits, to recite first the Song of Songs. The reasons are:

(a) The Song of Songs describes the people of Israel as the chosen bride of God. To the Jew the Sabbath is a spiritual bride that brings to him joy, happiness and contentment.

(b) The Song of Songs is a means of drawing the Jew closer to God, his beloved. The Shabbat is also a means of bringing the Jew nearer to God.[12]

Prayer service for Friday evening consists of two parts. The first is called *Kabbalat Shabbat*, "Welcoming the Shabbat." These prayers open with six chapters of the Psalms (95-99). The first five chapters were chosen because they speak about the messianic period when man will enjoy true peace and restfulness. Therefore, the Jew, on the Sabbath, anticipates a day of serenity similar, albeit remotely, to the future Eternal Shabbat. These are followed by Psalm 29 because in this chapter David employs the words "the voice of God" seven times to correspond to the seven benedictions of the *Amidah*, the silent prayer of the Shabbat evening service.[13]

The famous mystic poem, *Lekha Dodi Likerat Kallah*, "Come my beloved to greet the bride; we will welcome the Shabbat," follows.

Kabbalists were wont to go out into the field where they performed the ritual of *Kabbalat Shabbat*. Symbolically, they went out to receive the bride, the Shabbat. Until today there are those, particularly in Jerusalem, who remain outside of the Synagogue during Kabbalat Shabbat and do not enter until the second part of the service begins.[14]

In Yemenite communities the congregants stand during the *Lekha Dodi*, raise themselves on their toes and then bring their heels down. This is done throughout until the conclusion of the verse. This custom was initiated as a form of dancing in the days of the Talmud. (See Rabbi Hananel, Baba Kama 32a.)[15]

The second part of the service consists of the regular *Maariv* prayers with one major exception. The *Amidah* is comprised of seven instead of the normal nineteen, benedictions: the first three and the last three of the regular *Amidah* and one benediction hallowing the Sabbath Day. Since the other thirteen of the eighteen benedictions of the weekday *Amidah* are devoted to the supplicant's personal needs and requirements, it was considered inopportune to include these prayers on a day when the faith and trust of the Jew in God is complete.[16]

Kiddush, the sanctification of the day over a cup of wine, is a most important feature of the Shabbat. From the Scriptural passage "And you will call the Sabbath a delight" (Isaiah 58:13), the inference is drawn that the *Kiddush* must be recited at the place where the meal will be eaten. When "you call" (sanctify) the Shabbat, it shall be done "where you delight" (eat your repast). In other words, one may not perform the ritual of *Kiddush* in one room and then proceed to the dining table in another room. But why over wine? The passage "[We recall] your caresses [to be] more pleasant than wine." (Song of Songs I:2) is interpreted by the Sages (Pesaḥim 106 a) to mean, "When we are called upon to remember, we prefer to do so over wine." Since the Torah exhorts us to *remember* the Sabbath Day to keep it holy, we do so over a cup of wine. There are two requirements for the proper observance of the *Kiddush*. First, it must be recited over a cup of wine and, secondly, it must be carried out at the place of the Shabbat meal.

In ancient and medieval times, and even until comparatively modern times transient guests would appear in the Synagogue on Friday night and the community would provide them with food and lodging, either in the Synagogue or in an adjacent building. On behalf of these guests, the *Kiddush* was recited in the Synagogue immediately after the prayer service. Today, in most communities, we do not find transients being cared for on the Shabbat. This situation gave rise to a sharp conflict of opinion, whether to retain the ritual of *Kiddush* in the Synagogue even though no transients gather there any longer. Those who adhere to it do it on the premise that it is a venerable custom which should be allowed to continue. Furthermore, there may be some congregants who will not recite the *Kiddush* either willfully or because they are incapable of doing so. For their sakes we retain the *Kiddush*. On the other hand, the authorities who wish to abolish the *Kiddush* in the Synagogue argue that we would be taking the name of God in vain in the benediction of the *Kiddush* since no transients are present in the Synagogue.[17]

Regardless of whether one may have heard the *Kiddush* in the Synagogue, he must recite it in the presence of his family, or even by himself if he is alone, when he returns to his home, where he will sit down to have his meal.

A custom, albeit not an ancient one, is to chant before making *Kiddush* the traditional *Shalom Alekhem*, "Peace be with you, O you angels." Two reasons are proposed for this custom:

(a) In the hustle and bustle of preparing for the Shabbat, members of the household are prone to irritate one another and cause a rift among themselves. The angels of Heaven are called upon to restore peace to the household.

(b) According to a beautiful Midrash, when the Jew returns from the Synagogue to his home he is escorted by two angels, one good and one evil. When they enter the home and find the house illumined by the sanctity of the Sabbath candles, the table pleasingly set and everything bespeaking beauty and serenity, the angel of goodness pronounces: "May all your future Sabbath days be as this one", and the angel of evil perforce nods his consent. Since both angels agree and the angel of goodness made peace with the angel of evil, we address them as angels of peace.[18]

Women are obliged to make *Kiddush*, either by reciting it alone, or be being attentive to the recitation of the head of the house. Ordinarily, one would expect them to be exempt because *Kiddush* must be recited at a specific time and in a specific place. Hence, the principle of *mitzvah she-hazeman grama*, that women are exempt from commandments related to a time element, should apply. For example, they do not don *tefillin* because these are worn during the day only.

However, the ritual of *Kiddush* is incumbent upon them because, as we have noted, the Jew was exhorted to do both,-

"*Remember* the Sabbath" and "*Keep* the Sabbath" Since women are required to "*Keep* the Sabbath", the requirement to "*Remember* the Sabbath" over a cup of wine, is incumbent upon them too.[19]

In order to understand the ritual of breaking bread, commonly known as the *ha-motzi*, on the Shabbat, it is necessary to look to the Torah where we find a description of what occurred when the Children of Israel ate the manna in the desert. There it is related: "And when the layer of dew was gone up, behold upon the face of the wilderness a fine, scale like thing, fine as the hoarfrost on the ground. . . and Moses said unto them, 'It is the bread which the Lord gave you to eat'. . . and it came to pass on the sixth day they gathered *twice* as much bread. . six days you shall gather it, but on the seventh day it is the Sabbath, in it there shall be none" (Ex. 16, 11-27).

From this stems the ruling that on Shabbat we recite the benediction of *ha-motzi* over two loaves of bread (*Leḥem Mishne*), commemorating the two portions of manna which were given to each Jew on the sixth day for the Shabbat.[20]

Another reason for the two loaves is that there are many other features of the Shabbat that are two in number: in the days of the Temple the additional (*Musaf*) sacrifice of the Shabbat consisted of two sheep; two candles are kindled; there are two exhortations: *Remember* the Sabbath and *keep* the Sabbath.[21]

These loaves of bread are called *ḥallah.* To the uninitiated this may be somewhat misleading because they commonly believe that *ḥallah* is the name of the bread we eat on Shabbat. In truth, however, *ḥallah* designates that portion of the dough that, in ancient times, was given to the priest, and, in modern times, is burned. In order to remind the one who is baking bread that it is obligatory to set aside *ḥallah* it has become customary to call that loaf of bread a *ḥallah.*[22]

Others dispute this idea and argue that if the reason for calling it *ḥallah* is solely due to the piece of dough that is set aside, why do we not call the bread that we eat on weekdays *ḥallah* as well, since the same laws apply there, too? Therefore, they suggest that *ḥallah* is phonetically and scripturally almost identical with the word *kallah*, a bride. Since the Shabbat is compared to a bride, we call the bread that we eat on Shabbat *ḥallah*.[23]

It should be noted that not only do we spread a cloth over the Shabbat table but we also place an additional covering over the *ḥallot* as well. In other words, the *ḥallot* must be inserted between two cloths. Three ideas are brought out in this way:

(a) Bread is our staple food, yet on the Shabbat it takes a secondary role waiting for the *Kiddush* to be recited first over the wine. In order, figuratively, to spare the *ḥallot* this affront, they are covered.

(b) The *ḥallot* are symbolic to the manna in the desert. The manna was enveloped in a layer of dew beneath and a layer of dew above it.[24]

(c) If the *ḥallot* were to be uncovered from the very start it could lead one to believe that they were there merely for the purpose of satisfying one's hunger. They, however, are part of the respect and honor we pay the Shabbat. Hence, we cover the *ḥallot* until the moment we are ready to eat them as a gesture of respect and honor.[25]

Before reciting the traditional prayer of *ha-motzi* on the Sabbath one should uncover the *ḥallot*, look for the best-baked part, and pass the knife over it making a slight groove and then recite the blessing. During weekdays, the bread has to be cut into just short of severing it before making the blessing because to cut into it after reciting the blessing would be considered an undue *hefsek* (interruption) between the time that one recited the benediction and his eating of the bread. In the case of the two *ḥallot*, however, since they represent the two *full* measures of manna that the Children of Israel gathered, they, too, must be whole. Hence, if one were to sever a part of the *ḥallah* before the benediction the blessing would be made over one and one half loaves instead of over two complete loaves. For this reason one should make a slight indentation in the *ḥallah* thus reducing the undue waiting period and simultaneously assuring that the benediction is recited over two whole loaves.[26]

In some homes both loaves of bread are cut as a remembrance of two measures of manna that were picked on Friday in honor of the Shabbat. In many homes, particularly in the old communities in Israel, only one loaf is cut although there are two loaves on the table. Their argument is that while it is true that the Children of Israel picked two measures of manna, one was for Friday night and the other for the Sabbath day.[27]

It was already noted that it is equally incumbent upon women to comply with the rituals of Shabbat as it is for men because they too were charged with the obligation to "*Keep* the Sabbath." Thus, women too, should take care to fulfill the obligation to recite the blessings over two loaves. Since this may be inexpedient, the master of the house should wait until the entire household is seated before proceeding with the *ha-motzi*. In that manner they will fulfill their obligation merely by listening to the procedure.[28]

Kabbalists throughout the ages were accustomed to prepare twelve *ḥallot* for the Sabbath table in commemoration of the twelve loaves of shew-bread that were brought by the priests into the Temple every Shabbat.[29]

A custom that has received universal acceptance in all Jewish communities is that of eating fish on Shabbat in one form or another. It is difficult to determine exactly when this custom was initiated although it is reasonable to believe that it is of ancient vintage. Some of the reasons that have been suggested are:

(a) In describing the creation of the world, the Torah relates that God blessed His creation of the fifth, sixth and seventh days. On the fifth he created fish; on the sixth, man; on the seventh, the Shabbat. Only on these three days do we find, "And the Lord blessed." Therefore, if man will eat fish on the Shabbat he will remember and be assured that, ". . . a threefold cord cannot quickly be torn asunder" (Ecclestiastes 4:12).

(b) To remind the Jew that just as the fish cannot survive out of water so the Children of Israel cannot survive without the Torah which is compared to water.

(c) According to the Kabbalistic view, the Jew will partake of a great fish, the Leviathan, when the Messianic period arrives. By its tranquility, our Shabbat serves as a preview of the messianic era with its total serenity.

(d) The Hebrew word for fish is *dag*. The Hebrew letters are *Daled* and *Gimel*. The numerical value of the *Daled* is four which should remind us of our four matriarchs: Sarah, Rebecca, Rachel and Leah. The numerical value of the *Gimel* is three, symbolizing the three patriarchs: Abraham, Issaac and Jacob.

(e) Although a fish may be out of water, it can still survive if there is some moisture upon it. So it is with the Jew. Removed from the mainstream of Torah study during the weekdays because of his labors and toils, as long as he retains some of the inspiration of the Torah acquired during the Sabbath study period, he can yet survive.

(f) Fish have a unique habit. When a drop of water falls into a pond where they are swimming, they will open their mouths as if they had never tasted water before. Although steeped in the study of Torah all his life, the Jew opens his eyes in amazement on the Shabbat at every idea that is propounded by the scholars, as if he had never learnt anything before.[30]

On the morning of the Shabbat, the rituals of *Kiddush* and the two *ḥallot* are repeated, with one difference. The *Kiddush* before the meal on Friday night must be recited over a cup of wine. On Saturday morning, the *Kiddush* may be recited over other drinks such as whiskey, beer and even milk. The thinking behind this is the principle that the *Kiddush* on Saturday morning is only an act of deference and honor to the day. If a person prefers beer or whiskey to wine, let him honor the day with the beverage that offers him most pleasure. On Friday night however, the *Kiddush* is an act of sanctification and like every other act of sanctification in the Jewish religion, it must be performed over wine.[31] In general the whole practice of the Saturday morning *Kiddush* is based on the Scriptural Verse: "Keep the Sabbath Day holy." If the Torah went out of its way to emphasize, "Keep the Sabbath Day holy", the Rabbis concluded, the day, too, should have its sanctification.

In describing the experience of a pleasant, tension-free, enjoyable day one might say, "I ate three solid meals". *Shalosh Se'udot* denotes the three meals that are mandatory on the Shabbat, beginning with Friday evening and ending late Saturday afternoon. In the Talmud (Shabbat 117 b) the Sages derive this obligation from their interpretation of a Scriptural passage "Eat that *today*; for *today* is a Sabbath unto the Lord; *today* you shall not find it in the field." (Ex. 16:25) The Torah instructs the Jew in the desert what he should do with the manna on the Shabbat and employs the word "today" three times, the inference: you shall eat the manna three times during the Shabbat. Since the day has three periods, evening, morning and afternoon, one meal should be eaten during each particular period of the day.[32] A Kabbalist also offers the thought that the evening meal is understandable—he is hungry; the two daytime meals, however, teach a moral lesson. Particularly during the short wintry days one could not fill himself with food in the morning and still have an appetite in the afternoon. If he is to fulfill the requirement of the third meal he must restrain himself during the second meal. These mini-meals would consequently leave for him sufficient time for study periods during the day. If he can control his eating habits on a day of rest and relaxation he will, a fortiori, curb his eating periods on weekdays and limit his leisure time during his working day.[33]

At the Third Meal (*Shalosh Seudot*) the *Kiddush* and *hamotzi* come to the fore once more. Every authority agrees that *Leḥem Mishneh*, the two *ḥallot*, are necessary. On the question of *Kiddush*, however, there is a difference of opinion. Some authorities think that if there is a *Kiddush* during the first and second meals, there is no reason why this pattern should not be repeated in the third meal. Others, the majority opinion, argue that the question of *Kiddush* is not dependent upon the number of meals but on the changing nature of the day. That is to say, that during a twenty-four hour period there is the change from night to day. One *Kiddush* during the evening and one *Kiddush* during the daytime should be sufficient.[34]

Another line of thinking takes into account the number of meals a person eats during the week. Customarily one partakes of two full meals a day. On Shabbat, three meals are necessary to complete the number fifteen to correspond to the fifteen words in the priestly blessing, "The Lord bless you and keep you", etc., which ends with the word "peace". This means that without the third meal on Shabbat one could not enjoy the blessing of peace.[35]

Incidentally, *Shalosh Se'udot*, the name applied to the third Sabbath meal, may be a misnomer because these two Hebrew words mean *three* meals when, in truth, we are dealing with the *Third* Meal—*Se'udah Shelishit.* However, the name "three meals" is used advisedly because if one had eaten two solid meals before and then sits down to eat a third meal, it is indicative that he does so out of deference to the Shabbat and not to satisfy his hunger. Because of this he is only now being credited with the mitzvah of eating of all three meals.[36]

After finishing his *Shalosh Se'udot* the Jew returns to the Synagogue for the concluding Maariv service. In many oriental communities, particularly those of Yemen, the Maariv prayers were recited at home without the benefit of a Minyan, a religious quorum. In the mirth of the celebration of the concluding stages of the Shabbat many imbibed wine freely which beclouded their senses. It would be dishonorable and disrespectful for the congregational reader not to be completely sober. In order not to spoil an entire service, it was deemed best that each worshipper should recite his Maariv service on his own.[37]

In the early part of the evening *Amidah*, the eighteen benedictions that are recited silently, there is a special prayer designated to point up the difference between the sanctity of the

Shabbat and the profanity of the weekday. This officially concludes the Shabbat, although, as we will see later, the *Havdalah* ritual still has to be performed. The purpose of this additional prayer in the *Amidah* is to permit us to do such things as are ordinarily forbidden on the Shabbat, for instance the kindling of the *Havdalah* candle (see below). In early times, when the Jewish people were first driven into exile, they were impoverished. Their poverty made them unable to afford the wine needed for the *Havdalah*. Consequently the extra prayer in the *Amidah* was inserted. When their condition improved, the *Havdalah* over wine was reinstated. The authorities felt that this lacked patterned orderliness and therefore decreed that both the special prayer during the *Amidah* and the ritual of *Havdalah* should be observed by all Jews in whatever circumstances they might be.[38]

If we anticipated the arrival of the Shabbat and its *tosefet* (what we added from the day before) with a great deal of delight, it is appropriate that we should anticipate the departure of the Shabbat with regret, and postpone it beyond nightfall. It also follows that if we welcome the Shabbat over a cup of wine, we should bid it farewell over a cup of wine as well. According to the Sages, this is the thinking behind the pronouncement, "*Remember* the Sabbath Day", i.e. both at its commencement and at its conclusion.[39]

This ritual symbolizing the parting of the ways between the Jew and his bride of the day, the Shabbat, is called *Havdalah* (separation), in which he draws a line of demarcation between the holy and the profane, the Shabbat and the weekday, the Children of Israel and the Gentiles of the world.

From earliest times two other features were added to the Havdalah service, both touching on the central theme of the Jew's unique experience on the Shabbat: the kindling of a candle with multiple wicks in torchlight fashion and the inhaling of aromatic spices, each with its special benediction. The benediction over the aromatic spice takes precedence over that of the torch-like candle because the candle is utilized only on Saturday night as part of the ritual, while aromatic spices are available to us and can bring us pleasure on many occasions.[40]

One Kabbalist offers the opinion that the reason for *Havdalah* being recited over a cup of wine lies in the transformation of the Jew from his spiritual norms of life during the Shabbat to the materialistic pursuits of the weekday. During the Shabbat it is his soul that benefits from his sanctity; during the weekday all his five senses begin to operate. His sense of taste is the only one that requires personal contact with the object to be stimulated. Wine sharpens that sense of taste.[41]

In Jewish theology, every observant Jew is endowed on the Shabbat with the *Neshama Yeterah* (lit. "an extra soul"). This means something different to each of several theologians. To some of our thinkers the Jew literally acquires an additional soul for the duration of the Shabbat. This soul descends from its heavenly abode, permeating the Jew from the start of the day and departs at its close. Other theologians assert that this concept is merely symbolic as it characterizes the change that comes over the Jew on Friday evening when he divests himself of all tensions and pressures affecting him during the weekdays in his mundane efforts. Then, with one stroke, he suddenly finds himself relaxed, and free of all worry and pressure. This sudden transformation is called "*Neshama Yeterah.*" When this peace of mind leaves him on Saturday night and his thoughts once again revert to his weekday concerns, he senses that something precious has gone and left him impoverished.[42]

Therefore, the pleasant aroma of the *besamim* is intended to raise his spirits so that he should not sink into a state of depression immediately after the Shabbat.

Another thought on the purpose of the aromatic spices is the one that the Mystics propound: Because of the sanctity of the Shabbat the wicked are spared the pain of fire in purgatory. At the close of the Shabbat the fires flare up again and the soul is tormented at the sight of this ordeal. The *besamim* are intended to placate and ease the pain of the soul.[43]

The benediction recited over the aromatic spice is "Blessed art Thou . . . who created diverse spices."

When a holiday begins on a Saturday night no *besamim* are needed during the *havdalah* ritual. Immediately after the *Havdalah* the Jew will be sitting down to the festive meal of the holiday and no thought of sadness will enter his mind.[44]

While one cups his hand and gazes at his fingernails by the light of the candle he recites the benediction, "Blessed art Thou o Lord . . . who creates the lights of fire." Both mystical and pragmatic reasons are offered for the performance of these rituals at the *Havdalah* ceremony.

In the first place, if a candle produces a single flame why do we recite the benediction, "Who creates the *lights* of the candle?" The plural is employed because a flame has a spectrum of several colors. Why particularly over a torchlight candle? In order to discern this spectrum the better. But why is a candle chosen? Several reasons are propounded:

(a) One of the entities that did not become evident in the six days of Genesis was fire. The Talmud (Pesaḥim 54a) relates that man was the very last creature to emerge before the day of rest set in. This happened on Friday at sunset. What Adam experienced first, therefore, was dusk and subsequent darkness. On Saturday morning he realized that there was another time element, daytime. But then on Saturday night darkness set in again and he became panic stricken, thinking that the world was returning to its former state of void and darkness. God imbued him with wisdom and Adam took two flintstones, struck them against each other and thus created fire. All this happened on Saturday night.[45]

(b) Making fire on the Sabbath is one of the explicitly specified prohibitions. Producing sparks and fire in any shape or form is forbidden on Shabbat. On Saturday night when this is once again permitted, it seems as if fire was recreated by man.[46]

There are a number of suggestions made as to why one gazes at his fingernails during the benediction over the candlelight:

(a) A benediction is recited only over something that affords one some benefit. For example, we say a blessing over bread because we are going to benefit from it. By extending our fingertips and gazing upon them in the light of the candle, we benefit from the illumination.[47]

(b) If one is to benefit from the illumination of the candles, he can do so best by distinguishing the white crescent at the base of the nail from the color of the skin of the fingers.[48]

(c) The nails are one of the few things in the human body that continue to grow throughout life.[49]

(d) Referring back to Adam and the two flintstones, his fingertips were responsible for creating the light.[50]

It should be obvious to us why a person who is blind is exempt from performing the ritual of the *Havdalah*. He cannot benefit from the light.[51]

Many people are accustomed, at the conclusion of the *Havdalah*, to pour a little wine into a plate, extinguish the candle in the wine and to pass it over their eyes as a sign of their dedication to, and love for the ritual of *Havdalah*.[52]

It is customary, once the *Havdalah* service is concluded, to chant songs and recite poems whose central theme is Elijah the Prophet. The obvious question arises: what relationship is there between Elijah the Prophet and Saturday night? Three reasons are advanced:

(a) The Talmud (Erubin 43b) states that Elijah the Prophet who, according to the Kabbalists, will someday appear to herald the approach of the Messiah, will not come on a Shabbat. Therefore, on Saturday night as soon as the Shabbat is over we sing his praises and declare, so to say: "You could not come during the day but we expect you tonight."

(b)According to another mystical explanation, Elijah enters the portals of Paradise and inscribes the names of all those who observe the Shabbat properly.

(c) Since the Talmud asserts (Shabbat 118b) that if the Children of Israel would fulfill the laws of Shabbat meticulously, no nation in the world could dominate them, we announce to Elijah: "We have just concluded the proper observance of the Shabbat and it is time you came to herald the approach of the Redeemer."[53]

The Jew is so elated with the physical relaxation and rest he enjoyed, and with the spiritual uplift he received through the sanctity of the Sabbath that he is reluctant to relinquish and abandon the mood and the delights of the day. He is most anxious to hold on to and retain this feeling of fulfillment although the Shabbat is over. The Sages of the Talmud (Shabbat 119b) recognized this yearning and instituted the meal of *Melaveh Malkah*, "escorting the Queen". That is to say, on Saturday night we symbolically escort the Sabbath Queen out of our life until the following week by bidding farewell to her at this meal.[54] A Kabbalistic reason for *Melaveh Malkah*: there is a small bone in the human body which takes nourishment from no food except from that which is served at the *Melaveh Malkah*.[55]

In Rabbinic literature this meal is sometimes referred to as King David's banquet. The Talmud (Shabbat 30a) relates that when David requested of God: "Let me know, O Lord, my end and the measure of my days, what it is," (Psalms 39:8) God replied, "I cannot divulge the exact time. However, I promise you that you will pass away on a Shabbat." From then on, the King tendered a meal of thanksgiving every Saturday night in celebration of surviving yet another Shabbat day. Somehow this festive meal has become a tradition which persists till this very day.[56]

Another authority reasons: the numerical value of the Hebrew name of Elijah is fifty-two, which equals the Hebrew letters *Bet* and *Nun*: the numerical value of David is fourteen, equalling *Yud* and *Daled*. Scrabble these four letters and you arrive at the word *Nadiv*, benefactor. The inference is that through Elijah who will herald the Messiah, a descendant of David, we will witness the Messianic Period.[57]

SOURCES

1. *Arukh ha-Shulḥan* 250 par. 2.
2. *Arukh ha-Shulḥan* 249 pars. 4, 5, 6.
3. *Arukh ha-Shulḥan* 249 par. 1.
4. *Tur Oraḥ Ḥayyim* 256; *Arukh ha-Shulḥan* 256 pars. 1, 2.
5. *Dover Mesharim* p. 22.
6. *Arukh ha-Shulḥan* 263 par. 1.
7. *Ben Ish Ḥai* p. 226.
8. *Ta'ame ha-Minhagim* p. 124.
9. *Tur Oraḥ Ḥayyim* 263; *Avudraham* p. 78.
10. *Sefer ha-Mat'amim* p. 113.
11. *Minhage Yeshurun* p. 258.
12. *Sefer ha-Mat'amim* p. 112.
13. *Arukh ha-Shulḥan* 267 par. 2.
14. *Minhage Eretz Yisrael* p. 100.
15. *Halikhot Teiman* p. 5.
16. *Arukh ha-Shulḥan* 268, par. 1.
17. *Tur Oraḥ Ḥayyim*; *Bet Yoseph* 269, 273; *Arukh ha-Shulḥan* 269, pars. 1, 2, 3; 271 par. 1; 273, par. 1; *Avudraham* pp. 82-83; *Ben Ish Ḥai* p. 218.
18. *Avudraham* p. 86; *Minhage Yesurun* p. 269.
19. *Tur Oraḥ Ḥayyim*, *Bet Yoseph* 271; *Arukh ha-Shulḥan* 271 par. 5.
20. *Tur Oraḥ Ḥayyim* 274; *Arukh ha-Shulḥan* 274 par. 1.
21. *Ḥayye Avraham* p. 32b.
22. *Ta'ame ha-Minhagim* p. 121.
23. *Sefer ha-Mat'amim* p.112.
24. *Tur Oraḥ Ḥayyim* 271.
25. *Sefer ha-Mat'amim* p. 114.
26. *Minhage Yeshurun* 166.
27. *Minhage Eretz Yisrael* p. 107.
28. *Arukh ha-Shulḥan* 274 par. 4.
29. *Arukh ha-Shulḥan* 274 par. 3
30. *Sefer ha-Mat'amim* pp. 20-21.
31. *Arukh ha-Shulḥan* 289 pars. 3, 5.
32. *Arukh ha-Shulḥan* 274, par. 7.
33. *Ḥaye Avraham* 37a.
34. *Tur Oraḥ Ḥayyim*, *Bayit Ḥadash* 291.
35. *Ben Ish Ḥai* 136.
36. *Sefer ha-Mat'amim* pp. 122, 123.
37. *Halikhot Teiman* p. 9.
38. *Ta'ame ha-Minhagim* p. 182.
39. *Arukh ha-Shulḥan* p. 296, pars. 2, 3.
40. *Arukh ha-Shulḥan* 296, par. 6.
41. *Ḥaye Avraham* p. 38b.
42. *Avudraham* p. 102.
43. *Arukh ha-Shulḥan* 297, par. 1.

44. *Minhage Yeshurun* p.299.
45. *Arukh ha-Shulḥan* 298, par. 1.
46. Ibid; *Ta'ame ha-Minhagim* p. 186; *Minhage Yeshurun* 298.
47. *Tur Oraḥ Ḥayyim*, *Bet Yoseph* 298.
48. *Arukh ha-Shulḥan* 298, par. 7; *Ta'ame ha-Minhagim* p. 187.
49. *Arukh ha-Shulḥan* 298, par. 8.
50. *Sefer ha-Mat'amim* p. 127.
51. *Arukh ha-Shulḥan* 298, par. 17.
52. *Ta'ame ha-Minhagim* p. 188.
53. *Minhage Yeshurun* p. 296.
54. *Tur Oraḥ Ḥayyim*; *Bet Yoseph* 300; *Arukh ha-Shulḥan* 300, par. 2.
55. Ibid.
56. *Ta'ame ha-Minhagim* p. 190; *Minhage Yeshurun* p. 300.
57. *Ben Ish Ḥai* p. 256.

Rosh Ḥodesh

A whole complex of *minhagim* surrounds the New Moon which occupies a prominent position in Jewish religious practice.[1] In this connection we must first dispel a long-standing misconception. People ignorant of the origin and significance of these *minhagim* have dismissed them as a relic of heathenism, seeing in them traces of moon-worship. It cannot be too strongly emphasized how false such a view is, and that it betrays a complete misunderstanding of the Jewish attitude to nature.

Maimonides points out that the Torah itself (Numbers 28:14) has expressly enjoined that the Jewish calendar is to be lunar and not solar.[2] According to the Talmud, even Moses found difficulty in grasping this concept until God pointed to the new moon and told him *ka-zeh re'eh ve-kadesh*—this is the celestial body which you are commanded to sanctify, and at this stage of its renewal.[3] It is on the basis of this *aggadah* that, throughout the Rabbinic and Kabbalistic literature, we find the greatest Jewish minds grappling with the various ideas and interpretations that emerge from practices associated with *Rosh Ḥodesh.*

While it was known from very early times that the interval between one new moon and the next was approximately 29½ days, the exact date on which the month was supposed to have begun was originally determined by visual observation. During the Temple times, persons who claimed to have seen the new moon on the thirtieth day and were legally qualified witnesses would hurry to the *Bet Din* (Rabbinical court) in Jerusalem to report what they had seen. If, after examination, the testimony would be found to be reliable, the *Bet Din* would declare that day to be *Rosh Ḥodesh.* Flares were kindled on the mountain-tops, signaling to the population of Israel that they should celebrate the festival of the New Moon that very day. If, however, no reliable evidence reached the *Bet Din* on the thirtieth day, *Rosh Ḥodesh* was automatically observed (without any official announcement) on the thirty-first. Later, after the destruction of the Temple, when it was no longer practical to inform the whole people about the appearance of the new moon, and when, in addition, it was feared that the chain of *semikhah* (ordination), on which the Rabbis based their authority, would be broken and that the Jews would become dispersed throughout the world, a calendar was drawn up by Hillel II, which to the present day remains authoritative for determining the dates on which the months begin.[4]

The procedures of ancient times have left their mark on our present-day practice. For example, on the Sabbath preceding each new moon (with one exception, to be mentioned later) the advent of the coming month is heralded by reciting special prayers and by announcing publicly in the synagogue the exact time of the new moon's appearance—the day, hour, minute and second. This is done to commemorate the proclamation by the *Bet Din* in ancient times. The congregation stands throughout this ceremony, since the witnesses who reported the appearance of the new moon were required to stand while giving their evidence.[5]

According to some Kabbalistic writers, when God first created the world He intended it to be perfect in every respect. The sun was to shine by day and the moon, with equal brightness, by night. Adam's sin of eating from the forbidden fruit was the first imperfection to appear in the Divine scheme, and as a punishment for it God brought about an imperfection in the moon as well. Afterwards, the lunar disc, instead of remaining complete, would gradually wane until it disappeared altogether from the sky; it would, however be reborn and begin a new cycle of waxing and waning. Some pious Jews instituted a monthly fast, called *Yom Kippur Katan* (minor Yom Kippur) on *Erev Rosh Ḥodesh* (the eve of the new moon) as an act of penance for man's first sin. Even today many who do not fast recite special penetential prayers at the *Minḥah* service of this day.

Rosh Ḥodesh itself induces a holiday spirit and is marked in the synagogue by the recital of the *Hallel*-psalms, a special reading from the Torah, and a supplementary service *(musaf)*. It is forbidden to fast nor may any funeral eulogies *(hespedim)* be delivered on this day, since they cause grief to the assembled thereby marring the spirit of the festival.[6]

Although work is permitted on *Rosh Ḥodesh*, it has long been customary in many communities throughout the world for women not to work on this day. This *minhag* has various explanations. When Moses was up on Mount Sinai, receiving the Ten Commandments, the people, in rebellious mood, came to Aaron and demanded that he make a visible god for them to worship. Reluctant as he was to comply, he fell in with them in order to gain time, confident that Moses would soon return and put an end to the trouble. Had he ordered the men to bring their gold ornaments to serve as raw material for the construction of the idol, they would have immediately complied. He told them instead: "Bring me the jewelry of your wives and daughters." This maneuver had the desired effect. The Israelite women, knowing the evil pupose for which they were required, stubbornly refused to give up their adornments. Later on, however, when God's sanctuary was being built, they gladly donated their jewelry to make the sacred vessels. The sanctuary was set up for the first time on *Rosh Ḥodesh* of the month of Nisan, and in recognition of the women's courage and devotion, God gave them a special holiday—*Rosh Ḥodesh.*[7]

Another suggestion for this *minhag* is based on the parallel between the cycle of the moon's disappearance into darkness, followed by a radiant rebirth, and the woman's physical cycle. During more than one third of the month a husband is, according to Jewish law, forbidden to approach his wife; and the renewal of their marital relations is compared to that of the moon's rebirth.[8]

Although *Rosh Ḥodesh* does not rank as a full holiday and

men are permitted to work on it, it has several features in common with the major festivals. The Torah itself enumerates *Rosh Ḥodesh* among the major holidays (Numbers 10:10). References to the festive character of the day are to be found also in other sections of the Scriptures (I Samuel 20:18; Isaiah 1:13, 66:23; Hosea 2:13; Amos 8:5). In the synagogue four men—one more than on an ordinary weekday—are called up to the Torah. The additional *aliyah* corresponds to the additional sacrifice *(korban musaf)* which was offered in Temple times after the regular daily service *(korban tamid)* to which the daily *shaḥarit* service corresponds.

If *Rosh Ḥodesh* is regarded as a festival, why are not five persons called to the Torah-reading (this being the usual number on festivals) and why is this reading not followed by one from the Prophets *(Haftarah)*, especially since, as indicated above, there are several passages any of which might appropriately have been chosen? The answer is that, since *Rosh Ḥodesh* does not quite have the same level of sanctity as the other festivals and is not among the days on which work is forbidden, the synagogue service, already considerably lengthened, must not be prolonged further lest it cause hardship for people ready to go to work.

In recognition of *Rosh Ḥodesh* as a half-holiday, we remove our *tefillin* before the *musaf* service, which commemorates this holiday aspect of the day.[9]

As on other festivals, so on *Rosh Ḥodesh*, the *shaḥarit* is followed by a recital of the *Hallel*-psalms, but with a difference. On festivals the full *Hallel* is recited preceded by a *Berakhah* (benediction), which runs as follows: Blessed are You, O Lord our God, King of the universe, Who has sanctified us with Your commandments and commanded us to read the *Hallel*," after which Psalms 113-118 are read in their entirety. On *Rosh Ḥodesh* two of the longer psalms—115 and 116—are each curtailed by the omission of the first eleven verses. This shortened recital is called (not quite accurately) "half-*Hallel*." Halakhic authorities differ on the question as to whether the usual benediction should precede half-*Hallel*. Maimonides argues that the recital of *Hallel* on *Rosh Ḥodesh* is not a mitzvah (divine command), but merely a *minhag* (custom) which does not require an introductory benediction.[10] So Sephardim to this day omit the *Berakhah* on *Rosh Ḥodesh*. Most authorities, however, agree that *minhag Yisrael Torah hu*—a custom accepted by Jews is to be treated as if it were a Biblical command, so that the introductory blessing should be said.[11]

The principal reason given for reciting the *Hallel* on *Rosh Ḥodesh* is that, in his concluding Psalm 150, David sang twelve Hallelujahs, one for each of the twelve months. We repeat the last verse because seven times in each nineteen year cycle an extra month is added to compensate for the discrepancy between the solar and lunar years.[12]

We have mentioned above that the diminution of the moon's light has been regarded as symbolic for human guilt, and that this is the reason why some people fast on the eve of the new moon. On *Rosh Ḥodesh* the reappearance of the moon is taken as a sign of *kapparah* (atonement): God has forgiven man and indicates His pardon by allowing the moon's crescent to appear once more. The relief from guilt calls for celebration.[13]

A very interesting custom is that of *Kiddush Levanah*, the sanctification of the new moon, which is observed on an evening between the fourth and the fourteenth of the month, usually on the first Saturday night while the Sabbath atmosphere still lingers, and the Jew is still dressed in his Sabbath attire. A special *berakhah*, in which we thank God for the moon's reappearance, is followed by a series of prayers in which this renewal is linked with the spiritual renewal of the individual Jew and the rebirth of the Jewish people. Leading themes are God's creativity and the need for man's rededication to His service. Since, during this service we stand facing the moon and in certain passages the moon is poetically addressed in the second person, it might appear to the ignorant that we are according it Divine honor. For this reason we end the service with the *Alenu* prayer, in which we unequivocally reject every kind of idol worship, and declare our sole allegiance to the Creator of the universe.[14]

SOURCES

1. For a more detailed analysis and explanation of this mitzvah see my book *The Mitzvot*, pp. 9-12.
2. *Yad ha-Ḥazakah*, beginning of "Hilkhot Kiddush ha-Ḥodesh."
3. Rosh Ha-Shanah 20a.
4. *Yad*, "Hilkhot Kiddush ha-Ḥodesh" 5.
5. *Arukh ha-Shulḥan, Oraḥ Ḥayyim* 417.
6. *Arukh ha-Shulḥan, Oraḥ Ḥayyim* 418 par. 1, 2 and 420 par. 1.
7. *Pirkei de-Rabbi Eliezer* 45.
8. *Sefer ha-Mat'amim* p. 41.
9. *Oraḥ Ḥayyim* 423, par. 4.
10. *Yad*, "Hilkhot Ḥanukkah" 3:7.
11. *Oraḥ Ḥayyim, RaMa* 422, par. 2.
12. *Tur, Oraḥ Ḥayyim, Bet Yoseph* 422.
13. *Oraḥ Ḥayyim* 419; *Sefer ha-Mat'amim* p.42; *Otzar Yisrael* vol. 9, p. 249.
14. *Tur Oraḥ Ḥayyim* 426. See also Samson Raphael Hirsch, *Horeb*, (English transl.) Vol I, pp. 167-168.

Passover

The Festival of Pesaḥ is mentioned in the Bible in the following passages, forming the basis for the way we have celebrated it through the generations:

> And this day shall be to you for a memorial, and you shall keep it as a feast to the Lord; throughout your generations you shall keep it as a feast by an ordinance forever. Seven days shall you eat unleavened bread; the first day you shall remove leaven from your houses; for whoever eats leavened bread from the first day until the seventh day, that soul shall be cut off from Israel.
>
> (Exodus 12:14-15)

> And you shall observe the feast of unleavened bread; for on that very day I have brought your hosts out of the land of Egypt. Therefore shall you observe this day throughout your generations as an ordinance forever. In the first month, on the fourteenth day of the month in the evening, you shall eat unleavened bread, until the twenty-first day of the month in the evening.
>
> (Exodus 12:17-18)

> Seven days shall no leaven be found in your houses; for whoever eats anything leavened, that soul shall be cut off from the Congregation of Israel, whether he is a stranger, or one that is born in the land. You shall eat nothing leavened; in all your habitations shall you eat unleavened bread.
>
> (Exodus 12:19-20)

> And you shall observe this thing for an ordinance to you and to your sons forever. And it shall come to pass, when you come to the land which the Lord will give you, as He has promised, that you shall keep this service. And it shall come to pass, when your children shall say unto you: "What does this service mean to you?" that you shall say: "It is the Passover sacrifice of the Lord, for He passed over the houses of the Children of Israel in Egypt, when He smote the Egyptians and delivered our houses."
>
> (Exodus 12:24-27)

And they baked unleavened cakes from the dough which they brought out of Egypt, for it was not leavened; because they were forced out of Egypt, and could not linger, nor had they prepared for themselves any food.

(Exodus 12:39)

And Moses said to the people: Remember this day, in which you came out of Egypt, out of the house of bondage; for by strength of hand the Lord brought you out from this place; there shall no leavened bread be eaten. . . . Seven days shall you eat unleavened bread, and on the seventh day shall be a feast to the Lord.

(Exodus 13:3-6)

And there shall be no leavened bread seen with you, nor shall there be leaven seen with you in all your borders. And you shall tell your son in that day, saying: It is because of that which the Lord did for me when I came out of Egypt.

(Exodus 13:7-8)

And it shall be when your son asks you in the future saying: "What is this?" that you shall say to him:: "By strength of hand the Lord brought us out of Egypt, from the house of bondage."

(Exodus 13:14)

When your son asks you in the future, saying "What mean the testimonies, and the statutes, and the ordinances, which the Lord your God has commanded you?" then you shall say to your son: "We were the Pharaoh's bondsmen in Egypt; and the Lord brought us out of Egypt with a mighty hand. . . ."

(Deuteronomy 6:20-25)

. . . And you shall sacrifice the Passover offering to the Lord your God, of the flock and of the herd, in the place in which the Lord shall choose to cause His name to dwell there. You shall eat no leavened bread with it; seven days shall you eat unleavened bread, the bread of affliction; for in haste did you come out of the land of Egypt; that you may remember the day when you came out of the land of Egypt all the days of your life. And there shall be no leaven seen with you in all your borders seven days.

(Deuteronomy 16:1-4)

The Jew does not enter his religious experiences suddenly or casually. Indeed, the preparations for the various observances may be as exciting and important as the events themselves. This is the case especially with Passover which is preceded by and is a culmination of a period of intense preparatory activity. In fact, the production of *matzot*, the unleavened bread, that most essential symbol of the festival, begins months earlier with the grinding of the wheat into flour which is then carefully guarded from becoming moist until the baking. Very observant Jews produce special *shmura* ("guarded") *matzot* from wheat which they themselves have harvested the previous summer and which they have meticulously guarded against moisture all the while through the grinding and up to the baking.

With the advent of Nissan, the month in which Passover occurs, the preparations in and around the Jewish homes take on a feverish pitch. House-cleaning, shopping for a new wardrobe, buying of new dishes and food items are some of the chores in anticipation of the holiday.

These busy preparations, important as they are, are not the only distinguishing features of Nissan. The Torah already designated this month as the "chief of the months," the first month of the Jewish year, in recognition of several miraculous events that had occurred during it, leading to the final act of Redemption.

It was on the tenth day of Nissan that God commanded the Children of Israel to take a lamb, tie it to their bedposts lest it get blemished, and prepare it to be sacrificed on the fourteenth of the month. This was an especially defiant act in face of their Egyptian captors to whom the lamb was an object of worship and even more so since the lamb (Aries) is the zodiacal sign of the very month of Nissan. Yet, instead of severe reprisals against this perfidious act, the Egyptians accepted it with meek resignation.[1]

The Shabbat before Passover is known as *Shabbat ha-Gadol*, the Great Shabbat. What makes this greater than any other Sabbath? A number of answers have been suggested:

(a) It was on the tenth of Nissan, which that year fell on a Shabbat, that the Jews demonstrated their spiritual emancipation from Egyptian culture by taking the Paschal Lamb, as mentioned before. For this reason the Rabbis accorded this particular Shabbat a special place in the Jewish calendar.

(b) When the Egyptian first-born passed by Jewish homes and inquired why they were desecrating the Egyptian religion, they were told that the sacrificing of this lamb would precede the death of the Egyptian first-born, whereupon they turned to their parents and demanded that they allow the Jews to leave. The parents, annoyed at the impudence of their sons, refused, and the first-born then attacked their parents and slew them. This, also, occurred on the tenth day of Nissan, the Saturday before Passover.

(c) The Shabbat is fundamental to Judaism because it gives witness to the power of God who created the world in six days and rested on the seventh. Passover, on the other hand, testifies to God's personal contact with, and love for, the Children of Israel. On the Shabbat before Passover both ideas are demonstrated—power and love. Because of this, it is called the Great Sabbath.[2]

(d) A more pragmatic reason: it was, and still is, the custom for Rabbis to spend most of the Shabbat before Passover in explaining the complicated problems concerning the laws and rituals of the approaching holiday. It is a long and tiring day for the congregants and for the Rabbi. In this context, the Great Sabbath can also mean the "Long Sabbath."[3]

The actual excitement of the holiday begins on the night before, with the ritual of *bedikat ḥametz*, the search for the leaven. The Bible states: "Seven days *no leaven shall be found in your houses*," and "There shall *not be seen* with you any leaven in your borders seven days." These two prohibitions are known in Jewish literature as *bal yeraeh* and *bal yimatze*, leaven is not to be *seen* nor to be *found* on your premises during the Passover holiday. Every nook and corner of the house must be searched for *ḥametz*. That and more: not only is it necessary to remove all visible leaven but the Jew also verbally renounces ownership of all *ḥametz* that might exist in his household without his knowledge. This is known as *bittul be-lev*, literally, a renunciation within his heart. In order to comply properly with the rules of *bedikat ḥametz*, both prerequisites must be fulfilled: a physical search for the leaven and a mental renunciation of ownership.[4]

But why is it necessary to perform the *bedikat ḥametz* on the night before Passover? The Torah states "But on the first day you shall have put away leaven out of your houses," (Exodus 12:15) which the Rabbis interpret to mean that on the fourteenth day of Nissan all leaven must be removed from the premises. The Torah also says that when the Paschal Lamb was sacrificed shortly after noon on the fourteenth day of Nissan, all *ḥametz* was already to have been removed from the house. This search for *ḥametz* was to be carried out neither by the light of the sun nor even of the moon, but by the light of a candle, and at night, which is the only time when the light of a candle makes a visible difference.[5]

The procedure for *bedikat ḥametz* is as follows: first, to make sure that some *ḥametz* is present, even though the house has been cleaned, the mistress of the house places a number of pieces of bread in key places in her home so that when the blessing for the search for *ḥametz* is recited, God's name should not be taken in vain. It is the custom to place ten pieces of bread for the following reasons:

(a) In the story of Purim we are told that, on the thirteenth day of the month of Nissan, the scribes copied the decree to destroy all the Jews in the Persian empire. According to tradition, these scribes were the ten sons of Haman. Therefore, we burn ten pieces of bread on the fourteenth of Nissan to show that the Jews overcame the calamity these men plotted against them.[6]

(b) According to the Kabbalah the true significance of *bedikat ḥametz* is to remove the spiritual *ḥametz*, the evil inclination, from the heart. According to the Kabbalah, God created ten types of angels in ascending levels of merit, and also, in contrast, ten levels of impurity to which man can descend. Through the ritual of searching for the ten pieces of bread, we show our desire to search ourselves and destroy these imperfections within us.[7] Thus, just as the search for *ḥametz* illustrates that no matter how much the house has been cleaned some leaven may still be left, similarly, no matter how much a person may try to lead a good and righteous life, perfection has still eluded him.[8]

The practice in many homes is to use a candle, a feather, and a wooden spoon for the ritual of *bedikat ḥametz*. The candle is used because candlelight can penetrate into deep recesses. There are no explanations for the feather and the wooden spoon, except that they serve the purpose. The feather is used to brush the crumbs out of the holes and corners; the wooden spoon is easily burned when it is cast into the fire together with the crumbs the next day.

After *bedikat ḥametz*, the bread crumbs and the spoon and feather are set aside to be burned the next morning. *Ḥametz* may not be found on the premises after noon which, in this context, means midday rather than 12 a.m., that is, it means the midpoint of the day, as it is calculated by the number of daylight hours divided by twelve.* The Sages decreed that all visible *ḥametz* must be burned by the fifth "hour" of daytime, and that no benefit be derived from *ḥametz* by the beginning of the sixth hour although technically one should be permitted the use of *ḥametz* until even later. Here is an illustration of the latter restraint: When a man marries a woman he presents her with a ring and proclaims: "You are consecrated to me with this ring." If, instead of a ring, he gave her a loaf of bread and said: "You are consecrated to me with this loaf of bread," the marriage would be invalid if he did this after the sixth hour, because he is prohibited from deriving any benefit from *ḥametz* at that hour.[9]

*In Jewish ritual law, the day is divided into twelve parts. The simplest way to explain this is to give an example: Suppose, on a certain day, it becomes light at 6:00 a.m. and darkness sets in at 6:00 p.m. In this case, the daytime lasts for twelve hours, and each hour would be rightfully called one "part" of the day. During the winter season, however, when daytime is shorter the calculation must be adjusted. For example, if it become light at 7:00 a.m. and darkness sets in at 4:00 p.m., there are only nine hours of daylight. These nine hours are subdivided into twelve parts and each part is described as an hour. In summer, daytime is longer and if there are fifteen hours of daylight they, too, are subdivided into twelve parts and each part is called an hour.

Having searched for the *ḥametz*, the head of the family makes sure that there is none, except for the pieces he gathered during the seach, which he is now ready to dispose of. Next follows the *biur ḥametz*, the burning of the *ḥametz*. So we see that the process of disposing of the *ḥametz* by the fifth hour of the day before Passover is threefold: *bedikat ḥametz*, *bittul ḥametz* and *biur ḥametz*.

We have already mentioned that it is necessary that no leaven foodstuffs be present or seen (*bal yeraeh u-bal yimatze*) during the Passover holiday. What happens to all the other articles in a household that came into contact with or absorbed leaven during the year? What about the leftover foodstuffs that were used with *ḥametz*? The religious authorities were sufficiently pragmatic to realize how wasteful it would be to destroy these eatables. They therefore instituted that they be transferred for the duration of Passover to the ownership of a non-Jew. Technically, this would mean that the non-Jew owns the items but is holding them on the premises of the Jew. Since it would be difficult for every Jew to perform the legal transfer, it is customary that each member of the community sign a document of transfer to the rabbi who, in turn, transfers the document with the signature to a non-Jew. This document is redeemed from the non-Jew by the Rabbi immediately after Passover, and the various items are returned to their original owners. This transaction is called *mekhirat ḥametz*, the sale of the *ḥametz*.[10]

Matzah is an indispensable food for the Passover holiday. The Torah commands us to eat *matzah* only on the first night of the holiday. On the other days we may eat *matzah* or do without it. It has already been mentioned that the flour was carefully guarded from the time the wheat was cut until the dough was mixed so that no water or other fluid came in contact with it and hastened fermentation (leavening). The background for this specificaction is the Scriptual admonition "And you shall *observe* the unleavened." (Exodus 12:17) This means that the Jew must watch over the wheat from which the unleavened bread was made. So "watched" *matzah* is called *Matzah Shemurah*

(Guarded *Matzah*). Even the water used in the baking must be cold, so as not to hasten the process of fermentation, which begins eighteen minutes after water is added. In other words, any dough left unbaked for a period of eighteen minutes is disqualified. In Biblical and Talmudic literature *matzah* is known as *leḥem oni*, bread of poverty, because it is made of just two ingredients, water and flour. There is another type of matzah known as *matzah ashirah*, enriched *matzah*, so called because it is made with wine or oil, or milk, or eggs, instead of water.

All the rituals and ceremonials of the first night of Passover pertain to the Exodus from Egypt. Eating *matzah* that night is so important because it represents the unleavened bread that the children of Israel ate in their haste to leave Egypt. It is in remembrance of this that we, too, eat *leḥem oni. Matzah ashirah* is forbidden on the first night of Passover, although it may be eaten later in the week. Very observant Jews are not satisfied only with complying with the requirement of *matzah shemurah* for the first night, but use no other *matzah* for the remaining days of Passover.[11]

What is more, from the time the wheat is cut until the *matzah* is removed from the oven, every step in the process must be done *lishema*, for the purpose of the mitzvah of having *matzah* on Passover. This means that if the *matzah* were baked for any other purpose, and then one decided to keep some for the first night of Passover he would not have fulfilled the requirements of the holiday.[12]

We have previously spoken about the signal importance of the month of *Nissan* in the Jewish calendar, because the exodus from Egypt took place then. *Nissan* is so important that we should not display any unnecessary melancholy for the entire month. For example, no eulogies may be delivered at funerals and fasting is not permitted, with one exception: the fast of the first-born before Passover. The background to this fast day lies in the history of the Exodus. The word "Passover" indicates that when God went out to slay the first-born of the Egyptians, He "passed over" the homes of the children of Israel and spared their first-born. To show their gratitude, the first-born of the Jews, throughout the ages, were expected to spend the day before Passover in prayer and fasting. However later in Jewish history, the need to fast was circumvented by partaking of a *se'udat mitzvah* instead, based on the principle that when a feast is made in honor of some religious event, those who participated in the *mitzvah* are exempt from fasting, and take part in the *se'udah* also. If a first-born wished to be exempt from fasting on the eve of Passover, he had to take part in the performance of a *mitzvah* which calls for a *se'udah*. After a circumcision, for example, it is customary to serve a *se'udat mitzvah*. If a first-born attends the ritual circumcision of a baby on the morning before Passover, he need not fast. Also, the completion of the study of one of the tractates of the Talmud calls for a celebration. A first-born attending a celebration in honor of the completion of a tractate is thus exempt from fasting. This ritual is called *siyum bekhorim*—the concluding study period for the first born.[13] Even an infant who is a first-born must be represented by his father at the *siyum bekhorim*.[14]

The basic idea in celebrating the first night of Passover is the obligation of every Jew to relive the experience of his forefathers on the night they left Egypt. All the rituals and ceremonials connected with Pesaḥ are in keeping with this idea. In the year of liberation, the children of Israel slaughtered their Pascal Lamb during the afternoon of the fourteenth day of *Nissan*. They stopped all work and directed all of their attention to the requirements of the day: the Pascal Lamb, *matzot*, etc. It is for this reason that we, too, stop all unnecessary work from noon before the start of the holiday onwards, and direct all of our efforts towards the approaching celebration of Passover. Even personal care such as cutting the hair and nails must be done before noon so that one may totally concentrate his thoughts on the holiday.[15]

By the end of the morning of the fourteenth of *Nissan*, the Jew should have already gotten rid of all leavened food. But the celebration of the holiday does not start until nightfall. What can one eat in the meantime? One can eat anything unleavened, with the exception of *matzot*. The reason for this is the necessity to eat *matzah* that night with a relish. If he had already tasted *matzah* during the day, it would lose its novelty and appeal when he eats it again a few hours later. On the other hand, if during the day he eats no bread and also cannot eat *matzah*, in the evening the *matzah* impresses upon him its historical and ritual significance.

The Rabbis of the Talmud compare the consumption of *matzah* before nighttime to one who has intimate relations with his betrothed before marriage. Why did they choose betrothal as an analogy? The marriage ceremony includes *Sheva Berakhot*, seven benedictions. Only after these prayers have been recited is the groom permitted to have physical relations with the bride. During the Seder ritual there are also seven benedictions: over wine, washing the hands, etc. before we are permitted to eat *matzah*.[16]

Although it is proper to extend the Shabbat as well as the festivals at both ends by starting a little earlier and ending a little later (a practice known as *Tosefet Shabbat)*, where the Passover Seder is concerned, however, this principle does not apply. We do not begin our festivities until nighttime. The historical background for this is the Biblical account of the Paschal Lamb during the night of the Exodus. The children of Israel were instructed to offer the lamb during the day but to eat it only at nightfall.

Everyone who celebrates this holiday is considered during the Passover night as royalty. Members of the nobility have their tables set long before they actually sit down to eat. Therefore, today, we spend time in preparing all that is needed before we finally sit down to conduct the Seder.[17]

What preparations are we to attend to before the holiday begins? Before going into details a few introductory remarks are in place. The word *Seder* means order or program. There is a prescribed order to the performance of the rituals. It is not a haphazard arrangement but a structured and well programmed succession of ceremonials. Another suggestion as to why it is called a *Seder* emphasizes the fact that the order of all the holidays in the Jewish calendar follows a pattern set down by the events of the Exodus. We must also remember that the event of the Exodus was not a minor one, which could be minimized or even ignored as so many other events in human history. The concept of freedom is too important to be forgotten. Every generation must teach its young the story and the message of the Exodus. Therefore, whetting the curiosity of our children is a fundamental requirement in the celebration of Passover.

Several rituals are intended merely to prompt the children to ask, "Why are you doing this only on Passover night?" It is said that in Baghdad the father asks his son: "Imagine yourself leaving Egypt. Have you enough food for your journey? What will be your itinerary?" All this is done to arouse the child's curiosity over the events of the Exodus.[17a]

The word *Haggadah* is a Hebrew word which means telling. It also refers to the book which relates the story of the Exodus.

Before the Seder, one must make sure that there is enough wine for every member of the family to drink four cups. A number of suggestions have been made to explain the significance of the four cups:

(a) They represent the four expressions of redemption God used in assuring the children of Israel that they would be redeemed, "I will bring you out; I will deliver you: I will redeem you: I will take you to me as a people" (Exodus 6:6-7).

(b) The starting point of the Egyptian slavery and redemption from Egypt was the episode when the Egyptian butler told Joseph in prison of his dream of the cup of wine he was to set before his master (Genesis 40:11-13). In his tale, the butler used the term "the cup of Pharaoh" *four* times. "The cup of Pharaoh" meant torture, persecution, and enslavement for the Jew. To countermand these, God used four terms of redemption which spelled freedom for the Jew. So, we drink four cups of wine, hail-ing each of these four assurances of our redemption.

(c) The four cups of wine are to remind us of the four nations that later drove the Jews into exile—the Chaldeans, the Medes, the Greeks and the Romans.[18]

(d) There were four strong national characteristics which the children of Israel retained in Egypt, which enabled them to survive and finally witness the day of the Exodus: they did not change their Hebrew names; they did not change their Hebrew language; they possessed high moral standards; they had no informers among them.[19]

A chair or couch which can hold a pillow must be prepared for the head of the household. All year round Jewish people should not be ostentatious, but should show some measure of mourning for the destruction of the Temple. It is different on the night of Passover, however, when the Jew is encouraged to put on display all his finery, as evidence that he is free and independent of any tyranny. Even the pillow that he leans upon that night should be covered with expensive material. Other Rabbis say that in modern times reclining on a pillow is no longer any indication of being a free person, so that the custom no longer has any meaning; thus, while it is preferable to recline on a pillow during the Seder, it is not compulsory. The prevailing opinion, however, is that we ought to recline on a pillow even nowadays, so that we may relive the experiences of our ancestors during the Exodus.[20]

Another item that requires our attention before the holiday is the arrangement of three *Matzot* on a platter, or on a three-tiered case. Whereas, on Shabbat and every other holiday, two loaves of bread are necessary to commemorate the two portions of manna that the children of Israel gathered in the desert for the Shabbat, three *Matzot* are necessary for the Seder. Why?

(a) The Torah tells us that three angels appeared to Abraham and , "Abraham hastened into the tent of Sarah and said: 'Make ready quickly three measures of fine meal, knead it and make cakes'" (Genesis 18:6). The sages calculated that this occurred on

Passover, and that therefore the three *Matzot* on Passover night originated even before the Exodus.[21]

(b) As we will learn later, one of the three *matzot* will be broken and a part set aside for the *Afikoman*. We already know that on Shabbat and holidays we need two whole loaves for the benediction over bread. Because they take the place of bread, there must be two whole *matzot* on *Pesaḥ* as well. If, however, we took only two *matzot* and one was broken for the *Afikoman* we would no longer have two whole *matzot*. We, therefore take three *matzot*; one to be broken and two others for the purpose of the benediction.[22]

It is the custom to prepare a shroud-like garment known as the *kittel*, to be worn by the master of the house during the Seder. We have opposing views concerning the reason for wearing this garment:

When a person is in mourning he wears black; in happy moments he wears white. Passover is a joyous occasion for the Jew and, therefore, he wears a white garment.[23]

On the other hand, the *kittel* reminds us of the shroud in which the dead are buried; so that we should not be carried away by the joy of the holiday, rather one should remember that the only time one is totally free of any responsibility is when he is dead. Otherwise, one must be committed to the service of God. Also, the first day of *Pesaḥ* always occurs on the same day of the week as *Tisha be-Av*, the day of national mourning. And finally, what more appropriate time is there than on Passover night when the entire family is assembled that the father, by robing himself in the *kittel*, in essence says to his children: "You see me dressed in shroud-like attire. Remember, when my end comes, I will need your prayers for my soul.[24]

Another urgent matter that must be attended to before the Seder begins is the preparation of the plate that is to play an important role during the observances of the evening. There are different versions as to how the plate is to be arranged although there is no conflict as to the items to be displayed.

Visualizing the plate as a clock, the standard arrangement, is as follows: A broiled piece of meat, preferably covering a bone, is placed at one o'clock. This represents the Paschal Lamb which was roasted over a fire. The bone, called *zero'ah* (arm), the outstretched hand with which God delivered the children of Israel from bondage.

At four o'clock we place the *ḥarosetḥ*. This is a paste-like mixture of grated apples and almonds sprinkled with cinnamon and mixed with wine. It is to remind us of the mortar that the children of Israel used for making the bricks with which they built the Egyptian cities. Red wine is used in the mixture to remind us of the blood of the infants that were hurled into the Nile by the Egyptians; almonds, because the Hebrew word for almond is *shaked* which also means to accelerate. That is to say that God anxiously accelerated the end of Israel's enslavement. The apple is added because the Jewish women in Egypt were so brave that they went out into the forests and delivered themselves of their babies under apple trees where they would not be detected by the Egyptian taskmasters. The purpose of the cinnamon is to give the mixture a brownish color to resemble that of bricks.[25]

At six o'clock we place horse-radish which has a sharp, bitter taste to remind us of the bitter life that our ancestors experienced in Egypt.

At eight o'clock we put the *karpas*, which may be potato, onion, radish or any other vegetable over which we recite the benediction: "Blessed are You—who brings out the fruit from the earth."[26] The reason it is called *karpas* is that the word *karpas* unscrambled spells *perekh samekh* which means that sixty tens of thousands toiled: there were six hundred thousand Jews in Egypt, and this is the number represented by sixty tens of thousands.

At eleven o'clock we place a broiled egg. This custom is of a much later origin. When the Temple existed the Jews were required to bring a *korban ḥagigah*, an offering in honor of the Festival, three times a year: *Passover*, *Shavuot* and *Sukkot*. This was the Jews' expression of thanksgiving to God for having granted him the opportunity to come with his family to celebrate the Festival in Jerusalem. On Passover the *korban ḥagigah* was first offered and the *korban pesaḥ*, the Paschal Lamb, followed. Then after eating from the meat of the *korban ḥagigah* to satiety, they partook of the Paschal Lamb. In commemmoration of the *korban ḥagigah* we set aside an egg on the seder plate, opposite the piece of roasted meat and bone. Why an egg? Because in Aramaic, the vernacular of the Jews in Temple times, the word for egg was *be'ah* which also means to pray. Through prayer the Jews were delivered from Egypt.[27]

In the imaginary center of the clock we place a bitter herb such as lettuce. This we call *maror* which, in Hebrew, means bitter and has the same significance as horse-radish.

In addition, to the seder plate, a bowl of salt water is placed on the table to serve a double purpose; first, to represent the bitter tears which our ancestors shed as slaves; second, to dip the *karpas* into it so that it should taste bitter.

All preparations have been made, everything is ready, so that we can begin the Seder.

The service in the Synagogue on the night of Passover is the same as those of the other two major holidays with very slight variaton. However, some authorities wondered why the prayer of *al ha-nisim*, the acknowledgment of the miracles performed by God on behalf of his people, was not included. The Exodus was the end result of ten miracles, the ten plagues. Why should Passover, then, be different from Purim and Ḥanukkah when the miracles of those minor holidays are acknowledged by the recitation of the *al ha-nisim* prayer? There are two answers given for this:

(a) As soon as we return from the Synagogue and sit down to the festive table, we begin to relate the story of the Exodus which includes the ten plagues. The whole story is an obvious and sufficient acknowledgement of the miracles that God wrought in Egypt.

(b) The only two occasions when we recite the *al ha-nisim* are during the prayer service in the Synagogue on Purim and Ḥanukkah which are festivals instituted by the Sages of the Talmud. The holiday of Passover, however, was laid down already in the Torah which in itself is a recognition of the miraculous events prior to the Exodus.[28]

Why is this holiday popularly known as *Ḥag ha-Pesaḥ*, the holiday of Passover, when in the Torah itself it is referred to as *Ḥag ha-matzot*, the holiday of the *matzot*? In the 'Song of Songs' in the Bible—a unique kind of love song—we find the lover singing, "I am my friend's and my friend is mine" (6:3). The lover is totally caught up in the beloved, the beloved in the lover; Israel is given over to singing God's praises, and God to singing those of Israel. In the Torah, the name of the Festival is *ḥag ha-matzot*, the Festival of the unleavened bread as part of God's praise of Israel for keeping His commandments. The Jew, on the other hand, sings God's praises for passing over the first born of the Hebrews, and he, therefore, refers to the Festival by the name of Passover.[29]

After returning from the Synagogue and putting on his *kittel*, the Jew is ready for the Seder. The first item on the Seder program is the *kiddush*, the sanctification of the day over a cup of wine. This is no different from that of any other major holiday, except that a phrase proclaiming the holiday of Passover is included. When this rite is over, everyone must drink most of the cup of wine while reclining on the pillow on the left side. The next step is for the head of the family to wash hands without reciting the usual benediction. We wash our hands only before eating bread. This time, so as to arouse the curiosity of the children who continually ask questions, the father washes his hands although we are not going to eat bread, something that we do not do all year round.[30]

Following this, we dip a piece of potato (or any other vegetable used) into the salt water and after reciting the appropriate benediction, we eat it while reclining. There are several suggestions as to why we do this:

(a) Potatoes and other vegetables are commonly eaten *during* the meal, not before. This unusual practice of eating of vegetables before the meal on the night of Passover, is aimed to provoke the children to ask questions.[31]

(b) This first dipping has, as its background, the story of Joseph and his brethren which led eventually to the tragedy of the enslavement of the children of Israel in Egypt. Jacob presented Joseph with a striped shirt. His brothers became envious and contrived to sell him as a slave into Egypt. This was the beginning of a chain of events that led to the bondage. The last two letters of the Hebrew word *makhar*, "to sell", are *kaf* and *resh*. The first two letters of the Hebrew *pasim*, "striped," are *peh* and *samekh*. Put these four letters together and you have *karpas*. The vegetable is dipped into salt water to remind us of the excruciating experience of the children of Israel as slaves in Egypt, all of which came about because of Joseph's striped shirt which led to his being sold as a slave to Egypt.[32]

(c) We have already noted that *karpas* is the acronym for six hundred thousand Jews who were enslaved. But what is the significance of the dipping—and why particularly into salt water? While the Jews were in a state of enslavement they could not observe the *mitzvah* of circumcision. The tribe of Levi was a privileged sect in Egypt and all the Levites were circumcised. Then the time came for the Paschal Lamb to be offered. However, the Torah explicitly warned that the uncircumcised were forbidden to partake of the Paschal Lamb. When the masses saw the circumcised Levites preparing themselves for the offering of the Paschal Lamb they became envious. Immediately six hundred thousand men circumcised themselves. But according to the law of conversion, circumcision is not sufficient; immersion in a proper body of water is necessary. The only place they could perform the ritual of immersion was in the river Nile. Imagine six hundred thousand people entering a small area of the Nile! The water became unclean and cloudy. When a family dips some food in a small bowl of salt water, which in itself is a beclouded liquid, it becomes even more murky and reminds the Jew of the lengths to which the children of Israel went, in order to celebrate the Passover.[33]

The head of the house then takes the middle of the three *matzot*, and breaks it into two halves. One half he replaces between the two whole ones, the other half he wraps in a cloth and places beneath the cushion upon which he is reclining. It is set aside to be used later in the evening as the *Afikoman*, which will be discussed later. There are two reasons suggested for this ritual. The first half of the *matzah* is hidden so that children may inquire about this strange custom; the second half is returned to its former place so that when the master of the house will speak about the "bread of the poor" he will be able to point to the half of the *matzah* which represents the lot of the poor.[34] This ritual is called *Yaḥatz*. "dividing the *matzah*."

A custom of long standing is that children should be encouraged to find and steal the *Afikoman* from its hiding place. If the child succeeds, it is the custom to give him the gift he asks for as ransom. The purpose, of course, is to awaken his curiosity and prevent him from falling asleep.[35] However, amongst Yemenite Jews "stealing the *Afikoman*" was banned, because the idea of stealing, even in make-believe, is against the teachings of the Torah.[36]

In many homes, immediately after breaking the *matzah*, the person leading the Seder places one half of the *matzah* on his shoulder for a few moments to relive the experience of our ancestors, described in the Torah: "And the people took their dough before it was leavened, their kneading troughs being bound up in their clothes upon their shoulders."[37] (Exodus 12:34).

Maggid, the telling of the story, follows when the head of the household, holding aloft the two and one half *matzot*, begins with the exclamation: "This is the bread of affliction which our ancestors ate in the Land of Egypt!" Why does he lift the *matzot*? Taking their idea from the Bible, "He *raises* up out of the dust the poor, from the dunghill he *lifts up* the needy" (Psalm 113:7), the

Rabbis stressed that this *matzah* representing the downtrodden should be raised to dramatize the fact that there was a time when the children of Israel were poor and oppressed and God lifted and raised them up to the status of a free people.[38]

When a child hears the cry of his parent that, "this is the bread of the afflicted ," he will begin to ask questions, the four questions that are found in the taditional *Haggadah*. In fact, the Torah anticipated this curiosity and told us: "And you shall tell your son on that day. . ." (Exodus 13:8). So that the story of the Exodus should not become boring, it was necesary to stimulate curiosity and to emphasize the idea of asking questions. If there are no children to ask these questions, the wife asks them, and if a man is not married, he asks himself. . . The questions are an integral part of the ritual of the *Haggadah*.[39]

Then the story is unfolded. As it is so important that everyone at the table should relive the experiences of our forefathers during the Exodus, the *Haggadah* need not only be read in Hebrew, but *should* be read in the language that one understands best.

During the recitation of the *Haggadah* when the reader comes to the point where he enumerates the ten plagues, he is required to dip his finger into the cup of wine before him, withdraw it, and sprinkle the wine onto a plate. This is done for each of the ten plagues, as well as for the acronyms that Rabbi Judah gives for these plagues. The reasons for this strange ritual are:

(a) When the Torah speaks about the ten plagues brought upon the Egyptians it says: "Then said the magicians to Pharaoh, this is the *finger* of God." (Exodus 8:15)

(b) With each sprinkling of a few drops, the cup of wine becomes less; with each plague that God brought upon Pharaoh and his people, their opposition to freeing the Jews was lessened.[40]

(c) We sprinkle a little wine from the cup when we recite the three groups of plagues as designated by Rabbi Judah because the first group of three: blood, frogs, vermin were initiated by Aaron alone; the second group: lice, pestilence, boils, by Moses without the aid of his rod; the third group: hail, locusts, darkness and the slaying of the first born were accomplished by Moses with the aid of his rod. Rabbi Judah classified the plagues separately to show their different origins, and we thefore sprinkle drops of wine at the mention of each category.[41]

After telling the story of the Exodus, we drink the second cup of wine and are ready to begin with the other rituals of the evening. First, we wash our hands and recite the appropriate blessing, which we did not do when we washed our hands earlier. Now we are about to partake of the *matzah* for the first time. We take hold of the two and one half *matzot* and recite the traditional *ha-motzi.* This is done because on every Shabbat and holiday it is obligatory to recite the benediction over two loaves. We then drop one of the whole *matzot* and we recite a second blessing, *al akhilat matzah*, "and commanded us to eat unleavened bread." This second benediction is to show that we are fulfilling the requirement of eating *matzah.* The broken *matzah*, *leḥem oni*, assumes significance only when it is held and contrasted with one whole *matzah.* It would not have the same meaning if it was lost between two whole *matzot.* After both benedictions one should take a piece of the broken and a piece of the whole *matzah* and eat them together or in succession.[42]

The next item in the *Seder* is the *maror*—for which we take some bitter herbs, such as romaine lettuce, and dip it into the *ḥaroset.* Then we make the appropriate benediction and eat it. So we dip twice. Why is this necessary? One answer given is, again, to stimulate questions from the children. Another reason: In anticipation of the last plague, the slaying of the first born of the Egyptians, the Jews dipped twice into the blood of the Paschal Lamb: once, to smear it on the lintel of the door; the second time on the doorpost.[43]

Korekh is the next ritual to be performed. This involves placing some freshly ground horse-radish or other bitter herbs between two pieces of *matzah* and reciting, "This is what Hillel did when the Holy Temple was in existence: he took unleavened bread and bitter herbs and ate them together, in order to perform the mitzvah, 'with unleavened bread and bitter herbs they shall eat it.'" The background for this practice of Hillel's is that in Temple days the Paschal Lamb was sacrificed, and the Torah stresses that on that occasion the lamb and the *matzah* must be eaten together with the bitter herbs. Since the destruction of the Temple there is no offering of a Paschal Lamb and, therefore, we no longer can have the combination of the three. It follows then that we aren not compelled to eat the bitter herbs either. It is only by Rabbinic decree that we should continue to eat the bitter herbs on Passover. *Matzah*, however, is a separate commandment laid down by the *Torah*. On this basis we first eat a piece of *matzah* and then go to eat a piece of bitter herbs dipped in *ḥaroset*. Hillel, however, argued that the Torah specifically states that *matzah* must be eaten *with* bitter herbs. We should still be guided by the Biblical commandment of eating *matzah* and bitter herbs together although there is no longer any Paschal Lamb. To satisfy Hillel's view we take bitter herbs and sandwich them in between two pieces of *matzah* and eat them together.[44]

In many homes at the conclusion of the last mentioned ritual, a hard boiled egg dipped in salt water is eaten. Some ideas on the reason for this practice are:

(a) Salt water reminds us of mourning. We have already noted that the first day of Passover falls on the same day of the week as *Tishah Be-Av*, the national day of mourning for the destruction of the Temple.

(b) In the same vein, we remind ourselves of the words "May my tongue cleave to my palate if I do not remember you, if I recall not Jerusalem at the head of my joy" (Psalms 137:6). Since Passover is one of the most joyous occasions of the Jewish year, we remember, with grief, the destroyed city of Jerusalem.

(c) The salt water reminds us of Sodom which originally was a fertile area and then turned into a mass of salt. According to

Rabbinic tradition, this happened on Passover.

(d) All foodstuffs become softer and tenderer the more you cook them. The egg, however, is a substance that becomes harder the more it is cooked. The Jew, too, possesses that characteristic. The more you persecute him, the more he becomes hardened in his devotion and commitment to God and the Torah.[45]

Having concluded all the necessary rituals relative to the Seder plate we start the meal. Many Jews do not eat any food which contains *matzah* in any form other than dry *matzah*, for example, fried *matzah*, *matzah* dumplings, etc. This is due to the high regard we have for the *matzah* on Passover in that it is not merely a food, but has a significance of its own.

Tzafun—is a ritual which is performed at the end of the meal. This Hebrew word means "hidden," and refers to that half of the *matzah* which we had set aside at the beginning of the Seder for the purpose of the *Afikoman*. This ritual finds its roots in the idea that the Paschal Lamb had to be consumed not to satisfy hunger but solely as a remembrance of how the Children of Israel dealt with the Paschal Lamb during the Exodus. It was with this idea in mind that in Temple days they first ate heartily of the *korban ḥagigah*, the festival offering, and then, satisfied, partook of the *korban pesaḥ*, the Paschal Lamb. In our Seder rituals, when the meal which represents the *korban ḥagigah* is over, we eat a piece of *matzah*, representing the *korban pesaḥ*. It is interesting that in medieval Spain and even in modern homes in Jerusalem today, they do not hide the *Afikoman* but place that piece of *matzah* on the shoulder of a young boy who leaves the room and very shortly returns.

"Who are you?" he is asked.

"I am a Jew," he replies.

"Where do you come from?"

"From Egypt."

"Where are you headed for?"

"For Jerusalem," he answers.

"What are you carrying?"

"I am carrying a *matzah*!"

The origin of the word *Afikoman* is obscure. However, two suggestions have been made:

(a) In ancient times when a company would conclude a meal they would all call out *Afikoman* which was a combination of two words. . . *afiko*, "take out"; *man*, "the sweets".The idea is that the taste of the *matzah* representing the Paschal Lamb must remain with us for the rest of the night, so that we will continue to meditate and speak about the Exodus. The same rule applies today to the last piece of *matzah* which symbolizes the Paschal Lamb.

(b) *Afiko*, "remove"; *mane*, "dishes." That is to say, "We have finished our meal here; let us go to another place where they are still celebrating."[46]

As is customary we finish the meal with the recitation of the *Birkat ha-Mazon*, the Grace after Meals, and we drink the third cup of wine.

Another unique feature during the reading of the *Haggadah* is the opening of the door of the home when the people at the Seder cry out to God, "Pour out your wrath upon the heathen who will not acknowledge You, and upon the kingdom who invoke not Your name, for they have devoured Jacob and laid waste his dwelling!" Why must the door be opened? In ancient times the door was kept open because there were poor people wandering in the streets who could not afford the luxury of a Seder table. Therefore, the door was opened and from the inside of the home could be heard, loud and clear, "Let all those who are hungry enter and eat; all who are in distress come in and celebrate the Passover."[47] Nowadays when, fortunately, there is seldom anyone who has not prepared himself for the Passover celebration and the invitation to join in the Passover Seder has become obsolete, the opening of the door is delayed to that point in the *Haggadah* when we recite, "Pour forth Your wrath. . . ." Beginning with the seventeenth century and continuing up to comparatively modern times, the Jews in Eastern Europe were subject to pogroms and persecutions during the Passover season because the Gentile masses were incited on the pretext that the Jews had slaughtered Christian children and were using their blood in the making of *matzot*. In order to strengthen their case, the Christians would slay one of their own children, throw him into the courtyard of a Jewish home, call the police who would discover the body and, without further investigation, join the masses in killing Jews and destroying their property. Therefore, the door was left open so that if any such child was cast into the courtyard, the Jews would immediately dispose of it.[48] Another reason is to demonstrate our total commitment to God and our faith in His protection. We open the door and we say in effect: "God is our protector and the world cannot harm us."[49]

Before we open the door we pour an additional cup of wine. There are two opinions as to why this is called the Cup of Elijah.

(a) We noted earlier that the four cups of wine were instituted as a toast to the four expressions of deliverance of the children of Israel from their Egyptian taskmasters, as they were expressed in the Torah. The Sages were divided over the subject as to whether the expression "and I will *bring* them to the Promised land" has the same significance. It is a tradition that someday the Prophet Elijah will appear and solve all problems. He will then decide whether we should drink a fifth cup of wine commemorating the expression of, "I will *bring* them . . ." However, the cup of wine today is merely symbolic, and not intended for drinking.[50]

(b) According to an ancient tradition it was on the day that Elijah ascended to heaven amidst a pillar of fire that the first Emperor of Rome was enthroned. The Roman Empire eventually destroyed Jerusalem and the Temple and drove the Jews into exile. According to tradition, Elijah will herald the advent of the true Messiah who will deliver the Jews from their enemies. Therefore, it is appropriate to have the Cup of Elijah on the table before us when we call out, "Pour out your wrath. . . ."[51]

We fill up the fourth cup of wine and recite the complete *Hallel*, which is composed of Psalms 113-118. These are psalms of gratitude to God for the goodness He has bestowed upon the children of Israel at the time of the Exodus. At the conclusion of the *Hallel*, we drink the fourth and last cup of wine.

Further hymns are sung in Ashkenazi homes which never found their way into Yemenite or Sefardi communities.[52] Amongst these is the Song of "An Only Kid," *Ḥad Gadya*. It tells the story of an only goat that a father bought for two coins. The goat is eaten by a cat, which is bitten by a dog, which is beaten by a stick, which is burned by fire, which is extinguished by water, which is drunk by an ox, which is then slaughtered by a slaughterer who, in turn, is destroyed by the Angel of Death who, finally, is eliminated by God. Some Rabbis believe that this song, patterned after the song, "The House that Jack Built," was intended to amuse the children who stayed up during the entire Seder. Others think that this is an allegory in which the kid represents the persecuted Children of Israel whom the father (God) bought for two coins (Moses and Aaron or the two tablets). The persecutors of the Jews are themselves destroyed. The cat represents Assyria; the dog, Babylon; the stick, Persia; the fire, Macedonia; the water, Rome; the ox, the Saracens; the slaughterer, the Crusaders; the Angel of Death, Turkey, that ruled over Palestine. Finally, God destroys these foreign rules and vindicates Israel.[53]

There is yet another opinion that this song of *Ḥad Gadya* was instituted to create a lively discussion among those present at the Seder as to what actually the author intended. Everyone would speculate on its hidden meaning, and this would lead to an extended discussion of the Exodus.[54]

SOURCES

1. *Arukh ha-Shulḥan* 429. 1,2.
2. *Arukh ha-Shulḥan* 430. 1,4.
3. *Ta'ame ha-Minhagim* p. 207.
4. *Arukh ha-Shulḥan* 431. 15.
5. *Arukh ha-Shulḥan* 431. 11,24.
6. *Minhage Yeshurun* p. 133.
7. *Ta'ame ha-Minhagim* p. 213.
8. *Ta'ame ha-Minhagim* p. 212.

9. *Tur Oraḥ Ḥayyim* 443; *Arukh ha-Shulḥan* 443. 1,2,3,4.
10. *Tur Oraḥ Ḥayyim, Bet Yoseph* 448; *Arukh ha-Shulḥan* 448. 15,16,17.
11. *Tur Oraḥ Ḥayyim* 453; *Arukh ha-Shulḥan* 453. 12,13,17,18,20, 23; 459.5.
12. *Arukh ha-Shulḥan* 453. 23.
13. *Tur Oraḥ Ḥayyim, Bet Yoseph* 470; *Arukh ha-Shulḥan* 470. 1,5.
14. *Ta'ame ha-Minhagim* p. 215.
15. *Tur Oraḥ Ḥayyim* 468; *Arukh ha-Shulḥan* 468. 1,3.
16. *Arukh ha-Shulḥan* 471. 1,2,3; *Ḥayye Avraham* p. 41b.
17. *Arukh ha-Shulḥan* 472. 1,2.

17a. *Massa Bavel* 198.

18. *Otzar Yisrael* Vol. II, p. 185.
19. *Ta'ame ha-Minhagim* p. 224.
20. *Arukh ha-Shulḥan* 472. 3.
21. *Ta'ame ha-Minhagim* p. 227.
22. *Minhage Yeshurun* p. 137.
23. Ibid.
24. *Sefer ha-Mat'amim* p. 54.
25. *Arukh ha-Shulḥan* 473. 17.
26. *Arukh ha-Shulḥan* 473. 10.
27. *Sefer ha-Mat'amim* p. 55.
28. *Arukh ha-Shulḥan* 473. 2,3.
29. *Rabbi Levi Yitzḥak of Berditchev.*
30. *Ben Ish Ḥai* p. 111; *Arukh ha-Shulḥan* 473. 18.
31. *Arukh ha-Shulḥan* 473. 18.
32. *Ben Ish Ḥai* p. 111.
33. *Ta'ame ha-Minhagim* pp. 229,230.
34. *Arukh ha-Shulḥan* 473, 20.
35. *Ta'ame ha-Minhagim* p. 230.
36. *Halikhot Teiman* p. 22.
37. *Arukh ha-Shulḥan* 473. 20.
38. *Ta'ame ha-Minhagim* p. 231.
39. *Arukh ha-Shulḥan* 473. 3.
40. *Ta'ame ha-Minhagim* pp. 233, 234.
41. *Ḥayye Avraham* p. 42a.
42. *Arukh ha-Shulḥan* 475. 3.
43. *Minhage Yeshurun* p. 141.
44. *Sefer ha-Toda'ah* Vol. 2, p. 111.
45. *Sefer ha-Toda'ah* Vol. 2, p. 113.
46. *Arukh ha-Shulḥan* 478. 1,3. *Sefer ha-Toda'ah*, Vol. 2, pp. 114, 115.
47. *Minhage Yeshurun* p. 144.
48. *Sefer ha-Mat'amim* p. 55.
49. *Sefer ha-Mat'amim* p. 56.
50. *Ta'ame ha-Minhagim* 236.
51. *Sefer ha-Mat'amim* p. 55.
52. *Halikhot Teiman* p. 23.
53. *Otzar Yisrael* Vol. IV p. 249.
54. *Minhage Yeshurun* pp. 146, 147.

Shavuot

It is commonly accepted by the masses that Shavuot is *Zeman Mattan Toratenu*. . . the anniversary of the giving of the Torah to the Children of Israel. In fact, all present day observances of the holiday revolve around this theme. In the Scriptures, however, this holiday has three names, none of which has anything to do with the "Giving of the Torah." Furthermore, in the Talmudic period this holiday was designated by another name which had a different connotation altogether.[1]

In the Scriptures Shavuot is called by these names:

(a) *Ḥag ha-Katzir*, "the Feast of the Harvest" (Exodus 23:16), since that holiday occurs in the season (Sivan: May-June) when the wheat begins to ripen. It was from this wheat that two loaves of bread were baked and brought to the Temple as an offering, *Shete ha-Leḥem*, after which the new season's wheat could be used for the Temple meal offerings.

(b) *Ḥag ha-Shavu'ot*, the "Festival of the Weeks," designated by this name because of the Biblical references, "Seven weeks shall you count unto you" (Exodus 34:22; Deuteronomy 16:9). This refers to the seven weeks beginning with the second day of Passover, a period of forty-nine days, called *Sefirat ha-Omer*—"the counting of the Omer." Shavuot is celebrated following this period, on the fiftieth day.

(c) *Ḥag ha-Bikkurim*, the "Festival of the First Fruits." As was noted in (a), immediately after the ritual of offering the two loaves, wheat offerings could be brought from the new crop.

Later the Sages added the name *Atzeret*, "withdrawal." In the Torah, the last days of the two other pilgrim festivals (Passover and Sukkot) are referred to as *Atzeret* to indicate that on the seventh day of Passover and on the eighth day after the beginning of Sukkot, there must be a withdrawal from all menial labor. Shavuot too, was given the name of *Atzeret* by the Rabbis so as to emphasize the necessity of abstaining from menial labor on this holiday as well. In fact, for this reason the Sages referred to Shavuot by the name *Atzeret* exclusively. In other words, while Passover can be identified with *Matzot*, and Sukkot with booths, Shavuot has no specific identification other than the abstention from work. The Sages refused to adopt the theme of "Giving the Torah," in assigning a name to the Festival, because in their thinking it would be sacrilegious to limit the celebration of the "Giving of the Torah" to a single day. To them, every day of the year should be considered as a day of receiving the Torah anew. However, according to the calculations of the Rabbis (Shabbat 86b), it was on the sixth day of Sivan that the Jews stood at Mt. Sinai and were given the Torah. Since the Biblical significances of the day were only valid when the Temple existed, we stress the historical event of receiving the Torah on Mt. Sinai so as to enhance the meaningfulness of Shavuot now that the Temple service is not performed.

The question arises, however, how can the Torah apply the name "Weeks" to this holiday when, in truth, it is celebrated *after* the seven weeks had elapsed. The authorities were quite aware of the problem and proposed the following two reasons:

(a) Playing upon the word *shav'ua*, "week," which sounds almost exactly as the word *shevu'ah*, which means an oath, they propounded the idea that after the Children of Israel had spent seven weeks in the desert, God took an oath that He would never exchange His Chosen People for any other.

(b) The number "seven" has mystic overtones in Jewish lore and law. The seventh day is the Sabbath; the seventh year in the Jubilee cycle is the year of *shemittah*; another seven involves family relations: When a woman finishes her menstrual period, her days of impurity, she counts seven clean days after which she may resume her relationship with her husband. During their stay in Egypt, the Children of Israel were in a state of impurity. After the Exodus, they counted seven weeks and then were wedded to God, with the Torah serving as the marriage contract.[2]

But why did the Sages object to calling this holiday by its Biblical name, *Shavuot*? This was due to the fact that Shavuot refers to the holiday following the seven weeks from the beginning of Passover. Deviationists at that time, however, insisted that the count had started from Sunday following the first day of Passover, with the Festival always falling on Sunday. In order to avoid any confusion and misunderstanding, the Sages preferred calling the holiday by the name *Atzeret*.

A later historical event while not related to the other themes has some bearing upon the holiday of Shavuot. In his rebellion against the Romans, (70-132 C.E.) Bar Kokhba was joined and supported by Rabbi Akiva and twenty four thousand of his students. Rabbi Akiva was the leading Rabbinical personality of his time. Between Passover and Shavuot, an epidemic broke out amongst his disciples, many of whom died each day (Yevamot 62b). In remembrance of these heroic scholars the Jews have instituted, since the Gaonic period, a measure of mourning and abstain from weddings, haircuts and shaving.

Unfortunately, in later periods other catastrophes occurred during the period between Passover and Shavuot taking the lives of countless Jews. The Crusaders wrought havoc on many Jewish communities during their march from Europe to the Holy Land; there was a mass slaughter of Jews in France and Germany during the twelfth century; Chmelnitzki and his Cossacks carried out massacres and pogroms upon Jews in Poland in the middle of the seventeenth century. All these misfortunes occured during these weeks. However, the original and main reason for this period of mourning is the epidemic decimating Rabbi Akiva's pupils which, according to tradition, lasted thirty-four days out of the forty-nine days of the *Sefirah*.

Some differences exist concerning these thirty-four days and the period of mourning which commemorates them.

(a) Some authorities contend that the thirty-four days of

mourning begin with the first day of *Sefirah* and continue for thirty-three days. According to this opinion all the restrictions mentioned above would be lifted on the thirty-fourth day.

(b) Others maintain that the restrictions remain in force until Shavuot but only begin after the first fifteen days of *Sefirah.*

In either case, the thirty-third day *(Lag ba'Omer)* would be included in this period of restraint.

(c) Later authorities, on the other hand, accept the period of mourning of thirty-three or thirty-four days but leave it to the individual to choose his dates either from the beginning or towards the end of the Sefirah period but *Lag ba'Omer* (the thirty-third day of the Omer) is in any event excluded because on that day there was a relief from the epidemic.

Sephardi Jews observe the mourning period through the thirty-fourth day of the Sefirah, while most Ashkenazi Jews observe the mourning until the thirty-third day.[3]

Another manifestation of Jewish grief for the epidemic that struck down the disciples of Rabbi Akivah is the custom not to perform any menial labor from sunset to sunrise every day during the *sefirah* period until Shavuot. In early times both men and women refrained from doing any work during these hours. Later the custom was relaxed as far as the men were concerned and only women adhered to it. There are two reasons for this custom:

(a) For some unknown reason the disciples died just before sunset. Therefore, the people at that time had to close their shops and stop their labors in the evening to tend to the funeral arrangements and join in the funeral cortege. The women were particularly active in this task because arrangements had to be initiated even before the men could leave their daily tasks.

(b) When the Torah describes the holiday of Shavuot it instructs us to count *sheva shabatot,* "seven Sabbaths," the equivalent of forty-nine days. Then, on the fiftieth day, the holiday of Shavuot was to be celebrated. *Shabatot* is derived from the word Shabbat, to rest. In a totally different context, the Torah uses the word *Shabbat* (Leviticus 25:4) as meaning to refrain from specific work. There the Torah is speaking about the *shemittah* year when all agricultural activites must cease. The common denominator between *shemittah* and *sefirah* is the word *Shabbat*. Hence, the authorities deduced that just as in the *shemittah* year the Jew was forbidden to work so must he refrain from work during the counting of the "Seven Sabbaths." When the counting is actually done, i.e. at night, no labor should be performed.[4]

Generally one recites the *she-heḥeyanu* upon the performance of any seasonal mitzvah recurring in the calendar year. This is true of shofar, lulav, megillah, etc. Why do we not recite the *she-heḥeyanu* at the commencement of counting the Omer? Because this benediction is an expression of joy and an acknowledgment of God's grace. The counting of the Omer, on the other hand, is performed with a sadness in our heart as it is a reminder of the Temple, now destroyed, where this counting was in preparation for the Omer offering the following day.[5]

In preparation for the holiday of Shavuot it is customary to decorate the synagogue and the homes with flowers, shrubbery and foliage. (Sephardi Jews decorate the Scrolls with floral arrangements). In Lithuania Rabbi Elijah, the Gaon of Vilna, abolished this custom as of pagan and Christian origin. Most communities throughout the Jewish world, however, still observe this practice. The following reasons are given:

(a) According to the Mishnah (Rosh ha-Shanah 1:2) it is on Shavuot that the trees and their fruits are judged by God who decides whether the year will be one of abundance or scarcity. This judgment will affect the quality of the *bikkurim*, the first fruits, that are brought to the Temple. We embellish the synagogue with greenery to remind us to pray that the trees yield an abundance of fruit, which would add honor to the donor of the *bikkurim*.

(b) Shavuot is the holiday in which we celebrate the giving of the Torah to Israel on Mt. Sinai. Moses was the leading figure in this dramatic event. The long chain of events that led to Mt. Sinai had its beginning at the discovery of Moses amidst the reeds on the Nile. The foliage reminds us of the reeds where Moses was found and rescued.

(c) In contrast to all the surrounding mountains, Mt. Sinai was, according to tradition, unique in that a verdant oasis stood at its foot. This tradition stems from the instruction that God gave to the Children of Israel through Moses, to keep their flocks from grazing at the foot of the mountain. This prohibition implies that shrubbery grew there.[6]

In all Jewish communities most men, young and old alike, remain awake during the entire, or most of the night of Shavuot, occupying themselves with *tikkun lel shavuot*, (lit. the improvement, or restoration, of the night of Shavuot). This activity takes the form of intensive study which includes parts of the Scriptures, sections of the Mishnah and Talmud and chapters of the Kabbalah. There are three early sources for this custom:

(a) One Midrashic source has it that on the night preceding the giving of the Torah, many of the Children of Israel went complacently to sleep. They felt no eager anticipation for the most world-shaking event in human history that was about to unfold. This callous indifference was an affront to God. In order, therefore, to amend the wrong of our forefathers, we remain awake the entire night, awaiting the dawn of the next day when we will celebrate the receiving of the Torah at Mt. Sinai.

(b) According to another Midrashic statement, the Children of Israel at the foot of Mt. Sinai refused to accept any more than the Written Torah. God had to coerce them into accepting the Oral Law by raising Mt. Sinai over their heads and threatening to crush them underneath it. The Midrash further relates that Moses, standing on the peak of Mt. Sinai, enshrouded in clouds, could tell the difference between night and day only when he heard the masses of people, at the foot of the mountain, studying the Oral Law and then he knew it was night. Hence, we remain awake all night to rectify our ancestor's failure to accept the Oral law willingly and doing so only after being threatened with extinction. This is also the reason why we concentrate our study for the most part on the Talmud, the Oral Law.

(c) Another early source is the Zohar, the classic kabbalistic work. There, (Emor 98), Shavuot is described as the wedding day of the Children of Israel, the bride, and the Torah, the groom. Much had to be done by the bride to prepare herself spiritually for her wedding day. The Children of Israel bring to their marriage as a dowry their hours of study of the previous evening. Accompanied by this "trousseau" of learning, the Jewish People come to their Betrothed with the full recognition and appreciation of his virtues and value.[7]

Until about two hundred years ago the Jews of Yemen had never heard about the *tikkun lel shavuot.* They too, remained awake all night but instead of reading excerpts from the Mishnah and Talmud, they concentrated on the *Sefer ha-Mitzvot* by Maimonides.[8]

Until the middle of the eleventh century no one ever thought that the Torah would or should acquire a foreword or introduction. It was about that period that an outstanding Rabbinic authority and poet, Rabbi Meir the son of Rabbi Isaac of Worms (d. circa 1096) composed the famous poem *Akdamut*, "The Prelude." The reading of the Ten Commandments on the first day of the Shavuot Festival is dramatically introduced by the chanting of this vivid poem written in Aramaic. In rich imagery it depicts the angelic hosts singing God's praises on high, and His people Israel loving His Torah and singing God's praises before men.

"Could we with ink the ocean fill,
Were every blade of grass a quill,
Were the world of parchment made,
And every man a scribe by trade,
To write the love of God above
Would drain the ocean dry;
Nor would the Scroll contain the whole,
Though stretched from sky to sky."

It reaches its climax in the call, "Then let us rejoice that He blessed us and gave us the Law." This poem with its ninety-seven verses is a double alphabetical acrostic, with an additional acrostic giving the name of the author, "Meir, son of Isaac, may he grow in Torah and in good deeds. Amen. And be strong and of good courage."[9]

In the first part of this poem, the author gives exalted praises to God for creating the world, the angels to serve Him and the Children of Israel to praise and laud Him. The second part describes the repeated efforts of the peoples of the world to persuade the Children of Israel to abandon their ancient faith and assimilate. The plaintive tune with which the *Akdamut* is chanted was composed in London in 1870.[10]

Communities differ however on where the *Akdamut* should be chanted. Some call the first person (kohen) to the Torah, read one verse from the Torah and then begin to recite the *Akdamut*. The reason for this arrangement is to demonstrate the superiority of the Torah over any other literary creation, important and holy as it may be. Therefore, we commence with the reading of the Torah and then turn immediately to the *Akdamut*. The standard practice is to chant the *Akdamut* before the first person called to the Torah recites the blessing in order not to interrupt the reading of the Torah .[11]

Another custom universally observed in the synagogue on Shavuot is the public reading of the Book of Ruth. This is an ancient custom dating back to the days of the Talmud. In *Masekhet Soferim* (14:18), the Rabbis stated that half the Book of Ruth was read at the conclusion of the first day of Shavuot and the rest at the conclusion of the second day of the holiday (here the reference is obviously to the two days of Shavuot observed in the diaspora). In a later period, the authorities fixed the second day of Shavuot for reading the entire Book of Ruth. There are a number of reasons why this book of the Scriptures is read on Shavuot:

(a) To remind the Jew that just as Ruth's conversion to Judaism was attained through adversity and hardship, so knowledge of the Torah, which was received on Shavuot, is acquired only through assiduous study and unflagging diligence.

(b) The story of Ruth is the only historical event of great

spiritual significance that has any connection with the harvest. Therefore, we read the story of this great convert on Shavuot which also occurs during harvest time.[12]

(c) From the very beginning of her life, Ruth was destined to embrace Judaism and accept the yoke of the *mitzvot*. Before she took the final step she was obliged to observe the Noahide laws. The numerical values of the letters of her name add up to six hundred and six. (The *Resh* equals two hundred; the *Vav*, six; and the *Tav*, four hundred.) Thus the six hundred and six *mitzvot* which she accepted after conversion plus the seven she was obliged to keep before her conversion, add up to six hundred and thirteen. The Torah, by the count of most authorities contains six hundred and thirteen *mitzvot*.

(d) When Ruth became aware that David was to be descended from her, she became apprehensive, filled with misgivings and guilt feelings. Her non-Jewish origin troubled her. Similarly, the Children of Israel standing at Mt. Sinai ready to receive the Torah were for all intents and purposes non-Jews. In their prolonged enslavement in Egypt they could not circumcise their sons. They had to undergo the entire process of conversion, including circumcision and ritual immersion. Hence, on Shavuot, when we celebrate God's gift of the Torah to the Children of Israel, we read the story of Ruth as if to reassure her: "Have no fear; Before we received the Torah, we, too, were non-Jews."

(e) Tradition teaches us that King David died on Shavuot. His devotion to God knew no bounds. His Psalms attest to his faith in, and love for, God. His firm resolution to seek communion with God stood the tests of crises and tribulations. It is proper, then, that on the anniversary of his passing we read the story of Ruth from whom he was descended.

(f) "Why read the story of Ruth particularly on the day when we celebrate the acceptance of the Torah at Mt. Sinai?" queries an outstanding authority, and proposes the following answer. The Torah as we know it cannot be succinctly defined as "Scriptures," the Written Word. By all classical definitions, Torah must also include the Oral Law; one is inconceivable without the other. The Oral Law clarifies and expounds the written word. In Deuteronomy (23:4) we are instructed, "A Moabite shall not enter into the assembly of the Lord." According to the Talmud, the Oral Law, this implies that a Moabite *male* may *not* marry a Jewess, but that a Moabite *woman is* permitted to marry a Jew. Ruth was a Moabite. If not for the validity of the Oral Law, Ruth would not have been allowed to marry Boaz the Jew. In that event, King David would never have appeared on the scene. We therefore, read the story of Ruth on Shavuot because it was then that the Torah, comprised of the Oral Law and the Written Law, was fully accepted by the Children of Israel.[13]

(g) Although Ruth was a woman of high intellectual accomplishments and personal integrity, she achieved the fulfillment of her life only when she embarked on the course that led to her embracing the One God and His *mitzvot*. The moral to be learned from her is that no one should rely upon his intellecutal achievements in order to attain fulfillment in life. The only way to realize that goal is through total submission to the will of God.[14]

(h) The Talmud (Yevamot 47a) states: When a non-Jew expresses the desire to convert to Judaism we impart to him, among other things, the laws of charity. These include such *mitzvot* as *pe'ah*, and *shikḥah* and the like. When reaping his crops, the owner of the field was obliged to leave a corner of his field unharvested. This was called *pe'ah*. Another benefit granted the poor was the rule that forgotten sheaves were not to be recovered by the owner but left behind for the poor. This was called *shikḥah*. There were yet other ways of gleaning by which the needy could sustain themselves. All forms of gleaning differ from the popular concept of charity. In the case of charity the donor has a right to choose the recipient and the manner in which the gift was to be offered. In the case of gleanings, however, the donor had to renounce all his rights to the produce. Any poor person could come when he wanted and take what he wanted as if the produce belonged to no one.

The true test of a convert is when he accepts these laws

without questioning their validity and is ready to abide by them.

During her early life as a Jewess, Ruth suffered privation. She had to resort to gathering gleanings in the fields to sustain herself. Later she became the wife of Boaz, a wealthy landowner. Seeing her husband allocating produce for the poor, she heartily approved both the laws of charity and the laws of gleaning. She passed the test. It is for this reason that on Shavuot, the holiday of the harvest, we read about the famous convert who met the requirements of conversion as set down by the Rabbis.[15]

It is a universal custom in Jewish homes, with the exception of Yemenite Jews, to serve dairy foods on Shavuot. Some eat dairy food, and then, after a short while, partake of a meat dinner. Others eat dairy food only. A number of reasons have been advanced:

(a) It was only when the Jews received the Torah that they realized that specific laws governed the proper slaughtering of animals and the extraction of the blood. They suddenly discovered that all their utensils were not kosher because they had been used for non-kosher food. Since, according to tradition, the Torah was given to them on a Sabbath day when work is forbidden, they had no opportunity to make their utensils kosher by scalding *(hag'alah)*. Thus they had no alternative but to eat dairy food.

(b) The numerical values of the Hebrew letters of *ḥalav*, milk, add up to forty. This was to remind us of the forty days and nights that Moses spent on Mt. Sinai in preparation for the giving of the Torah to the Children of Israel.

(c) One of the Noahide laws which applied to the Jews before they received the Torah was the injunction against eating part of an animal while it was still alive. Milk comes under that category. However, upon receiving the Torah, on Shavuot, milk became permitted to them.

(d) In Genesis (18:1-18) we are told of three men, really angels, who visited Abraham and Sarah to foretell the birth of Isaac. "And he took cream and milk and the calf which he had dressed and set it out before them." They ate milk and meat at the same time. By either partaking of milk products alone or of eating both but with an interval between them as prescribed by the Torah, we show that we stand on a higher level than the angels and therefore deserved to receive the gift of all gifts, the Torah.

(e) The Jews who made their exodus from Egypt required circumcision. They were, therefore, compared to infants who are circumcised on the eighth day after birth. The food of infants is milk.

(f) According to the calculations of the Sages, Moses was taken out from the reeds of the Nile by Pharaohs daughter on the day of Shavuot. Jochebed, Moses' mother, was summoned to nurse the baby. According to tradition, Moses refused to be nursed by any Egyptian woman. "Can it be possible that the holy mouth that was to utter the word of God should suck at the breast of a pagan?" We eat dairy products to remind us of the breast feeding of the infant Moses.

(g) Meat contains blood. This is symbolic of the red hot passions of sin. Milk is white and is symbolic of purity. By studying the Torah which was presented to the Jew at Mt. Sinai on Shavuot, and by observing the tenets, the *mitzvot*, we can avoid the flames of passion and emerge purified.

(h) Earlier we established that Shavuot, in a way, was a continuation of Passover. In fact, on the second day of Passover there began the preparatory period of forty-nine days, which ended with Shavuot. Some authorities would bring the two holidays even closer in ritual and significance. They maintain that Passover and Shavuot should have similar features to indicate this continuity. Today, we place two food products on our seder plate: one to symbolize the *korban pesaḥ*, the pascal lamb, the other to symbolize the *korban ḥagigah*, the festival sacrifice. Shavuot, therefore, should also have two separate food products to correspond to those of Passover. We thus partake of two separate meals, one dairy, one meat. However, these two meals may not be eaten together because we are forbidden to mix meat and dairy products. if we are to separate them it would mean that two separate loaves of bread would have to be prepared, one for each meal. These two loaves, in turn, would remind the Jew of the two loaves that were brought into the Temple as the first offerings of the wheat harvest on Shavuot. Without the dairy meal there would be no necessity for the presence of two loaves on the table.

(i) Dairy food is the customary diet for infants, and by eating it, we indicate that no matter how much one has studied the Torah, he is like an infant who has not even begun to fathom the depth of God's word.

(j) By chemical process the body converts blood into milk. Eating milk products on Shavuot symbolizes that, through Torah and *mitzvot*, the *middat ha-din*, the attribute of strict justice, can be transformed into *middat ha-raḥamim*, the attribute of mercy. In other words, God will deal with man with compassion rather than with inflexible justice. (In Kabbalah, white is the symbol of *Ḥesed*—mercy, red is the symbol of *Din*—strict justice.)

(k) We have dealt before with the custom of remaining awake all night *(tikkun leil shavuot)* in remembrance of *Mattan Torah* when the Children of Israel were awake all night awaiting the dramatic moment when the Torah would be given to them. When that momentous event came to an end they suddenly felt hungry. They could not wait to go through the process of koshering their meats and so they resorted to dairy meals and produce which were readily available.[16]

Yemenite Jews never adopted the custom of eating dairy products on Shauot for any of the reasons cited above. They abide by the Midrashic statement that Abraham, the first Jew, observed all the six hundred and thirteen *mitzvot* and that he handed down this tradition to his progeny. At Mt. Sinai, therefore, the Children of Israel already had kosher utensils, and kosher meat was available.[17]

Jewish communities in Arab countries observed the custom of ascending to the roof of the synagogue on Shavuot and throwing apples down to the ground. The origin of this custom is traced to the similarity of the exclamation of the Children of Israel at Mt. Sinai to the growth of an apple. The fruit of the apple begins to develop before the leaf. Similarly the Children of Israel proclaimed *na'aseh ve-nishma*, "We will do and we will listen," whereas the logical order would have been, "We will first listen and then act." They, however, announced their resolution to perform the *mitzvot* before they could listen and analyze them.[18]

SOURCES

1. *Arukh ha-Shulḥan* 494:2.
2. *Ta'ame ha-Minhagim* p. 279; *Sefer ha-Mat'amim* p. 57.
3. *Tur Oraḥ Ḥayyim, Bet Yoseph, Darke Mosheh, Derishah* 493; *Sefer ha-Toda'ah* p. 245-246; *Ta'ame ha-Minhagim* p. 279; *Arukh ha-Shulḥan* 493: 1-7; *Otzar Yisrael* Vol 10 p. 30.
4. *Tur Oraḥ Ḥayyim* 493; *Sefer ha-Toda'ah* p. 247; *Arukh ha-Shulḥan* 293:9.
5. *Ḥayye Avraham* p. 43b.
6. *Sefer ha-Mat'amim* p.58; *Sefer ha-Toda'ah* p. 273; *Ta'ame ha-Minhagim* p. 279; *Arukh ha-Shulḥan* 494:6; *Otzar Yisrael* Vol. 10, pp. 30-31.
7. *Sefer ha-Toda'ah* Vol II p. 283; *Ta'ame ha-Minhagim* p. 279; *Sefer ha-Mat'amim* p. 58.
8. *Halikhot Teiman* p. 32.
9. See *Rabbinical Council of America Prayer Book* p. 504.
10. *Otzar Yisrael* Vol. 2, p. 182.
11. *Sefer ha-Toda'ah* Vol. II p. 275; *Otzar Yisrael* Vol. 2, p. 182.
12. *Avudraham* p. 128.
13. *Sefer ha-Toda'ah* Vol. II p. 301.
14. *Ḥayye Avraham p. 45a.*
15. *Minhage Yeshurun* pp. 198-199.
16. *Rama, Hilkhot Shavuot* 494:3; *Sefer ha-Mat'amim* p. 59-60.; *Ta'ame ha- Minhagim* p. 281-282; *Arukh ha-Shulḥan* 494 par. 5.
17. *Halikhot Teiman* p. 31.
18. *Minhage Eretz Yisrael*, Zemanim p. 50-51.

Tish'ah Be-Av

There are four types of fast days in the Jewish calendar. Two are ordained in the Torah: Yom Kippur which has a set date, the tenth of Tishri, and a fast undertaken by an individual for personal reasons in fulfillment of a vow. The other two types are post-Biblical in origin and were instituted by later authorities. These are: the "Four Fast Days" and the Fast of Esther, and fasts on occasions of communal or personal crises. We shall not deal in this chapter with the fasts of Yom Kippur and Esther, nor with fasts in connection with vows or crises. The first two will be dealt with in their proper places; the other two types are beyond the scope of this work. Here, we shall concentrate on "The Four Fast Days", with a more detailed analysis of *Tish'ah be-Av*.[1]

The four fasts are:

(a) *Tzom Gedaliah*—the Fast of Gedaliah (ben Aḥikam) which occurs on the third day of Tishri. Gedaliah was an official appointed by Nebukhadnezzar to govern the Jews who remained in their homeland after the Temple had been destroyed in 586 B.C.E. and the vast majority of Jews driven into exile in Babylonia. Gedaliah maintained that the remnant should be loyal to the Chaldeans (Babylonians). Opponents of this course assassinated him. In retaliation Nebukhadnezzar inflicted severe reprisals upon the Jewish people. Because of the calamitous consequences, a fast day was instituted.

(b) *Asarah be-Tevet*—the Tenth Day of Tevet. It was on this day that Nebukhadnezzar laid siege on Jerusalem. This was the beginning of all the subsequent calamities that befell the Jewish people and it has been designated as a fast day.

(c) *Shiv'ah-asar be-Tammuz*—the Seventeenth Day of Tammuz. Five disasters occured on this date:

(1) Moses, descending from Mt. Sinai, discovered the people worshipping the Golden Calf and broke the two Tablets of Law.

(2) During the siege of Jerusalem the *Korban Tamid*, the twice-daily sacrifice that was brought in the Temple amidst song and music, was abolished at the command of Nebukhadnezzar.

(3) In the year 70 the Romans breached the walls of Jerusalem during their siege. Prior to the destruction of the First Temple the walls of Jerusalem were breached on the ninth of Tammuz. This too, should have warranted a fast day but the Rabbis were reluctant to institute two fast days so close together.

(4) On the same day the Romans publicly burned a Scroll of the Law and

(5) they set up an idol in the courtyard of the Temple.

(d) *Tish'ah be-Av*—the Ninth Day of Av. Five tragedies occurred on this day:

(1) It was on this date that the Children of Israel who left the Land of Egypt, were prohibited by the decree of God to enter the Promised Land. (Numbers 14:34).

(2) The First Temple was destroyed.

(3) The Second Temple was destroyed.

(4) Betar, the last fortress to hold out against the Romans in the Bar Kokhba revolt, fell in the year 135 and the fate of the Jewish People was sealed.

(5) A year after the fall of Betar, the Temple area was plowed. Already the Prophet Zachariah predicted the Four Fasts: "So says the Lord of Hosts, the Fast of the Fourth (month—Tammuz), the Fast of the Fifth (month—Ab), the Fast of the Seventh (month—Tishri), and the Fast of the Tenth (month—Tevet) shall be unto the House of Judah occasions for joy and happiness and pleasant holidays" (Zechariah 8:19). The Rabbis of the Talmud (Rosh ha-Shanah 186) were perplexed by this

paradox: How could the prophet call these days both Fasts and Holidays? The Rabbis resolved this seeming contradiction in terms by explaining that during periods when Jews abandon the practices of the Torah these days are to be fast days; when the Children of Israel would adhere to their traditions, they would become holidays.

Thus all four Fast Days are connected by the common motive of the Destruction of the Temple and the Exile.

The period between the seventeenth day of Tammuz and the ninth day of Av is called *Ben ha-Metzarim*, "between the straits." This stems from the verse: "And her pursuers overtook her within the straits" (Lamentations 1:13), referring to the tragic days that hemmed in the Children of Israel between the seventeenth of Tammuz and the ninth of Av.[2]

In order fully to appreciate the laws, customs and ceremonials of *Tish'ah be-Av*, we must remember several basic facts:

(a) *Tish'ah be-Av* is a day of intensive, not casual, mourning for the destruction of the Temple and Jerusalem.

(b) Coexisting with this sense of grief is a subtle sense of joy. One authority makes the telling point that there is significance in the fact that the Sabbath before *Tish'ah be-Av* is called *Shabbat Ḥazon*, the shabbat of vision, because the Prophetic portion read on this day begins with the word *ḥazon*. He points out that the Prophet (Habakkuk 2:3) comforts the Children of Israel with the words, *ki od ḥazon la-mo'ed*—"there is yet a vision of a joyous occasion." *Hazon* and *mo'ed* are placed in juxtaposition, indicating that even as the Jew begins his period of grief, he envisions the sadness turning to happiness.[3]

The Talmud (Ta'anit 26b) lays down the law that from the first day of the month of Av through the ninth day— according to some authorities, even extending to the tenth—the Jew is expected to curtail his joys.[4] This curtailment applies to the wedding ceremony as well, even to one without a festive meal; and also to the engagement of a couple if celebrated with a festive meal. Also, when a child is born or a business transaction is successfully concluded, which events at other times would be marked by a celebration, we are bidden, during these nine days, to keep our joy to a minimum. Although the period of mourning has been extended to begin with the seventeenth day of Tammuz,[5] the more stringent laws of mourning do not start until the first day of Av.

To illustrate the differences of opinion concerning some of the rules connected with *Tish'ah be-Av*, let us examine those pertaining to eating meat. The Talmud forbids meat only during the *se'udah ha-mafseket*, the last meal before the fast. A meat dish is a sign of a joyous occasion. In preparing for a time of grief such as *Tish'ah be-Av* there is no place for lavish dining. However, during the rest of the three weeks meat is permitted. Another opinion holds that this ruling covers the entire period from the first through the ninth of Av because during that period the Temple was under attack and all animal sacrifices ceased. According to a third view the abstention from meat begins already with the seventeenth day of Tammuz because the *korban tamid* was abolished on that day. Today no observant Jew limits the restriction to the eve of *Tish'ah be-Av*. There are those who refrain from meat during the nine days while others abstain from it throughout the three weeks.[6]

An interesting offshoot of this division of opinion is to be found in the debate concerning a *siyum*, the conclusion of the study of one of the Sacred Books which warrants a celebration at which refreshments are served. One authority permits the circumvention of the prohibition against eating meat during the nine days by arranging his studies in such a manner that he will conclude one of the Talmudic Tractates (a *Siyyum*)during that period.[7] Another authority, however, condemns this practice as a mere subterfuge.[8]

While some laws of *Tish'ah be-Av* are similar to the laws of mourning for a parent, other *Tish'ah be-Av* prohibitions are identical with those of Yom Kippur. Thus, the Jew is forbidden on this day of mourning to eat, drink, wash, anoint himself, wear shoes, have conjugal relations or to study the Sacred Books. The last injunction is based on the verse "The precepts of the Lord gladden the heart" (Psalms 19:9). The deprivation of food and drink is self-explanatory. Nothing in the slightest form of nourishment may be taken on that day. Washing refers only to that of self-indulgence. However, after leaving the toilet or in order to remove dirt from one's hands, one is permitted to wash. Again, anointing oneself for pleasure is forbidden; for hygienic reasons it is permitted. Leather shoes alone are prohibited; cloth or rubber shoes may be worn.

It is obvious why the pleasure of conjugal relations is forbidden on *Tish'ah be-Av*. However, the question arises as to whether sexual relations are permitted when *Tish'ah be-Av* falls on a Saturday and the fast is postponed to the next day, Sunday. Since the day is actually *Tish'ah be-Av*, should one refrain from this pleasurable experience, or shall we say, that since food and drinks are permitted on that day, so why not other pleasures as well? The later authorities ruled that this physical pleasure is forbidden because one can forego it for an extra day, but one cannot fast two days in succession.

Although *Tish'ah be-Av* is held to resemble Yom Kippur, there is a basic difference between them: on Yom Kippur only one whose life might be endangered by fasting may eat; on *Tish'ah be-Av* a sick person may eat even where there is no question of danger to life.[9]

The observance of *Tish'ah be-Av* begins with the *seudah hamafseket*, the last meal before the fast. Instead of an elaborate repast, a modest meal is eaten, consisting of one course, usually hard-boiled eggs and bread. Egg is the customary food for mourners. Being round, it reminds us of death which, circle-like, must return as an experience for every human being. There was a difference of opinion between the Rabbis of France and Germany during the Middle Ages concerning cooked foods of several ingredients such as meat, potatoes, rice and beans. The question revolved around the point as to whether this was to be regarded as a one course meal, or, because of its many ingredients, a meal of several dishes. In Germany, the authorities took up a very strict position on this matter; in France they were more lenient. Today, we accept the lenient viewpoint.[10]

According to the strict rules of mourning on *Tish'ah be-Av* one must either stand, or else sit on the floor, but not on a chair or a bench. This was to be observed even during the *se'udah ha-mafseket.* In that spirit, too, the observant Jew was advised not to eat his meal in the company of others, and thereby avoid the necessity of reciting the Grace after the Meal with *zimmun*, the ritual for saying Grace in company. *Zimmun* is indicative of permanence, the habitual and the durable. One would prefer not to make this mournful meal a recurring experience.[11]

Before proceeding to the synagogue one must remove one's leather shoes. After the maariv service, all lights are extinguished with the exception of some candles and the worshipers seat themselves on the floor or on a stool less that three handbreadths high. Until this day, among the Yemenite Jews, the leading personality of the community stands up and cries out: "Tonight marks (the exact number of years) since the destruction of the Second Temple and as yet redemption has not come. Know ye that whoever has not been privileged to witness the building of the Temple, is regarded as having witnessed the destruction within his own lifetime."[12] Following this a solitary candle is lit and the recitation of the Book of Lamentations is begun.

As noted before, the mode of behavior on *Tish'ah be-Av* is similar to that of the mourner during his *Shiv'ah* period. With respect to *tefillin*, however, there is a slight difference. A mourner is exempt from putting on his *tefillin* only during *aninut*, the period between death and burial, when his grief is most intense. However, during the rest of the mourning period, he is to observe the *mitzvah* of *tefillin.* The saddest period of *Tish'ah be-Av* is the morning, when the Jew recites the elegies *(Kinot)* over the destruction of the Temple, hour after hour. Therefore, mourner-like, he does not put on his *tefillin* because they are considered as spiritual ornaments which are inconsistent with the spirit of a day of mourning. This is based on a play of words in the verse "He has cast down from heaven unto the earth *Tif'eret Israel* (the glory of Israel)" (Lamentations 2:1). The root of the word *Tif'eret* is *Pe'er* which means ornament. The ornament that the Jew wears every day is *tefillin.*[13] Another authority recommended the placing of some ash on the spot of the head where the *tefillah* normally lies. He, too, plays on the word *Pe'er* and equates it with *Efer*, "ash", which has the same letters as *Pe'er.*[14] However, it must be remembered as pointed out, that *Tish'ah be-Av* is not devoted to unmitigated grief. It contains an element of hope and joy. Therefore, the order of confession that is observed in our daily prayers (*Nefilat Appạyim)* is omitted. Also, from midday on, we are permitted to sit on chairs but not to wear leather shoes. During the afternoon service, *(Minḥa)* we once again put on our *tefillin* and we begin to reduce the intensity of grief that has pervaded us during the day and to entertain thoughts of comfort.[15]

In the mood of the day, when we are filled with mental anguish over the destruction of the Temple, visiting the cemetery and praying at the graves of close relatives and saintly personalities is in order. However, it is customary to make such visits alone and not in the company of others, because in company one can be easily led to frivolous talk and unbecoming behavior.[16] Until this very day, one can observe the Jerusalem elders circling the walls of the Old City to remind themselves of the tragic event commemorated by *Tish'ah be-Av.*[17]

A difference of opinion exists with respect to a circumcision that falls on *Tish'ah be-Av*. It is indeed a time for celebration when a father inducts his son into the Jewish fold through the ritual of circumcision. It is also a source of joy for others who participate in its performance, such as the *Mohel* and the *Sandek* (the person who holds the baby during the ceremony). Thus, a conflict of emotions arises. On one hand, *Tish'ah be-Av* is a day of intense grief; on the other hand, circumcision is an occasion of overwhelming joy. Yet a *berit* may not be postponed. Therefore, one opinion holds that we may follow the rule *zerizim makdimim* and hasten to perform the *mitzvah* at the earliest opportunity, in this case immediately after midday. The other opinion counsels to perform the *berit* before the afternoon service when we prepare ourselves for prayers of comfort and solace. The practice prevailing today is to follow the first opinion.[18]

SOURCES

1. *Arukh ha-Shulḥan, Oraḥ Ḥayyim* 562.
2. *Sefer ha-Toda'ah*, Vol. II p. 370.
3. *Sefer ha-Mat'amim* p. 13, and Rashi to Habakkuk 2:3.
4. *Tur Oraḥ Ḥayyim* 551.
5. *Darke Moshe* 551.
6. *Tur Oraḥ Ḥayyim*, end of 551. See also *Bet Yoseph* and *Darke Moshe*, ibid.
7. *Darke Moshe*, end of 551.
8. *Arukh ha-Shulḥan* 551.
9. *Arukh ha-Shulḥan, Oraḥ Ḥayyim* 554.
10. *Arukh ha-Shulḥan, Oraḥ Ḥayyim* 552.
11. *Sefer Ben Ish Ḥai* p. 174.
12. *Otzar Yisrael* Vol. X p. 319.
13. *Tur Shulḥan Arukh* 555; *Arukh ha-Shulḥan* 555 par. 3; *Sefer ha-Mat'amim* 131.
14. *Darke Moshe, Oraḥ Ḥayyim* 555.
15. *Arukh ha-Shulḥan, Oraḥ Ḥayyim* 555 par. 2.
16. *Sefer ha-Toda'ah* Vol. II, p. 379.
17. *Sefer ha-Toda'ah* Vol. II, p. 379.
18. *Arukh ha-Shulḥan, Oraḥ Ḥayyim* 559 par. 8.

Rosh Ha-Shanah

According to Jewish theology there is a day in the year when every human being is required to give an account of his life during the year that has passed. On that day he stands before the Heavenly Bar and there the verdict will be rendered whether or not he deserves another year of life. The scales of judgment may be tipped either way. Satan stands there to indict him. Armed with accusations, incriminations and denunciations he charges that this person is incorrigible and irredeemable; he sins continually; she brazenly defies the word of God—in short this man or woman deserves to die. To gain a deeper understanding of the full significance of the High Holy Days, Rosh ha-Shanah and Yom Kippur, it would be well to draw an analogy from warfare. A general does not hurl his forces into battle without thorough preparation. He meticulously trains his troops, plans the logistics, studies strategy and leaves nothing to chance. The lives of his troops are in his hands and he will do whatever humanly possible to avoid loss of life. So it is with the Jew on Rosh ha-Shanah, on the day he engages in battle with Satan. His is a spiritual confrontation with those forces that would condemn him and deny him another year of life. So he does not procrastinate. He begins his preparations a full month earlier, on the first day of Elul, girding himself with prayer and good deeds, drawing closer to God in order to adequately defend himself against all calumnies.

As one of the means of preparation, beginning with the first day of Elul we sound the shofar every morning, except on Saturday. While Maimonides explains that the shofar is blown as the means of stirring the Jew to repentance, other reasons also have been advanced:

(a) The Psalmist (81:4) exhorts the people, "Sound the shofar at the New Moon at the designated time for our Festival Day." *Ḥodesh*, the new moon, can also be interpreted as month. The inference, therefore, is: blow the shofar for a month before the appointed time, which is Rosh ha-Shanah. The purpose is to confuse Satan, by causing him to hear the sound of the shofar prior to the holiday. This will prevent him from knowing when the Day of Judgment will fall. He will then be unable to level his accusations.[1]

(b) Another reason is based on the *Aggadah* (Pirke de-Rabbi Eliezer 46). We learn that after the Children of Israel created and worshipped the Golden Calf Moses, outraged by this abomination, shattered the tablets. He was then instructed by God to ascend Mt. Sinai again and there to receive a second set of tablets. As Moses began his ascent, a shofar was sounded in the camp of the Israelites reminding them not to repeat their sins. This episode occurred on the first day of Elul. Accordingly, we too begin to sound the shofar on the first day of Elul to remind us that we must ever remain alert to the seductions of sinfulness which recur daily in our lives.[2]

(c) In the Song of Songs (6:3) Solomon sings: *Ani le-dodi ve-dodi li.* "I belong to my friend and my friend is mine." The first letters of these four Hebrew words form the word "Elul". In other words, before the Day of Judgment, during the month of Elul, it is best that I be close to my friend (God) and I will be sure that my friend (God) will be close to me. Furthermore, all four words end with the letter *Yud* . The numerical value of *Yud* is ten. Four *Yuds* equal forty, reminding us that there are forty days from the first of Elul through Yom Kippur.[3]

Another ritual that begins during the month of Elul is the recitation of *Seliḥot*, penitential prayers. While the sounding of the shofar during Elul is universally observed, the Sephardi community follows a different course from the Ashkenazi with regard to *Seliḥot.* The Sephardim are consistent. They recite *Seliḥot* each morning, the same as they blow the shofar each morning, throughout the month of Elul. The Ashkenazim only begin their penitential prayers on the midnight of Saturday preceding Rosh ha-Shanah, provided that it is at least four days before the holiday. The concept of *Seliḥot* is based on an Aggadah (Tanna de-be Eliyahu Zuta Chap. 23) in which it is related that King David was troubled by the question, how could the Children of Israel attain atonement for their sins? God replied that if the Children of Israel would gather and confess their sins before Him, following the order of the prayers of penitence, He would forgive them. On Rosh ha-Shanah, we too are most anxious to receive God's pardon. Hence, we gather and confess our sins before the Holy Day.[4]

We can readily appreciate the consistency of the Sephardi community. However, why did the Ashkenazim restrict their *Seliḥot* services to the week or two preceding Rosh ha-Shanah? One suggestion is that in expounding the commandments of Rosh ha-Shanah the Torah proclaims: "And you shall bring an offering unto the Lord." This is interpreted to mean that on Rosh ha-Shanah the Jew must be as contrite as if he himself were being brought as an offering to God. The laws governing the nature of the sacrifice specify that the animal must be isolated for four days beforehand to ensure that it is free of any disqualifying blemish. Thus, four days before Rosh ha-Shanah, the day when we are symbolically to offer ourselves as a sacrifice, we begin our intensive prayers of penitence to rid ourselves of any defects hindering our spiritual commitment to God.[5]

Another reason for the four days: we will learn later that the period of self-effacement and contrition extends till Yom Kippur. Actually, the time for penitence should begin with Rosh ha-Shanah and end with Yom Kippur, ten days later. Now, many Jews not only pray but also fast during these *Aseret Yeme Teshuvah*, the Ten Days of Penitence. They cannot, however, fast all ten days. Four of these days are excluded—no fasting being permitted on the two days of Rosh ha-Shanah, *Shabbat Shuvah*, and the day before Yom Kippur. To complete the ten days we observe four more days of intensive spiritual activity prior to Rosh ha-Shanah.[6]

But why must these *Seliḥot* services begin on a Saturday night?

(a) It is a time easily remembered by all.[7]

(b) The world was created in six days. The last being to be created on the eve of the Sabbath was man. On the Sabbath day, everything came to a standstill with activities resumed at the close of the Sabbath. Man's primary activity is to serve and worship God and to illustrate our devotion to this primary duty we begin our fervent prayers on *Motza'e Shabbat*, when we usher out the Sabbath.[8]

(c) Almost invariably on the Saturday preceeding the first *Seliḥot* service, we read: *Attem nitzavim ha-yom*—"You are standing this day before the Lord" (Deut. 29:9). The numerical values of the letters of the three Hebrew words add up to six hundred and ninety four. The two Hebrew words *la-amod li-seliḥot*, "arise for the penitential prayers," also total six hundred and ninety-four. The implication is that on the Saturday of this portion we must stand before God and recite our prayers of penitence.[9]

The name *Rosh ha-Shanah* is not found in the Torah. instead the day is referred to in this manner: "In the seventh month on the first day of the month shall be a solemn rest unto you, a memorial proclaimed with the blast of horns, a holy convocation" (Lev. 23:24). If it is the beginning of a New Year, why is this day designated as the first day of the seventh month? Why not the first day of the first month which according to Jewish tradition is Nisan? For the Jewish people as a nation Nisan is indeed the first month, because that was the month in which the Children of Israel left Egypt and emerged as a free, independent people. The *Rosh ha-Shanah* that we are dealing with here is a New Year for the *individual* and his obligations to God and his fellow man.

Still, why are the High Holy Days celebrated in the month of Tishri?

(a) Since the Torah employs the world *shevi'i*, which means "seventh," "the seventh month," it was thought to be the proper month for a confrontation with Satan because *sova* ("to be satiated") is phonetically similar to *shevi'i*. The implication is that we are not afraid to face our accusers during a month that is replete with special mitzvot through our observance of Rosh ha-Shanah, Yom Kippur, Sukkot and *Hoshanah Rabba.*[10]

(b) This is the season of the year when the farmer begins to gather in his produce from the fields. There is a long list of obligations that the farmer must assume with respect to the poor and destitute during this season. He must give tithes; he may not recover sheaves that he had inadvertently left behind; he may not retrieve clusters of grapes that he forgot to pick; he is obligated to leave the corners of his fields unharvested—all for the benefit of the poor, the widow and the orphan. Armed with all these *mitzvot*, the Jew is ready to face the Satanic forces that would accuse him before the Heavenly Bar of Justice.

(c) The Zodiac sign for Tishri is a scale. Man's sins and good deeds are accurately weighed. A scale is meant not to measure but to weigh. That is to say, there are good deeds that on the surface may appear small and insignificant yet in reality may be very weighty indeed. The same consideration applies to transgressions. Consequently, the Day of Judgment was set in Tishri with the hope that, although we might have sinned, some of the minor good deeds we had performed would outweigh our bad deeds, and the heavenly Court would decree for us another good year of life.[11]

Rosh ha-Shanah is the only holiday that falls on the first day of the month. Why? Above we referred to the call of David (Psalms 81:4) to his people concerning the time designated for the holiday. The Hebrew word for "designated" is *keseh*. This Hebrew word has another connotation: *kisui*, a cover. The implication is that of all the holidays Rosh ha-Shanah is the only one when the moon is not visible. Other holidays are observed when the moon is nearly or completely full and shines with all its radiance and the Jews, too, celebrate those holidays with radiant pride and elaborate ceremony. Rosh ha-Shanah, on the other hand, falls on the first of the month when the moon is completely hidden. The Children of Israel are compared to the moon. Consequently, they stand before their God on Rosh ha-Shanah contrite and humble, stripped of all personal aggrandizement. Furthermore, the entire concept of Rosh ha-Shanah as a Day of Judgement is concealed and is not openly mentioned in the Torah. This was done purposely to prevent man from saying: "I will wait for the Day of Rosh ha-Shanah to repent since the Torah designated it as the Day of Judgement."

This concealment is also the background for the custom of omitting the "Blessing of the Coming Month" on the Sabbath preceding the holiday. While it is customary to sanctify every month by reciting the appropriate prayers on the Sabbath preceding the advent of the new month, Tishri is the exception. We do not announce the coming of Tishri to prevent the Satanic forces from knowing precisely on what day Rosh ha-Shanah would fall and preparing their accusations beforehand.[12]

An interesting aspect of Rosh ha-Shanah is the fact that it is celebrated for two days in *all* Jewish communities including Eretz Israel. In other holidays there is a difference between Israel and the Diaspora—they are all celebrated for one day in the Holy Land, while in the Diaspora they last two days. Rosh ha-Shanah is universally celebrated for two days. Why? The Torah ordains "On the *first day* of the seventh month etc." (Lev. 23:24). The Torah specifies *one* day. How do we come to keep two?

This is one classic illustration of the power of tradition in Jewish life. The Jewish calendar is a lunar calendar. It is the appearance of the new moon that determines when our holidays occur. From early history the new month was declared to have begun when two witnesses arrived and testified before the *Bet Din* that they saw the new moon. Once the *Bet Din* was satisfied that this testimony was correct, they proclaimed that day to be the first of the new month. This was the simple procedure followed in the Holy Land. The Diaspora communities, on the other hand, had to await the arrival of messengers who informed them of the date of the new moon and on the basis of this information they would know on which days to celebrate the holidays. Often, the messengers did not arrive on time. It was, therefore, decided that they would celebrate two consecutive days for each holiday knowing for sure that the *Bet Din* had proclaimed a new month on either the 30th or the 31st day from the previous New Moon. Hence, the *yom tov sheni shel galuyot*, the added second holiday of the Diaspora, was instituted.

Rosh ha-Shanah was treated somewhat differently. On the twenty-ninth of Elul, the *Bet Din* eagerly awaited the arrival of the two witnesses. Having counted the days of Elul they knew that the witnesses should arrive sometime on the twenty-ninth day of the month and according to the time of their arrival the court would designate the day of Rosh ha-Shanah. Although they were certain of the day when the new moon would appear, they could do nothing until the witnesses arrived. Rosh ha-Shanah being a sacred day, however, they provisionally required the day be observed as the first of the month and, occasionally, if the witnesses only arrived in the evening, they retained the sanctity of that day and proclaimed the next day, as well, as Rosh ha-Shanah. In other words, these two days were not a result of any doubt in the Diaspora, but of the definite observance at times of a holiday even in Eretz Israel. It is for this reason that the two days of Rosh ha-Shanah have come down to us throughout the ages as a *yoma arikhta*, a long, extended day.[13]

Another reason: the Jerusalem Talmud (Rosh ha-Shanah Chap. 1) teaches that man's fate is decided on Rosh ha-Shanah. In Jewish jurisprudence, a court dealing with a capital case may not pronounce its verdict on the same day but must wait till the next day to allow time for further reflection. On Rosh ha-Shanah, when man's life hangs in the balance, the Heavenly Court is accordingly not to arrive at its verdict on the same day. Hence, a second day is added.[14]

Later on, after a calculated calendar was established, there could no longer be any doubt about the appearance of the new moon. Yet the old tradition of observing two days of the holidays was retained until this day.

Since the two days of Rosh ha-Shanah are considered as a *yoma arikhta*—an extended day—the later authorities grappled with the following problem. If these two days of Rosh ha-Shanah are to be considered as one long day, should the *Sheheḥeyanu* (blessing of thanksgiving) be recited on both nights or only on the first? In absence of a final decision it is recommended that on the second night a new garment be worn or a new fruit eaten, which of itself would require that the blessing be said. In this way, one recites the *Sheheḥeyanu* on the second night as well, as a definite obligation with respect to the garment or the fruit and as a doubtful obligation with respect to the holiday.[15]

With the previous paragraphs as background, let us now trace the rituals and customs of Rosh ha-Shanah. We begin with the services in the Synagogue the night before. For other seasons, each country and community has its own distinctive synagogue melodies. Not so on the High Holy Days on which the prayers are chanted with the same melody handed down from generation to generation.

At the conclusion of the services, each worshipper wishes the others: "May you be inscribed for a good year." The origin of this custom is a Talmudic passage (*Rosh ha-Shanah* 16b): Three books are opened before the Lord on Rosh ha-Shanah. In one book he inscribes the names of the truly righteous who are immediately assured of another year of life. In the second book, the names of the truly wicked are immediately inscribed for death. The third book is for those who are neither completely righteous nor completely wicked. Their fate remains suspended until Yom Kippur, when it is sealed. We demonstrate our high regard for our fellow-man by saying to him in essence, "We have found you to be a righteous person and so we hope you will be inscribed immediately in the Book of Life." Since, according to the Kabbalah the verdict on the righteous is pronounced during the first three hours of the holiday, it is appropriate that we wish our friends a year of life as soon as the holiday begins.[16]

After returning from the Synagogue and reciting the *Kiddush*, the family sits down to their meal. It is curious that in many Jewish communities the *ḥallot*, the loaves of bread, are baked in the form either of a ladder or of a bird. The bird-like *ḥallah* is an allusion to the Scriptural passage: "As fluttering birds so will the Lord of Hosts shield Jerusalem" (Isaiah 31:5).[17] Those who have the ladder-like *ḥallah* take their cue from the character of the day. On Rosh ha-Shanah man's destiny is determined, whether he will live or die, whether he be poor or rich etc. Thus, on this day, life is likened to a ladder. Man will either ascend or descend; will succeed or fail.[18]

The menu for the first night of Rosh ha-Shanah is an indication of the hopes, fears, and trepidation that pervade the Jew on that day. They reflect his sense of insecurity and uncertainty. This too, is an illustration of leaving nothing to chance but grasping every possible straw that may help man on this Day of Judgment. As first course, the head of a ram or a fish is served and the prayer recited: "May the coming year bring about our achieving the status of the head [of society] rather than [its] tail." The head of a ram is also intended to recall the ram that was substituted for Isaac.[19]

Fish is a popular food for the night of Rosh ha-Shanah and when eating it we pray that our numbers increase just as fish multiply.[20] On the other hand, the Jews of Iraq refrained from eating fish because the Hebrew word for fish is *dag* which is similar to *da'agah*, the Hebrew word for worry and anxiety.[21]

Another item on the menu: an apple dipped in honey. There are two reasons proposed for this practice:

(a) An apple has the three qualities of taste, appearance, and fragrance. The Jew sincerely supplicates God for the three major gifts in life: worthy children, longevity and adequate sustenance.[22]

(b) In the ancient Temple, it would have been inexpedient for the priests to remove the ashes of the burnt offerings beyond the Temple walls after each sacrifice. They, therefore, moved the ashes to the side of the altar temporarily until a heap accumulated which in its shape resembled an apple. Later, all the ashes were removed at one time. The apple we eat on Rosh ha-Shanah is also intended to remind us that Isaac was almost slaughtered and his ashes would have been part of the apple-like heap. The honey recalls to our minds that the fate of Isaac was sweetened, and we hope that our fate too will be sweet.[23]

Pomegranates grace the Rosh ha-Shanah table. By eating one, we express the prayer and hope that on this Day of Judgement the Heavenly Court will find us filled with as many good deeds and meritorious accomplishments as the number of the seeds in a pomegranate.[24]

Most people dip a piece of *ḥallah* in honey because the numerical value of the letters of the Hebrew word *devash*, "honey," is three hundred and six which is the same as the numerical value of the Hebrew words *Av ha-Raḥamim*, "O Father of Mercy."[25]

The type of vegetables we eat is also significant. Peas are eaten for the same reason as the pomegranate because the Aramaic word for peas is *rubiya*, derived from *rav*, an "abundance"; leeks are eaten because the Hebrew word for leek is *karti*. The root of this word is similar to *karet* which means to cut off, excise. With this food we pray that God will eradicate our enemies. Many people eat beets because the Aramaic for this word is *silki*, similar to *histalek*, remove. We pray that our enemies *yistaleku*, vanish from our midst. Dates are favorites on Rosh ha-Shanah. The Aramaic name for this fruit is *tamra* and *tam*, which is similar, means to end. May the influence of our enemies come to an end. Finally, in many homes a dish of pumpkin is served. The word for pumpkin is *kara*, which also means to tear. Our prayer: May any unfavorable verdict against us be torn up at the last moment.[26]

Nuts, on the other hand, are avoided because the Hebrew word for them is *egoz*, the numerical value of which is the same as that of *ḥet*, (the final aleph omitted) which means "sin." We wish to dismiss all thoughts of sin on Rosh ha-Shanah.[27]

The meal ends with the *Birkat ha-Mazon*, the Grace after Meals.

Hallel, the prayer of joy and adoration recited on all other festivals, does not form part of the Rosh ha-Shanah morning service. Why should Rosh ha-Shanah be different? One reason is based on a Talmudic passage (*Rosh ha-Shanah* 32b): the angels came before the Lord and inquired why His children did not recite the *Hallel* on Rosh ha-Shanah and Yom Kippur. He replied, "How can they recite *Hallel* on so awesome a day when the Books of Life and Death are open before Me and no man knows what his fate will be."[28] Another reason proposed is that it would be foolish and arrogant for man to celebrate the day with happiness and song as if he were certain that he would win a favorable verdict.[29]

The shofar to be blown on Rosh ha-Shanah is made from a ram's horn. Cows' horns are disqualified because of the association with the Golden Calf worshipped by the Children of Israel in the desert. On the Day of Judgment nothing is to be left to chance; we simply do not wish to provide our accusers before the Heavenly Court with the argument that we are the offspring of those who worshipped the Golden Calf. The ram's horn, on the other hand, provides us with a powerful defense: one of our ancestors, Isaac, was prepared to give up his life and become a sacrifice at the bidding of God. It was the last minute substitution of a ram that gave the episode a happy ending. Furthermore, a ram's horn is twisted and, when it is made into a shofar, it is sounded with the wide end tilted downward. The motive for this procedure is to remind the Jew on the holy day that he must not be arrogant but rather humble and contrite.[30]

When the Torah (Lev. 23:24, 25:29; Numbers 29:1) gives us instructions concerning Rosh ha-Shanah and Yom Kippur, it uses the term *teru'ah*, denoting the sounding of the horn (shofar), three times. The first reference in Leviticus and the reference in Numbers deal with Rosh ha-Shanah; that of Leviticus 25:9 with the emancipation of slaves on the day of Yom Kippur of the Jubilee year. The Rabbis understood that all three references were to be combined to impart a single idea. In the first place, it indicated that on Rosh ha-Shanah the *teru'ah* was to be sounded three times to correspond to the threefold reference. Secondly, a *teki'ah*, a smooth, straight sound must both precede and follow the *teru'ah*. Two reasons have been suggested:

(a) Dealing with the shofar blasts of the Jubilee year, it is stated: "Then shall you make proclamation with the blast of the *horn* on the tenth day of the seventh month; on the Day of Atonement you shall make proclamation with the *horn* throughout all the land"(Lev. 25:9). A proclamation is prefaced by a simple loud sound. Since the phrase "Proclamation with the blast of the horn" precedes the word *teru'ah*, and the same phrase follows this word, the Rabbis deduced that a *teki'ah* must precede and follow the *teru'ah* on Rosh ha-Shanah. Therefore, a *teki'ah* followed by a *teru'ah* and then another *teki'ah* must be sounded. And since the word *teru'ah* is mentioned three times, three sets must be blown, giving a total of nine soundings of the shofar that are mandatory on Rosh ha-Shanah.[31]

(b) A *teki'ah*, the simple sound of proclamation, usually heralds good news. The other sounds of the shofar, as we will soon see, are broken sounds. These suggest ill tidings. The sequence of the sounds of the shofar should remind man of the vicissitudes of life. This pattern calls to mind the story of the person who bought himself a ring. On it, he had inscribed: "This shall pass." In troublesome days he looked at the ring and was consoled by the inscription. In days of prosperity he was subtly reminded that this, too, could change. We blow the *teki'ah* and we rejoice over our good fortune. Immediately afterwards we hear the broken sounds conveying the sobering message that life can have its tragedies, too. But one is not to remain in a state of depression because another *teki'ah* comes next; good fortune may once again be one's portion in life.[32]

When the Torah uses the word *teru'ah*, it does not specify the exact type of sound this term covers. With proper manipulation, a variety of sounds can be produced from a *shofar*. Here, again, the Sages searched for clues. They found that the Aramaic translation of *teru'ah* is "*yevava*," which denotes a "moan" or "wail." Proof that this is the meaning is found in Judges (5:28) where the word *va-teyabev* "and she moaned" is used. In other words, the *teru'ah* is a moaning-wailing sound. But even here there can be a difference. A person who cries may make a groaning sound; he can also be sobbing, gasping for breath. It is due to this uncertainty, and to satisfy all opinions, that in addition to the single sound of *teki'ah* the Sages also instituted the sound of *shevarim* which is similar to three groans, and *teru'ah* which is suggestive of short sobs or gasps for breath.

Here, then is the procedure to be followed: First we sound the *teki'ah*, next the *shevarim-teru'ah* and then another *teki'ah*. This is done three times. The second phase is *teki'ah*, *shevarim*, *teki'ah*, sounded three times. Last, *teki'ah*, *teru'ah*, *teki'ah*, sounded three times. This makes a total of thirty sounds.[33]

The Sages went a step further. They decreed that during the day of Rosh ha-Shanah a hundred blasts must be blown. Referring back to Judges (Chap. 4), we find Sisera, a Canaanite general, going out to do battle against the Children of Israel. Yael, a Rekhabite woman, beheads him and completes Israel's victory. In the meantime, Sisera's mother anxiously awaits the victorious return of her son. As time passes, and he does not return, she bemoans her fate. She comforts herself with the thought that he will return bringing rich spoils with him. This self-centered consolation takes place amidst her lamentations and waiting. How could a mother think in terms of spoils when not only was her son in danger of losing his life in battle, but many sons of other mothers would fail to return home? There are one hunded and one letters in that part of the Scripture (Judges 5:28-29). We sound the shofar for each letter of this brazen, inconsiderate and callous moaning of an arrogant mother. The question arises: why do we sound the shofar one hundred times instead of one hundred and one times? The answer proposed is that the Jewish concept of motherhood is that no matter how brutal a woman may be to others, she has true motherly feelings for her own child. While Sisera's mother might have been callously indifferent to the fate of Jewish mothers' sons, we credit her with genuine feelings for her own son. On this account, we subtract one sound from the one hundred and one.[34]

Saadiah Gaon (882-942) gives ten reasons for sounding the shofar on Rosh ha-Shanah.

1. God completed the creation of the heavens and the earth on Rosh ha-Shanah thus establishing His sovereignty over the Universe. We herald our acknowledgement of His being King with blowing the shofar.
2. Rosh ha-Shanah is the beginning of the Ten Days of Penitence. The shofar admonishes us to repentance.
3. It is to remind us of the momentous occasion when we stood at the foot of Mt. Sinai and received the Torah amidst the sound of the shofar.
4. It is to impress upon us the importance of the Prophets, and their exhortations which are compared to the blasts of a shofar.
5. The broken blasts (*shevarim)* of the shofar remind us of the destroyed Temple. We must pray for its rebuilding and the restoration of its services.
6. We must remember and emulate Abraham's readiness to obey God and sacrifice his son Isaac. It was a ram that was substituted for Isaac, hence the use of a ram's horn.
7. The stirring sounds of the shofar prompt us to address our prayers to God with broken hearts and feelings of awe.
8. It helps us recognize the solemnity of the day and to be imbued by its sanctity.
9. To remind us of the day of the ingathering of the Jews into the Land of Israel, an event which will be heralded by the blasts of the shofar.
10. To impress upon us the belief in the resurrection of the

dead, which will also be heralded by the shofar sounds in the Messianic era.

The shofar must be blown from the narrow end, and never from the wide. The basis for this is the verse in Psalms (118:5): "Out of my distress I called on the Lord." The Hebrew word for distress is *metzar*. It is derived from *tzar*, "narrow." Accordingly, the verse is interpreted to convey that "out of the *narrow* (part of the shofar) I called upon the Lord."[35] We also noted previously that the shofar should be tilted somewhat downward. It is customary for the person blowing it to hold it against the right side of his mouth with the notion that the left side of man is already protected against his would-be accusers by virtue of the fact that he wears his *tefillin* on his left arm. The shofar will cover his vulnerability on the right side.[36]

What happens when a circumcision is to take place on Rosh ha-Shanah? On any Sabbath or other holiday, this ritual is performed after the people have returned home from the Synagogue. On Rosh ha-Shanah the circumcision is performed before the shofar is blown. The reasons behind this are:

(a) Circumcisions occur more often during the year than the celebration of Rosh ha-Shanah. Therefore, the law of *tadir ve-she-eno tadir, tadir kodem* applies—the more frequently performed mitzvah takes precedence over the less frequently performed mitzvah.[37]

(b) Abraham was the first to circumcise himself. The shofar reminds us of the binding of Isaac. It is appropriate that we pay tribute to Abraham by first circumcising the child and then listen to the sound of the shofar which honors Isaac, his son.[38]

In ancient days, the shofar was sounded even on the Sabbath Day. So intense was the solemnity of the day and the environment, that no one would dare violate the Sabbath by carrying the shofar in forbidden areas. Once the Temple was destroyed the Sages decreed that in those cities where a duly ordained *Bet Din* held session it was permissible to blow the shofar on the Sabbath day. The court could be relied on to ensure the proper observance of Shabbat.[39] When these courts of ordained judges ceased to function a decision was reached that nowhere in the world, not even in the Holy Land, should the shofar be blown on Shabbat. The laxity in religious observances among the masses made the violation of that day a distinct possibility.[40]

While the congregation recites the introductory prayers prior to *Teki'at Shofar*, the sounding of the shofar, the shofar itself is kept hidden from view. This custom is based on a Midrash (Bereshit Rabba 56) where we are told that when Abraham arrived at the location where Isaac was to be sacrificed, he stopped to build an altar. During the time that he was busy erecting the altar and until he was ready to proceed with the sacrifice, he hid his son for fear that some passerby would throw a stone and cause a blemish in Isaac, thus disqualifying him for an offering. It was mentioned several times that the shofar serves as a reminder of Isaac's heroism. Symbolically, we reenact the *Akedat Yitzḥak*, the binding of Isaac, by hiding the shofar.[41]

Thus far we have been speaking about the mitzvah of *Teki'at Shofar*, the *blowing* of the shofar. This may be somewhat misleading. Actually, the commandment requires that we *hear* the sound of the shofar. In other words, the main obligation is not the blowing of the shofar but the listening to its sound. Therefore, if one stands from a distance and sees the shofar being blown but does not hear the sounds with his ears, he has not fulfilled his obligation. It is for this reason that the person blowing the shofar recites the benediction, "Blessed are You. . . who commanded us to *hear* the sound of the shofar."[42]

The series of sounds that emanate from the shofar are sounded once before the *Amidah*, the silent prayer, and a second time when the congregational Reader repeats the *Amidah*. The first sounding of the Shofar is referred to as *Meyushav*, "seated"; the second is *Me'umad*, "standing." This means that although it is customary today to remain standing while listening to the shofar, this really is optional during the first sounding as contrasted with the *Me'umad* when one is obliged to remain standing. Some communities sound the shofar even during the silent *Amidah*.

What need was there for the second sounding of the shofar? Would the purpose not be achieved with one series of *Teki'at Shofar?* The purpose of the multiple soundings of the shofar is again to confuse man's most vicious adversary, Satan. The intensity and passion with which the Children of Israel adhere to this mitzvah, to the extent that although they were requested by God to blow the shofar only once on Rosh ha-Shanah they proceed to sound it twice will silence Satan and render him incapable of hurling his accusations. In fact, he may become so confused as to conclude that he is hearing the shofar of the Messiah.[43]

However, one authority inquires: "Is it not possible that Satan will not become bewildered after all?" The Rabbis, therefore, offer the following suggestion: The Sages of the Talmud assert that the highest level of repentance is achieved when one acts not out of fear of punishment but for the love of God. His sins are then transformed into virtues. If we would sound the shofar once on Rosh ha-Shanah, this could be interpreted as performing the mitzvah out of fear; when we repeat it again and again we give unmistakable evidence that we do the mitzvah out of love. In that case Satan dare not expose our sins before the Celestial Court for fear that our demonstrated love for *mitzvot* would turn his allegations into virtues and meritorious acts.[44]

Why is the *Teki'at Shofar* deferred till shortly before the Musaf (additional Service)? Why is it not performed in the Shaḥarit (morning service) according to the principle of *zerizim makdimim*, "the diligent hasten to perform the mitzvah early?"

The answer is found in an historical event which occurred long ago during a certain period in history, when a foreign power ruled the Holy Land. The tyrannical rulers forbade the Jews to sound the shofar, interpreting it as a call to arms against them. The Jews circumvented the decree by postponing sounding the shofar until very late in the lengthy prayer service as part of Musaf. In that manner, the military authorities would thereby realize that the sounding of the shofar was not a call to arms, but an integral part of the service. Although the decree was rescinded, *Teki'at Shofar* was not restored to the morning ritual. Instead, it was instituted prior to Musaf but was retained in the Musaf service as well. Even at the time when their lives were at stake, the Jews still found a way to perform the rite of *Teki'at Shofar*.[45]

Another important feature of the service is the three-fold prayer of *Malkhuyot*, wherein we proclaim God as our King; *Zikhronot*, wherein we acknowledge the desire of God to remember every one of his creatures, even the lowliest; *Shoferot*, whereby we reaffirm our dedication to the Torah which was given to the Children of Israel at Mt. Sinai to the accompaniment of the blast of a shofar.

At the conclusion of each one of these sections the shofar is sounded. We referred to these shofar soundings before as *Me'umad*. While the Musaf *Amidah* of every other holiday is comprised of seven benedictions—the first and last three of the standard *Shemoneh Esreh* and a single benediction in between which deals with the significance of the particular day—on Rosh ha-Shanah, the *Amidah* consists of nine benedicitons: the first and last three of the *Shemoneh Esreh* plus the *Malkhuyot*, *Zikhronot* and *Shoferot* insertions.

What was the motive impelling the *Anshe Knesset Hagedolah*, the Men of the Great Assembly in the days of Ezra and Nehemiah, to insert these three additional sections? Several explanations have been suggested:

(a) God assures the Children of Israel that if they will enthrone Him as King to the sound of the shofar, He will remember them and grant them a year of good life.[46]

(b) In her prayer to God (I Samuel 2:1-10), Hannah mentioned the Ineffable Name nine times. Therefore, on Rosh ha-Shanah, the day on which, according to the Sages of the Talmud (Berakhot 29a), she conceived Samuel, we recite nine reverent benedictions.[47]

What is the composition of these special prayers? For each section four verses were selected from the Torah, the Five Books of Moses; three from the *Nevi'im*, the Prophets; and three from the *Ketuvim*, the Hagiographa—a total of thirty verses for the *Malkhuyot*, *Zikhronot* and *Shoferot*, ten verses for each.

One opinion speculates that the ten verses of each section corespond to the ten Hallelujahs (Psalms 150:1-6). Among these Hallelujahs is one that refers to the sound of the shofar. Another opinion favors the thought that the number is to correspond to the Ten Commandments which were expounded at Mt. Sinai to the sound of the shofar. Another line of thinking is that the world came into being after God had said ten times, "Let there be. . . ."[48]

We mentioned previously that all the sounds emanating from the shofar totaled thirty. We also mentioned that during the day one must hear one hundred sounds. Now, in those communities where the shofar is sounded twice, the total will be sixty; in those communities where they will blow the shofar a third time during the silent prayer the total reaches ninety. In both cases the number is short of one hundred. To complete the one hundred notes at the conclusion of the entire service, in those communities where *Teki'at Shofar* takes place three times, totaling ninety sounds, they add another ten; those that blow the shofar twice add forty sounds.[49]

It is customary not to sleep during the day of Rosh ha-Shanah. This is a day to be dedicated to prayer, meditation and soul searching. Hence, there should be no time for sleeping. Another authority gives the following reason. According to Jewish jurisprudence a man cannot be condemned to death unless he is present at the trial to defend himself. The question arises: how can the Heavenly Court judge man on Rosh ha-Shanah when he is absent from the scene and cannot face the prosecutor? When man is asleep and his soul temporarily returns to Heaven, Satan argues that the soul of man is present, and therefore, the prosecutor and defendant can continue with the proceedings. On the other hand, if he is awake during the entire day of Rosh ha-Shanah, body and soul remaining on earth, he is not present at his trial and the trial cannot proceed.[50]

The last distinguishing feature of the day is the age-old ritual of *Tashlikh*, the casting away of sins. Although this ritual has come under severe censure by some, the foremost Rabbinic authorities throughout the ages did uphold it.

Tashlikh calls for the Jew to approach a body of water, even a well, where he recites Psalms in addition to the verses "You shall cast all their sins into the depths of the sea" (Micah 7:18-19). During the recitation of these prayers he shakes out his pockets, symbolically ridding himself of all his sins by casting them into the water.

What is the origin of this ritual? Three suggestions have been offered:

(a) Water can be spilled on the ground without much effort and become mud. Man should humbly recognize that he, too, like water can be dislodged from his elevated status and reduced to ignoble lowliness.

(b) The lesson of fish in water should have a sobering effect upon man. A fish may swim about hither and thither unsuspectingly when, with lightning suddenness, it is caught in a net. So it is with man. He may feel secure in the thought that he is not the one to sin or transgress. However, sin is a trap which can with alarming suddenness be sprung upon him.[51]

(c) A Midrashic passage (Tanḥuma, va-Yeira 22), connects the *Akedat Yitzḥak* with the *Tashlikh* ceremony. When Abraham and Isaac were on their way to perform the sacrifice, we are told, Satan tried desperately to obstruct them. He set up a barrier in front of them in the form of a deep body of water. Undismayed, Abraham forged ahead. When, however, the water reached to his neck he cried out to God that his intention of fulfilling God's command was being thwarted. What should he do. Thereupon God ordered the waters to recede and Abraham continued on his way. This demonstration of dedication and submission to the will of God should serve as an inspiration to all of us. By performing the *Tashlikh* service near a body of water, we have the lesson of Abraham's devotion brought home to us.[52]

SOURCES

1. *Sefer ha-Minhagim* p. 39.
2. *Tur Oraḥ Ḥayyim* 681; *Perishah* 581:1; *Arukh ha-Shulḥan* 581 par. 1.
3. *Sefer ha-Toda'ah* Vol. 2, p. 434.
4. *Minhage Yeshurun* p. 184.
5. *Minhage Yeshurun* p. 185.
6. *Arukh ha-Shulḥan* 581 par. 2.
7. *Minhage Yeshurun* p. 185.
8. *Arukh ha-Shulḥan* 581 par. 3.
9. *Sefer ha-Minhagim* p. 39.
10. *Ḥayye Avraham*, p. 46a.
11. *Ḥayye Avraham*, p. 45b, 46a.
12. *Sefer ha-Toda'ah*, Vol. 1, p. 10.
13. *Tur Oraḥ Ḥayyim*; *Bet Yoseph* 600; *Arukh ha-Shulḥan* 600 pars. 1,2; *Sefer ha-Toda'ah* Vol. 1, p. 11, 12.
14. *Minhage Yeshurun* p. 193.
15. *Arukh ha-Shulḥan* 600 par. 4.
16. *Minhage Yeshurun* p. 186.
17. *Minhage Yeshurun* p. 183.
18. *Sefer ha-Mat'amim* p. 99.
19. *Arukh ha-Shulḥan* 583, par. 3.
20. *Avudraham* p. 143.
21. *Massa Bavel* p. 222.
22. *Ben Ish Ḥai* p. 205.
23. *Ta'ame ha-Minhagim* p. 310.
24. *Tur Oraḥ Ḥayyim* 583; *Arukh ha-Shulḥan* 583 par. 2.
25. *Sefer ha-Mata'mim* p. 100.
26. *Tur Oraḥ Ḥayyim* 583; *Arukh ha-Shulḥan* 583 par. 1; *Ben Ish Ḥai* p. 204.
27. *Darkei Moshe* 583:1; *Sefer ha-Toda'ah* Vol. 1, p. 15.
28. *Tur Oraḥ Ḥayyim* 584.
29. *Ta'ame ha-Minhagim* p. 312.
30. *Tur Oraḥ Ḥayyim* 586; *Arukh ha-Shulḥan* 586 pars. 1, 2.
31. *Tur Oraḥ Ḥayyim* 590; Arukh ha-Shulḥan 590 pars. 1, 2.
32. *Ben Ish Ḥai* p. 201.
33. *Tur Oraḥ Ḥayyim* 590; *Arukh ha-Shulḥan* 590 pars. 3, 4; *Sefer ha-Toda'ah* Vol. 1 p. 17.
34. *Sefer ha-Toda'ah* Vol. 1, p. 18.
35. *Arukh ha-Shulḥan* 590 par. 21.

36. *Sefer ha-Minhagim* p. 43.
37. *Arukh ha-Shulḥan* 584 par. 4.
38. *Ta'ame ha-Minhagim* p. 313.
39. *Yad ha-Ḥazakah*, Hilkhot Shofar, chap. 2.
40. *Arukh ha-Shulḥan* 598 par. 10.
41. *Minhage Yeshurun* p. 189.
42. *Tur Oraḥ Ḥayyim* 585; *Arukh ha-Shulḥan* 585 par. 5.
43. *Arukh ha-Shulḥan* 585 par. 2.
44. *Ta'ame ha-Minhagim* p. 317.
45. *Arukh ha-Shulḥan* 585 par. 3; *Sefer ha-Toda'ah* Vol. I p. 21.
46. *Arukh ha-Shulḥan* 591 par. 1.
47. *Sefer ha-Toda'ah* Vol. 1, p. 23.
48. *Arukh ha-Shulḥan* 591 par. 7; *Sefer ha-Toda'ah* Vol. 1 p. 24.
49. *Sefer Eretz Yisrael* p. 54.
50. *Ḥayye Avraham* p. 46b.
51. *Minhage Yeshurun* p. 192.
52. *Sefer ha-Toda'ah* Vol. I, p. 27.

Yom Kippur

As mentioned before, three books are opened before God during the High Holy Days. In them, the names of the wholly righteous, the wholly wicked and those who are on the borderline are inscribed. It is safe to say that any man born of woman belongs in the last category. His fate hangs in the balance from Rosh ha-Shanah until Yom Kippur, the Day of Atonement. Sufficent evidence has accumulated that, during the past year, man has sinned to such an extent that he should be indicted and convicted. However, he is not prepared to give up the battle. During the *Aseret Yemei Teshuvah*, the Ten Days of Penitence, he makes a major, strenuous effort to correct his ways and tip the scales in his favor. With every ounce of his spiritual strength he repents; he will submerge himself totally in prayer, soul-searching, communion with God and supplication for forgiveness, and be divested of all other interests. Not even marriages may take place during the Ten Days of Penitence to allow man to become totally absorbed in seeking repentance. He is determined to comply with the Scriptural verse in its fullest measure, "For on this day shall atonement be made for you, to cleanse you; from all your sins shall you be clean before the Lord" (Leviticus 16:30). Man himself shall not be the judge as to whether he is clean. He is to stand *before the Lord*; that is to say: God will determine whether he has cleansed himself adequately from all his sins.[1]

Why are these days called the Ten Days of Penitence when Rosh ha-Shanah and Yom Kippur are only seven days apart? Because the penitential days begin with Rosh ha-Shanah and extend to include Yom Kippur together with the intermediate days they were designated as the *Ten* Days of Penitence.[2]

During this period the effort to right oneself with God continues without interruption. Even on the Sabbath between Rosh ha-Shanah and Yom Kippur, *Shabbat Shuvah*, the reading from the Prophets begins: "Return O Israel, unto the Lord your God; for you have stumbled in your iniquity" (Hosea 14:2-10).

How does one achieve repentance? All the great theologians throughout the centuries agree on one procedure:

(a) *Hakkarat Ha-Ḥet*, "acknowledgment of the sin." Ofttimes people rationalize that what they are doing is not sinful. Thus, the first step in repentance is to concede that wrongdoing is synonymous with sin.

(b) *Vidduy*, "confession." The second step in reaching a state of repentance is to confess one's sins. The sinner manifests his grief and sorrow over his deplorable way of life when he proclaims: "I have sinned."

(c) *Kabbalah le-Haba*, "resolution." It is not sufficient for man to proclaim his wrongdoing and transgression. What is even more important is that he must realize and resolve, without any mental reservations, that he will not revert to his errant ways.

Who can honestly make this resolution? No matter how determined the effort may be, can we truly expect man never to return to sinful conduct? Yet, although we may recognize our shortcomings, a strenuous effort must be made to correct our ways. It is to meet this challenge to man to uplift himself morally that pious Jews who feel that they may have sinned in some respect resolve that they would exert every possible human effort never to repeat this wrong. In other words, they concentrate on this particular defect.[3]

A custom that has prevailed in many Jewish communities throughout the world for centuries and which was the cause of a great deal of contoversy and apologetics is that of *Kapparot*, the expiatory offering. This ritual, which takes place during the night and early morning preceding Yom Kippur, involves taking a live white fowl, swinging it around one's head while reciting: "This is my atonement; this is my ransom; this is my substitute." As if saying: if on Yom Kippur it is decreed that I must die, then this fowl which will be shortly slaughtered, should serve as my substitute. In his magnum opus *Yad ha-Ḥazakah*, Maimonides makes no mention whatsoever of this ritual. Some of the early Rabbinic authorities opposed it because it smacked of sorcery. On the other hand, equally great authorities not only sanctioned this custom but encouraged it because of the ancillary ceremonial: when the fowl was eviscerated the innards were thrown into the streets where the birds would feed upon them. Several reasons have been suggested for this custom:

(a) By displaying our quality of mercy in providing food for the free-roaming birds, we hope that God will extend his mercy upon us and forgive us our wrongs.[4]

(b) The common name for fowl is *tarnegol*; *gever* is another name. *Gever* also means man. Hence, let *gever*, man, take a *gever*, a fowl, as a substitute.[5]

(c) Theoretically, birds sustain themselves by theft. The intestines are the receptacles of their stolen goods. Before the awesome day of *Yom Kippur* begins, one would like to dissociate himself from such transgression by discarding the innards before eating the fowl.[6]

(d) There is also a charity aspect: The slaughtered fowl is not usually consumed by the one who performs the ceremonial. Instead, he either gives it to the needy or, if he insists upon eating it himself, he gives the money value of the fowl to charity.[7]

In those communities where this practice was observed, some very serious difficulties arose. The *shoḥetim*, the ritual slaughterers, were mobbed by people who came with their fowl and insisted that they be attended to immediately. There was no opportunity for the slaughter-knife to be examined as frequently as dictated by Jewish law. Consequently, the knife might have become dulled and the slaughter of many chickens thereby invalidated. The latter day Rabbis were most fearful that with all their desire to enter Yom Kippur free of any deliberate sins people would, nevertheless, inadvertently consume *trefa*, i.e. non-kosher food. These Rabbinic authorities strove with all their might to abolish the ritual of *Kapparot*, but to no avail. The masses were captivated by the ceremonial and to this very day cling to its observance.[8]

Every holiday, as indeed every day, begins with the *maariv* (evening service) of the night before. Yom Kippur is somewhat different. The importance of the day already makes itself felt at *minḥah*, the afternoon service. After concluding the regular *amidah*, the eighteen benedictions recited silently, we recite the *vidduy*, the confessional prayer. By approaching the day of *Yom Kippur* with trepidation, we demonstrate our awareness that we are contaminated with sin. Accordingly, we confess and enumerate all our sins now, even before Yom Kippur begins. This confession may appear to be entirely out of place at this time. The Sages deemed it fit, however, that one should not enter into the sanctity of Yom Kippur before he purges himself by his confession. Furthermore, as we shall soon learn, before Yom Kippur begins, one is to eat a full meal. Is it not possible that, for one reason or another, he will be in no position to recite his confession at the *maariv* service after eating his fill? Therefore, to be certain that the day will begin properly, he recites his confession in the afternoon before the commencement of Yom Kippur.[9]

For each sin that we enumerate in the confession formula, we pound our hearts with our fist. One explanation is that by so doing a person addresses his heart with the accusation: "You are the cause of this sin."[10] Another is based upon a rule in Biblical law which states that, in cases of capital punishment, the hand of the condemning witness must cast the first stone. Since we are condemning the heart as the culprit responsible for our transgressions, we strike it heavily with our hand.[11]

It can justly be presumed that one who has already acknowledged his sins and confessed to them is morally conditioned not to repeat them.

Jewish religion, however, goes a step further than merely requiring these formal steps in achieving atonement. The Rabbis add a personal dimension that is perhaps even more important than the religious element. Every item of the formal confession starts with the words, "For the sin that I have committed against You (God), etc." What of the sins that man commits against his fellow-man? The rule is explicit: no complete atonement can be effected until not only God, but our fellow-man whom we have wronged, is placated, as well. A personal apology and request for forgiveness is necessary. This is the thought underlying the passage in Pirke de-Rabbi Eliezer (Chap. 15): When the celestial prosecutors concede that the Children of Israel are comparable to the angels of heaven, amongst whom peace and contentment prevail, God listens and forgives His children.[12] In Baghdad it was customary for the beadle to call out to the crowded Synagogue: "My friends, now is the time for each one to ask forgiveness of his fellow-man." This solemn call to friendship had a very electrifying effect on the Congregation.[13]

Returning from the Synagogue after the *minḥah* service, we eat the *Se'udah ha-Mafseket*, the last meal to precede the fast. The Sages (Berakhot 8b) add an unexpected dimension to this meal. They state: eating and drinking on the eve of Yom Kippur is equivalent to fasting on Yom Kippur. How is this possible? What is the logic behind this seeming paradox? Several explanations are suggested:

(a) Basically Yom Kippur is a holiday. Holidays are generally celebrated by eating and drinking. On this holiday of Yom Kippur, however, we are commanded to fast. Hence, the lavish meal we eat before Yom Kippur is intended to be a substitute for the one on the day of fasting. On this account the Rabbis regarded the *Se'udah ha-Mafseket* as being equivalent to fasting.

(b) When one reduces his intake of food before a fast he conditions his stomach not to feel the pangs of hunger as acutely as when he fasts after eating to satiety. Conversely, fasting after an ample meal one's desire for food on the fast day will be all the stronger and more painful.[14]

(c) The simplest and most logical explanation is that it is

necessary for one to strengthen himself adequately for th deprivation that will face him the next day.[15]

In many homes the bread that is eaten at the *Se'udah ha Mafseket* is baked in a wing-like mold. This is to signify the con cept that the intense spiritual mood of Yom Kippur makes th Jews resemble angels; and angels have wings.[16]

This dichotomy that characterizes the day of *Yom Kippur* a a day of supreme spiritual experience and soul searching on th one hand and as a festive occasion on the other expresses itself i several ways. In Talmudic times, we are told (Ta'anit 26b maidens would dress themselves in white robes on Yom Kippu and go out into the fields to sing and dance. Today, we cover th table for the *Se'udah ha-Mafseket* with a holiday cloth and cove the beds with the finest spreads.[17] Although we spend virtual the entire twenty-four hour period of Yom Kippur in th Synagogue in prayer, fast and meditation, the day is still a holi day and should be treated as such. Another reason for spreadin a festive cloth over the table is to remind us when returning fro the Synagogue after the *Kol Nidre* service, that this is a solem day and we must avoid any desecrations.[18]

Before leaving for the Synagogue, both ordinary candles an memorial candles are lit. There are two reasons why we light th standard candles similar to those on the Sabbath eve.

(a) Yom Kippur is a holiday and, out of respect for its solem nity, we light candles as on Sabbath and all other holidays.

(b) According to tradition Moses descended from Mt. Sin with the second set of the Tablets on Yom Kippur. The Scriptur state: "For the commandment is a lamp and the law is light (Proverbs 6:23). That is, God's Torah is compared to a ligh Hence, we light a candle for the Torah which was handed us o Yom Kippur.[19]

The reasons for the memorial candles which commemora the souls of our beloved are as follows:

(a) The Scriptures state: "A *lamp* of the Lord is the *soul* man" (Proverbs 20:27).

(b) We commonly refer to this day as Yom Kippur, the Day of Atonement. In Rabbinic literature this day is called *Yom ha-Kippurim*, the Day of Atonements, in the plural. The inference is that not only should we entreat God for forgiveness for the living but also for those who have passed on.[20]

Before leaving for the Synagogue both men and women attire themselves in white garments. There are two reasons for this custom:

(a) White is the color of the attire of angels. On Yom Kippur, when the Jew observes a day free of sin, he is compared to the angels.

(b) The white clothes worn by women and the *kittels* worn by men should remind us of the shrouds in which the dead are laid to rest. This should stir us to even greater efforts in prayer and repentance.[21]

Describing Yom Kippur, the Torah states: "On the tenth day of the month shall you afflict your souls and you shall do no manner of work" (Leviticus 16:29). Thus we learn that on Yom Kippur, as on the Sabbath Day, no work is permitted. Afflicting one's soul is normally equated with fasting. The Sages of the Talmud (Yoma 73b) specified five deprivations that are to be considered as "afflicting the soul." In addition to the ban on eating and drinking, it is also prohibited to wash for the sake of pleasure, anoint the body with oils, to wear shoes, and to have conjugal relations. Washing the face and hands on Yom Kippur is considered as affording pleasure. Therefore, only the fingers should be washed. Only the wearing of leather shoes is considered pleasurable; cloth or rubber shoes are not. An outstanding authority propounds a novel thought on the wearing of shoes on Yom Kippur. According to him, man began to wear shoes from the earliest time because he did not want to touch the soil which had been cursed by God after Adam first transgressed God's command (see Genesis 3:17). However, on the Day of Yom Kippur man acts like an angel. Consequently, the earth, too, becomes sanctified and he has no reason to prevent himself from coming in contact with the soil.[22]

The five prohibitions were introduced to represent the Five Books of Moses. The moral is that one must submit to the way of life taught by the Pentateuch without any consideration for bodily pleasures. Another reason: they represent the five senses with which man either observes the laws of God or transgresses them. Lastly, they represent the five services of Yom Kippur, namely: *Ma'ariv* (Evening), *Shaḥarit* (Morning), *Musaf*(Additional), *Minḥah* (Afternoon), *Ne'ilah* (Closing).[23]

The Synagogue service begins with the *Kol Nidre* prayer. Several introductory remarks about *Kol Nidre* are appropriate. In the first place, contrary to popular belief, the prayer of *Kol Nidre* is neither more nor less important than any other prayer of the day.[24] It is a declaration having to do with the violation of vows. Why is so much stress placed on this subject on Yom Kippur night? Because the day of Yom Kippur atones for every sin that man commits, except for the non-fulfillment of a vow to give charity. In view of the stringency of this ruling it takes a public pronouncement of regret and an official act of annulment to cleanse one of this sin.[25] Furthermore, speech is the human characteristic that distinguishes man from all the rest of the animal kingdom. But, if speech holds no sanctity for man and he says what he does not mean and means what he does not say, in essence he is no better than the lower animals. In this light, when one makes a solemn vow and treats it casually, he commits a serious transgression which requires repentence.[26]

Interestingly, there is a sharp difference of opinion on the pertinence of *Kol Nidre*. One opinion is that this ritual is for the release from vows that were not fulfilled during the past year. For fear of being punished for this sin we ask to be released from the vows. Other authorities disagree: How can one be released from vows that he has already broken? They argue, therefore, that the release of *Kol Nidre* pertains to vows in the forthcoming year. In other words, it is a declaration that if one should make a vow and, for one reason or another, perchance not fulfill it, he should not be held responsible.[27]

In some communities before chanting *Kol Nidre* three Scrolls of the Law are removed from the Ark and placed on the table of the center platform *(Bimah)*; in others seven Sifre Torah are taken out; most communities remove all of them.

The custom of bringing three Scrolls to the *Bimah* is explained as follows: The three persons holding the Torah Scrolls constitute the panel required for release from vows. Others hold the view that the Scrolls represent the three sections of the Bible: Pentateuch *(Torah)*, Prophets *(Nevi'im)*, and Hagiographa *(Ketuvim)*. A third opinion would have the three Scrolls represent the three Patriarchs: Abraham, Isaac and Jacob. Those that subscribe to the number seven are influenced by the Kabbalistic concept that there are seven Heavens between the earth and the Seat of God. Those who remove all the scrolls from the Ark do so lest people assume that the scrolls left behind are defective and disqualified.[28]

On the center *Bimah* at least two men, holding the Scrolls in their arms, flank the Reader as he chants the *Kol Nidre*. The reasons are:

(a) These three men represent the *Bet Din*, the court that releases an individual or a community of all vows. (See preceding paragraph.)

(b) In the Torah (Exodus 17:12), we are told that Amalek came to do battle with the Children of Israel in the desert. While the struggle lasted, Moses, accompanied by Aaron and Hur, went up a nearby mountain to offer supplication to God. "And Aaron and Hur stayed up his hands, the one on the *one side*, and the other on the *other side*."[29]

Kol Nidre must be recited before darkness sets in. According to Jewish jurisprudence no court may issue verdict at night. If the improvised court, standing with the Sifre Torah, are to release the Congregation from all vows, this must be done while it is still day.[30] For the same reason we are enjoined to arrive at the Synagogue before dark and cover ourselves in our *talesim* for one does not don a garment with *tzitziot* (fringes) during the night.

The prologue to *Kol Nidre* is the solemn declaration pronounced by the Reader: "By the authority of the Heavenly Court and by the authority of the earthly court, with the consent of the Omnipresent and with the consent of this congregation we declare it lawful to pray with sinners." Logically, or perhaps illogically, a pious person may not wish to find himself in reverent prayer in close proximity to a sinner. The religious person who has spent an entire year in total commitment to God's will may feel it denigrating to mix in company of those who have defied God's word. The Rabbis of the Talmud (Menaḥot 27a), however, insisted that both righteous and unrighteous Jews must worship together, tied by the common bonds of their heritage. They even go a step further (Keritot 6b), "A fast in which none of the sinners of Israel participate is no fast." They compare the various elements in society with the ingredients that comprised the incense offering in the Temple. One of these elements was *Galbanum*, which has a most unpleasant odor. Yet, without this ingredient, the incense would be unfit. It is for this reason that the *Kol Nidre* service is preceded by the prologue, to announce to the entire Congregation that it is permissible for all sections of Jewish society, saint and sinner alike, to join together in prayer.[31]

This prologue has a historical background. It was instituted during the days of the Spanish Inquisition when apostasy was rife. Many Jews simply did not have the courage to defy the decree of the land. They allowed themselves to be baptised. Nevertheless, they were in a state of continual anguish tormented by their guilty conscience. The only time they allowed themselves to join in prayer with their former co-religionists was when they stealthily entered the secret places of worship on Yom Kippur. It was on such occasions that the proclamation, "We declare it lawful to pray with the sinners", was instituted.[32]

The *Kol Nidre* itself is chanted three times. Each time the Reader begins on a higher note. Severals reasons have been suggested for this custom:

(a) This is analogous to one who enters a royal court. When

he addresses the Emperor the first time he is so overawed that his voice is scarcely audible. On his second visit he is less apprehensive and he speaks a little louder. On the third visit, he feels quite at home and at ease, and speaks with confidence and clarity.[33]

(b) The reason that the prayer is repeated three times is traced to Jewish judicial practice where the court pronounces its decision three times. Thus, in absolving a person from a vow the court would declare "You are released" three times. Accordingly, the Congregation makes its declaration three times.[34]

(c) Repetition lends emphasis. We repeat the *Kol Nidre* to emphasize the severity of the sin of violating vows. If there is any member of the Congregation who did not listen properly to the significant message of *Kol Nidre* the first time, perhaps he will be more attentive when the Reader raises his voice for the second time, and most attentive for the third time. While the Cantor is chanting the *Kol Nidre*, the Congregation should join in quietly with him. The reason: just as the reader who chants the *Kol Nidre* releases the Congregants from their vows, so too the Congregants release him and those surrounding him from their vows.[35]

The prayer *Kol Nidre* concluded, we begin the *maariv* services, and here something unique occurs. It is customary that after one exclaims, *Shema Yisrael* ("Hear O Israel, the Lord our God, the Lord is One"), he recites the verse, "Blessed be the name of His Glorious Majesty forever and ever" in an undertone. On Yom Kippur this verse is called out loud. Why? It is related in the Midrash *(Rabba, va-Etḥanan)* that when Moses went up to Mt. Sinai he heard the angels reciting this verse in adoration. When he returned to the people he disclosed his discovery to them, and requested them to recite this verse, but silently. This would be analogous to one who stole a precious jewel from the royal court. Presenting it to his wife, he instructed her not to wear it in the open lest the theft be discovered. On Yom Kippur, however, when the Jew is compared to the angels he has no fear of displaying the gem that belonged to the angels.[36]

The next morning the Jew returns to the Synagogue and becomes absorbed in the *shaḥarit* (morning) service in which special prayers pertinent to Yom Kippur are inserted. After *shaḥarit* we remove two Scrolls from the Ark for the Torah reading; one for the section in the Book of Leviticus (16:1-34) which begins with the untimely death of the two sons of Aaron, the High Priest, who were punished for bringing a strange fire into the Tabernacle, and continues with the Yom Kippur sacrificial service. There are a number of reasons why the death of the two sons is mentioned in the section describing the sacrificial service of the Day of Atonement.

(a) The death of the righteous, as exemplified by the two sons of Aaron, should stir us to profound grief and result in soul-searching.

(b) No matter how saintly a person may be, he must ever be alert to the pitfalls of sin. Here were two young men, priests themselves and sons of the High Priest, reared in an atmosphere and environment of holiness and yet even their great father had to witness their demise because of a transgression.

(c) These two men did not commit a cardinal sin calling for capital punishment. They had been guilty of a simple transgression. Nevertheless, they died by the Hand of Divine Providence. This is to teach us that we must not assume the attitude that some sins are inconsequential.[37]

(d) We read this portion of the Torah because it speaks about the order of worship for the Day of *Yom Kippur.*[38]

From the second scroll we read from Numbers (29:7) in which the Torah deals with the additional sacrifice *(Musaf)* of the day.

Finally, we read from the Prophets (Isaiah 57:14-58:14). The reason that this section of the Prophets was chosen is that its theme is repentance.

After the Torah and Haftorah readings we recite the *Yizkor*, the memorial prayer for the departed. Previously we indicated that on Yom Kippur even the dead are in need of atonement. Other reasons for the *Yizkor* on Yom Kippur are:

(a) During the course of the memorial prayer we pledge to donate to charity. According to Kabbalistic thinking, children can elevate the souls of their parents to a higher level of peaceful repose in the spiritual realm *(Gan Eden)* by offering charity in their memory.

(b) What greater source of satisfaction and delight can the souls of parents have than observing from on high their children absorbed in prayer and fasting and conducting themselves in accordance to their legacy.[39]

The central feature of the *Musaf* service that follows soon after is the recounting of the order of sacrifices offered by the High Priest during the day of Yom Kippur. In Temple times the Jew could obtain atonement in addition to his inner repentance through the various offerings brought on his behalf by the High Priest. This is the inference of the verse "And he (the High Priest) shall have made atonement for himself and for his household and for all the assembly of Israel" (Lev. 16:17). When the Temple was destroyed and the sacrificial service was suspended, the Sages decreed that the Jews should gather in the Synagogue on Yom Kippur and recite the Biblical passages pertaining to the order of worship in the Temple. This, the Sages contended, was the meaning of the verse, "And let us repay the steers of the sacrifice with (the prayer of) our lips." (Hosea 14:3)

During the original service in the Temple, the High Priest prostrated himself ten times when he pronounced the Ineffable Name. Today, although we are not allowed to utter the Ineffable Name, we prostrate ourselves three times as we recite the three confessions made by the High Priest: for himself, for his household and for his people.[40]

In previous times it was customary to spread out hay or grass upon the floor of the synagogue for Yom Kippur. The background for this custom is the warning in the Torah, "Neither shall you place any figured stone in your land, to bow down to it" (Lev.

26:1). Since the floors of the synagogue were usually made of stone, to prostrate oneself on it was forbidden. Therefore, the straw or grass was used to cover the stone. In most congregations today, the worshippers use mats or cardboard on which to prostrate themselves. Another reason for the old custom was to bring some comfort to the tired and aching bare feet of the congregants.[41]

The next service of the day is *Minḥah* (Afternoon Service). Yemenite Jews would return to their homes after the *Musaf* service to change from their white garments into their habitual holiday attire. This was done in remembrance of the High Priest who changed his garments on Yom Kippur before the *Korban Tamid* of the afternoon. In most communities clothes are not changed during the entire day of Yom Kippur.

Two outstanding features mark the *Minḥah* service: We read the portion of the Torah (Lev. 18:1-30) that deals with the sins of incest and immorality. This may be astonishing, but several reasons have been suggested.

(a) As we are instructed not to "expose the nakedness" of various kin, so do we ask God not to uncover our spiritual nakedness and explose our shameful sins before the world.

(b) A great many of man's transgressions can be traced to illicit sexual behavior. Yom Kippur, we hope, obtains atonement for these.

(c) We already noted that on Yom Kippur the women adorn themselves. Therefore, on this day, this portion is read from the Book of Leviticus to warn the menfolk against the pitfalls of impure thoughts.[42]

The next outstanding feature is the reading of the Book of Jonah, which follows immediately upon the reading in the Torah. Two reasons are given:

(a) Just as Jonah failed in his attempt to flee from God, so must we accept the indisputable fact that no one can escape from God.

(b) Repentance does indeed save man from Divine punishment. The entire city of Nineveh had become corrupted and God was determined to destroy it, yet because they repented they were saved.[43]

The last and final prayer service of the day is that of *Ne'ilah* (Concluding Service). The word *Ne'ilah* means "Closing." There are several reasons why this period of the day is called *Ne'ilah.*

(a) The doors of the Temple were closed at this hour of the day.

(b) This is the time of the day when the Gates of Heaven are being shut to the Yom Kippur prayers.

(c) In these prayers, pious Jews lock themselves in complete communion with God in their last appeal for atonement for their sins.[44]

The final passage of *Ne'ilah* is *ashamnu*, the confession which is recited in the silent *amidah.*

Thus in the five services of the day, in addition to the *Minḥah* preceding Yom Kippur, we make confession ten times. This is intended to atone for our transgressions of the Ten Commandments and all their ancillary laws.[45]

As an epilogue to the Yom Kippur prayers we proclaim three verses: "Hear O Israel, the Lord our God, the Lord is One" is recited once; "Blessed be the name of His Glorious Kingdom for ever and ever" is recited three times to convey that God *was* King, *is* King and *will be* King forever; finally, "The Lord is our God" is recited seven times to escort the *Shekhinah* through the seven Heavens back to its original abode after having rested upon us on earth during Yom Kippur.

The very last act of the day is a blast of the shofar, for which a number of explanations have been suggested:

(a) To commemorate the sounding of the shofar at the close of Yom Kippur in the Jubilee year during Temple days which signalled the emancipation of slaves.

(b) To demonstrate our confidence that during the past ten days we have emerged victorious from the struggle we waged with Satan. A victorious army returns from battle with the flourish of trumpets and horns.

(c) To commemorate once more the heroism of Abraham and Isaac who were ready for self-sacrificing, but sacrificed a ram instead.

(d) Before Moses ascended Mt. Sinai the second time, he instructed the Childen of Israel to sound the shofar when they would see him descending with the tablets. He returned on Yom Kippur.[46]

SOURCES

1. *Sefer ha-Toda'ah* Vol. I, p. 32.
2. *Sefer ha-Toda'ah*, Vol. I, p. 31.
3. *Sefer ha-Toda'ah*, Vol. I, p. 35.
4. *Arukh ha-Shulḥan* 605 par. 4.
5. *Tur Oraḥ Ḥayyim* 605.
6. *Sefer ha-Toda'ah* Vol. I, p. 40.
7. Ibid.
8. *Arukh ha-Shulḥan* 605 par. 5
9. *Arukh ha-Shulḥan* 607 par. 1.
10. *Arukh ha-Shulḥan* 607 par. 8.
11. *Sefer ha-Mat'amim* p. 101.
12. *Tur Oraḥ Ḥayyim* 606; *Arukh ha-Shulḥan* 606 par. 5.
13. *Ben Ish Ḥai* 208.
14. *Arukh ha-Shulḥan* 604 par. 4.
15. *Sefer ha-Toda'ah* Vol. I, pp. 41, 42.
16. *Sefer ha-Mata'amim* p. 101.
17. *Sefer ha-Toda'ah* Vol. I, p. 43.
18. *Minhage Yeshurun* p. 69.
19. *Sefer ha-Minhagim* p. 48.
20. Ibid.
21. *Sefer ha-Toda'ah* Vol. I p. 48.
22. *Ta'ame ha-Minhagim* p. 331.
23. *Sefer ha-Toda'ah* Vol. I, p. 43.
24. *Arukh ha-Shulḥan* 519 par. 3.
25. *Ḥayye Avraham* 46b.

26. *Sefer ha-Toda'ah* Vol. I, p. 51.
27. *Tur Oraḥ Ḥayyim* 519; *Arukh ha-Shulḥan* 519 par. 4; *Avudraham* p. 151.
28. *Ḥayye Avraham* p. 46b.
29. *Sefer ha-Toda'ah* Vol. I, p. 50.
30. *Sefer ha-Minhagim* p. 49.
31. *Arukh ha-Shulḥan* 519 pars. 1, 2.
32. *Sefer ha-Toda'ah* Vol. I, p. 51.
33. *Sefer ha-Toda'ah* Vol. I, p. 50.
34. *Ḥayye Avraham* p. 47a.
35. *Ta'ame ha-Minhagim* pp. 333-334.
36. *Arukh ha-Shulḥan* 529 par. 7; *Sefer ha-Toda'ah* Vol. I, p. 52.
37. *Ḥayye Avraham* p. 47b.
38. *Arukh ha-Shulḥan* 521 par. 2.
39. *Sefer ha-Toda'ah*, Vol. I, pp. 55, 56.
40. Ibid. pp. 57, 62, 63.
41. *Arukh ha-Shulḥan* 523 par. 8; *Sefer ha-Mat'amim* p. 102.
42. *Bet Yoseph* 522; *Ḥayye Avraham* p. 47b.
43. *Ḥayye Avraham* p. 47b.
44. *Sefer ha-Toda'ah* Vol. I, p. 65; *Ta'ame ha-Minhagim* p. 339.
45. *Sefer ha-Toda'ah* Vol. I, p. 52.
46. *Sefer ha-Toda'ah* Vol. I, p. 66.

Sukkot

Immediately after the conclusion of Yom Kippur, it is customary to begin to build the *sukkah* in preparation for the forthcoming festival of Sukkot which begins four days later. What prompts this haste to prepare for the next holiday is the maxim *"mitzvah ha-ba'ah le-yadekha al taḥmitzenah,"* "when the opportunity for a good deed presents itself do not let it sour," that is, do not postpone it. Since preparations for the Sukkot holiday will have to be completed within the next few days, this warrants immediate attention.[1]

Furthermore, the Jew had just gone through a great deal of soul-searching and mental anguish. From Rosh ha-Shanah through Yom Kippur he stood before the Heavenly bar of justice pleading for another year of life, health and happiness. During these ten days he endured much tension because he did not know what the verdict would be. Even after Yom Kippur, with his fate decided he may still not feel relieved because of his trepidation for the future: he has sinned and he has no assurance as to God's forgiveness. Therefore, God speaks to the Jew, "Come to me and dwell in my presence in this *sukkah* and rest assured that you are forgiven."[2]

The Torah refers to this holiday as the Feast of Tabernacles, and also as the Feast of the Ingathering of the Fruits (Lev. 23:34, 39). The Scriptures goes out of its way to emphasize the aspect of the ingathering of the fruits in order to underscore the importance of celebrating the holiday in the fall when the farmer has gathered in his produce. To prevent the Holiday occurring in another season, a leap month is periodically inserted in the spring to effect the necessary adjustment. Accordingly, the middle of the month of Tishri (Sukkot begins on the 15th) always falls in the autumn.

With respect to the name "Sukkot," we find a difference of opinion among the Sages (Sukkah 11b): Rabbi Eliezer holds that the "tabernacles" were in reality the heavenly clouds that surrounded the Children of Israel in the desert protecting them from all hostile elements. Rabbi Akiva contends that the "sukkot" referred to real booths. The Torah also provides us with the motive behind the mitzvah: "That your generations may know that I made the Children of Israel to dwell in booths when I brought them out of the Land of Egypt" (Lev. 34:43). In addition, the mitzvah of *Sukkah* is to provide us with a moral lesson of the highest importance: The children of Israel, leaving Egypt, entered the desert. They could neither sow nor till nor grow any produce in the sandy wastes. They did not even have permanent homes and were compelled to dwell in huts and tents. It was only their trust in God that sustained them through forty years of the most trying conditions. The *sukkah* is intended to remind the Jew of every generation to look to God's beneficence.

Why then does this holiday occur in the fall? Would it not be more appropriate to dwell in the *sukkah* in the spring to coincide with Passover?

(a) If it was called for during the spring or summer time the meaning of the *sukkah* would be misconstrued: the Jews stay in huts because they are airier than their stuffy homes. In the fall, however, as the rainy season begins, people seek the shelter of a permanent home. It is then that the Jew is bidden to dwell in a hut, when he is obviously doing so only because of God's command.

(b) In the autumn when man has gathered in his crops and feels elated with his bountiful harvest, he is prone to become haughty and arrogant and given to forget that he owes his prosperity to God. He is therefore instructed to leave his worldly possessions and live in a fragile hut in order to remind him that nothing is permanent, and that his success may be as insecure as the walls of this *sukkah*.

(c) In the context of the opinion that the *Sukkot* of the desert were Divine clouds the reasoning behind the postponement of the Festival to the 15th of Tishri is as follows: when the People of Israel left the land of Egypt they were immediately enshrouded in these clouds. Then followed the episode of the Golden Calf and in His anger God removed these clouds. Thrice, Moses went up to Mt. Sinai to plead the cause of his people. On the tenth of Tishri, on Yom Kippur day, he brought with him the laws concerning the *Mishkan*, the Tabernacle, as a sign of God's forgiveness. For the next four days the Children of Israel brought together all the materials necessary for the building of the *Mishkan* and on the fifteenth day of Tishri they started its construction, and showing His pleasure, God restored the clouds. Then an exchange of acts of faith took place. God took his *Shekhinah*, the Divine Presence, from His Heavenly Abode and let it rest on the *Mishkan*; the Children of Israel, on their part, removed themselves from their homes and dwelt in a *sukkah*, meaning the Divine clouds, the symbol of God's everpresent protection.[3]

From the Scriptures (Lev. 23:33-44; Deut. 16:13-17), three aspects of the holiday of Sukkot emerge.

(a) The *sukkah* and its construction.
(b) Sukkot as a Festival and Holiday.
(c) The Four Species

While the Torah is quite explicit concerning some of the details of the Festival, it is less specific regarding the Four Species (*Arba'ah Minim*). It is also rather vague in respect to the construction of the *sukkah*. Two key words will guide us through most of this presentation: *ba-sukkot teshevu*, "You shall dwell in booths." From these two words, the Sages (Sukkah 28b) derive a paradoxical feature of the *sukkah*. It must be a dwelling place with all the features of a regular dwelling, but remains a booth with all the insecurity it entails. We must bring into the *sukkah* the finest of linens and tableware, decorate it lavishly, and even sleep there. All the same, if inclement weather sets in were are instructed to leave the *sukkah* and return to our permanent homes. The word *teshevu* determines the reasoning behind all this:

teshevu ke'en taduru—"to dwell" indicates normal standards of living. It conveys that we are to live as we are accustomed to, i.e. conditions which would force us to leave our permanent dwelling free us of our obligation to dwell in the *sukkah.* To summarize the paradox, the *dirat arai* ("temporary dwelling place") *(sukkah)*, acquires the characteristics of the *dirat keva*, the permanent dwelling place.

The *sukkah* must be erected in an open space under the sky. This implies that if a *sukkah* is built indoors, under dense foliage, or under any roofing, the *sukkah* is disqualified.[4]

Two components make up a *sukkah:*

(a) the walls, which are less significant, and

(b) the roof which is the more significant. In fact, the word *sukkah* stems from the same root as the word *skhakh* (covering). When we speak of a *dirat arai*, an improvised dwelling, we are not referring so much to the walls which may be sturdy, or merely strong enough to withstand a normal breeze, as to the *skhakh.* All that is required are at least three walls that are no higher than twenty cubits and no lower than ten handbreadths. On the other hand, the rules concerning the *skhakh* are more complex. These rules are not defined in the Torah; they are *Halakha l'Mosheh mi-Sinai*, oral traditions transmitted to us through the ages from the days of Mt. Sinai.[5]

The *skhakh* must consist of material of the plant world—such as foliage. The Sages inferred this from the verse: "You shall make booths unto yourselves for seven days after you have gathered in from your threshing floor and winepress" (Deut. 16:13). They assert that the words "threshing floor and winepress" purport to impart that those materials which are associated with a threshing floor or a winepress are to be used for *skhakh.* This would include branches and leaves, trees, straw or other types of plant life. To use food products as a roof covering for the *sukkah*, however, is forbidden, because food is susceptible to uncleanliness when it becomes moist, and anything that is susceptible to defilement cannot serve as *skhakh.* Similarly, wooden slats may be used as a *sukkah* covering because they are cut from trees, provided they are not too wide. If they are wide they are used for permanent construction and a *sukkah* is not to have permanence.[6]

Another fundamental requirement of the *skhakh*, known to us through tradition, concerns its density. Here applies the rule of *tzilltah merubah me-ḥamata*, the *sukkah* must be more shaded than exposed. Furthermore, one must be able to look up through the *skhakh* and see the larger stars. Also, the *skhakh* must not be so dense as to prevent heavy rain from penetrating.

One authority advances this reason for the *skhakh* having to be penetrable: On the last day of Sukkot, we pray for rain. The question arises: Why must we wait for the last day? Why not pray for rain on the first day, just as we pray for dew on the first day of Passover? The answer is, on the first day of Sukkot when all the activities of the Jew are conducted in the *sukkah*, it would be detrimental if he prayed for rain and rain did come, thus driving him out of his *sukkah*. The moral to be learned from this is that while rain is generally a blessing, it can also be a curse, depending upon the will of God. Now, if one should arrange the *skhakh* so densely that not a drop of rain could penetrate, one may forget that rain could be a detriment.[7]

Finally, a ruling of supreme importance pertaining to *skhakh* is that the walls must be standing before the roofing is laid. This means that one must not suspend the *skhakh* over a certain area and then proceed to build the walls beneath that covering. The background for this ruling is "Thou shalt make unto yourself booths" (Deut. 16:13). The proper procedure is first to build the walls and then put a roof on. This is inferred from the word, *ta'aseh*, "you shall make," in a normal manner. If one suspends the roof and then builds the walls, he violates the principle, *ta'aseh ve-lo min ha-asui*, "you shall make and not use something already made in the process of erecting a *sukkah*." Another example of this principle: one builds a *sukkah* beneath the branches of a tree. These branches are disqualified as *skhakh* because the covering may not be rooted in the ground but must be detached. After completing the *sukkah* beneath these branches he severs the branches from the trunk and retains them as *skhakh*. This is not permissible since it violates the principle of *ve-lo min ha-asui*. When the *sukkah* was finished the branches were unfit since they were attached to the ground; the fact that he cut them off later is of no consequence.[8]

During the seven days of the holiday no profane use may be made of the *sukkah* materials, not even removing a sliver from the walls to serve as a toothpick. This ruling applies to every part of the *sukkah* including the *skhakh* and the ornaments with which the interior is decorated. The Rabbis of the Talmud (Sukkah 9a) deduced this rule as follows: The Torah expresses itself thus: "On the fifteenth day of this seventh month is the Feast of Tabernacles for seven days unto the Lord" (Lev. 23:34). It is significant that the words *Sukkot*, "feast," and "unto the Lord" are combined in a single sentence. In the view of the Rabbis who expound the Torah, the word *Ḥag*, "Feast", refers to the *Korban Ḥagigah*, the holiday sacrifice which the Jews brought to the Temple. In the same phrase the Torah also speaks of *Sukkot*. Hence, the Torah compares *Sukkot* to the sacrifice. Thus, as in the case of the *Korban Ḥagigah*, the Festival Sacrifice, one could not partake of the meat before performing the requisite preliminary rites, so it is in the case of a *sukkah*. Not until the final termination of the holiday, may one derive other benefits from it. During the seven days of the holiday the *sukkah* is considered dedicated to the fulfillment of God's command.[9] Even after the holiday is over, the *skhakh* which indeed is the essential part of the *sukkah*, must be treated with some measure of respect because of its prior sanctity. Therefore, it should be carefully set aside or burned, and not discarded.[10]

As mentioned before, the Biblical commandment includes the two key words around which the whole concept of Sukkot revolves: "You shall *dwell* in *booths* seven days." "To dwell" implies living, in all its aspects. This means that one must eat, drink, spend every moment of the day there and even sleep there in the company of his wife. However, the Rabbis were pragmatic and permitted leaving the confines of the *sukkah* briefly. Furthermore, during the short period one is out of the *sukkah*, he may drink water or eat fruit or a small quantity of bread. Also, as noted before, in inclement weather—in heavy rain or freezing cold—one does not have to remain in the *sukkah* while becoming soaked to the bone by rain, or frozen by the cold. The exception is the first night of Sukkot, when the Jew is expected to enter the *sukkah*, usher in the Festival with Kiddush (the sanctification of the day), and eat a piece of bread the size of an olive regardless of the weather. The reason for this is the comparison made by the Sages between the festivals of Sukkot and Passover. Both holidays fall on the fifteenth day of the month, Passover in Nisan, and Sukkot in Tishri. Since they have the day of the month in common, the Sages (Sukkot 27a) find another common factor: just as on Passover it is imperative that one partake of the matzah on the first night of the holiday, so is it incumbent upon the Jew at least to recite the Kiddush and to eat a small quantity of bread in the *sukkah* on the first night, even when conditions are such that he cannot remain there for any length of time.[11]

The Jew begins the celebration of all other holidays by reciting the Kiddush. On Sukkot, however, when he enters his *sukkah* he begins not with the Kiddush but with the Kabbalah-inspired custom of inviting the *Ushpizin*, the guests. Who are these guests who are invited to join him in the *sukkah*? Abraham, Isaac, Jacob, Joseph, Moses, Aaron and David. Each day, as he enters the *sukkah*, he welcomes one of these seven great ancestors.

Why are these seven singled out for this honor? The following reason has been suggested: The greatest joy that a parent can have is to witness his progeny walking in paths that he trod himself. Similarly the greatest joy an offspring can have is the opportunity to be proud of his progenitor. The most sublime sentiments of father and son are experienced when they walk together. In the case of Abraham, God speaks to him "Get you out of your land and your birthplace and go to the land that I will show you" (Genesis 12:1). Abraham followed God's instructions and left for an undisclosed destination. So the Children of Israel leave their comfortable homes and dwell in insecure booths because God instructed them to do so.

What does the Torah tell us about Isaac? "And there was a famine in the land and he went and dwelled in Gerar" (Genesis 26:1). There he experienced hardship because he was in *Galut*, in exile. The same happened to the Children of Israel as well. They were driven from exile to exile and yet did not question God's motives. Even when they enjoy a respite in the *Galut* they leave their homes and dwell in a *sukkah* to obey God's commandment.

In the case of Jacob, his father urged him to leave his home and go to Padan Aram (Genesis 28:2). Jacob had already acquired the privileges and blessings of the first-born. Yet, instead of enjoying his good fortune he went to Laban where he toiled for twenty years. The same pattern is followed by the Children of Israel. After the successful gathering of the harvest before Sukkot, they do not revel in their security but leave all their worldly possessions to dwell in a *sukkah* at the bidding of God.

Concerning Joseph, the Psalmist says, "They forced into fetters his feet, in irons was his body put" (Psalms 105:18). This was Joseph's experience when he was sold as a slave into Egypt where he was imprisoned. Yet his faith in God did not waver and his trust did not weaken. So is it with the Children of Israel, no matter how severely they were harrassed and persecuted, they remained steadfast in their commitment to God.

The Psalmist also speaks about Moses and Aaron "You lead like a flock your people by means of Moses and Aaron" (Psalms 77:21). These two greatest of Jewish leaders could have enjoyed all the wealth and prestige at their command, yet they forsook all these materialistic privileges to follow the word of God and lead their flock for forty years in a desert. Similarly the Jews forego the comforts, conveniences and pleasures of a well established home life to dwell in a *sukkah* with all its discomforts, only because God requests them to do so.

Finally, why is the presence of David called upon on the last day of Sukkot? David himself gives the answer: "The Psalm of David when he was in the Wilderness of Judah. O, God, You are my God; early will I seek You, my soul thirsts for You; my flesh longs for You in a dry land, and it is faint without water" (Psalms 63:1, 2). Even in the desert David was neither thirsty for water nor hungry for bread but for communion with God. The same applies to the Children of Israel. They may possess beautiful homes with splendid furnishings and appointments, yet that is not what the Jew strives for. Coming closer to God is of much greater significance to him. To emphasize this attitude, he removes himself from the safety of his home and does God's bidding by dwelling in a *sukkah.* Thus, we invite these *Ushpizin,* each one on a separate night, to join us in the *sukkah.* Directed toward our innermost sentiments, we are elated that we are emulating the Godly characterisitics of our *Ushpizin.*

According to another line of reasoning, we invite these exalted and noble guests as an exhibition of the supreme contribution that they made to the welfare of mankind. Abraham invited every stranger into his home. He taught each one of them the meaning of loving-kindness. Isaac was prepared to submit himself to be offered to God as a sacrifice. He exemplified unparalleled heroism and commitment to God. In willingly accepting menial labor, Jacob displayed the quality of humility. Joseph overcame the drive of his passions in the incident with the wife of Potiphar. He taught the world a lesson that man, if he so desires, can conquer his basest instincts. Moses and Aaron exemplified the concept of service to God. Without the illumination of these two contributions, the world would be in darkness until this very day. Finally, David, the Psalmist and Sweet Singer of Israel, established a dynasty which ruled in the past and will rule in the future with untainted justice and awe-inspiring dignity.

Thus by ushering these symbolic guests into the *sukkah,* we say to them figuratively, "Although the world has not learned to live by your examples, we hope and pray that eventually it will acknowledge your ways of life and come to live by them.[12]

In addition to the observance of the mitzvah of dwelling in the *sukkah* with respect to eating, drinking and sleeping there, we perform during this period the ritual of the *Arba'ah Minim*, the "Four Species." The Torah instructs us, although not with precise definition, "On the fifteenth day of the seventh month when you have gathered in the fruits of the land, you shall keep the Feast of the Lord seven days. And you shall take unto yourselves on the first day the fruit of goodly trees, branches of the palm trees, boughs of thick trees and willows of the brook, and you shall rejoice before the Lord your God for seven days" (Lev. 23:39-41). What exactly is the "fruit of a goodly tree"? What precisely are "boughs of thick trees"? The Torah does not explain. Here again their identifications are a matter of tradition handed down from generation to generation from the days of Mt. Sinai.

The fruit of goodly trees is identified as the *Etrog*; branches of palm trees, the *Lulav*; the boughs of thick trees, the myrtle *(Hadas)*; willows of the brook, twigs of the willow tree *(Aravot)*.

Why must one take in hand these particular four species? Various reasons have been proposed:

(a) The simplest answer is the fact that the Torah commanded us to do so.

(b) The *Etrog* has both fragrance and pleasant taste. Similarly there are Jews who possess the knowledge of the Torah and also perform meritorious deeds. The palm tree from which the *Lulav* is taken bears a delicious fruit but has no fragrance. Analogously, there are those who possess a great deal of Torah learning but are void of good deeds. The *Hadas*, the myrtle branch, is noted for its aroma but does not bear edible fruit. Similarly, there are people who perform good deeds but possess no knowledge of the Torah. The twig of the willow tree has neither fragrance nor fruit, corresponding to those who neither are learned in Torah nor perform praiseworthy acts. The Lord says, "Let all four species be held together so that the more virtuous may protect and complement those that lack virtues."[13]

(c) We are commanded to take the *Etrog* which is shaped like a heart to atone for the sinful desires of our hearts; to take myrtle, the leaves of which resemble the eyes, to obtain forgiveness for the lustful gazing of our eyes; to take the willow twigs with their leaves formed like lips to seek forgiveness for any reprehensible words that we may have uttered with our lips. And why the *Lulav*? Because just as the *Lulav*, tall as it may be, has only one core (spine), so the Children of Israel, too, have only one mind and heart in their devotion to their Father in Heaven.[14]

(d) Sukkot occurs in the fall on the threshold of the rainy season. Rainfall is vital for human existence: if it is abundant it means prosperity; should there be drought, famine is the result. The Four Species are especially dependent on rain for their growth. Holding them in our hands we beseech God to grant us sufficient rain just as He did for these plants.[15]

The Four Species and their distinguishing features are:

(a) *Etrog* (a member of the citrus family)—The Torah refers to it as the fruit of a goodly (beautiful) tree because both the fruit and the tree have the same pleasant taste. The biblical term *hadar*, beautiful, can also be interpreted as *ha-dar*, "the one that dwells": the *Etrog* is one of the very few fruits that for several years can remain on the tree after it has ripened.[16]

Generally, the *Etrog* has two stems, one at each end. The stem by which it is attached to the tree is called the *oketz*; the protruberance at the other end which has the appearance of a flowering bud is called the *shoshanta*, the "blossom", commonly known as the *pittam*, the "nipple." There are some *etrogim* that have no *pittam* or one that is inconspicuous. Observant Jews are divided as to which of these two types of *Etrogim* they prefer. Those who seek out only the *etrog* with the *pittam* do so because this is the singular, distinguishing feature of this fruit; those who prefer the other type of *Etrog* do so because they are apprehensive that the *etrogim* with the *pittam* may be a hybrid produced by grafting.[17]

If the *pittam* is broken off, the *Etrog* becomes unfit for the performance of the mitzvah. However, if the *oketz* was removed, the *Etrog* is still usable. The reason is simple: with the *oketz* removed there was no damage done to the body of the *Etrog*. The *pittam*, however, is ingrained in the *Etrog* and when it is broken off, the *Etrog* becomes deficient.[18]

The size of the *Etrog* is immaterial, as long as it is at least the size of an egg. In fact, members of the Sephardic community seek out only the huge, over-sized kind. If the *Etrog* is smaller than the size of an egg it indicates that it has not ripened and cannot yet be called a "fruit" in the broader sense.[19]

(b) The *Lulav* (palm frond)—it is the branch of a palm tree with long leaves lying one upon the other. These leaves converge to a point which must be as perfect as possible.

(c) The *Hadas* (myrtle)—These twigs should be entirely covered by leaves growing out three at a time from the same level on the stem. Two-leaved branches are permissible if three-leaved ones cannot be found.

(d) *Aravah* (willow)—The twigs have long leaves, with smooth or finely serrated edges on red stems. While willow trees usually grow near bodies of water, this is not a prerequisite for the *Aravah*.

Three of the Four Species (*Arba'ah Minim*), the *Lulav*, *Hadas* and *Aravah*, have to be bound together. To accomplish this, leaves of *lulav* are woven to form a sheath with two pockets and a hole in the center through which the *lulav* is passed. In one of the two pockets two *Aravot* are inserted; in the other, three *Hadassim* are placed. In addition, the leaves of the *Lulav* proper are held together by three rings made of *Lulav* leaves. The three rings represent Abraham, Isaac and Jacob.[20]

The Torah speaks of the "fruit" in the singular, indicating one *Etrog*. It also speaks of the *Aravot* (willows) in the plural, meaning two. When the Torah speaks of the *Hadas* (myrtle), it describes it in three words: *anaf*, *etz*, and *avot: a bough* that is *thick* and grows on a *tree*. Hence the necessity for three *Hadassim*.[21]

The *Hadas* must stand slightly higher than the *Aravah* when placed in the two-pocketed sheath into which the *Lulav* has been inserted. The reason for this arrangement is the superiority of the *Hadas* over the *Aravah*. The *Hadas* possesses a fragrance which is lacking in the *Aravah*.[22]

The Four Species are to be held in the manner in which they grow. For example, the *Lulav* must not be held with the tip turned downward. The basis of this rule is in Exodus (26:15): "And you shall make the boards for the Tabernacle of acacia wood *standing up*." Normally, when one erects a building he lays down the planks horizontally. In the case of the Tabernacle in the desert, the Torah specifies that the planks should be placed vertically, i.e. in the same manner as the tree grows. The same procedure must be followed with respect to the Four Species.[23]

Why indeed did the Rabbinic authorities require the three species to be tied together? The Torah makes no such requirement. And, if it is required, why do we not bind the *Etrog* to the rest? The reasoning is as follows: in the Torah we find Moses singing, "The Lord is my strength and song and He is become my salvation; this is my God and I will glorify *(anvehu)* Him" (Exodus 15:2). *Anvehu* can also be derived from the word *na'eh* which means "beautiful." The implication is that whatever Moses would do for the sake of God, he would do in an aesthetic manner. There is a certain aesthetic majesty to holding the *Etrog* and the *Lulav* encircled by the bouquet of the *Haddasim* and the *Aravot*.[24]

The *Etrog*, however, must not be tied together with the other three species for the following reason: It was already noted that sometime during the Sukkot holiday we pray fervently for the blessings of rain. Since an abundance of rain is essential for the crops it does not affect the Jew only. Accordingly, the Jew beseeches God to bestow His beneficence on all of mankind. Previously, we spoke about the difference between the Four Species in respect to fragrance and taste. This is true of the various strata found in society. There are peasants tilling the soil who are illiterate. These are represented by the *Aravah* , the willow that has neither taste nor fragrance. On a higher plane are those who are occupied with the functions of government, such as military and legislative, where a hierarchy of organization exists. Like the *Lulav*, whose leaves are graduated, one underneath the other, so are these government functionaries placed in categories reaching up to the pinnacle—the king. On a higher level yet stand the learned men of science who are represented by the *Hadas* with its fragrant but barren leaves. Since each one of these three species possesses some deficiency, they are grouped together. The element of society which enjoys the highest level of fulfilment is the one that lives a life of religious commitment and full devotion to serving God—a life of wholesome taste and a soul-satisfying aroma, as represented by the *Etrog*. Hence, the *Etrog*, the symbol of purpose and direction in life, cannot be tied together with those species that are imperfect and deficient.[25]

We are faced with still another question. If the *Lulav* is not the most important of the Four Species, why is the benediction worded: "Blessed are You O Lord . . . and commanded us to take the *Lulav*?" Since the *Etrog* is compared to the heart, why not recite the benediction over the *Etrog*? Two reasons are advanced:

(a) In the arrangement of the Four Species as they are held, the *Lulav* towers over the others and is the first to catch the eye.[26]

(b) Of the trees on which the Four Species grow, the palm tree is the tallest and most imposing.

Finally, another problem relative to the performance of this mitzvah: If we first take these Four Species in hand and *then* recite the benediction, we will be violating the rule of *over la-asiatan*, as explained on p. 32. On the other hand, we recite the benediction over every commandment while holding the object of the particular mitzvah in our hand. How do we comply with one rule without violating the other? This can be resolved in either of two ways:

(a) Taking the *Lulav* into one's hand and leaving the *Etrog* untouched. In this manner one recites the benediction *al netilat*

Lulav, "You did command us to take the *Lulav*." After the recitation of the benediction, he takes the *Etrog* and joins it with the *Lulav*. Recited before he picks up the *Etrog*, his benediction will have been *over la-asiatan*. This is the procedure followed by Sephardi Jews.[27]

(b) Taking the *Lulav* into the right hand and the *Etrog* with its *pittam* turned downward in the left hand while reciting the benediction. In this way one has not fulfilled the *mitzvah* of the Four Species because, as we have already noted, they must be held in the manner that they grow and in this case the *Etrog* was held upside down, and complied with the rule of *over la-asiatan*. After the benediction he turns the *Etrog* with the *pittam* up for the proper performance of the commandment.[28]

What is one to do with the Four Species? He holds the *Etrog* in his left hand and the *Lulav* in his right hand. This is done because the *Lulav* combined with the *Hadassim* and the *Aravot* constitute the majority of the Four Species. Then he draws both hands together and waves the species *(na'anu'im)*: three times each to the east, to the north, to the west and to the south, towards the heavens and towards the earth to show that the presence of God is everywhere. This waving in the six directions is common to Jews everywhere. However, a minority of authorities argue that God's omnipotence can be confirmed by merely waving the Four Species either north and south or east and west because if He rules over one axis He obviously rules over the other axis as well. Thus, according to this view, only four directions are necessary. The prevailing former opinion objects to this because waving east and west, or north and south, and then heavenward and earthward, is making the sign of the cross. Therefore, they advocate the waving to six directions.[29]

But what is the reason for this ritual of waving? Three reasons are suggested:

(a) Sukkot is the beginning of the rainy season. We, therefore, wave the species in all directions as if saying: "Omnipotent Father, just as these Four Species cannot grow without an abundance of water, so are we totally dependent upon adequate rain at the right time."[30]

(b) Sukkot follows closely on Yom Kippur. We emerge from a day of fast and prayer in trepidation, unsure of our fate for the coming year. Therefore, the joyous waving of the Four Species on Sukkot was introduced to uplift our spirits. This is based on the verse: "Then shall all the trees of the forest sing for joy" (Psalms 96:12). The Rabbis interpret the verse as conveying: "Then *with* all the trees of the forest shall they (the Jews) sing for joy." The trees of the forest refer, of course, to the palm, the myrtle, and the willow.[31]

(c) Another authority takes the opposite view. We emerge from Yom Kippur full of joy and happiness, confident that we have been granted another year of life. Just as a general returning victoriously from battle holds his baton aloft and waves it jubilantly in all directions to the cheering masses, so do we wave the Four Species. We wave the Lulav, wreathed in beautiful foliage, in all directions to display our exuberance at having overcome the forces of evil which confronted us before the Lord on Yom Kippur.[32]

An intriguing ritual that took place in the days of the Temple and which has its echoes to this very day is *Simḥat Bet ha-Sho'evah*, the joyous drawing of water. Throughout the ages the Jews have been subject to calumnies charging them with some form of worship, worshipping many gods including the god of water. Anyone that understands both the mentality of the Jew and appreciates the need for rain for the welfare of humankind must reject these slanderous allegations.

When the sacrifical service was in existence in the Temple, certain sacrifices were accompanied by the pouring of a flask of wine on the altar. During the seven days of Sukkot an additional libation, one of water, was poured on the altar during the regular morning sacrifice. This was known as *Nisukh ha-Mayim*. The Torah does not mention this water libation; it was a ritual that had its origin at Mt. Sinai. There are two reasons propounded for this ritual:

(a) By pouring the water on the altar in the House of God, the Jew indicated his acknowledgement that he was totally dependent upon God. Water is easy to obtain yet it can be withheld by God.

(b) Water is a common commodity: to produce it requires no toil on the part of man. It is the product of rains that are provided by God. By pouring water on the altar, the Jew, thereby, displays his humility. He comes before God pleading for rain not with pride at his personal accomplishments but with a token of water, rain drops, which he obtained without effort.

From where was the water for the libation procured? Close by the Temple area was a pool of water called *Shilo'ah (Siloam)*. The priests would go down to this stream with elaborate ceremony, draw water and bring it to the Temple. This was done every day during the seven days of Sukkot. Each evening huge gold candelabra were lit in the Temple court and singing and dancing commenced. This was known as *Simḥat Bet ha-Sho'evah* which preceded the *Nisukh ha-Mayim*. Until this very day Jews celebrate *Simḥat Bet ha-Sho'evah*, although there is no Temple, nor sacrifices nor libations. The message of this celebration is significant; it is to acknowledge the insignificance of man and his total dependence upon God.[33]

The seventh and last day of Sukkot is called *Hosha'na Rabba*, the great day of the call for help. The Torah does not differentiate between it and the rest of Sukkot; it is merely the last day of the Festival. It was in the days of the prophets Haggai, Zechariah and Malachi that added sanctity was bestowed upon this day and special rituals initiated.

During the Temple days, the Jews took an extra branch of the willow, beside those which formed part of the Four Species, and during Musaf, the additional sacrifice, they circled the altar once, holding aloft this branch. On the seventh day of Sukkot, they circled around the altar seven times. They would then flail the willow branch on the ground. Today we do not take a separate willow branch, but we march around the *bimah* (center platform) with the Four Species. One of the Torah

Scrolls is taken from the Ark first and held on the *bimah* while the procession circles it. On each of the first six days of *Sukkot* we recite different verses dealing with the omnipotence of God, our attachment to the Temple which we hope to rebuild, the atonement for our sins on Yom Kippur, our devotion to the people of Israel who observe the Sabbath, and the tribulations of our people during their dispersion. On the seventh day, *Hosha'na Rabba*, we carry all the Scrolls to the *bimah* and repeat all these verses, one at each *hakafah* (procession). All this is in memory of the rituals in the Temple.

Why is this day called *Hosha'na Rabba*? And why has it acquired superior sanctity over the other days, to the extent of being compared to Yom Kippur? Several explanations have been given to all these questions:

(a) The Court on High is compared to the mundane judicial system. Here on earth when a man was convicted for his crime in a lower court he is allowed to appeal to a higher court. If he fails in his plea before the higher court, he has recourse to the Supreme Court. In each case he hopes and prays for acquittal. So is it with the heavenly Bar of Justice, which contemplates man's destiny on Rosh ha-Shanah. Certain that he was not found sufficiently just and righteous to be acquitted immediately, one believes that on Yom Kippur one's case is once again argued before the Heavenly Tribunal. Here too, man is uncertain about the success of his appeal. So, on the last day of Sukkot, we gather in the Synagogue again and in our last quest for atonement, we cry out: *Hosha'na!*, "Help O Lord!" Hence, the name *Hosha'na Rabba*, "the day of great [cry for] help."

(b) In their Midrashic idiom, the Sages relate: God spoke to Abraham saying: "I am One and you are one. I am prepared to designate one day for atonement of the sins of your children. That day shall be *Hosha'na Rabba*. If they do not receive my forgiveness on Rosh ha-Shanah, I will forgive them on Yom Kippur—if not then, they will be forgiven on *Hosha'na Rabba*." Why was this promise given particularly to Abraham? The Rabbis reply that God said "One of my names is *Eheyeh* the numerical value of the letters of which add up to twenty-one. You, Abraham, are the twenty-first generation from Adam. I will designate the twenty-first day of the month of Tishri as a day of forgiveness. The twenty-first day is *Hosha'na Rabba.*[34]

(c) The Day of Atonement is the tenth day of Tishri. The Hebrew letter *Yud* has the numerical value of ten. Five days after Yom Kippur, Sukkot follows. The letter *Heh* has the value of five. Six days later is *Hosha'na Rabba.* The Hebrew letter *Vav* has the numerical value of six. Of these three Hebrew letters is constituted the Ineffable Name of God.[35]

But why circle the *Bimah* seven times and why did they do so around the Altar in the Temple? The following reasons are all predicated on the fact that *Hosha'na Rabba* is a day for profound religious dedication and devotion.

(a) In I Chronicles (29:11), David addresses God thus: "Yours O Lord, are the *greatness* and the *might*, and the *glory*, and the *victory*, and the *majesty*. . . . the *Kingdom*, and You are *exalted* as the head above all." The Psalmist enumerates seven attributes of God. We circle the *Bimah* seven times corresponding to these seven attributes and hope, as David did, to find favor in the eyes of God on this solemn day of *Hosha'na Rabba.*[36]

The Sephardi communities recite verses after each *hakafah* recalling the seven great personalities of the *Ushpizin* (see p. 223) who in the Kabbalah correspond to the abovementioned seven divine attributes (*Sefirot).*

(b) We march around the *Bimah* to symbolize that our prayers on this day are to pierce the seven Heavens that, according to the Kabbalah, separate the earth from the Heavenly Throne of God.

(c) Joshua circled Jericho seven times and the walls collapsed. We, too, circle the *Bimah* in fervent prayer in the hope that the walls of our sins and transgressions will collapse and we will obtain atonement from our Heavenly Father.[37]

Finally, why do we flail the *Aravot* (willows) on the ground?

One authority[38] holds that there is no rational explanation for this ritual and we are obliged to perform it solely on the basis of a long tradition. According to another opinion[39] this ritual is a lesson in Jewish history. Because the Jewish people defied God, they were condemned to centuries of exile where they were persecuted, humiliated and brought to their knees. However, it is God's design that the Jew should not be obliterated from the face of the earth. Despite the chastisement and persecution suffered through the various periods of their history the Jewish people shall survive. We beat the twigs of the willow upon the ground to demonstrate that much as it is flailed, it is not completely destroyed; so it is with the Jews.

Another reason for this ritual: No Jew, however pious, is totally free of sin. Defiance of, and ignoring God's word warrants the penalty of the law. Symbolically, one thrashes the willow twigs as a sign of the punishment one would deserve for his transgressions.[40]

Lastly, we have already noted that each of the Four Species possesses a distinguishing characteristic which the others lack. On the bottom rung of the ladder is the willow which has neither taste nor fragrance. We also indicated that the leaves of the willow resemble the lips. On *Hosha'na Rabba*, a sacred day indeed, we engage ourselves in a ritual involving the branch of a weeping willow as if declaring: "We resolve that henceforth the words of our lips will be untainted and pure, and sin will no longer be part of our lives."[41]

It is not commonly known that another holiday follows immediately after Sukkot. *Shemini Atzeret* (the Eighth Day of Solemn Assembly) is a separate holiday distinct from Sukkot. This is derived from the words of the Torah, after concluding the directives for the seven days of Sukkot: "On the eighth day you shall have a solemn assembly, etc." This day is to be observed with all the rites and prohibitions of all other holidays. The Rabbis of the Midrash (Bamidbar Rabba 21) provide the motive behind this added day of festivities: During Temple days the morning devotionals were inaugurated with a sacrifice called

Korban Tamid shel Shaḥarit. On significant days such as Sabbath, Rosh Ḥodesh and holidays, an additional sacrifice was offered signifying the uniqueness of the day. This was known as *Korban Musaf*, the additional sacrifice. During the seven days of Sukkot, a total of seventy bullocks were offered corresponding to the seventy nations of the world. During Sukkot, we have prayed for peace and prosperity, not for ourselves alone but for all mankind. On *Shemini Atzeret* a single bullock was sacrificed for *Musaf.* God speaks to the Children of Israel, as it were, and says, "Through your sacrifices during the seven days of Sukkot you have entreated me to bestow My beneficence upon all mankind. The time has come when you, My people, and I should celebrate by ourselves; just you and I. You have offered sacrifices for the benefit of all other nations. Now bring a single bullock as a sacrifice to Me for your own benefit alone."[42]

In the Diaspora, *Shemini Atzeret* is immediately followed by *Simḥat Torah* (Rejoicing in the Law) which is celebrated with great exhilaration and joyous abandon. *Simḥat Torah* is not mentioned either in the Torah or in the Talmud. It evolved in the Middle Ages and is being celebrated in the diaspora on the second day of *Shemini Atzeret* of which it is the *Yom Tov Sheni shel Galuyot* (see p. 183). In other words, *Shemini Atzeret* which is celebrated for one day in the Holy Land lasts one more day in the Diaspora. Therefore in Israel all the rituals and customs of both days are incorporated into one entire day of *Shemini Atzeret* while in the Diaspora *Simḥat Torah* with all its ceremonies are observed on the following day. The holiday is called *Simḥat Torah*, the Joy of the Torah, because on that day the Jew rejoices that he was privileged to conclude his annual Torah-reading cycle.

Some of the highlights of this day are:

(a) *Hakafot* (Processions of Encirclement)—All the Scrolls of the Torah are removed from the Ark and the congregants, holding them aloft, carry them around the *Bimah*, the center platform, singing and dancing. Children take a very lively part in the procession, in commemoration of the Temple days when, once in seven years, on the last day of the holiday, all men, women and children from near and from afar gathered in the Temple to listen to the King reading the Torah.

Children today march around carrying aloft flags not unlike soldiers marching. Just as when an army parades, each regiment proudly carries its colors, so too, in the procession of the *Sifre Torah*, the children carry flags to impress upon them the thought that we are God's army and our only battle is for Torah.[43]

(b) In the morning every man attending synagogue is called up to the Torah. Even the little children are gathered up to listen to the reading of one portion. One adult recites the blessings which are repeated by the children. This ceremony is called *Kol ha-Ne'arim* ("all the youngsters"). Some find the basis for this practice in the last words of the Torah: "Before the eyes of *all* Israel."

(c) Immediately after the final words of the Torah have been read, the reading of the first Chapter of *Bereshit* (Genesis) follows. The reason is to obviate the instigation of the Satan who otherwise may viciously argue: "Lord, behold Thy favorite children. They finish the study of the Torah and have no desire to continue with it."[44]

(d) In our thinking, the Jew, so to speak, is wedded to the Torah. To study it and to observe its tenets is his spiritual life and love. It is for this reason that the man who is called up to the Torah to read the concluding portion is called *Ḥatan Torah*, the Bridegroom of the [completion of the study of the] Torah; the one following him is called *Ḥatan Bereshit*, the Bridegroom of the Beginning, i.e., Genesis.

(e) It is customary for the "Bridegrooms" to invite the congregants and their families to a banquet either following the service or at the conclusion of the Festival *(Neilat ha-Ḥag)*.

SOURCES

1. *Arukh ha-Shulḥan* 625 par. 5.
2. *Sefer ha-Toda'ah*, Vol. 1, p. 75
3. *Sefer ha-Toda'ah*, Vol. 1, p. 74.
4. *Tur Oraḥ Ḥayyim* 626; *Arukh ha-Shulḥan* 626 par. 1.
5. *Tur Oraḥ Ḥayyim* 633; *Arukh ha-Shulḥan* 633 pars. 1, 2, 3, 10.
6. *Arukh ha-Shulḥan* 629 par. 1, 10; 631 par. 4.
7. *Arukh ha-Shulḥan* 631 par. 6.
8. *Arukh ha-Shulḥan* 626 par. 10.
9. *Tur Oraḥ Ḥayyim, Bet Yoseph* 638; *Perishah* 638 par. 2; *Arukh ha-Shulḥan* 638 par. 1, 2.
10. *Arukh ha-Shulḥan* 638 par. 12.
11. *Tur Oraḥ Ḥayyim, Bet Yoseph* 639.
12. *Sefer ha-Toda'ah*, Vol. 1, p. 82, 83.
13. *Avudraham* p. 159, based on *Midrash Rabbah.*
14. Ibid., based on *Midrash Tanḥuma.*
15. Ibid.
16. *Arukh ha-Shulḥan* 648 par. 1.
17. *Tur Oraḥ Ḥayyim* 648; *Arukh ha-Shulḥan* 648 pars. 17, 27.
18. *Arukh ha-Shulḥan* 648 par. 18.
19. *Arukh ha-Shulḥan* 648 par. 45.
20. *Ta'ame ha-Minhagim* p. 347.
21. *Tur Oraḥ Ḥayyim* 651; *Arukh ha-Shulḥan* 651 par. 1.
22. *Arukh ha-Shulḥan* 651 par. 8.
23. *Sefer ha-Toda'ah*, Vol. 1, p. 89.
24. *Arukh ha-Shulḥan* 651 par. 5.
25. *Ḥayye Avraham* p. 49a.
26. *Ḥayye Avraham* p. 48b.
27. *Sefer ha-Toda'ah*, Vol. 1, p. 89.
28. *Arukh ha-Shulḥan* 651 pars. 12, 13.
29. *Avudraham* p. 158.
30. *Sefer ha-Toda'ah*, Vol. 1, p. 92.
31. *Arukh ha-Shulḥan* 651 par. 21.
32. *Avudraham* p. 158.
33. *Sefer ha-Toda'ah*, Vol. 1, pp. 101, 103, 106.
34. *Sefer ha-Toda'ah*, Vol. 1, p. 121; *Minhage Yeshurun* p. 112.
35. *Ḥayye Avraham* 49b.
36. *Sefer ha-Toda'ah*, Vol. 1, p. 122.
37. *Avudraham* p. 160.
38. *Sefer ha-Toda'ah*, Vol. 1, p. 124.
39. *Minhage Yeshurun* p. 116.
40. *Ḥayye Avraham* 49b.
41. *Sefer ha-Mat'amim* p. 64.
42. *Sefer ha-Toda'ah*, Vol. 1, pp. 106, 125.
43. *Sefer ha-Mat'amim* p. 65.
44. *Ta'ame ha-Minhagim* p. 360.

Hanukkah

The Feast of Lights, as Ḥanukkah has come to be called relatively recently, is one of the most beloved festivals of the Jewish year and one which is celebrated almost universally by all groups and factions of Jews, even by the secularists.

Yet halakhically speaking Ḥanukkah is only a minor festival which is not of Biblical origin, one that has originated in the time of the Second Temple, several hundred years after the Biblical period.

Despite this lack of Biblical status—or perhaps because of it—Ḥanukkah is especially rich in *minhagim*, as many of its observances and ceremonies are customs that have evolved through the ages and very often vary from place to place.

For a full understanding of the rituals and customs of Ḥanukkah, it is important to be familiar with its historic background as related in the Talmud and other primary sources.

After the death of Alexander the Great of Macedon, who had conquered the entire Middle East, his empire was divided among his generals. Palestine was ruled by the Ptolemies of Egypt, after which she became a province of Syria under the Seleucids. Initially, the Syrians treated the Jews relatively well. Later, however, the infamous Antiochus Epiphanes, issued decrees forbidding the Jews to observe the laws of their religion and ordering them to worship the Greek idols. The forcible Hellenization of the Jewish masses made the situation desperate and drastic action had to be taken if the hallowed Jewish way of life was to be saved from disintegration. Mattathias the Hashmonean son of Johanan the Priest, and his sons rose to the challenge. They went out to do battle with the armies of Antiochus and led by Judah the Maccabee emerged victorious, despite their being outnumbered. Then on the twenty-fifth day of Kislev, 165 B.C.E. the victorious Maccabeans reconquered Jerusalem where they found the Temple desecrated and all its sacraments defiled except one cruse of pure oil with the seal of the High Priest upon it. This oil was used for the lighting of the Menorah and, although there was sufficient oil to burn for one day only, it miraculously lasted for eight days.

This period of eight days was devoted to the rededication of the Temple and the Altar. Hence the name of the festival: *Ḥanukkah*, "dedication" in Hebrew.

According to another explanation the name *Ḥanukkah* is a composite of *Ḥanu Kaf He*, which means "they rested on the twenty-fifth", alluding to the fact that after waging war the Maccabees rested on the 25th day of Kislev.

From the historical background described above, it becomes apparent that there are two aspects to the celebration of Ḥanukkah: the first, to commemorate the military victory; the second, remembrance of the miracle of the cruse of oil.

Concerning the latter, the question is being asked: why celebrate the festival for eight days as a symbol of the miracle, when, in truth, we should be celebrating seven days only since there was sufficient oil to burn for one day.[1] One answer is that the single day's supply was divided into eight parts in the hope that the oil would burn for eight days, which was the time needed to produce new oil. The miracle happened and on each of the eight days an eighth of the necessary quantity of oil burned for a full day. Others maintain that we celebrate eight days to commemorate the eight days that it took the Hasmoneans to reinstate the full sacrificial service in the Temple. The discovery of the cruse of oil was seen as the consent of Heaven to this rededication.[2] It was also a reenactment of Moses' dedication of the Tabernacle in the desert (Lev. 8) and of Solomon's celebration of the erection of the First Temple (I Kings 8).[3]

There is a difference of opinion also on the question as to what, indeed, was the necessity to wait eight days. One explanation is as follows: a person who became impure by coming in contact with a dead person remained in that state for a period of seven days. On the third and seventh day of that period he was sprinkled with *me ḥatat*, the water mixed with the ashes of the red heifer. On the eighth day he became purified. Since the Hasmoneans came in contact with the corpses of the fallen on the battlefield, they subsequently had to wait seven days to purify themselves and not before the eighth day were they able to produce the holy oil. Other authorities reject this reasoning because the laws of purification dictate that when an entire community is impure it may proceed legitimately to perform the Temple service. Accordingly, the Hasmoneans could have started to make the new oil immediately although they were impure because of their contact with the dead. Therefore, they hold, to produce oil required eight days because it took four days to travel to the Galilee to obtain the necessary olives and four days back to Jerusalem. Hence, the very finding of the jug of oil itself was a miracle.[4]

Since Ḥanukkah commemorates a military victory as well as the miracle of the oil, why is the celebration centered around the miracle of the oil while the military victory is passed over? One reason is the admonition of the prophet to the people of Israel that "not by strength and not by might" but by the spirit of God shall they prevail. Another reason is that in the days of the Hasmoneans the military victory was indeed celebrated with fanfare. However, with the loss of our sovereignty later, it was more appropriate to stress the spiritual strength of Israel as represented by the light of the menorah.

Why was there no provision made for a festival meal on Ḥanukkah as is the case with Purim? The underlying reason is that through the miracle of Purim Haman was prevented from destroying the Jews physically. To commemorate this event it was logical that a celebration of a physical nature be instituted. The Syrians were determined to annihilate the Jew spiritually. Conversely, their defeat called for expressions of praise and gratitude to God through total commitment to Him. Nevertheless, the custom is to set the table on Ḥanukkah slightly more elaborately than during an ordinary week-day because one cannot really enter into a spiritual celebration without some physical joy. Sephardim, in fact, do arrange feasts on Ḥanukkah.[5]

An outstanding Sephardi sage suggests that Purim calls for a feast because the danger that arose at that time was the result of God's ire against the Jewish people, for partaking of the non-kosher food at the banquet of the Ahasuerus. That danger was averted at the banquet that Esther made for Ahasuerus and Haman. Since both the evil design and its nullification were the results of banquets, it was deemed proper for the Jews of future generations to celebrate the deliverance at banquets. These circumstances do not apply to Ḥanukkah.[6]

Among Ashkenazim, Ḥanukkah nights have long been an occasion for playing cards and other games of chance. Most authorities deplore and condemn such activities as a frivolous waste of time. One game, however, is not only popular, especially with children, but it is one of the time-honored traditions of Ḥanukkah. The *dreidel* is a spinning top made of wood or lead (lately also of plastic). Its four sides are embossed with the letters *nun*, *gimmel*, *heh*, *shin*, the initials of the sentence "*ness gadol hayah sham*," a great miracle happened there, an allusion to the miracle of the oil. It is also customary for parents to distribute coins *(Ḥanukkah gelt)* among the small fry.

Two basic premises in relation to lighting the Ḥanukkah lights are *pirsumei nissa* and *le-shem mitzvah*. *Pirsumei nissa*, to publicize the miracle of the oil, is the reason why until relatively recent times, the Ḥanukkah lights were placed outside, at the entrance to the house. This was to induce passers-by to stop and gaze at the lights and be inspired by their significance. This, too, is the reason why the lights must be placed no lower than three handbreadths and no higher than ten cubits—only within these measurements does the eye notice their presence. Today, we light the Ḥanukkah menorah indoors in order not to vex the non-

Jewish population. Even indoors the light must be placed where it will be easily noticeable, near an entrance or, preferably, near a window. Indoors, the *pirsumei nissa* would apply to one's family and neighbors.

Le-shem mitzvah implies that the candles must be lit and used exclusively for the sake of the festival. To this end a *shammash* (a service candle) is placed apart from the Festival lights to make sure that the illumination from which we benefit is derived from the *shammash* and not the festival candles. Also, the festival lights are not to be placed in a spot that is used for other candles such as dinner tapers or Sabbath candles so as to be clearly identified with the mitzvah of Ḥanukkah.[7]

Still another basic premise is the Talmudic decision that *hadlakah osah mitzvah* as opposed to *hanaḥah osah mitzvah*. This is the subject of a Talmudic dispute whether the final placement of the lamps or candles is the fulfillment of the mitzvah or whether it is the act of lighting that makes the mitzvah valid. If *hanaḥah osah mitzvah*, then one may perform the mitzvah by placing an already lit menorah on the proper place at the appropriate time. However, the law is that *hadlakah osah mitzvah*, i.e. it is the kindling that consummates the mitzvah. Accordingly, even if the lights were placed in their proper spot but were kindled elsewhere or before the proper time, they must be extinguished and then rekindled as a specific act of the performance of the mitzvah.[8]

The Ḥanukkah lights have to burn for at least one half an hour. If one filled the receptacle with enough oil to burn for the required half-hour and for one reason or another it did not burn that length of time, he need not rekindle the light. However, the spirit of the Law, would dictate to rekindle the extinguished wicks as a matter of *hiddur mitzvah*, "enhancement of the mitzvah."[9]

According to the Talmud (Shabbat 21b), one light on each of the eight days is sufficient to remind us of the miracle of the lights. For that reason, one who, for example, is traveling on a train and obviously is in no position to display eight candles in his compartment can meet the requirements by kindling one light only. The more zealous observers, according to the Talmudic passage cited above, would kindle one light for each member of the family. Those who are even more meticulous in their observance kindle an extra light for each additional day because otherwise there would be no visible indication as to which of the eight days he was celebrating. For instance, if one kindled nine lights because he had a wife and seven children there would be no way of telling whether these nine lights represented the second, third, or fourth day of the festival. This distinction that the Talmud draws between the ordinary, the more zealous and the most meticulous was valid only in the days of the Talmud when the Ḥanukkah lights were kindled on the outside of the house. Today there is no need for this distinction since all lights are lit indoors and each member of the family kindles his in a different place. However, to repeat, basically one light suffices.[10]

Assuming that everyone would wish to fulfill the mitzvah in the most meticulous manner, the question arose concerning the method of setting out the lights and kindling them during all days after the first. Do we set out and kindle the lights beginning with the last and proceeding to the first or vica versa? Simply put, do we kindle the lights from left to right or from right to left? The accepted ruling is that we light from left to right.

The School of Shammai prescribed that we kindle eight lights on the first night diminishing the number by one each day, till we light only one candle on the eighth. The reasons are:

(a) To indicate how many more days there *remain* to the festival. Thus, on the first day the eight candles show that there are eight days left.

(b) There is a Biblical precedent for this procedure. On the first day of the holiday of Sukkot, in Temple times, the Children of Israel sacrificed thirteen bullocks for the burnt offering and on each successive day they brought one less. Similarly, on

Hanukkah the maximum was kindled first and with each day one less.

The School of Hillel disagreed and proposed that we start kindling the lights with the minimum and lead up day-by-day to the maximum. Here, also, two reasons are offered:

(a) It is more appropriate to have some visible indication of how many days have been celebrated already.

(b) The principle of *ma'alin ba-kodesh ve-lo moridin* applies to the Ḥanukkah lights as well. According to this rule, one must follow an ascending and not a descending order in holy matters.

As in most other matters, in this dispute too, we follow the rule of the School of Hillel.

An interesting question presents itself: Why is it that each individual is expected to perform all mitzvot individually while in the case of the Ḥanukkah lights the head of the household performs the mitzvah for the entire family if circumstances are such that the members of the family do not kindle for themselves. The answer is: Remembering the miracle of the oil by gazing at the Ḥanukkah lights—*pirsumei nissa*—is the objective of the mitzvah. Kindling the lights is merely a means to *pirsumei nissa*. Thus, although the head of the family kindles the lights, the rest of the family is instrumental in carrying out the intent of the mitzvah by looking at them and becoming party to *pirsumei nissa*. It is for the same reason that a blind person should not kindle Ḥanukkah lights.[11]

The Talmud (Shabbat 21b) states that the Ḥanukkah lights be kindled at sunset and must continue to burn for half-an-hour into the night. The reason for this is *pirsumei nissa*. At dusk , people begin to leave their work and on their way home their attention will be captured by the sight of the Ḥanukkah lights. As to what the Rabbis meant by the words "at sunset", there is a sharp difference of opinion between Maimonides and the Tur. Did the Talmud mean immediately after the sun sets or immediately before the sun sets? The Tur argues that the Rabbis intended that the Ḥanukkah lights be kindled after the sun sets and therefore the mitzvah is to be performed immediately after the Maariv service. Maimonides asserts that the Rabbis intended the lights to be kindled as the sun begins to set. This dispute between Maimonides and the Tur would apply only in those times when the lights were kindled outside and the fulfillment of the *pirsumei nissa* depended solely upon passers by. Today, however, we kindle our lights indoors and depend on our families for *pirsumei nissa* and the question of sundown should be irrelevant. Nevertheless, the custom of kindling at sunset prevails.[12]

Many people throughout the world light candles made of wax or paraffin for the sake of convenience. However, since the purpose of the Hanukkah lights is *pirsumei nissa*, those that are meticulous use only olive oil and wicks involved in the original miracle.[13]

As noted above, the Ḥanukkah lights may not be used for any personal benefit. To do so would be *bizzuy mitzvah*, the disgracing of the mitzvah. We pointed out that this was the reason for the *shammash*, the service candle, being added. In the Middle Ages the custom was to place an extra light, in addition to the *shammash*, slightly removed but in the same row as the Hanukkah lights. The purpose of this extra light was to make sure that no benefit was derived from the additional illumination of the Ḥanukkah lights. So widespread was this custom that when one passed by a house and saw six candles he knew immediately that it was the fourth day of Ḥanukkah. The fifth light was the *shammash* and the sixth was the extra light for illumination. Later, the authorities dismissed the custom of the extra light because the *shammash* served the same purpose.[14]

Let us now examine the actual ritual of kindling the Ḥanukkah lights. The wicks and oil or the candles are arranged in a row. The *shammash* is kindled and one is ready to recite the benedictions.

The blessings to be recited over the Ḥanukkah lights are as follows:

Blessed are you O Lord Our God, King of the Universe Who

has sanctified us with Your commandments and commanded us to kindle the light of Ḥanukkah.
Blessed are You O Lord, Our God, King of the Universe Who has performed miracles for our Fathers in the days of yore and in our times.
Blessed are You O Lord Our God, King of the Universe Who has given us life and sustained us and brought us to this happy season (recited only on the first night).

Here again we have a difference of opinion among the authorities. One school of thought advocates the recitation of the first benediction prior to the kindling of the Ḥanukkah lights and the second benediction following the kindling of the lights, in keeping with the rule of *over la-asiatan*, that the benediction should be said immediately *preceding* the performance of the mitzvah. This Talmudic rule would apply only to the first benediction but not to the second (or third on the first day). Others disagree and argue that where several benedictions are recited successively they are not to be separated and recited at different times. Therefore, they contend, since the first blessing must be recited prior to the kindling of the lights because of *over la-asiatan*, the others are to be recited beforehand as well.[15]

With respect to the first blessing the question arises: Where did God command us to kindle Ḥanukkah lights? In fact, there is no mention of it in the Torah because the Ḥanukkah episode occurred much later. The answer proposed is that both Ḥanukkah and Purim derive their validity from the verse, "According to the Law which they shall teach you, you shall do" (Deut. 17:11). This refers to the decrees of future Rabbinic authorities who will enact new laws in Jewish life. Since the Hasmoneans were the spiritual leaders of their day, and they ordained the holiday of Ḥanukkah and all of its features, it is binding upon the Jew with the same authority as if it were a direct Biblical commandment. Hence, when we recite in our blessing, "That You commanded us", it refers to the commandment to follow the decree of the Hasmoneans.[16]

In the first blessing, *le-hadlik ner* etc. there is a difference of opinion as to whether we conclude it with the words *ner shel Ḥanukkah* or, *ner Ḥanukkah* ("the light of Ḥanukkah", or "Ḥanukkah light"). Those that advocate "*shel Ḥanukkah*", see no difference between the blessing of Ḥanukkah lights and the blessing over the Sabbath candles where the wording is *shel Shabbat.* Those that prefer *ner Ḥanukkah* draw a contrast between the festival and the Sabbath light in that one may derive personal benefit from the Sabbath light; one may not, however, derive any personal use from the Ḥanukkah light. Hence, *ner Ḥanukkah* is appropriate because it conveys the message that it is a light for a specific purpose.[17]

Once we have recited the benedictions, another difference of opinion arises as to what we do next. Some authorities rule that the last wick set is to be the first wick kindled. This means that when, for example, we have six lights, the sixth light is to be kindled first and we then proceed from left to right. Their thinking is based on the premise that the last light symbolizes the added day of the miracle. Other authorities who recommend that we start from the first and move on towards the left are guided by two reasons:

(a) The Jewish way is to proceed from right to left as is indicated by Hebrew reading and writing.

(b) During the sacrificial service in the Temple when the priest sprinkled blood on all four corners of the altar, he proceeded from his right and continued toward the left.[18]

As we noted above, when the Ḥanukkah lights were kindled in the doorways, they were placed opposite the *mezuzah* so that when one entered the house he had the *mezuzah* on the right and the Ḥanukkah lights on the left. When he left, the Ḥanukkah lights were on his right and the *mezuzah* on his left. This was to serve as a message that when the Jew is driven out into a hostile world, the inspiration of the Ḥanukkah lights, representing God's watchfulness over him, was to be the strength of his right hand.[19]

One authority associates the concept of being surrounded with *mitzvot* with the notion that as one enters his house wearing his *tzitziot* and with a *mezuzah* on his right and the Ḥanukkah candles on his left, he is calling for "*Tzemaḥ*" (The word comprises the initials of *tzitziot*, *mezuzah*, and *Ḥanukkah.*) In Kabbalistic literature *tzemaḥ*, a sprout, is another name for the Messiah. Messiah will appear because of our observance of the Ḥanukkah lights, the *mezuzah* and the *tzitziot.*[20]

Since the festival of Ḥanukkah lasts eight days, *Shabbat* must enter the picture. Therefore, a question of priorities may arise. For every Shabbat of the year there is need for *leḥem mishneh*—the two loaves of bread, wine for *kiddush*, Sabbath candles, and the *havdalah* candle. On the *Shabbat* of Ḥanukkah we also need oil and wicks for the Ḥannukkah lights. If one is so improverished that he cannot afford to acquire all these necessities, which takes priority?

In theory, *leḥem mishneh* takes priority over all because it is of Biblical significance relating to the manna in the desert. Another reason is *shelom bayit*, the peace and tranquility of the family. When the mistress of the house can set an adequate table, it contributes to the beauty and serenity of the home. If one has sufficient funds for the *leḥem mishneh* but must make a choice between Sabbath candles and oil for Ḥannukah he should give priority to the former because it too enhances the *shelom bayit*. If he is faced with a choice between oil for Ḥanukkah and wine for *kiddush*, the former takes precedence although *kiddush*, too, is a Biblical Commandment. The reason is twofold: first, if one already has the two loaves he may recite the *kiddush* over them, thus foregoing the purchasing of wine and enabling him to buy Ḥanukkah candles. Secondly, the importance of *pirsumei nissa* adds weight to the choice of Ḥanukkah lights. Finally, if one must choose between oil for Ḥanukkah and *havdalah* candles the preference should go to the former, again because of *pirsumei nissa*.

All this is in theory. In practice, however, the ability to cover more of the necessities is broadened when we remember that basically one Ḥanukkah candle or wick is sufficient to satisfy the requirements of the Law.[21]

Although the Sabbath Day ordinarily starts with the kindling of the Sabbath candles when all work ceases, one may yet make mental reservations that he will perform some menial task for a few minutes after the kindling of the Sabbath lights. This is permissible by Jewish Law. However, over the question whether on Friday evening one should first light the Ḥanukkah lights or the Sabbath candles, most authorities agree that the lighting of the Ḥanukkah candles must take first place. The reason given is that otherwise this would be a violation of the Laws of the Sabbath since the Ḥanukkah candles could have been lit before. Another authority, on the other hand, suggests that the kindling of the Sabbath candles take priority because of *tadir ve-she'eno tadir, tadir kodem*—those *mitzvot* that are performed frequently are to be given priority over those *mitzvot* that are merely periodic. We, today, accept the former ruling.[22]

As to *Havdalah*, almost all authorities agree that at the conclusion of the Sabbath, in the synagogue the *havdalah* ritual is performed before the congregation disperses to their homes. This was intended to prolong the Sabbath Day. In the *Amidah* of the *maariv* service one mentioned the differentiation between the Sabbath and the weekday and this suffices to permit him to light the Ḥanukkah candles immediately afterwards. However, the real reason, according to most authorities is *pirsumei nissa.* If *havdalah* was recited first, the congregants might leave and forget about the Ḥannukkah lights. While the worshippers are waiting for the *havdalah* ritual and, in the interim the Ḥanukkah candles are kindled, we fulfil *pirsumei nissa.* On the other hand, in the home, where the *pirsumei nissa* depends upon the family, the *havdalah* is recited first.[23]

The Talmud (*Arakhin* 10b) is quite specific that during all eight days of Ḥanukkah the complete *hallel* is recited. Addressing themselves to the question, why Ḥanukkah should be different from Passover when the complete *hallel* is recited only on the first day and the abbreviated *hallel* on the remaining days, the authorities propose several reasons:

(a) Each day is markedly different from the day before. The day on which six candles are kindled is different than the day on which five candles are kindled. This may be compared to the seven days of Sukkot when, in Temple times the number of sacrifices brought on each day was different from that brought on the preceding day. On Sukkot, too, the complete *hallel* is recited every day.

(b) In the original drama of the cruse of oil, each day witnessed renewal of the miracle. We, therefore, recite the complete *hallel* to commemorate the miracle that occurred each day.

(c) During Ḥanukkah we read the Biblical portion which deals with the individual gifts brought by the chiefs of the Twelve Tribes of Israel to the Tabernacle at its inauguration. It is out of respect for each separate, generous donation of these heads of the tribes that we recite the complete *hallel.*[24]

In many communities throughout the Jewish world, it is customary to serve dairy products on Ḥanukkah. The most acceptable reason is that Judith, the daughter of Johanan, one of the leaders of the Hasmoneans, was taken to the home of a Syrian Satrap where she was to satisfy his lust. At this meeting she first served him generous portions of cheese which he washed down with a great deal of wine. He became inebriated and fell into a deep slumber. Thereupon Judith decapitated him and brought his head to the Hasmoneans who flaunted it in the face of the enemy. This demoralized and routed the hostile forces. Hence, because cheese was one of the factors in the military victory, we commemorate that event with dairy dishes. Other authorities dispute this reason because the episode involving Judith took place before the miracle of Ḥanukkah and in fact, is totally irrelevant to Ḥanukkah.

A different and fascinating reason is suggested by one authority: as was noted above the Syrians waged an all-out war upon the Jewish spirit and faith. Their evil decrees included those that forbade the observance of circumcision, the Sabbath and the holidays. The Hebrew word for circumcision is *milah*; that of the Sabbath day, *Shabbat*; and that of the new moon which has a direct bearing on every holiday, *ḥodesh*. The first letter of *ḥodesh* is a *ḥet*. The second letter of *Shabbat* is *bet*; the third letter of *milah* is *lamed*. Together, *ḥet*, *lamed*, *bet* form the word *ḥalav*, "milk." Therefore, we eat milk products to remind us of the destructive decrees issued by the Syrians.[25]

SOURCES

1. *Oraḥ Ḥayyim*, *Bet Yoseph* 670.
2. *Sefer ha-Toda'ah*, Vol. I p. 174-175.
3. *Arukh ha-Shulḥan*, *Oraḥ Ḥayyim* 670, par. 5.
4. Ibid., par. 3.
5. *Sefer ha-Toda'ah*, Vol. I, p. 172.
6. *Ḥayye Avraham* p. 50a.
7. *Tur Oraḥ Ḥayyim* 671.
8. *Arukh ha-Shulḥan*, *Oraḥ Ḥayyim* 675.
9. *Arukh ha-Shulḥan*, *Oraḥ Ḥayyim* 673.
10. *Arukh ha-Shulḥan*, *Oraḥ Ḥayyim* 671.
11. *Arukh ha-Shulḥan*, *Oraḥ Ḥayyim* 675.
12. *Arukh ha-Shulḥan*, *Oraḥ Ḥayyim* 672.
13. *Arukh ha-Shulḥan*, *Oraḥ Ḥayyim* 673.
14. *Arukh ha-Shulḥan*, *Oraḥ Ḥayyim* 673.
15. *Tur*, *Darkhe Mosheh*; *Arukh ha-Shulḥan*, *Oraḥ Ḥayyim* 676.
16. *Ta'ame ha-Minhagim* p. 365.
17. *Arukh ha-Shulḥan*, *Oraḥ Ḥayyim* 676.
18. Ibid.
19. *Sefer ha-Toda'ah* Vol. I, p. 186.
20. *Ben Ish Ḥai* p. 42.
21. *Tur Oraḥ Ḥayyim* and *Arukh ha-Shulḥan*, *Oraḥ Ḥayyim* 678.
22. *Tur Oraḥ Ḥayyim* and *Arukh ha-Shulḥan*, *Oraḥ Ḥayyim* 679.
23. *Arukh ha-Shulḥan*, *Oraḥ Ḥayyim* 681.
24. *Tur Oraḥ Ḥayyim* and *Bet Yoseph* 683.
25. *Ben Ish Ḥai* p. 44.

Tu Bi-Shevat

In some Anglo-Saxon countries, particularly in the United States, the fifteenth day of the month of Shevat has been called Arbor Day. Arbor Day is usually identified with planting trees and as applied to *Tu bi-Shevat* (fifteenth day of the month of Shevat) it is a misnomer: *Tu bi-Shevat* has little, if anything, to do with planting trees.

What then is the significance of *Tu bi-Shevat*?

In the first Mishnah of Tractate Berakhot we are told of four different occasions in the Jewish calendar that are called *Rosh ha-Shanah*, the beginning of a new year.

(a) *The first day of the month of Nisan.* This day was identified as the anniversary of the coronation of the king. In other words, if a king was crowned in Adar, the month preceding Nisan, his reign was deemed to have started its second year on the first day of Nisan although he had reigned for only one month. This was necessary for the purpose of dating in various legal documents.

(b) *The first day of Elul.* Everyone who had ten new animals born among his flock during the year had to set aside one as a tithe to be sacrificed in the Temple. When did the year start and when did it end? The year for the tithe of animals was reckoned from the first day of the month of Elul. The tithing, therefore, applied to the animals born from that date until the end of the month of Av.

(c) *The first of Tishri.* The Biblical regulations of the *Shemittah* and Jubilee years took effect from the first of the month of Tishri. Transcending the practical importance of this day, the first day of Tishri has become the *Rosh ha-Shana* par excellence since according to the teaching of the Rabbis in that same mishnah this is the day on which every human being passes before the Lord as sheep before the shepherd and has his destiny determined for the coming year. Tradition has it that this day is the birthday of the world, the anniversary of the sixth day of Creation.

(d) *Fifteen of Shevat (Tu bi-Shevat).* The fruits of the trees, too, are subject to the laws of tithing. What constitutes the fiscal year for the tithing of the fruits of the trees? The year ran from the fifteenth day of Shevat until the middle of Tevet. This is the true significance of *Tu bi-Shevat.* We can see, therefore, that this day is in no way related to Arbor Day.

Of these four *Rosh ha-Shanahs,* the first two have no practical significance today. The other two, the first of Tishri which is the popular *Rosh ha-Shanah* and *Tu bi-Shevat* are celebrated with numerous customs and ceremonies, more for the first of Tishri and less for *Tu bi-Shevat.* The *Rosh ha-Shana* proper, being the Day of Judgement, is one of the most solemn holidays of the year as it concerns the welfare of the individual as well as of mankind. *Tu bi-Shevat* as the New Year of the trees symbolizes the Jew's profound concern about his homeland, its trees and fruits.[1]

The Jew in his sensitivity to everything created by God imagines that, just as the human being on *his Rosh ha-Shanah* beseeches God to grant him a year of fruitfulness, health and success so, indeed, do the trees, in their own inexplicable way, pray to God for the same beneficence. And just as man on *his Rosh ha-Shanah* trusts that God has granted *him* his wishes, so he is happy in his trust that God has granted the trees and their fruits another year of fruitfulness on *their* New Year day.[2]

Ashkenazi Jews celebrate *Tu bi-Shevat* by partaking of fruits that grow in Israel. Also, in the synagogue service, memorial prayers and *Nefilat Appayim* are omitted. Sephardi Jews remain awake through the night of *Tu bi-Shevat* and study all the Biblical, Talmudic and Kabbalistic sources related to the fruits of the land. They stop briefly at intervals, each time to eat a different fruit and then continue with their studies. They particularly stress the idea propounded by the books of the Kabbalah that when a Jew offers the proper blessing and then partakes of the fruit, he saves that fruit from falling into decay, contrary to the purpose of God's creation.[3]

On *Tu bi-Shevat* 1915 a group of teachers in Jerusalem took their students to Motza where each planted a tree in honor of the day.[4] Perhaps this is the origin of the contemporary custom of planting trees on this day by the school children of Israel.

SOURCES

1. *Sefer Ha-Toda'ah* p. 213.
2. Ibid.
3. *Sefer Eretz Yisrael* p. 59.
4. *Otzar Yisrael*, Vol X p. 34.

Purim

The historical background of Purim is to be found in *Megillat Esther* (the Scroll of Esther) in the Bible. The Festival does not begin as a happy occasion; we make a practice of fasting on the day before Purim—*Ta'anit Esther*—because, in the story, Esther asked the Jewish people to fast, out of sympathy for her, for three days before she risked her life by entering the King's audience-chamber.[1] We should remember, however, that *Ta'anit Esther* does not occur on the actual date of the fast as it was instituted by Esther. What we do is merely a symbolic evocation of the Fast that Esther underwent with the Jews of her time. The original Fast of Esther occurred in the month of Nissan, eleven months before the month of Adar when the deliverance of Purim took place. We could ask: even if our fast today is only symbolic, why do we fast only one, and not three days as the Jews did in the days of Esther? Because of their critical situation, the Jews at that time were intensely motivated and could fast for three days. Even nowadays, some very religious people fast for three days, not one after the other, but one day each week, for the three weeks before the Festival.

When Purim falls on Sunday, we do not fast on the day before because it is a Sabbath. The fast is observed instead on the previous Thursday. Two reasons are given as to why we do not fast on Friday.

(a) Even the preparation for the Sabbath on Friday is characterized by joy. Obviously, fasting has no place in the household that is happily busy with the preparations for the Sabbath.

(b) If people were to fast and spend additional time in prayer and study, they would have little time and strength left for the preparation of the Sabbath.[2]

The Soferim, the group of Sages that lived from the time of Ezra to the beginning of the Tannaitic period, issued the ruling that the *Megillah*, the Book of Esther, must be read on the evening of Purim which, as we will soon see, falls either on the fourteenth or fifteenth of Adar, and reread the next morning. The reason why it is read twice is to be in line with the proclamation of the Psalmist, "So that my glorious soul may sing praise to You, and never be silent. O Lord my God, *forever* will I give thanks to You"(Psalms 30:13). To encapsulate *forever* in a period of one day, we must read the *Megillah* both during the night and in the daytime. The Sages characterize the *Megillah* as *Hodayah*, a book of thanksiving, in keeping with the words "Forever will I give *thanks* to You." It is because the *Megillah* has been considered the equivalent of thanksgiving and praise that *Hallel*, which is usually said on every festive occasion, is omitted on Purim. In other words, the *Megillah* takes the place of the *Hallel*.

To stress the importance of reading the *Megillah*, the Rabbis ruled that even the Jew whose whole time was occupied with Torah study, and the Priests who performed the sacrificial services had to stop what they were doing for the sake of the reading of the *Megillah*. This decision stems from the verse "In the multitude of people is the King's glory" (Proverbs 14:28). This means that we must thank God for the deliverance of Purim when many people are present, so as to give the event due publicity.

There is only one exception to this rule: When one comes across an abandoned corpse, one must put aside whatever one is doing, no matter how important it may be, and occupy oneself with the arrangements for burial. This duty is called a *Met Mitzvah*, which takes precedence even over the reading of the *Megillah*. The other *Mitzvot*, however, are only to be postponed until after the *Megillah* reading if there will still be time to perform them later. If a priest has to make the choice between listening to the *Megillah* and, for example, performing his Temple service, he has to forego the Mitzvah of *Megillah.* The basis for this is the fact that the practice of reading the *Megillah* is Rabbinic, and the other *Mitzvot* Biblical in origin. Under ordinary circumstances, a Rabbinic decree cannot invalidate a Biblical Mitzvah.[3]

The *Megillah* (9:19-31) lists the four ways in which the Jew observes Purim:

(a) Reading the *Megillah.*

(b) Giving charity *(mattanot la-evyonim).*

(c) The giving of gifts of food to others *(mishloaḥ manot).*

(d) The Festive Meal *(Purim se'udah).*

In the *Megillah* we find that a distinction is made between the way the Jews living in walled or unwalled cities celebrated Purim. So the Rabbis of the Talmud later laid it down that in cities that had had walls since the time of Joshua Purim was to be celebrated on the fifteenth day of the month of Adar, and in all other cities on the fourteenth.

In the city of Shushan (in Persia) Purim is celebrated today on the fifteenth of Adar, yet it was not a walled city in the time of Joshua. Nevertheless, because the main events described in the Book of Esther occurred in Shushan, it is honored by being considered a walled city, thus putting it in the same category as Jerusalem. The question then springs to mind as to why the time of Joshua is specifically mentioned? Why not simply date back to the days of Mordecai and Esther? It was Joshua who began the intensive drive to annihilate Amalek, and according to tradition, Haman was a descendant of Amalek.[4] If the *Megillah* is so insistent that we make a difference between walled and open cities, patriotism dictates that Jerusalem should at least have the same status as Shushan. This is why it is necessary to go back to the days of Joshua when Jerusalem was a walled city. In cities, however, such as Tiberias, which may or may not have had walls in the days of Joshua, Purim is celebrated both on the fourteenth and the fifteenth of Adar. Cities that are currently open but were walled during the days of Joshua are viewed as if they still have walls today.

During the Jewish leap year, when there is an extra month of Adar, Purim is celebrated on Adar II.[5]

There are five *Megillot* (Scrolls) in the Bible: The Song of Songs, Ruth, Lamentations, Ecclesiastes and Esther. Yet, when people speak of *the Megillah*, they are always talking about the Book of Esther. The fact is that in the narrative itself the event of Purim is referred to both as *Sefer*, "Scroll," as in *Sefer Torah* (Esther 9:32), and *Igeret*, "letter" (ibid. 9:29). This is why a kosher *Megillah* must be written on parchment and in the same script as a Torah Scroll, but when it is read it must be folded like a letter (*Igeret*), to fit both descriptions.

Since this dramatic story was intended not only for the intellectuals, but for a mass audience, one might think that the *Megillah* could be translated into any language which can be understood by both the reader and the audience. However, this is not so; the *Megillah* can only be read in Hebrew. There are several reasons for this:

(a) *Trop*—the musical notations attached to the Hebrew words and dictating the melody. No other language would fit this particular tune.

(b) The Rabbis simply did not want the *Megillah* to be debased into a conglomerate of several languages.

Providing that he reads from a kosher *Megillah*, everybody may quietly join in with the reader; however, if he is reciting by heart, or reading from a text that does not meet the requirements of a kosher *Megillah*, he may not read aloud. This is why, when it is the custom for the congregation to read several verses aloud themselves, the reader must repeat them after the voices of the people have died away, since many in the congregation may not have read them from kosher *Megillot*.

When the reader and the congregation following him reach

that point in the story that deals with the hanging of the ten sons of Haman, the ten names must be recited in a single breath. This custom stems from the Talmud (Megillah 16b), "Even in our recitation Haman and his ten sons should be exterminated at one time, [i.e. in one breath] so that we may comply with the words in the Bible: 'May the sinners die out from the earth, and the wicked be no more.'" (Psalms: 104:35)

In different Jewish communities throughout the world, to maintain the interest of the young, the congregation used to join with the reader in reciting several verses from the *Megillah* aloud. The verses usually so treated are: 2:5; 8:15-16; 10:3.

In Yemenite congregations the community usually joins the reader in reciting the verse: "So they hanged Haman . . . " (Esther 7:10). The reason for this is that the five-fold expression of redemption used with reference to the exodus from Egypt was compared to the terms used in the redeeming of the Jews from the plots of Haman.[6]

There are various small gadgets used in the synagogue on Purim, to make noise whenever the name of Haman is mentioned. These used to be flat stones or wooden paddles, on which the word "Haman" was inscribed. By pounding them together the word would be erased in a short time. The source of this custom is the Biblical verse: "For I will utterly blot out the remembrance of Amalek from under the Heavens" (Exodus 17:14). Haman's ancestors were the Amalekites. The Talmud (Soferim 14:18) rejects all customs that have no Biblical foundation. Most other authorities agree that if a custom gains currency in Jewish life, there must be some rationale behind it. Therefore, the modern noisemakers that do not have the name of Haman inscribed on them, are not disapproved of. The later authorities were, however, of the opinion that if the noisemakers interfered with concentration on the *Megillah*, it was better that it should be read in a private home in the presence of only a *minyan*, even if that was contrary to the maxim, "In the multitude of people is the King's glory" (Proverbs 14:28).[7]

In Yemenite communities noisemakers were forbidden because they were considered contrary to the synagogue decorum.[8]

Before beginning the *Megillah* the reader recites three benedictions.

(a) *Barukh Attah . . . al mikrah Megillah*—"Blessed are You . . . concerning the reading of the *Megillah*."

(b) *Barukh Attah . . . she'asah nisim la—avotenu bayamim hahem bazeman hazeh*—"Blessed are You . . . Who wrought miraculous deliverances for our fathers in days of old and this season."

(c)*Barukh Attah . . . she'heḥeyanu ve-kiyemanu ve-higianu la-zeman ha-zeh.* "Blessed are You . . . Who has kept us alive and preserved and brought us to this season."

These benedictions are recited before both the evening and the morning readings. When anything new enters the yearly cycle of Jewish life, it is marked by the *she'heḥeyanu* benediction. For example, when we purchase a new garment, when a child is born, a new Festival welcomed, a new fruit eaten, we say the blessing. It follows then, that each year when we read the *Megillah*, we should recite the *she'heḥeyanu*. However, the authorities are divided as to whether this blessing is necessary for the morning reading of the *Megillah*, or whether, since we have already welcomed in the Festival with this blessing the evening before, there is no longer any need for it to be recited again in the morning. Maimonides holds this latter view, but later authorities argue that since the major features of Purim, such as the festive meal, the special food gifts to friends, and money gifts to the poor are carried out during the day, these call for an additional *she'heḥeyanu* to be said at the reading of the *Megillah* in the morning which will also cover the other features of the day. The custom today is to follow the opinion of the latter authorities, and say the blessing both times.

An interesting question arises in connection with the first benediction: ". . . and has commanded us concerning the *reading* of the *Megillah.*" Several authorities ask why we do not end with the words *lishmo'a mikra Megillah*, "to *listen* to the reading of the *Megillah*," since everyone in the congregation, except for the reader, is *listening* and not reading. Should not the *Megillah* be compared to the Shofar where the benediction is, *lishmo'a kol shofar*, "to *listen* to the sound of the Shofar"? The answer given is that, in case of the Shofar, the *sound* is of main importance and if the sound produced by the Shofar cannot be clearly heard, one has not fulfilled the mitzvah of the Shofar. This is why *listening* is stressed. In the case of the *Megillah*, the important factor is *reading* and if one does not hear the reader but reads the *Megillah* for oneself, one has fulfilled the requirements of the mitzvah.

As we noted before, *Hallel* (Psalms 113-117) is not recited on Purim because the Book of Esther is one long continuous expression of God's praise. This is strange in view of the fact that every major holiday and festival in the Jewish calendar calls for the recitation of the Hallel during the synagogue service. Why should Purim be different? The answer that is given is based on a Talmudic passage (Megillah 14a) where one of the Sages reasons that in one of the psalms of Hallel we say, "Bless you, the servants of the *Lord.*" Since the destruction of the Temple we are not servants of God, but of Ahasuerus. In other words, physically we may be free but spiritually we are still subject to foreign influences.[9]

If, according to *Halakhah*, the *Megillah* is equivalent to Hallel, can a person who has no *Megillah* recite the Hallel in its stead? The authorities are divided about this.[10]

When Purim falls on Sunday, the preceeding night two obligations arise simultaneously: *Havdalah* and the *Megillah*. Which takes precedence? Here too, there is a difference of opinion. Several authorities maintain that *Havdalah* should be recited first and the *Megillah* read afterwards because otherwise we would enjoy the benefit of the light without first saying the *Havdalah* prayer. Others say that the prayers referring to light recited before the end of the Sabbath are enough to express our gratitude to God for the blessing of light, and that therefore the *Megillah* should precede the *Havdalah*. In most Jewish communities today the *Megillah* takes precedence. There are two reasons for this:

(a) After listening to the *Havdalah* service in the synagogue one must recite it again at home so that the whole family can hear it. So, if one will eventually have to fulfill the mitzvah of *Havdalah* again at home in any case, why this duplication which would cause unnecessary postponement of the reading of the *Megillah*.

(b) The Sages have always urged us to extend the Sabbath as long as possible. Reading the *Megillah* first is a good pretext for doing this.[11]

Tefillin should be worn during the reading of the *Megillah* at the *shaḥarit* service. The basis for this is the verse, "For the Jews there was light, with joy and gladness and honor" (Esther 8:16). *Vi(ye)kor* is the Hebrew world for "honor." the Sages interpreted this word to mean *tefillin*, as they are the Jew's badge of honor. Therefore, when the Jew recalls what his ancestors experienced in Persia, he keeps wearing his *tefillin*.[12]

We have already noted that the second feature of the Purim celebration is the distribution of money-gifts among the poor. This is based upon the passage (Esther 9:22) in which we are told that the Jews in those days celebrated their victory over Haman by distributing gifts to those in need. The Hebrew word for "poor," *evyonim*, is in the plural. This is the basis for the ruling that money must be given to at least *two* poor people. Also, because the Bible uses the general term "poor," it is all right to fulfill this *mitzvah* by giving money to non-Jews. Who receives the money is of secondary importance; the giving is what is essential. If one gives a money gift to a husband and wife, it counts as if he had helped only one person. So important is the emphasis on these money-gifts that, if necessary, one must reduce one's expenditure on the *Se'udah*, in order to give generously to the poor.

The purpose of these gifts is that the poor enjoy a festive meal—the recipient is not, therefore, allowed to squander the aid given him on anything else, but can only spend it on the Purim meal.

In addition to distributing alms to the poor, it is obligatory to perform the ritual of *Maḥatzit ha-Shekel.* In the Torah (Exodus 30:11-16) we are commanded that every Jew, from the age of twenty and upwards, contribute a *half-shekel* once a year to the Temple towards the cost of the public sacrifices. The Sages of the Talmud (Shekalim I) instituted that these contributions were to be made during the month of Adar, the month in which we celebrate Purim. As a remembrance of the half-shekels that were brought to the Temple, Jews still donate similar amounts to a special charitable fund. To keep alive the idea of the *half*-shekel, later authorities suggested that although their comparative values may differ, the monetary unit normally designated as "half" should be used: for example, half a dollar, half an Israeli lira, half a pound sterling. Since, in treating this subject, the Torah employs the word half-shekel three times, we, too, give three coins which are the equivalent of these. However, the Biblical restriction on this obligation to those twenty years old and above is not carried out strictly; even children are taught to give.

Also, in the chapter dealing with the half-shekel the Torah uses the term *over al ha-pekudim*, to show that all Jews had to be accounted for. Since *over* and *ubar* (embryo) have the same spelling, this prompted Rabbi Moses Isserles, author of the glosses on R. Joseph Karo's *Shulḥan Arukh* to interpret the verse to mean that a woman who was with child should also make her Purim contribution. This donation of *Maḥatzit ha-shekel* is made just before the reading of the *Megillah.*[13]

From the same verse (Esther 9:22) we learn that Purim at the time was celebrated by the sending of food gifts to friends. The actual Hebrew phrase is *mishloaḥ manot ish le-re'ehu. Manot* is the plural form of *manah* meaning food portion. So, the gift must consist of two different kinds of foods. *Ish le-re'ehu* "one to another," suggest that to send to one person alone is enough. This sending of food gifts to friends is also a specific feature of the *day* of *Purim*, with the emphasis placed on the word *day*. The authorities are divided as to whether this law has been fulfilled if the parcels of food are sent a long time before Purim even if they arrive on the day of Purim. The question is whether this ritual takes effect at the same time the food gift is sent, or when it is received.[14]

The question is asked: why do we not recite a blessing before performing this mitzvah as we do over all other *mitzvot*? An answer suggested for this is that one may think that the recipient is a friend when in fact he is not. This would cause the blessing to be in vain.[15] Again, the idea of reading the story of Esther on Purim, and that of distributing money to the poor, and the festivities during the day are all understandable. But, what need is there for the sending of gifts to friends? What is there about Purim that would especially warrant this custom? Two reasons have been suggested:

(a) In the Book of Esther (9:16) we are told that the victory of the Jews over Haman was partly due to "the remaining Jews that were in the King's provinces rallying *together* and standing up for themselves and procuring rest from their enemies." It was the solidarity of the Jews that helped to vanquish Haman. We therefore send gifts to one another to indicate that we are still a people united by a common bond.

(b) A second reason is a characteristically ethical one. We send gifts to each other to show that no one person can live completely by himself, nor achieve his goals all by himself. No matter how self-sufficient he may be, he must inevitably depend upon others in society.[16]

The last of the four features of Purim is the enjoyment of festive food and drink. The obligation to have the *Se'udah*, too, stems from the same passage (Esther 9:22); "To make them days of entertainment and joy," which the Sages interpret to mean to eat and drink. In the Talmud, the Rabbis even seem to imply that it is a mitzvah to drink intoxicating liquor till one can no longer distinguish between praising Mordecai and cursing Haman, the hero and villain of the story. In Hebrew this is called *ad de-lo yada*. Is such intoxication in keeping with the spirit of the Jewish religion? Although a few Rabbis have no qualms about advocating complete intoxication on this one occasion, most are not quite so emphatic on this point, and have the following suggestions to make as to how to fulfill the *ad de-lo yada:*

(a) Maimonides and R. Moses Isserles propose that one should drink enough liquor or wine to become mellow and sleepy. In this state of oblivion, one would be unconscious of the difference between blessing Mordecai and cursing Haman.

(b) In the days of the Talmud it was the custom on Purim to recite a very long poem that ended with the words, "Cursed be Haman and blessed be Mordecai." So if a person drank even a little more than he was accustomed to, even though he had not become completely intoxicated, it would be difficult for him to recite the poem till the end. Hence, *ad de-lo yada* would imply that he did not know how to read that poem to the final words, "Blessed be Mordecai and cursed be Haman."

(c) The Rabbis did not mean that one was to become so drunk as not to know which of the two, Haman or Mordecai, deserved to be blessed or cursed. They were only suggesting that one should be in such a mental state that one would not be too clear about the issue.

(d) One should drink *ad de-lo yada*, until one was *approaching* the point when he could no longer distinguish between Mordecai and Haman, but not up to and beyond it.[17]

Although Purim is a minor and not a major holiday, it is not really in keeping with the spirit of the festival to do manual work; nor are funerary eulogies or mourning permitted. Weddings, however, are permitted on Purim because of the overriding importance of the first mitzvah in the Torah, *piryah ve-rivyah*, the duty to propagate the human race.[18]

A curious aspect of the *Megillah* is the fact that God's name is not mentioned in it at all. Three reasons are given for this:

(a) The Rabbis of the Talmud say that Esther pleaded with the spiritual leaders of her day to record the historical event in which she had been involved, so that future generation might value her supreme dedication to God and her people. The Sages therefore told the story as an historical event in which Esther was the heroine, and they were not explicit about the part God played in this miracle. So the name of God does not appear in the narrative.

(b) In the Purim story, Esther married a non-Jew, and this was God's unique and inexplicable way of saving His people from annihilation. However, people who come to read the Book of Esther could conclude that intermarriage was perfectly acceptable because of this precedent. If God's name were to be included in the *Megillah* such readers might not realize that God's hand had guided these unique events, but would assume that God sanctions intermarriage.

(c) "Where is there an allusion to Esther in the Torah?" asked the Rabbis. Playing on the words in the Scriptures, "*ve-anokhi haster astir panai*," "And I shall surely hide My face" (Deuteronomy 31:18), the Rabbis take *astir* to allude to "Esther" which is spelled and almost sounds the same. They therefore suggest that in the Book of Esther, *astir*, "I will hide," God does not reveal Himself and His Name is not mentioned.[19]

A quaint Purim custom is that of eating *hamantaschen*, three cornered cakes filled with poppy seeds or prunes. This particular shape is based on the Midrash which tells how Haman's political strength grew from day to day and how he thought that he would succeed where others had failed in annihilating the Jews. He became less confident when he reflected that the *three* Patriarchs would intercede on behalf of their children before the Heavenly Throne.[20]

In most Jewish communities throughout the world people

disguise themselves and put on masks and costumes on Purim. There are four reasons for this:

(a) People who disguised themselves either as Haman or as Mordecai would give others the opportunity of reaching the state on Purim of not being able to distinguish between Haman and Mordecai.

(b) To emphasize the essential idea of Purim that, just as in masquerade, only the exterior is changed, and the inner self concealed, so the Jews in Persia, who kneeled before the idols of Haman in deference to the royal decree, only paid an external kind of homage—an outer gesture which did not reveal their true inner feelings.

(c) We have already noted the reference to Esther the Rabbis find in the Torah (Deuteronomy 31:18). Just as God masked Himself in the presence of Moses, and there is that hidden reference to Esther in the verse, so many people disguise themselves on Purim.

(d) According to tradition, Haman was descended from Amalek, who, in turn was a descendant of Esau. So, all the hatred that the Esaus, Amalekites and Hamans throughout the centuries harbored against the Jew stemmed from the fact that Jacob disguised himself as Esau and stole their father's blessing. By disguising ourselves on Purim, the day of the victory over Haman, we show our belief that Jacob was right to do what he did and that his action was legitimate and approved by God.[21]

It must be emphasized here that while Purim is associated with joy and festivity, the real significance of the Festival is in the way God dealt with the enemies of Israel. This idea is pinpointed in Rabbinic literature when we find Yom ha-Kippurim, the major fast day in the Jewish calendar, is held to be a derivative of *ke-purim*—"like Purim." If Yom Kippur is compared to Purim, then Purim is holier than Yom Kippur. In any event, Purim and Yom Kippur must have in them something similar, although one is a fast day and the other a feast day. On

Purim the fast precedes the feasting; on Yom Kippur the feasting precedes the fasting. Purim stands above Yom Kippur because during the latter, the Jew sanctifies himself and draws close to God by self-denial, while on Purim he achieves the same end in a more difficult way, through joy and pleasure. It is much easier to come closer to God by fasting than through the pleasure of the senses.[22]

Maimonides (Yad, end of Hilkhot Megillah) repeats the Midrashic idea that in the days of the Messiah, when all holidays and festivals will be forgotten, Purim will still be celebrated. All the Prophetic Books will lose their relevance except the Book of Esther. The following explanation is offered for this: All holidays have their source in an act of sanctification on the part of the Jew. In the time of the Messiah there will be nothing that man can do to add to the general atmosphere of sanctity. Purim, however, was an historical drama that unfolded entirely by Divine Providence. So, when the Jew celebrates Purim in the time of the Messiah, he would really learn to appreciate what God had done, and from his vantage point as a human being, really be able to sanctify the Festival.

Why should the *Megillah* outlast all other Prophetic Books? The reason is that the Torah, the Five Books of Moses, consists of a set of laws that guide the Jew throughout his life. The Prophets, in their visions and exhortations, merely substantiate and reinforce the teachings of the Torah by showing the consequences of a life that does not follow the Word of God. When the Messiah will arrive, the Torah will be a *sine qua non*, with no need of any admonitions, enforcements or substantiations. The Book of Esther, however, is a text apart. It was not intended to add to the Five Books of Moses. The *Megillah* is a story which is a link in the long chain of Jewish effort to eradicate Amalek, the symbol of injustice, depravity and godlessness in the world. This struggle will end when Israel and mankind will be rid of Amalek and what he represents, in the time of the Messiah. The Book of Esther is the outstanding example of the long struggle between Israel and

Amalek. Therefore, in the days of the Messiah, the Book of Esther will still be studied to remind the Jew of the millenia of constant warfare that he had to endure until the final victory.[23]

SOURCES

1. See Esther Chap. 3 verse 7.
2. *Tur Oraḥ Ḥayyim, Bet Yoseph, Arukh ha-Shulḥan* 686.
3. *Tur Oraḥ Ḥayyim, Bet Yoseph, Perishah* 687, *Arukh ha-Shulḥan* 687.
4. *Avudraham* p.112.
5. *Tur Oraḥ Ḥayyim, Bet Yoseph, Arukh ha-Shulḥan* 688.
6. *Halikhot Teiman* p.41.
7. *Tur Oraḥ Ḥayyim, Bet Yoseph, Darke Mosheh, Arukh ha-Shulḥan* 690.
8. *Halikhot Teiman* p.41.
9. *Tur Oraḥ Ḥayyim, Bet Yoseph, Bah, Arukh ha-Shulḥan* 692-693.
10. *Oraḥ Ḥayyim Sha'are Teshuvah* 693:2.
11. *Bet Yoseph, Tur Oraḥ Ḥayyim, Arukh ha-Shulḥan* 693.
12. *Arukh ha-Shulḥan* 693.
13. *Tur Oraḥ Ḥayyim, Bet Yoseph, Darke Mosheh, Arukh ha-Shulḥan* 694.
14. *Arukh ha-Shulḥan* 695.
15. *Ta'ame ha-Minhagim* p.383.
16. *Tur Oraḥ Ḥayyim, Bet Yoseph, Baḥ, Darke Mosheh, Arukh ha-Shulḥan* 695.
17. *Tur Oraḥ Ḥayyim, Bet Yoseph, Arukh ha-Shulḥan* 695.
18. *Sefer ha-Toda'ah* Vol. I, pp. 284, 286.
19. *Sefer ha-Mat'amim* p.87.
20. Ibid.
21. *Sefer ha-Toda'ah*, Vol. I, pp. 280-281.
22. *Sefer ha-Toda'ah*, Vol. I, p.285.
23. *Sefer ha-Toda'ah*, Vol. I, p. 285-286

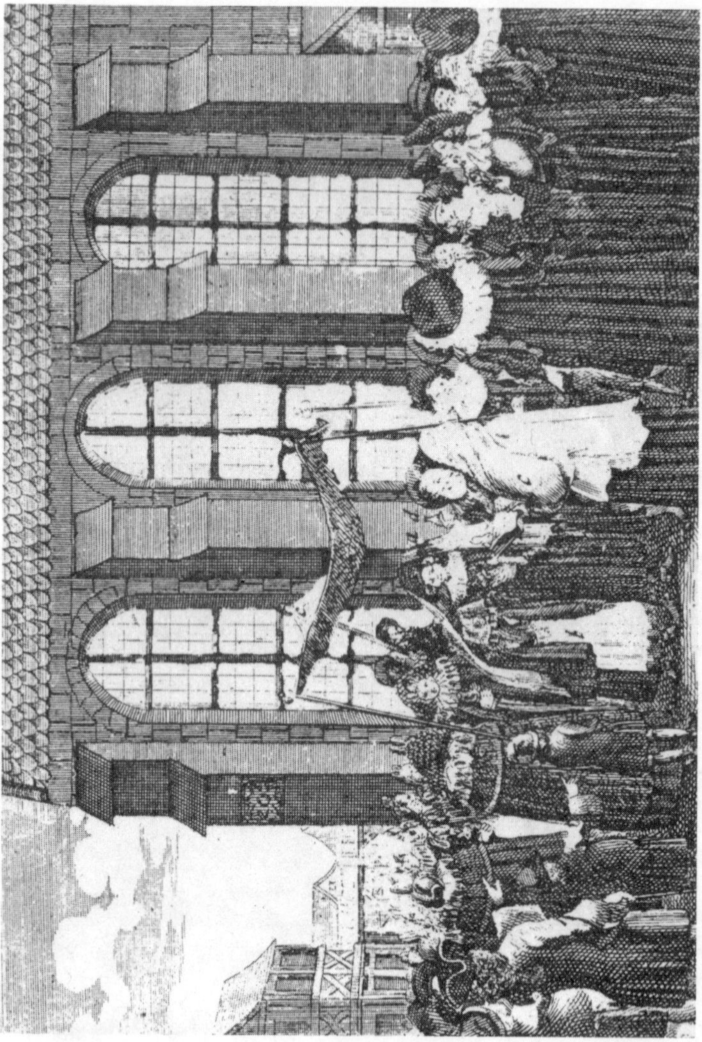

Marriage

The most elaborate ceremony in Judaism and the one which abounds in customs more than any other religious observance is that of marriage. This unique attention lavished on the marriage ceremony reflects the very special place matrimony occupies in Jewish life both as a means to the fulfilment of the commandment "Be fruitful and multiply" (Gen. 1.28) and as a condition of spiritual and mental well-being. There are numerous statements in the Talmud extolling married life and expressing the high esteem in which the wife was held by our Sages.

> One who does not have a wife lives without joy, without bliss, without happiness (Yevamot 62b)
>
> A man without a wife is not a human being (Yevamot 63a).
>
> A man should always refrain from causing distress to his wife (Bava Metzia 59a).
>
> A man should always pay due honor to his wife for his house is blessed only on her merit (ibid.).
>
> He who loves his wife as himself, and honors her more than himself about him is written "and you shall know that peace is in your tent" (Yevamot 62b).
>
> A man should always honor his wife beyond his means (Ḥullin 84b).

In order to fully comprehend the meaning and origin of the various customs and ceremonies connected with a Jewish wedding, it is important that we first acquaint ourselves with the several stages of development that the institution of marriage itself has undergone in Jewish history.

Prior to the giving of the Torah, a man married a woman by simply taking her into his home by mutual consent and having relations with her.[1] When the Torah was given the Jew was commanded to acquire a wife by marrying her in the presence of two witnesses. The two witnesses represent society which thereby takes cognizance of the act of marriage. This procedure is implied in the words of the Torah: "If a man take a wife and comes onto her. . ." (Deut. 22.13). By means of inference from another Biblical passage, the Rabbis interpreted the verb "take" to imply acquisition which in turn means a contractual transaction. A marriage, therefore, in its legal aspect is a meeting of minds between a man and a woman for the purpose of concluding a marriage contract. Yet it would be wrong to misconstrue this seemingly business-like framework of marriage in Judaism as devoid of all tenderness and love between husband and wife. The Rabbinic statements cited above abundantly demonstrate that love and mutual respect between husband and wife are essential for the stability of their life together. At the same time, the Sages realistically recognized that without a legal transaction executed with all the requisite formality the union of two strangers might be but a casual and therefore unstable liaison.

The Sages therefore established that this transaction is to take the form of an acquisition. And since it is the man who acquires the wife (a practice which preceded Torah law), he must indicate in some tangible way that his intention in acquiring the woman as a wife is legitimate, honorable and serious. The woman, on the other hand, has to consent to her being acquired as a wife of her own free will and is not to be coerced into marriage.

Accordingly, the Talmud (Kiddushin 2a) states that a wife can be acquired in one of three ways: through her acceptance of an object of monetary value, such as a coin or a ring; through a written document in which the man declares his intention to marry her; through cohabitation. (In practice, this latter was forbidden by the Rabbis as promiscuous.)

This act of acquisition is called *erusin* (betrothal) and it is only the first step in the Jewish wedding procedure. It is also referred to as *kiddushin*, the basic meaning of which is "separation," since through the act of betrothal the bridegroom separates his bride from belonging to anyone else but himself. It also means "consecration": indeed, far from being a mundane act, matrimony in Judaism is the mutual consecration of husband and wife for the purpose of fusing their lives into one holy union.

Through *kiddushin* the bride becomes an *arusah*, his betrothed, a status in Jewish law in which she is considered his wife only to the extent that she is forbidden to marry any other man, and if he desires to dissolve the betrothal, he would have to present her with a bill of divorce *(get)*. Otherwise, they have no obligation to each other and are forbidden to cohabitate.

The next step is the *nissuin*, "elevation," the consummation of the marriage by receiving the wife into the house of the husband. This is effected by the act of the *ḥuppah*, "enveloping," generally a canopy which symbolizes the house which the newly wed couple set out to build together. The final step of consummating the marriage is the *yiḥud*, the seclusion of the bride and groom.

In ancient times, and among Oriental Jews as recently as the early part of the last century, the bride was allowed a year between *erusin* and *nissuin* to enable her to prepare for her wedding and to acquire her trousseau.[2] Nowadays it has become the universal practice to perform the *kiddushin (erusin)* and *nissuin* immediately one after the other in order to avoid the problems and difficulties arising from a prolonged period of an unconsummated marriage.

Against this basic historical and legal background of the Jewish marriage, let us now describe and examine the origins of the many customs and traditions which permeate the wedding ceremony with such profusion. Although it may lack the power of law, tradition is an indispensable ingredient of Judaism as it provides the continuity which binds the Jewish present with the Jewish past. This binding power of tradition is especially evident in the wedding customs, which even in their contemporary form reflect all the traditions of past centuries.

We shall discuss only those wedding customs which are rooted in Jewish tradition. Customs such as flower girls, bridesmaids, ring bearers, best man and ushers and many other similar practices are recent borrowings from the non-Jewish environment and are alien and even contrary to the Jewish concept of marriage as it developed throughout the centuries.

According to some authorities many wedding customs hark back to the time when God "betrothed" the People of Israel with the Torah under the canopy of Mt. Sinai.[3] Others see the idyllic relationship of Adam and Eve as the prototype of the Jewish bridal couple.

Let us now analyze the wedding ceremony as it is conducted today. The festivities usually begin in the synagogue on Sabbath morning before the wedding. In Rabbinic literature (Masekhet Soferim Chap. 11, Pirke de-Rabbi Eliezer Chap. 17), it is related that King Solomon, wishing to imbue the populace with the virtue of *gemilut ḥasadim*, kindliness and generosity, provided two entrances in the newly built Temple: one through which bridegrooms passed and the other through which mourners passed. When the people saw a young man passing through the bridegrooms' entrance, they offered their congratulations and good wishes. When a mourner entered the other gate, condolences were offered. After the destruction of the Temple, the Rabbis ordained that the bridegroom should be invited to the synagogue and called up to the Torah to receive the congratulations and best wishes of the congregation.

At the conclusion of the reading of the Torah for the bridegroom, it is the custom to shower him with nuts. The Hebrew word for nut is *egoz*, whose numerical value is seventeen, the same as the numerical value of the short form of the Hebrew word for sin, *ḥet*, as well as that of the Hebrew word *tov* which means good. By showering the groom with nuts, we symbolically tell him that as a bridegroom all of his sins are forgiven and all will be good with him. In some communities, the congregation showers the bridegroom with almonds and raisins. This too, is a message to the bridegroom. There are almonds that are sweet and others that are bitter; there are grapes (raisins) that are sweet and others that are sour. So are wives: some can be true helpers in life; others can be shrews. The man can merit the good wife only by his own virtues.[4]

On the day of the wedding it is customary for the bride and groom to fast. The following reasons are given:

(a) Marriage is the beginning of a totally new phase in the life of the young couple. In this respect the wedding day may very well be compared to Yom Kippur when a person is given a new lease on life and all his previous sins are forgiven. From this analogy it follows that just as one fasts on Yom Kippur, so do the bride and the groom on the day of their wedding.

(b) When the Jew is in a state of profound contrition, he fasts and prays to be forgiven for his sins. On the day of his wedding, when so much of their future is at stake, the bridal couple fasts and prays fervently that God should bless them with happiness.

(c) When the Children of Israel stood at the foot of Mt. Sinai, betrothing themselves to God by accepting the Torah, they were so ecstatic and oblivious to their physical needs that they forgot to eat. In emulation of that event, bride and groom fast on the day of their wedding.

(d) The meal served at the wedding reception is usually a lavish affair involving drinking hard liquor, which in turn may lead to a state of inebriation. The couple-to-be-married must be in a state of sobriety to be fully aware of the legal formalities which are the most important element in the marriage ceremony.[5]

For that reason, in some communities the custom of fasting is practiced only by the bridegroom and not by the bride. The guests in the groom's quarters before the wedding are generally served liquor. Were the groom to join in the feast, he might become inebriated. On the other hand, the ladies visiting the bride in her quarters are not likely to be served hard liquor and the probability of her intoxication is remote.[6]

The first ritual performed at a wedding is what is popularly known by its Yiddish name, *"badeken die kallah."* The groom is escorted by the guests to the place where the bride is waiting and covers her face with her veil. The assembled guests then recite the blessing that was pronounced over our Matriarch Rebecca: "Our sister, may you become the mother of thousands, of ten thousands" (Genesis 24:60). A number of reasons have been offered for this custom:

(a) When Rebecca accompanied Eliezer to become the wife of Isaac, the Torah relates: "And she said to the servant, 'Who is this man who walks in the field to meet us?' And the servant said, 'It is my master (Isaac)! And she took her veil and covered herself" (Genesis 24:65).

(b) Some undisciplined men attending the wedding may cast a lustful eye on the bride.

(c) Another occasion when one covers the eyes is when the *Shema Yisrael*, "Hear O Israel", is recited. At that time we do so to indicate that we have blind faith and trust in God. So it is with the bride who covers her eyes in order to demonstrate her total commitment to her husband and her unquestioning trust in him. The custom of Oriental Jews, and in the old community of Jerusalem until this very day is to cover the entire face of the bride and for others to lead her while she is blindfolded. This is the practice also among Hassidim. In most Jewish communities, however, the veil is made of tulle or lace which allows the bride to see and comprehend whatever takes place at the ceremony.[7]

(d) To protect the bride from *ayin ha-ra*, the "evil eye." Although it defies rational explanation, the fear of being harmed by "evil eye" has very much been a part of Jewish folk belief from ancient times. Protective amulets to ward off its harms are worn to this very day by Oriental Jews. Various remedies have been employed throughout the ages by Jews of all countries to cure its ill effects. We can only surmise that the "evil eye" is a phenomenon akin to jealousy. At a wedding, too, when the bride is radiant with happiness and the occasion is joyful, someone whose life was not similarly blessed may begrudge her good luck and jealously look upon her with an "evil eye", wishing her ill. It is to protect her from such harm that the bride's face is covered.

(e) To avoid the embarrassment of any possible change of heart on the part of the groom, should he at the last minute notice some blemish on the bride's face and decide to call off the wedding.[8]

While in some Sephardi communities the wedding ceremony would be held in a synagogue as befitting the solemnity of the event, the Ashkenazi tradition is to conduct the ceremony outdoors, for two reasons:

(a) The merriment of the wedding could lead to licentious behavior and conduct unsuitable for a synagogue.

(b) Since almost every wedding takes place at night, it is appropriate that the stars be a symbol of God's blessing to Abraham: "That I will greatly bless you, and I will exceedingly multiply your seed as the stars in Heaven" (Genesis 22:17). Today, most of the ceremonies in the Western Hemisphere are conducted indoors whereas in Israel almost all are performed outdoors.[9]

The marriage ceremony must be conducted in the presence of a *Minyan*, a quorum of ten men. The source for this ruling is the Book of Ruth (4:2), where we find Boaz courting Ruth: "And he took ten men of the elders of the city and he said, 'sit ye down here.'" The Rabbis (Ketubot 7b) interpret this verse to mean that Boaz assembled this quorum in preparation for his marriage to Ruth.[10]

The groom, accompanied by his escorts holding candles, is led to the canopy. According to the Midrash the concept of escorts, *shoshvinim*, dates back to Adam and Eve when the angels Michael and Gabriel escorted Adam to his marriage with Eve. The custom for the escorts to hold candles again harks back to Mt. Sinai when Israel was "wedded" to God: "And there were voices and lightning" (Ex. 19:15). Another explanation: the Hebrew word for candle is *ner*, the numerical value of its letters being two hundred and fifty. Double that number (to correspond to the two candles held by the two escorts) and the total is five hundred. The numerical value for the Hebrew words *peru u-revu*, "be fruitful and multiply," is also five hundred.[11]

But why should the groom enter the *Ḥuppah* first? Here, too, the background is the "marriage" between God and the Children of Israel at Mt. Sinai. The Torah tells us: "The Lord came from Sinai" (Deut. 33:2). He was at Mt. Sinai first and came to greet His "bride," the Children of Israel. Another thought: the Torah relates: "And he brought her (Eve) to Adam" (Genesis 2:22).[12]

The bride accompanied by her escorts, also carrying candles, reach the canopy and begin to circle around the groom three times. The idea of this encirclement is found in Scriptures where the Prophet speaks about the bliss of the Messianic Age and says: "The woman will go around her husband" (Jeremiah 31:21). In this, their most joyous moment, the bride circles around her groom to demonstrate that he is to be the center of her life. Another thought: by making a complete circle around the groom, the bride figuratively indicates that by marrying her, the husband's life has become complete and fulfilled.

The reasons for the *three* encirclements are:

(a) They symbolize the three basic provisions that the husband may not deny his wife: food, raiment and conjugal rights.

(b) The Prophet Hosea (2:21, 22) comforts the Children of Israel during a distressing period of their history and relates the words of God: "And I will *betroth* you unto me forever, and I will *betroth* you unto me in righteousness and in justice and in loving-kindness, and in mercy. And I will *betroth* you unto me in faithfulness and you shall know the Lord." God used the word "betroth" three times. In commemoration of that prophecy, the bride circles around her husband three times.[13]

In some communities the bride encircles her husband seven times. While no source could be found, one might surmise that it is in keeping with other encirclements in religious life such as

Hakafot, the procession of the Torah Scrolls around the *Bimah* on *Simḥat Torah*, which also takes place seven times.

Following the encirclement, the bride takes her place on the right side of the groom. This is based on the verse "The Queen stands on your right hand in fine gold of Ophir" (Psalms 45:10).

With the bridal couple under the *ḥuppah*, the actual wedding ceremony begins. Few realize that what is taking place is two distinct ceremonies performed in immediate succession: *erusin* or *kiddushin* (betrothal) followed by *nissuin*, the marriage proper. As explained earlier, traditionally a certain length of time would elapse between these two procedures, a practice which was later abolished by the Rabbis for practical reasons.

(A vestige of the ancient *erusin* which far preceded the *nissuin* survives to our days in the form of the *Tenaim* [lit. "conditions"]. Generally taking place at the time of the engagement of the young couple, it is celebrated by a festive meal at which an agreement is drawn up between the two affianced and their parents setting forth the date and place of the wedding and any other conditions and stipulations pertaining to the marriage. After the signing and ceremonial reading of the *tenaim* document, a china plate is broken by the two mothers, and the young couple is declared as affianced. More recently even the *tenaim* ceremony is often performed at the time of the wedding, just before going to the *ḥuppah.)*

Before the act of *erusin*, the officiating Rabbi recites two benedictions over a cup of wine: one is the usual blessing of "*bore peri ha-gafen*" which one pronounces before drinking wine; the other is the *Birkat Erusin*, "Benediction of Betrothal," an expression of praise to God Who sanctifies His people Israel through the *ḥuppah* and *kiddushin*.

Originally these blessings used to be recited by the groom himself, a practice later abandoned to save embarrassment for the unlearned who might be unable to recite it.[14]

After these benedictions both the groom and the bride are

given to drink from the cup

As explained before, betrothal in Jewish law is a transaction in which the man "acquires" the woman for his wife by presenting her with an object of value in the presence of two witnesses while declaring his intention of taking her for his wife. By her mere acceptance of this object of value, she demonstrates her assent to his declaration and becomes his wife.

Accordingly, after the two benedictions were pronounced, the bridegroom places a ring on the bride's finger before two witnesses and declares: "Hereby you are consecrated to me with this ring in accordance with the laws of Moses and Israel."

As is the case with all legal procedures, the two witnesses must not be related to either party in the marriage nor to each other.[15]

The marriage is just as valid if in place of a ring some other object or, for that matter, a coin was presented to the bride. In fact in Yemenite and other Oriental communities a coin is used for betrothal.[16] This is in accordance with the Mishnaic dictum that one of the ways of acquiring a wife is by means of money. It is interesting to note that in Baghdad, where a coin was used instead of a ring, the bride wore silk gloves as a sign of dignity and honor to demonstrate that her acceptance of the coin not be construed as receiving charity.[17]

In most communities, however, a ring is used for the following reasons:

(a) A chain is formed by interlocking rings. The ring which the groom presents to his bride symbolizes the new link which they are just about to add to the long chain of generations of the Jewish people.[18]

(b) Just as a ring has no beginning and no end, so may the devotion and love of the newly wed couple for each other be never ending.[19]

(c)In Scriptures we find several instances where the presentation of a ring marked the conferring of power and authority.

Pharaoh removed his ring and gave it to Joseph when he appointed him vicerory; Ahasuerus did the same when he invested first Haman then Mordecai with certain powers. Similarly, by placing a ring on his bride's finger the groom elevates her to the position of the mistress of the house.[20]

With the betrothal ceremony *(erusin)* thus completed, the marriage ceremony *(nissuin)* commences with the reading aloud of the *Ketubah*, the Marriage Contract. Setting forth the mutual obligations of the newly-weds, both monetary and conjugal, the Ketubah embodies the principle that a marriage is valid only when there is a meeting of minds and with the full consent of the bride and groom. The Ketubah which was prepared before the marriage ceremony is now read aloud under the *ḥuppah* to impress upon the married couple the solemnity of their obligations to each other.

The *Ketubah* is validated by the signatures of two witnesses (in some communities it is also signed by the bride and groom).

The reason for reading the *Ketubah* between both sets of benedictions is to underscore the idea that although today we combine *erusin* with the *nissuin* in one ceremony, they are actually two separate functions.[21]

The next ceremony under the *ḥuppah* is the recitation of the *Birkhat Nissuin* (also called *Birkhat Ḥatanim)* consisting of the seven marriage benedictions popularly know as *Sheva Berakhot.* Actually there are six marriage benedictions which are preceded by the blessing over wine. Because *erusin and nissuin* are two separate rituals, a different cup of wine is used for each. After these benedictions, too, the groom and bride, now already husband and wife, are given to drink from the cup.

At this point, before leaving the *ḥuppah*, the bridegroom breaks a glass placed under his foot in commemoration of the destruction of the Temple. This happiest event in the lives of the newly-wed couple cannot pass by without reflecting for a moment on the greatest national tragedy that befell the Jewish people. For the same reason, in some Sephardi communities a wreath of olive leaves is placed upon the heads of the bride and groom during the wedding ceremony. The olive leaves which have a bitter taste are an outward manifestation of the bitterness in the hearts of the Jewish people over the destruction of Jerusalem and the Temple.[22]

Others think that the reason for breaking a glass under the canopy is the Kabbalistic notion that the Angels of Destruction are intent upon marring this happy event as well. Hence, a glass is broken, to satisfy their design.[23]

As we use the word *ḥuppah* today, it refers to a canopy or some other type of covering held over the head of the bride and groom. This may even be in the form of a *tallit.* In ancient times *ḥuppah* was referred to as the residence where the conjugal act took place. Obviously, today, the consummation of the marriage does not take place in what is presently known as a *ḥuppah.* The *ḥuppah* symbolizes the home that the groom is providing for his bride, but it cannot serve the purpose it was originally intended for. Therefore immediately after the wedding ceremony, the bride and groom are led into a private room for a short period of seclusion where they break their fast. This is known as *Yiḥud* and it completes the wedding ritual.

In addition to the breaking of the glass there are other dramatic overtones to the marriage ceremony. In many circles, particularly among Hassidim, the groom stands under the *ḥuppah* in the white robe known as a *kittel.* Two reasons, both along the same line, have been proposed.

(a) By wearing this shroud-like garment, the groom is reminded of the day of death and thus admonished to refrain from passionately pursuing the pleasures of this world.

(b) White is synonymous with purity. Wearing the white *kittel* demonstrates that the groom has been cleansed of all his sins.[24]

Amongst Yemenite Jews, the groom would approach his mother at the beginning of the marriage ceremony and ask her forgiveness for all the wrong he ever did to her. As an act of contrition, he kneels and kisses her knees. She expresses her forgiveness and presents him with the coin with which he will marry his bride.[25]

It is an ancient tradition dating back to Biblical times to celebrate the marriage of a virgin for seven days following the wedding. This festive period is known as *sheva berakhot* ("Seven Blessings") because during these seven days, when there are guests present who were not at the wedding or did not participate previously in one of the festive meals following the wedding, the same seven *berakhot* of *nissuin* that were recited under the *ḥuppah* are repeated after each meal.

Two episodes in the Scriptures serve as precedents for a week's celebration.

(a) When Jacob discovered the ruse that Laban had perpetrated against him and demanded that the younger daughter Rachel be given to him as a wife, Laban replied, *Male shevu'ah zot*—"Fulfill the week of this one and we will give you the other as well" (Gen. 29:27). "The week" refers to the week of celebration following Leah's wedding.

(b) When Samson married Delilah and his guests came to celebrate we find, "And Samson said to them, 'I will propound to you a riddle; if you can in any wise tell it to me within the seven days of the feast'" (Judges 14:12). Here too, the seven days represent the festive week following Samson's wedding.

The procedure of this celebration is as follows: after the washing of the hands, bread is broken and a meal is served. At the conclusion of the meal, Grace is recited over a cup of wine. At this point there is a difference between the Sephardi and Ashkenazi communities. In the latter a second cup of wine is used for the purpose of the seven benedictions because of the principle "*en osim mitzvot ḥavilot, ḥavilot,*" *mitzvot* are not to be performed in bundles. In other words, if one cup of wine was used for Grace we may not assign it another function—that of the *sheva berakhot*, the seven benedictions. Sephardim, on the other hand, use one cup because, they contend, the principle of not performing *mitzvot* in bundles applies only to those that are of Biblical origin. The mitzvah of reciting *sheva berakhot* during the week following the wedding is of Rabbinic origin.[26]

Some very interesting and unique wedding customs have evolved during the centuries:

(a) While it is not obligatory, many choose to hold the wedding during the first half of the month. It is an expression of the hope that just as in this period of the month, the moon waxes larger and larger until it reaches its full stature, so may it be with the good fortune of this couple. This is not to be construed as superstition but merely a good omen for a happy life.[27]

(b) In Baghdad, three roasting spits were set into the ground of the courtyard surrounding the groom's home during the sixth day of the week in which he was married. The groom would leave his home, extract these spits from the ground and throw them behind him. This was a symbol of casting off evil spirits.[28]

(c) Based on the writings of the medieval Kabbalist, Rabbi Yehudah he-Ḥasid, the custom evolved not to marry a woman whose name is identical with that of a man's mother. Were both the bride and her mother-in-law to have the same name, an embarrassing situation could arise when the husband would call his wife and his mother would answer the call.[29]

(d) It is customary for the bride to present her future husband with a *tallit* before the wedding. The basis for this custom is in the Torah: "You shall make yourself fringes upon the corners of your garments" *(tallit)*. This verse is immediately followed by "If a man take a wife. . . ." (Deuteronomy 22: 12, 13). The inference is that first he acquire a *tallit* and then a wife. Since the bride is the one who is instrumental in fulfilling the second passage, she presents him with a *tallit* in fulfillment of the first passage.[30]

Another reason: In Talmudic times, an unmarried man did not cover his head with a *tallit*. This was the sign that he was still a bachelor. By becoming his wife, the bride changes his status and henceforth he is expected to wear a *tallit* as is the practice of all married men. In keeping with that tradition, the bride presents the groom with the *tallit*.[31]

An interesting question is why we do not recite at the wedding a benediction over our fulfilment of God's commandment to take a wife unto ourselves, just as every other mitzvah warrants a benediction. The authorities propound the thesis that the wedding is not a mitzvah in itself, an end in itself, but a means for the fulfilment of a mitzvah, that of being fruitful. We are called upon to recite benedictions only over mitzvot themselves and not over the means to that end.[32]

SOURCES

1. Maimonides, *Yad Haḥazakah*, Hilkhot Ishut, Chap. 1
2. *Massa Bavel* p.201
3. *Arukh ha-Shulḥan*, Even ha-Ezer 34, par. 4; *Ta'ame ha-Minhagim* p. 407.
4. *Sefer ha-Mat'amim* p. 33.
5. *Arukh ha-Shulḥan*, Even ha-Ezer 61, par. 21; *Sefer ha-Mat'amim* p. 33.
6. *Ta'ame ha-Minhagim* p. 403.
7. *Sefer ha-Mat'amim* p. 33.
8. Ibid p. 36
9. *Minhage Yeshurun* p. 32.
10. *Arukh ha-Shulḥan*, Even ha-Ezer 62, par. 11.
11. *Ta'ame ha-Minhagim*, p. 407.
12. *Sefer ha-Mat'amim* p. 34; Ibid Part 2 p. 23.
13. Ibid p. 35; *Minhage Yeshurun* p.35.
14. *Arukh ha-Shulḥan*, Even ha-Ezer 34, par. 8.
15. Ibid 27, par. 1.
16. *Halichot Teman* p. 139.
17. *Ben Ish Ḥai* 188.
18. *Sefer ha-Mat'amim* p. 30.
19. Ibid p. 39
20. *Minhage Yeshurun* p. 36.
21. Ibid p. 37.
22. *Avudraham* p. 196; *Arukh ha-Shulḥan*, Even ha-Ezer, 65,par. 5.
23. *Sefer ha-Mat'amim* Part 2, p. 22; *Ta'ame ha-Minhagim* p. 412.

24. *Ta'ame ha-Minhagim* p. 407.
25. *Halikhot Teman* p. 139.
26. Ibid p. 152.
27. *Arukh ha-Shulḥan*, Even ha-Ezer 64, par. 13.
28. *Massa Bavel* p. 203.
29. *Ta'ame ha-Minhagim* p. 402.
30. *Sefer ha-Mat'amim* p. 29.
31. *Minhage Yeshurun* p. 27.
32. *Ta'ame ha-Minhagim* p. 420.

Birth

Of the numerous ceremonies connected with the life-cycle of a Jew none possesses the drama and exultation that characterizes the rite of circumcision. It is not just the fulfilment of one of the many precepts of Judaism; it is the rite through which the newborn male enters the Jewish fold.

The ceremony is known in Hebrew as *Berit Milah*, the "Covenant of Circumcision"; also as *Berito shel Avraham Avinu*, the "Covenant of our Father Abraham." Indeed, it was our Patriarch Abraham who was commanded by God:

> This is my covenant which you shall keep between Me and you and your seed after you: Every male among you shall be circumcised. And you shall be circumcised in the flesh of your foreskin, and it shall be a sign of covenant between Me and you. And he that is eight days old shall be circumcised among you, every male throughout your generations. . .(Gen. 17:10-12).

Thus, circumcision was the first commandment given the progenitor of the Jewish people even before the rest of the Torah was given. It was in fulfilment of this covenant that Abraham circumcised his son Isaac on the eighth day of his birth (Gen. 21:4).

From the explicit words of the Torah we deduce two basic laws:

(a) It is incumbent upon a father to circumcise his own son. Abraham did not delegate anyone else to circumcise Isaac, but performed the ritual himself. However, if the father for some reason is unable to perform the ritual himself, he may delegate a proxy to perform it in his stead. If the father had died it becomes the obligation of the *Bet Din* of the community to do so. If there is no *Bet Din*, a concerned member of the community must attend to this matter.[1] If one reaches manhood uncircumcised, he himself must see to it that he undergoes circumcision without further delay.

(b) The circumcision must take place on the eighth day unless for reasons of health it must be postponed until the physical condition of the child permits it.

Why was the eighth day designated in the first place? According to the Zohar the circumcision ritual is compared to the offering of a sacrifice on the altar of the Temple, and the Torah forbids us the separation of the newborn animal from its mother for seven days. Only on the eighth day may it be brought as a sacrifice.[2]

Why was the male organ chosen rather than any other part of the body to indicate the covenant between the Jew and God? The answer is in the words of God to Abraham: "You shall walk before me and be *whole*," which the Rabbis interpreted as follows: If any other part of the body should have been severed, Abraham would not have been whole. The foreskin of the male is the only part of anatomy that can be removed without mutilating man. Another reason given is that the removal of the foreskin diminishes the sexual drive allowing man to turn his thoughts to loftier matters.[3]

The Rabbis of the Talmud state that circumcision outweighs all other commandments in the Torah. When one who was uncircumcised as an infant attains adulthood and neglects to circumcise himself he is subject to the severe penalty of *karet* (extirpation). The Torah relates that even Moses, the greatest of all prophets, nearly lost his life by divine intervention because he was tardy with his son's circumcision. The Rabbis further deduced the paramount importance of this mitzvah from the fact that in Chapter 17 of Genesis, where God instructs Abraham concerning circumcision, He uses the term "covenant" thirteen times. This is not found in connection with any other mitzvah.[4]

Since the Torah very explicitly states that the circumcision must take place on the eighth day, it cannot under any circumstances be performed before that day. What if one inadvertantly or intentionally circumcised his son before the eighth day? In such case the child is to be entered into the Covenant of Abraham on the eighth day by *hatafat dam berit*, the drawing of a drop of blood from the skin of the glans. The same ceremony of *hatafat dam* must be performed if, through some quirk of nature, an infant is born without a foreskin, in fulfilment of the commandment thereby sealing the covenant between the Jew and God.[5]

In Jewish ritual the day begins at sunset and ends at sunset, with twilight being of doubtful status whether it is the end of the previous day or the beginning of the next. Now, what of a child born during this twilight period? (For halakhic purposes, a child is considered born the moment his head emerges from the womb.) Do we count the eight days from the preceding or the following day? The problem is of special importance when the child was born Friday after sunset. Generally, we are to perform the *berit* on the eighth day counted from the day of birth. In the case of the child born at twilight on the eve of Sabbath, the *berit* is postponed to Sunday of the following week, i.e. to the ninth day. Although performance of the mitzvah of circumcision takes preference over the laws of *Shabbat*, this is so only when the *Shabbat* being the eighth day of birth is not in doubt.[6]

As mentioned earlier, if the infant is in less than perfect physical condition, the *berit milah* is postponed until his complete recovery. Moreover, no *berit milah* is to be performed when there is any indication that it may endanger the life of the person to be circumcised. Thus, when two brothers died in succession as a result of their circumcision, indicating that they had suffered from hemophilia, the third son of the same mother must not be circumcised lest he too suffer the same fate. Even when two cousins, the sons of two twin sisters, died as a result of circumcision, none of the subsequent sons of the two families are to be circumcised. "And he shall live by them (the commandments)" (Lev. 18:5), to which our Sages added: "And he shall not die through them" (Yoma 85b). The performance of the *mitzvot* should bring life and joy; not cause death.[7]

Thus far we have dealt with the strictly halachic aspects of *berit milah* as laid down in the Torah and interpreted by the Rabbis. Most of the customs surrounding the *berit* ceremony, however, are rooted in the mystical teachings of Kabbalah. The mystery of birth (and the same goes for death) cannot adequately be explained by rational means. Where the human logic fails, mysticism takes over. It was the Zohar that first endowed the mtizvah of *milah* with an aura of sublime sanctity comparing the act of circumcision to an offering; equating the child with the sacrifice, his blood with the blood of the sacrificial animal; the knees of the *sandek* (see below) with the altar. Both acts have the power of effecting atonement and Divine forgiveness.[8]

Being invested with this extra significance, the actual *berit milah* is preceded by a series of customs most of which are based on kabbalistic teachings. The first in the series of ceremonies is the *Shalom Zachar* ("Peace, or welcome, to the male child"), a festive gathering of friends and family in the home of the parents of the newborn on the first Friday night following the birth. The following reasons are proposed for this custom:

(a) The Sabbath is characterized by peace. In greeting we say "Shabbat Shalom"; we usher in the Sabbath by singing "Shalom Alekhem." In the throes of childbirth the woman may have felt resentment and animosity toward her husband who was responsible for her travail. With the birth of the child, the pains have subsided, the joy of having a new baby permeates the house, peace once again reigns between husband and wife.

(b) The numerical value of "zakhar," a male child, is two-hundred and twenty-seven, the same as the numerical value of "berakhah," a blessing.

(c) The Talmud relates that the embryo in its mother's womb enjoys a state of sanctity because, while resting there, it is taught the entire Torah. Just before it is born an angel taps him on the lips, causing the child to forget all that he learned. When the child is about to be born into a world where free will and free choice between right and wrong are granted to man, it has to emerge as one who is free to choose and not as one whose sancitified state leaves no room for choice. At the *Shalom Zachar* we gather symbolically to offer our comfort to him for having lost his state of sanctity which would have enabled him to lead a life of spiritual values without the necessity of exercising his free will. For the same reason, it is customary to serve peas and lentils at the *Shalom Zachar.* Because of their round shape, these symbolize mourning.

(d) An integral part of every human being is his soul which, prior to birth, dwelled in the heavenly abode of the *Shekhinah* in a state of total peace. Now that the child is born, his soul has been moved from its tranquil and serene location and transported to a world of wickedness and strife. Hence we come to comfort the soul by wishing it peace.

(e) An opposite line of reasoning: For nine months the child was entombed in the dark, bleak dungeon of the womb. At birth he was liberated and brought into a world of sunshine and we welcome him with greetings of "Shalom."[9]

(f) Some Sephardi Jews celebrate this *Shalom Zakhar* on the night before the circumcision. Their custom is to bring the chair of Elijah the Prophet (which will be discussed later) from the synagogue to the home. This chair would be adorned with flowers and fragrant leaves. Singing and dancing would ensue.[10]

The next step takes place on the night before the circumcision when the *Mohel*, the person who performs the circumcision, visits the infant to examine him. Before departing, he places the scalpel to be used for the operation under the baby's pillow.

The reasons:

(a) According to the Kabbalists this will serve as a protection against Satan who makes every effort to prevent the child from entering into the covenant of Abraham.

(b) If the day of circumcision falls on a Saturday, the surgical instruments must be brought beforehand to the place where the *berit milah* will be performed. Therefore, in order not to differentiate between a weekday and a Saturday, the scalpel is always left with the infant prior to the event.

(c) If an infant is in poor health, circumcision is postponed for the time when the child's condition is sufficiently improved. By leaving the scalpel with the baby, the *Mohel* signals that the child is healthy, and that the circumcision will take place the next day.[11]

The night before the *berit milah* is called "Wachnacht" (Yiddish for "vigil"). It is customary to gather the school boys of the neighborhood around the baby's crib where they recite the *Keriat Shema* aloud. The father of the child together with other men of the family and friends spend the night in study and prayer. The reason of this custom is again based on Kabbalah, namely to guard the child from the attempts of Satan to harm him and thus prevent him from entering the holy covenant.[12]

On the day of the *berit milah*, if it falls on a day when there is *Keriat ha-Torah* (i.e. Shabbat, Monday and Thursday, Feast or Fast day), the father is honored with being called up to the Torah in recognition of his carrying out the law of Torah by circumcising his son. In most communities this honor is bestowed on the father on the Shabbat preceding the *berit milah*.[13]

Circumcision must take place as early as possible on the eighth day in keeping with the Talmudic maxim that *zerizim makdimim*, the diligent hasten to perform the mitzvah. The act of conferring holiness upon an infant surely deserves to be performed without any delay.[14]

A *minyan*, a quorum of ten man, should be present at the circumcision ceremony, including the father of the infant, the *Kvater*, the *Mohel* and the *Sandek*. The *minyan* is necessary as all acts of sanctification in Jewish life require this quorum. Also, by their presence at least ten men in Israel will be able to testify that this father fulfilled his obligation in bringing his child into the covenant of Abraham.[15]

The *Kvater* (roughly corresponding to the English "godfather") initiates the ceremony of circumcision. It is customary for his wife, the *Kvaterin*, to take the boy from his mother and hand him to the *Kvater* who, in turn, hands him to the father who stands in front of the circumcision chair. The reason that the father is not permitted to receive the child from the mother is the fact that the latter is in a state of impurity because of the birth and thus the husband may not come in close contact with her.

In one opinion the origin of the word *Kvater* is: *K* in Hebrew is a prefix, meaning "like"; *Vater* is Yiddish for "father," hence "*Kvater*" means "like a father." In other words, since the real father has no heart to circumcise his child, he appoints a *Kvater* to be his surrogate.[16] Another explanation is: the Yiddish word *Kvater* and the Hebrew word *Koter*, to offer incense, are spelled alike in Hebrew characters. Therefore, since as mentioned, the circumcision is compared to the bringing of a sacrifice in the Temple, it is the *Kvater* who performs a function comparable to the burning of the incense in the Temple.[17]

When the child is brought in for the ritual, those present call out, "*Barukh ha-ba*," "Blessed is he that comes." There are several reasons proposed:

(a) In Hebrew the numerical value of *ha-ba* is eight. Hence what we mean is: "Blessed is the one who arrives to be circumcised on his eighth day."[18]

(b) The letters of *ha-ba* in Hebrew are the initials of the Hebrew words in the scriptural passage "that cleave unto the Lord your God" (Deuteronomy 4:4). That is to say, by virtue of this circumcision, the infant will cling to God's *mitzvot*.[19]

(c) As we shall see further, Elijah the Prophet plays an important part in the circumcision ritual. Thus, when the infant is being brought to the chair of Elijah, we call out "*Barukh ha-ba*," "Blessed is he (Elijah) who has arrived to witness the circumcision."[20]

(d) The Hebrew letters of *Barukh ha-ba* stand for the initials of ***B**e-simha **r**abah **V**e-Ameru **kh**ulam **h**ineh **ba** Elijahu*, "Let all proclaim with great joy, 'Here comes Elijah.'"[21]

The *berit milah* takes place following the morning prayers

when the father still wears *tallit* and *tefillin*. One opinion in the Talmud would have the mitzvah of circumcision outweighing all other mitzvot combined. Another opinion states that the mitzvah of *tzitzit* (*tallit*) outweighs all other *mitzvot*. Therefore, it befits a father of the child to be circumcised to wear a *tallit*.[22] As for *tefillin*, the Torah refers to them as a "*sign* upon your hand," while circumcision is referred to as a "*sign* of the covenant." Hence, it behooves the father to wear *tefillin* at the circumcision of his son.

The *Mohel's* scalpel must be double-edged. There are two reasons:

(a) If it had only one sharp edge, the *Mohel* might begin cutting with the dull side and by applying pressure he would cause unnecessary pain to the infant.

(b) If the *Mohel* encounters a very tough foreskin blunting one edge of the knife, he can immediately turn the knife over and complete the surgery with the other edge.[23]

Candles are lit and held by those present, throughout the *berit milah*. One reason has a Scriptural background (Exodus 2:2): "And she (Jocheved) saw him (Moses) that he was a goodly child." The Rabbis explain that when Moses was born the whole house became filled with light. We light candles illuminating the room in the hope that this infant too, will be a good Jew. Another purpose for the lighting of the candles is to make passers-by aware of the ritual being performed so that they too, will enter and join the festivities.[24]

The *Sandek* referred to before is the man who holds the baby on his lap while the *Mohel* performs the circumcision. Commenting on the verse, "Take hold of shield and buckler," (Psalms 35:2), the Rabbis relate that David said to God, "I praise you with all my limbs: upon my head I place the *tefillin* and upon my knees I hold the infants to be circumcised and I act as their *Sandek*."[25]

As to the meaning of the word *Sandek*, one interesting speculation is that it perhaps stands for the initials of *Sanegor*

na'aseh din kategor, which means "the accusor (Satan) has become the defending counsel." In other words, by holding the child while he is being entered into the Jewish fold, the *Sandek* aids in defeating any evil designs Satan may have with respect to this child and the Children of Israel.[26]

Here again, in the sacrificial to which the circumcision ritual is likened, the *Sandek*, while holding the child, performs the function of the altar. Indeed, according to some sources his is the most important function in the entire circumcision ritual.[27]

Women do not serve as *Sandek*; it would be in poor taste for a woman to observe the surgical procedure on the genitals of a male.[28]

Before the ritual begins, the chair of Elijah is being prepared for the *Sandek* to sit on when holding the baby. The source for this custom is the Midrash which relates that until the reign of King Ahab, the ritual of circumcision was strictly observed by all Jews. Under the evil influence of Queen Jezebel, the Ten Tribes of Israel abolished it. Elijah, the Prophet admonished the King and his Queen that he would bring down a famine upon them if they did not reinstate the ritual. Whereupon Jezebel sought to kill Elijah. He fled and the Lord appeared to him and said, "Your whole life is dedicated to a passionate zeal for My covenant. By your life, I promise you that the Children of Israel will not perform any circumcision until you come there to witness it yourself." This is how Elijah came to be known as the "Angel of the Covenant," for whom a chair is set aside at every *berit milah*.[29]

The Midrash goes even further and relates that after being promised that he would be present at all circumcisions, Elijah argued with God saying, "How may I, who fought the spiritual battle of the Lord, be present in the company of a father and guests who may not be observant of the *mitzvot*?" Whereupon the Lord assured him that for his sake He would forgive the sins of those who were close by the Chair of Elijah. It is for this reason that many people, at a circumcision, endeavor to stand, even for a brief moment, near the Chair of Elijah.[30]

Another reason for the Chair of Elijah: when Phinehas, the grandson of Aaron the High Priest, became aware of the promiscuous behavior of an Israelite with a Moabite woman, he became incensed at the debasement of the sign of the covenant between God and Israel and killed them both in order to extirpate sexual lewdness from Israel. According to tradition, Phinehas was Elijah.[31]

In many Sephardi communities there is a special chair in the Synagogue designated as the "Chair of Elijah." On the night before the circumcision this chair is brought to the home of the infant. An ornately embroidered cloth is placed upon the chair which is adorned with scented flowers and plants. The Scroll of the Law is placed upon the thus bedecked chair and during the entire night visitors come to kiss the Scroll and wish the family and child well. The next morning, the chair is returned to the Synagogue to be used in the circumcision ritual.[32]

The father, wearing *tallit* and *tefillin*, takes his stand to the right of the *Mohel*. As already mentioned, ideally the circumcision should be preformed by the father himself. If he is unqualified to do so, he verbally delegates the Mohel as his agent. This too is due to the comparison of circumcision to the sacrificial service: In the Temple, the Israelite who brought his sacrifice to God delegated the Kohen to perform the rite on his behalf, while he stood by.[33]

The *berit milah* rite in actuality consists of three distinct operations:

(a) *Milah* proper, which is the surgical removal of the foreskin from the crown of the genital. This operation leaves behind a membrane covering the genital.

(b) *Periah*, the tearing of this membrane with the thumbnail and index finger back to the corona.

(c) *Metzitzah* (lit. suction), the sucking out of the blood either orally or through a glass tube to facilitate healing.

The halakhic principle is that circumcision without *periah* is not considered valid.

While the *Mohel* is cutting away the foreskin, he recites the blessing "Blessed are You, O Lord our God, King of the Universe Who has sanctified us with Your commandments and commanded us concerning circumcision." While he completes the procedure, the father of the infant recites the blessing "Blessed Are You. . . and commanded us to enter him into the covenant of Abraham our father." By this time the *Mohel* will have finished with the entire operation and the assembled guests respond: "Just as he entered into the covenant, so may he be introduced to the study of the Torah, to the nuptial canopy and to good deeds."

Exactly when the *Mohel* is to recite his blessing is the subject of a difference of opinion among the authorities. The general rule is that a blessing is to be recited "*over la'asiatan*," immediately before the performance of the mitzvah. Because of this, some authorities contend that the *Mohel* should recite his blessing before he begins to remove the foreskin. On the other hand, the removal of the foreskin does not complete the circumcision; the *periah* does. It is on this basis that others rule that the blessing be recited after the *milah*, just before the *periah*. The custom today is to compromise and pronounce the blessing while the *Mohel* is excising the foreskin.[34]

It would be logical to assume that the *Sheheḥeyanu* which is recited on the occasion of every seasonally recurring joyous event, should be recited by the father at the circumcision of his newborn son as well. Yet there is a difference of opinion whether the father should recite this blessing at the rite of circumcision. Those who oppose it base their ruling on the following arguments:

(a) Circumcision is not limited *only* to the father but can also be performed by others in the community.

(b) According to halakhah a status is presumed established only after thirty days have passed. For example: the redemption of the first born is performed only after the infant is thirty days old in order to be assured that it is a *ben kayama*, a viable child. At circumcision, the child is only eight days old and his viability is not yet established. Thus, the *Sheheḥeyanu*, the expression of gratitude to God for permitting us to live to see this event, is yet premature.

(c) It would be incongruous to recite a prayer of joy while the infant is subjected to pain.

Those that advocate the recital of the *Sheheḥeyanu* counter that, although another person may perform the rite, he does so as the surrogate of the father. As to the second objection, although the child's life is still in doubt, most children do survive.Lastly, even though there is some discomfort to the child, it is a very joyous occasion and should be subject to the same law as a holiday, when the *Sheheḥeyanu* is recited.

In practice Jewish society is divided on this issue: In Eretz Israel the *Sheheḥeyanu* is pronounced; in the diaspora communities it is omitted.[35]

The response of the guests, "So may he be introduced to the study of the Torah, to the nuptial canopy and to good deeds," is based on the Rabbinic decree that it is the father's duty to teach his son, to secure a wife for him and to lead him in the path of righteousness (Kiddushin 29a). At thirteen the child is expected to fulfill the commandments of the Torah; at the age of eighteen he is expected to marry and, thereby having removed all temptations, to lead a pious life.

But is it correct to say "Just as he entered the covenant of Abraham. . .", since he did not enter, rather he was entered by others? The answer proposed is that no one performs any mitzvah without some ulterior motive. He either hopes to earn a reward or is afraid of Divine punishment. We, therefore, express the hope that "Just as he (the child) entered the convenant of Abraham" without any ulterior motive, so he will perform good deeds later on in life as well, purely out of piety.[36]

Having removed the foreskin, the *Mohel* places it in a receptacle filled with earth. There are several reasons for this:

(a) The Scriptures relate that God promised Abraham, "I will make thy seed as the dust of the earth" (Genesis 13:16).

(b) We have already indicated several times that the lap of the *Sandek* is considered the equivalent of the altar in the Temple. Since the altar was made of earth, we put the foreskin into a dish containing earth.[37]

(c) When the Children of Israel wandering in the desert circumcised their newborn sons they interred the foreskins in the sands of the desert. Later, when Balaam was hired by Balak to bring down a curse upon them, he countered by saying, "Who can count the dust of Jacob?" According to the Rabbis of the Talmud this meant that Balaam was deeply impressed by the fact that, weary as they were, the Jews circumcised their young and covered their foreskins with earth. He thus intimated to Balaam that such brave people would never be overcome.[38]

(d) Another reason for covering the foreskin with earth is to teach us a lesson in faith: From infancy, Jews may be persecuted and be trodden upon like dust. Yet their faith must never waver in the promise of God to Jacob that his seed would be numerous as the dust of the earth.[39]

(e) The dust used in covering the foreskin serves as a lesson in humility. All our lives we tread on dust. However, the end is that man dies, and when he is buried that same dust is heaped upon *him.*[40]

(f) The Scriptures teach, "If your enemy be hungry feed him bread" (Proverbs 25:21). It is also written "And the serpent . . . dust shall be his food" (Isaiah 65:25). The Serpent was man's very first adversary. The evil inclination which the serpent symbolizes pursues man all his life. Hence, we throw the foreskin into the dust as if we were saying to this infant: "We have just fed the serpent of evil his bread, beware of him all the days of your life."[41]

After the surgery, the *Mohel* recites the following prayer:

> Blessed are You, O Lord our God, King of the Universe, Who has sanctified the well-beloved (Isaac) from the womb and has set Your statute in his flesh, and has sealed his offspring with the sign of the holy covenant. Therefore, in reward of this, O

living God, our Portion and our Rock, deliver from destruction the dearly beloved of our flesh, for the sake of the covenant You have set in our flesh. Blessed are You, O Lord our God, Who has made the covenant.

Our God and God of our fathers, preserve this child to his father and to his mother, and let his name be called in Israel . . . son of . . . Let the father rejoice in his offspring, and let the mother be glad with the fruit of her womb; as it is written: "Let your father and your mother rejoice, and let her that bore you be glad." And it is said: "And I passed by you and I saw you weltering in your blood and I said unto you: 'In your blood shall you live.' Yea, I said: 'In your blood shall you live.'" And it is said: "He has remembered His covenant forever, the word which He commanded to a thousand generations: (the covenant) which He made with Abraham, and His oath unto Isaac, and confirmed the same unto Jacob for a statute, to Israel for everlasting covenant." And it is said: "And Abraham circumcised his son Isaac when he was eight days old, as God commanded him." O give thanks unto the Lord for He is good; for His loving kindness endures forever. This little child, may he become great. As he had been entered into the covenant, so may he be introduced to the study of the Law, to the nuptial canopy, and to good deeds.

The reason we repeat the sentence, "In thy blood you shall live" is to underscore a basic doctrine of Judaism: Man through his own efforts can attain the benefits of both worlds, the mundane and the heavenly.

When the *Mohel*, in his concluding benedictions, comes to the words: "In your blood you shall live," he dips his finger into the wine and with it wets the baby's lips. The source is in the Midrash: When the Children of Israel in the desert worshiped the Golden Calf, Moses instructed the tribe of Levi to take their swords into their hands, grind the calf to dust, cast it into the water and force the sinners to drink. In this manner he was able to determine who had worshiped the calf and who had not. This was similar to the procedure used in the case of a *sotah*, the wife suspected of infidelity (Numbers 5:12).

The Jews in the desert were circumcised, but without *periah* because of the dangers of the journey. Realizing that a number of people would die on account of the Golden Calf, and conscious that they would not enter into their Heavenly rest because they were not completely circumcised, Moses instructed Aaron to do the *periah* and Joshua to put the water to their lips, while he, Moses, performed the *milah*. We, in constrast, wet the lips of the infant and bless him with the words, "In your blood shall you *live*." With the generation of the desert it was a matter of preparing the sinners for *death*; in the case of this infant we pray that *milah*, *periah*, *metzitzah* and the wetting of the lips will prepare him for a long and noble life.[42]

It is only following the circumcision that the infant boy is given a name. This is based on two Biblical sources:

(a) When God said to Abraham, "As for Me, behold, My covenant is with you" (Genesis 17:4), He gave Abraham his full name, i.e. Abraham instead of Abram. Thus we see that the name is given at the time when the covenant (the *Berit*) is made.

(b) "And Abraham called the name of his son, that was born to him Isaac. And Abraham circumcised his son Isaac when he was eight days old" (Genesis 21:3,4).

At the conclusion of the entire ritual, those present are treated to a meal which is considered a *se'udat mitzvah*. This, too, has its origin in the Bible. In Genesis (21:8) we read, "And Abraham made a great feast on the day that Isaac was weaned." The Rabbis of the Talmud play upon the word *higamel*, which means "weaned." The numerical value of *Heh* is five; that of *Gimmel* is three—a total of eight. The *Mem* and *Lamed* comprise the word *mal*—"circumcise." The allusion is that Abraham made a feast on the eighth day when Isaac was circumcised.[43]

On the first Shabbat after her recovery from confinement, it is customary for the mother to attend synagogue services, and for the father to be called up to the Torah. Two reasons are offered:

(a) During childbirth the mother's life was in jeopardy. Now that she has overcome that danger, she comes to the synagogue to express her gratitude to God for her safe delivery.

(b) In the days of the Temple, a new mother was required to offer a sacrifice. Today, accompanying her husband to the synagogue where she witnesses his being called to the Torah and reciting the appropriate benedictions serves as a substitute for the sacrifice.[44]

The elaborate rituals and the profusion of customs observed in connection with the birth of a boy are due to the high drama of the rite of curcumcision and the singular position which the *berit milah* occupies among the commandments of the Torah.

The birth of a daughter calls for much less ritual and it is generally observed with a simpler ceremony. Nevertheless it is an occasion for rejoicing which is centered around and usually follows the naming of the daughter.

The general custom is to name the newborn daughter in the synagogue after the father was called up to the Torah. This usually takes place on the first Shabbat following the birth.

In some communities the father is called up to the Torah and the daughter is named the first day after birth on which there is Torah reading such as Monday or Thursday.[45]

It is customary for the parents of the just named daughter to treat the congregation to a festive *Kiddush* of drinks and pastries. On this occasion the guests offer their prayerful wishes to the parents that may they "introduce her to the fulfillment of Torah, to the nuptial canopy and to good deeds" as befitting a true daughter of Israel.

SOURCES

1. *Tur Yoreh De'ah* 260-261;
   Arukh ha-Shulḥan Yoreh De'ah 260 pars. 1, 4; 261 pars. 1, 2.
2. *Ḥayye Avraham* p. 52b.
3. Ibid 53.
4. *Tur Yoreh De'ah* 260; *Perishah* 260.

5. *Tur Yoreh De'ah* 263; *Arukh ha-Shulḥan* 263 par. 13.
6. *Tur Yoreh De'ah* 262; *Arukh ha-Shulḥan* 262 par. 14.
7. *Tur Yoreh De'ah* 263.
8. *Zohar*, Koraḥ.
9. *Sefer ha-Mat'amim* p. 75-76; *Ta'ame ha-Minhagim* p. 385.
10. *Massa Bavel* p. 200.
11. *Sefer ha-Mat'amim* p. 77.
12. *Ta'ame ha-Minhagim* ibid.
13. *Shaare Efraim*, ch. 2, par. 8.
14. *Arukh ha-Shulḥan* 262 pars. 8, 9.
15. *Sefer ha-Mat'amim* p. 76-77.
16. *Sefer ha-Mat'amim* p. 78.
17. *Arukh ha-Shulḥan*. Yoreh De'ah 265 par. 35.
18. *Avudraham* p. 191; *Sefer ha-Mat'amim* p. 78.
19. Ibid.
20. *Arukh ha-Shulḥan* 265 par. 14.
21. *Ḥayye Avraham* p. 54a.
22. *Sefer ha-Mat'amim* p. 79.
23. *Ta'ame ha-Minhagim* p. 386.
24. *Sefer ha-Mat'amim* pp. 78, 79.
25. *Midrash Shoḥer Tov*. Chap. 35.
26. *Ta'ame ha-Minhagim* p. 391.
27. *Arukh ha-Shulḥan* 265 par. 35.
28. *Perishah* 265, par. 20.
29. *Pirke de-Rabbi Eliezer* Chap. 29.
30. *Ta'ame ha-Minhagim* p. 387.
31. Ibid.
32. *Massa Bavel* pp. 131, 200.
33. *Tur Yoreh De'ah* 365.
34. *Tur Yoreh De'ah*, beginning of 365; *Bet Yoseph* and *Perishah* 365; *Arukh ha-Shulḥan* 365, pars. 8, 10, 12.
35. *Arukh ha-Shulḥan* Yoreh De'ah 365, pars. 27, 28; *Ta'ame ha-Minhagim* p. 388; *Sefer Eretz Yisrael* p. 23.
36. *Ta'ame ha-Minhagim* p. 389; *Avudraham* p. 190.
37. *Sefer ha-Mat'amim* p. 78.
38. *Pirke de-Rabbi Eliezer*, Chap. 29.
39. *Minhage Yeshurun* p. 100.
40. Ibid.
41. *Ta'ame ha-Minhagim* p. 390.
42. *Pirke de-Rabbi Eliezer*, Chap. 29; *Avudraham* p. 191; *Sefer ha-Mat'amim* p. 79; *Ta'ame ha-Minhagim* p. 390.
43. *Pirke de-Rabbi Eliezer*, Chap. 29; *Ḥayye Avraham* p. 53b; *Arukh ha-Shulḥan*, Yoreh De'ah 265, par. 37.
44. *Sefer ha-Mat'amim* p. 46.
45. *Ta'ame ha-Minhagim* p. 396.

Pidyon ha-Ben

Another hallowed rite connected with birth, but much less frequently performed than *Berit Milah*, is *Pidyon ha-Ben*, the Redemption of the First-Born Son.

Why are we commanded to redeem our first-born son? From whom, when and how are we to redeem him? The answers to these questions are all clearly set out in the Torah. Immediately after the last of the Ten Plagues—the slaying of all the first-born of the Egyptians—God spoke to the Jewish People:

> Sanctify unto Me all the first-born that opens the womb among the Children of Israel. . . and all the first-born of man among your sons shall you redeem. And it shall be when your son asks you in time to come, saying: What is this? You shall say to him: By strength of hand the Lord brought us out of Egypt, from the house of bondage; and it came to pass, when Pharaoh would hardly let us go, that the Lord slew all the first-born in the land of Egypt,. . . therefore. . . all the first-born of my sons I redeem. (Ex. 13:1-3; 2:15)

The implication is clear: by delivering the Jewish people from Egyptian slavery, and more specifically in return for His slaying all the first-born of the Egyptians, God has sanctified the first-born of Israel and consigned them to His service. Through this designation the first-born were to be entrusted with the sacrificial service in the Tabernacle that was to be built.

After the Jewish people, including their first-born, sinned by worshipping the Golden Calf, God commanded Moses, "Take the Levites instead of all the first-born among the Children of Israel; and the Levites shall be mine" (Numbers 3:45). Because of their participation in the debacle of the Golden Calf, the *Bekhorim* (the first-born) became unfit for the service of God and were replaced by the Tribe of Levi which did not take part in that abomination.

How were the *Bekhorim* to be replaced by the Levites? Through *Pidyon Bekhor*—redemption of the first-born—details of which are quite clearly defined in the Torah.

> Everything that opens the womb of all flesh which they offer unto the Lord, shall be yours; however, the first-born of man you shall surely redeem . . . And their redemption money—from a month old shall you redeem them—shall be according to your valuation, five shekels of silver . . . (Numbers 18:15-16).

In this passage we find spelled out the four key elements of the mitzvah of *Pidyon Bekhor* or, as it is more popularly know, *Pidyon ha-Ben*, Redemption of the (first-born) Son.

(a) "Everything that opens the womb" (*peter reḥem)*—for the purposes of *Pidyon ha-Ben*, first-born means the *mother's* first child. Thus a man can have several *bekhorim* from several wives, but a woman can have only one first-born, even if she should give birth to the first sons of several husbands in succession.[1]

(b) "You shall surely redeem" is the basic stating of the precept of *Pidyon ha-Ben*.

(c) "From a month old you shall redeem them." The redemption is to take place on the thirty-first day after the birth. While fixing the time appears to be a *gezerat ha-katuv*, a scriptural decree without apparent reason, in one authority's opinion the rationale is that after thirty days the status of the child's viability has been established.[2]

(d) "Five shekels of silver" is the precise amount the father is required to give the *Kohen* (member par excellence of the Tribe of Levi) for redeeming his *bekhor*. With the silver contents of modern currencies fluctuating, it is difficult to establish the exact equivalent of five shekels. Five United States silver dollars are considered as having the proper amount of silver. More recently the State of Israel had special *Pidyon ha-Ben* coins minted for this purpose.

The *Kohen* may voluntarily return to the father the coins received from him. But to do so by prior agreement would render the redemption invalid. According to some authorities, to expect the *Kohen* to return the money, even without prior agreement to that effect, invalidates the transaction.[3]

Not every *bekhor* is subject to the mitzvah of *Pidyon ha-Ben*. The following are exempt:

(a) The son of a *Kohen* or a Levite. As we learned before, the very act of redemption became necessary because the Tribe of Levi took the place of the *bekhorim* as the functionaries in the Temple service. Thus the members of this tribe do not have to be redeemed.

(b) The son of the daughter of a *Kohen* or a Levite, even if the father is an Israelite. The reason is that the status of a *bekhor* is defined by the term *peter reḥem*, "opener of the womb." In other words, the mother is the determining factor, and since she is of priestly stock, her offspring is exempt from *Pidyon ha-Ben*.[4]

(c) A child born following a miscarriage, since this child did not open the womb; the aborted one did. For the same reason, a child delivered by caesarean section is also exempt.[5]

As we have seen, the time prescribed for *Pidyon ha-Ben* is the thirty-first day after birth. However, if that day falls on a Sabbath or a holiday, when no monetary exchange is permitted, the ceremony is to take place immediately after.[6]

The Torah places the obligation to redeem the *bekhor* upon the father. If the child is an orphan, or if he is not redeemed for any other reason by the time he becomes *bar mitzvah*, it is his obligation to redeem himself. Until modern times, it was customary to hang around the neck of an orphan *bekhor* a small medallion with an inscription as to his status as a reminder that upon reaching maturity he has to redeem himself.[7] Nowadays either a relative or the *Bet Din* performs the *Pidyon ha-Ben* of an orphan, or acts as a surrogate for the father if the latter for any reason is unable to do it himself.

There is however an opinion that in performing the mitzvah of *Pidyon ha-Ben* the delegation of a surrogate is not permitted, and that the father must personally carry out the ritual. And one outstanding authority offers an explanation: The sanctified status of the first-born came as a result of the slaying of the Egyptian first-born. This latter act was carried out by God Himself rather than through an intermediary. Conversely, the concomitant mitzvah should be performed by the father himself and not delegated to a stranger.[8]

The actual process of the ceremony of *Pidyon ha-Ben* is not mentioned in the Torah. The ritual as we know it today was instituted during the Gaonic period (circa 600-1050). The proceedings are as follows: After the assembled have washed their hands in preparation to breaking bread at festive tables, the traditional blessing over the bread is recited. The meal is interrupted and the father of the infant brings the child to the table while holding the five coins in his hand, and declares to the appointed *Kohen*, "This is my first-born, the one who opened the womb of his mother and he is to be redeemed for five shekels."

After receiving the child, the *Kohen* asks the father, "Which do you prefer? To give me your first born or to redeem him for five silver coins?"

The father replies, "I prefer to redeem my son and here is his redemption money as I am obliged to do according to the law of the Torah."

Before handing over the money, the father recites the following two benedictions: "Blessed are You Lord, Our God, King of the Universe who has sanctified us by His commandments and has bidden us to redeem the first-born son." "Blessed are You, Lord, Our God, King of the Universe Who has granted us life, sustained us and permitted us to celebrate this joyous occasion."

Upon the conclusion of the recitation of these two benedictions, the father presents the money to the priest and the latter, holding the redemption money over the head of the infant pronounces, "This is instead of that, this in commutation for that, this in remission of that." He then concludes the ceremony with the priestly blessing addressed to the child: "May the Lord bless you and keep you; May the Lord make His countenance to shine upon you and be generous unto you; May the Lord lift up His countenance upon you and give you peace."

As to the above dialogue between the *Kohen* and the father, two outstanding authorities ask a very pertinent question: In the Torah we are distinctly told "However, the first born of man you shall surely redeem" (Numbers 18:15). If so, how can the *Kohen* put it up to the father which he prefers, the child or five silver coins? Does the father have a choice? Does not the Torah explicitly command him to *surely* redeem his son?

One authority explains that the question put to the father is purely rhetorical and it is aimed to arouse the passionate desire of the father to keep his son. And it is an expression of this sentiment when the father says to the *Kohen*, "Here are five silver coins, and these may be my entire wealth, but return my child to me."[9]

The second authority offers a more analytical answer. We have previously noted that in the wake of the Exodus from Egypt God sanctified the first-born and mustered them into His service. it was later on that the priestly duties were taken away from the first-born and transferred to the Levites. However, the first-born remained with a vestige of sanctity which would restrict them in many ways. The purpose of the *Pidyon ha-Ben* is to release them from this status of sanctity. As it is inconceivable that parents should want their eldest son to live the life of a recluse, the priest asks the father, "Which do you prefer, that the child remain in a state of sanctity or that he be redeemed from his life of holiness with five silver coins?"[10]

It is customary for the father to present the child at the *Pidyon ha-Ben* ceremony on an ornate, richly decorated plate which is further adorned with pieces of jewelry and other precious objects as well as sweets. All this seems to be aimed at making the child appear even more adorable to the father so that he be most eager to redeem him. It is also a *hiddur mitzvah*, a beautification of a mitzvah.

The festive meal served on this occasion is declared a *se'udat mitzvah*, a meal to partake of which is considered a meritorious act. The Kabbalists went a step further and invested this meal with great mystical meaning. According to them to partake of food served at the *Pidyon ha-Ben* earns as much merit as fasting for 84 days which is sufficient to expiate even the greatest sin. One Kabbalistic authority finds an allusion to this in the Torah. At one point, when relating the redemption of all the *bekhorim* in the desert (Numbers 3:49) instead of the word *pidyon*, the unusual spelling of *pidyom* is used. This is interpreted as *peh-dalet (= 84) yom*, meaning, eighty-four days.[10]

SOURCES

1. *Tur Yoreh De'ah, Bet Yoseph, Perisha* 305.
2. *Avudraham* p. 193.
3. *Arukh ha-Shulḥan*, Yoreh De'ah 305 pars. 27-30.
4. *Tur Yoreh De'ah* 305; *Arukh ha-Shulḥan* 305 pars. 56, 58.
5. *Arukh ha-Shulḥan*, 305 par. 63.
6. Ibid. par. 42.
7. Ibid. pars. 13, 14.
8. *Ta'ame ha-Minhagim* p. 398.
9. *Ta'ame ha-Minhagim* p. 397.
10. *Arukh ha-Shulḥan* 305 pars. 35, 37.
11. *Ta'ame ha-Minhagim* p. 399.

Bar Mitzvah

A most important milestone in the lifecycle of a Jew is reached when he becomes thirteen years old. On that day he becomes *bar mitzvah*, lit. son of commandment, meaning that in the eyes of Jewish law he has now come of age. From now on he is subject to all the obligations as well as all the privileges of an adult as pertains to the observance of the various *mitzvot.*

That a boy reaches halakhic maturity at the age of thirteen is related in the Mishnah (Aboth 5:21): ". . . at thirteen (the age is reached) for the fulfillment of the commandments. . . ." The Talmud (Nazir 29 b) infers this from the Biblical narrative (Gen. 34:25): ". . . Simeon and Levi . . . took each *man* his sword . . ." According to Rabbinic tradition Levi was only thirteen years old at that time and the Torah refers to him as a "man."

While the concept of *bar mitzvah* itself is already mentioned in the Talmud, the custom of celebrating it with any kind of festivity is relatively recent. The earliest reference to any celebration is by a fifteenth century authority who declares that it is as incumbent upon the father to make a festive meal on the day his son becomes *bar mitzvah* as it is on the day of his wedding.[1]

The *bar mitzvah* ceremony as it has developed through the ages centers around the two most conspicuous rituals which the celebrant commences to observe on this day: one is *tefillin* which he is obligated henceforth to put on every weekday morning; the other is being called up to the Torah from which he had been barred before as a minor.

After the boy is called up to the Torah and recites the appropriate benedictions, the father pronounces a peculiar blessing:

Barukh she-petarani me-onsho shel zeh—"Blessed is He Who has now freed me from the liability of this one." This is based on the Midrash (Bereshit Rabbah 63, 10): Rabbi Eleazar said: A father is obligated to occupy himself with the upbringing of his son till he becomes thirteen; thereafter he should say "Blessed is He Who has freed me from the liability of this one." The underlying meaning is that the father is responsible for the misdeeds of his minor son since they are the result of a lack of proper upbringing by the father. On this day, as the son reaches manhood, the father is relieved of further responsibility for him.[2]

It is traditional for the *bar mitzvah* boy to deliver a talmudic discourse at the festive meal, generally pertaining to a halakhic aspect of the mitzvah of *tefillin*. According to an outstanding Rabbinic authority, the meal at which such discourse is delivered is considered a *seudat mitzvah*, a meal to partake of which is considered a pious deed.[3] The welcoming of a new member to the community of Torah observing Jews is indeed a cause for celebration.

On the Shabbat prior to his thirteenth birthday, it is customary to call up the boy to read the Maftir, the concluding part of the weekly portion, and the Haftarah, the prophetic reading. In many communities the boy reads the entire *Sidrah* and acts as the *sheliaḥ tzibbur* (leader of the congregation) on the Sabbath following his thirteenth birthday. This demonstrates his being accepted by the community as an adult.

As mentioned before, one of the outstanding events of the day on which a boy becomes *bar mitzvah* is his putting on tefillin for the first time. In some communities, however, he begins to practice this mitzvah one month earlier so that he can be fully acquainted with the procedure by the time it becomes obligatory. Lubavitch hassidim begin to put on *tefillin* two months in advance, one month without pronouncing the blessings and the second month with the blessings.

The contemporary custom of celebrating the *bar mitzvah* with lavish and ostentatious parties has no basis in Jewish tradition and it is in fact contrary to the spirit if not the letter of Jewish law and morality.

SOURCES

1. *Arukh ha-Shulḥan*, Oraḥ Ḥayyim 225, par. 4; *Magen Avraham* loc. cit., par. 5.
2. *Rama*, Oraḥ Ḥayyim 225, par. 2.; *Arukh ha-Shulḥan* ibid.
3. *Yam shel Shelomoh* on Bava Kamma Ch. 7; *Arukh ha-Shulḥan* ibid.

Death and Mourning

The Sages of the Mishna (Avot 4:22) teach us that we are born involuntarily and die involuntarily. A person has no say in being born, and in God's good time, he passes on without being able to avoid it. However, there the analogy ends. The pangs of birth, both for the infant and its mother, are rewarded with the experience of life. The pangs of death result in a void and in a confrontation with the unknown that can be a crushing experience for the living. Because we know nothing about death and we cannot explain rationally what happens after death, our emotions become shattered when we encounter the death of a close relative or friend.

Nevertheless, man is resilient. He refuses to surrender completely to this unknown. If rational reflection cannot serve him, he will resort to the non-rational. Where reason stops, mysticism takes over. Consequently, in matters of death and mourning the mystical breaks through the barriers of the rational religion, and the Jew seeks relief from the trauma of his loss and finds the answer to his search for comprehension in mystic conceptions.

It would be useful to bear in mind certain fundamental principles of Jewish thinking as they relate to the dead. In the first place, the Jew is expected to remember that man was formed from dust of the earth and, after his sojourn in the physical world, returns to the dust of the earth. This popular maxim has far-reaching implications. Is cremation permissible according to Jewish Law? Is it permissible, according to Jewish Law, to place a body in a vault on a shelf? To both questions the answer is a categorical "No!", since in both instances the body is not returned to the *earth*.

Another basic principle: the body of a deceased person is entitled almost to the same respect and dignity accorded to the living. Here, the principle of *lo'eg la-rash*, ridiculing the unfortunate, applies. For example, one should not wear a tallit in the proximity of a deceased, because the living person thereby is guilty of arrogance. He deliberately demonstrates his fulfilment of a mitzvah in the presence of the unfortunate, the deceased who cannot perform the mitzvah.

Finally, Jewish thinking impresses upon us that the element which confers on man a certain measure of sanctity is his soul. The body is composed of metals, chemicals and various organic matter. The body is profane; it is for this reason that we are asked to wash our hands upon leaving a cemetery. We cleanse ourselves symbolically of the impurities and defilements represented by the interred bodies. To accord respect and reverence to a cemetery is correct and proper; to ascribe sanctity to it is alien to our thinking.

The rule is that when death takes place the eyes of the deceased must immediately be closed, preferably by a son or some other member of the family. Several reasons are offered:

(a) According to the Kabbalah, man is not privileged to observe simultaneously both worlds, the physical and the spiritual. As long as his eyes are open to this world, he cannot behold the glory of the other world. Therefore, upon death, the eyes of the deceased are closed immediately.

(b) Others take an opposite view. Upon death, man comes to meet his Heavenly Maker. It is unbecoming for those eyes which are beholding the *Shekhinah* to also look upon mundane things.

(c) The believing Jew looks forward to the day of Resurrection. One cannot open his eyes to a radically new phenomenon unless they were first closed.[1]

(d) While a person is alive his eyes are responsible for the pursuit of sinful things. His eyes saw and he lusted; his eyes noticed and he became greedy. The son or another member of the family closes the eyes of the deceased as if saying, "Our father was never guilty of such behavior. His eyes only looked for the benefit of his children and family."[2]

(e) That the son is expected to close the eyes of his departed father is deduced from the Torah, where God speaks to the apprehensive Jacob and assures him, "And Joseph shall put his hand upon your eyes" (Genesis 46:4).

(f) In some communities it is customary to spread dust on the eyes of the deceased to underscore the moral: "See what happens to eyes that lusted. They are now like the dust of the earth."[3]

Immediately after death the body is covered and placed on the ground. The reasons for this practice are:

(a) A deceased person is an unbecoming sight. Before people come to attend to him, his body should be covered so that the dead person be remembered as he was when alive and not as he is when dead.[4]

(b) In the laws of ritual purity as promulgated in Leviticus and expounded by the Sages of the Talmud, the dead body is a primary source of *tum'ah*, defilement, and it imparts impurity to what it rests on with the exception of soil. By placing the body on the ground we avoid the ritual defilement.[5]

Once the body is placed on the floor, candles are lit and placed beside it. The basis for this custom is the scriptual verse "For the commandment is a lamp and the law is light" (Proverbs 6:23). The Scriptures also compare the soul of a person to light: "The soul of a man is the lamp of the Lord" (Proverbs 20:27). Therefore, a lit candle is placed near the one whose soul had just departed in order to express what is taught in yet another scriptual verse: "When you walk, it shall lead you; when you lie down, it shall watch over you" (Proverbs 6:22). That is to say that the light of the good deeds performed by the deceased during his lifetime will accompany his soul to its heavenly rest.[6]

Among Yemenite Jews the custom of lighting candles is unknown.[7]

A custom that has come down to us from ancient times dictates to pour out in front of the houses all stored-up water in the vicinity of the home of the deceased. There are a number of attempts to account for this custom:

(a) Since water used to be a precious commodity which was not to be wasted, the sudden appearance of a puddle of water in front of a home would serve as a sign that a death had occurred there.

(b) When spilled, water spreads in all directions. So, it is hoped, will God's attribute of loving-kindness spread over the soul of this newly departed person.

(c) In the religious life of the Jew, water is of prime importance as a cleansing and purifying agent. Nevertheless, water is now being wasted to remind us that what man pursues as things of value are in truth worthless.

(d) According to the Aggadah, the Children of Israel were accompanied in the desert by a rolling stone that poured forth water. In the Scriptures we find, "And Miriam died there and was buried there. And there was no water for the Congregation" (Numbers 20: 1, 2). The moment this saintly woman died, the waters, which had flowed heretofore only in her merit, ceased issuing from the stone. We want to demonstrate that the same is true of the deceased lying before us. He was a righteous man, and we pour out all the water indicating symbolically that as a result of his demise there is no water.[8]

One authority minimizes this custom as not especially important. In fact, he contends that in a densely populated area pouring water on the ground may cause unforeseen difficulties, especially in the winter.[9]

Every organized Jewish community has its *Ḥevrah Kadishah*, "Holy Society," whose members are dedicated to the burying of the dead. Why the appellation "holy" when they are exposed to the impurity and defilement of the dead bodies? The name, it is suggested, is a euphemism: to save them the embarrassment that would arise from being called "The Society of the Defiled," they are referred to as the "Holy Society." Another reason: "Holy" is synonymous with ritual preparation. These people are always ready for their grim task of preparing the body for proper burial. Indeed, one must be inclined to piety and holiness to participate reverently in burying the dead.[10]

It is this *Ḥevrah Kadishah* that washes the body and dresses it in white linen shrouds. To prevent families in vieing with each other in providing elaborate garments for the dead, the Sages of the Talmud ordained that the dead should all be clothed in simple, white, linen shrouds—the rich and the poor alike (Mo'ed Katan 27b). One authority, however, without challenging the basic rule of a white linen shroud does recommend to choose linen of a better quality. His opinion is based on the concept of Resurrection. It would be most appropriate for the dead to rise dressed in the finest linen to greet the Messiah.[11]

Another reason for white linen: In Temple times, Yom Kippur was the only day in the year when the High Priest would enter the Holy of Holies, dressed in simple, white, linen garments. There he would make confession and ask forgiveness for his sins and for the sins of the people. From this we gather that when one stands alone in confrontation with his Maker, he should be humble and contrite, wearing simple, white, unadorned linen garments.[12]

After the body is dressed, if the deceased was a man, it is wrapped in a *tallit*. Why is the *tallit*, a sacred object, inserted in the defilement of a burial casket? In fact, there is a disagreement concerning this practice. In the opinion of some authorities the deceased should be enwrapped in a *tallit* in order to avoid *lo'eg la-rash*, scoffing at the dead. In the chapter on *tallit* and *tzitzit* we learned how this mitzvah is meant to remind us on all six-hundred and thirteen *mitzvot*. Now, when the *Ḥevrah Kadisha* who attend to the body and the people who follow the funeral procession all wear garments with *tzitziot*, it would be an affront to the deceased who cannot fulfill this mitzvah. Therefore, it is suggested, the body should be taken out to the cemetery wrapped in a proper *tallit* with its *tzitziot*, but before interment one of the fringes should be removed thus rendered unfit for religious use. In this way violation of the prohibition against *lo'eg la-rash* will be avoided without consigning a kosher *tallit* to the grave.

Those who oppose the placing of a *tallit* in a coffin argue that if we were to bury everyone in a *tallit* including those who during their lifetime had been lax in the performance of this *mitzvah*, it would be a most blatant case of *lo'eg la-rash*, ridiculing the deceased, to cover a dead person in a *tallit* when he never wore one in his lifetime. The prevailing practice is to enwrap the dead in a *tallit*.[13]

The ritual of *keri'ah*, the rending of a garment as a sign of mourning, is performed at different stages in the various Jewish communities. There are those who perform this ritual immediately following the death of the relative. Others do so before the funeral procession commences; some wait until interment.[14]

What is the source for this custom? In recounting the death of Aaron's sons, the Torah relates that God ordered Aaron: "The hair of your head you shall not grow long, and your garments you shall not rend" (Leviticus 10:6). Since God deemed it necessary to instruct him *not* to rend his clothes, we deduce that in all other instances of bereavement relatives are required to do so. Another source for the rite of *keri'ah* for a bereaved is the passage: "Then arose the King (David) and rent his garments" (II Samuel 13:31). A pragmatic reason for *keri'ah* is advanced by one authority. Taking into account the shock experienced by the mourner upon learning of the death of his relative, in order to divert his grief and his thoughts of the dead, he is asked to rend his clothes. This wanton destruction of property should divert his thoughts from his grief and bring him relief if only for a brief moment.[15]

Grief at the loss of a mother or father is generally more intense than at the loss of a brother, sister, son, daughter, or spouse —the seven relations for whom Jewish law requires *keri'ah*. Accordingly, in the case of a mother or father, the clothes are rent on the left side opposite the heart; in the case of the others, on the right side.

There are additional distinctions between the *keri'ah* for a parent and that for other relatives: For a parent we rend every garment we happen to be wearing except the one touching the body; for others we only tear the outer garment. Where it becomes necessary to change the torn garment during the initial period of mourning, the *shiv'ah*, we do not rend the garment into which we have changed; for parents we do. If the news of the death of a close relative reaches us thirty days after the event, we are exempt from *keri'ah*; in the case of a parent, the rite is mandatory regardless of the time that has elapsed in between. The garment torn for a parent may never be rewoven or invisibly repaired; for a relative we may do so after thirty days.[16]

Keri'ah is performed while the mourner is standing. The precedent for this is the scriptural verse, "Then *arose* Job and rent his robe" (Job 1:20). The tear must be at least a handbreadth in length, again based on a scriptural precedent. When the messenger informed David that King Saul and his son Jonathan had fallen in battle, David, we are told, took hold of his clothes and rent them (II Samuel 1:11). By the words "took hold" it is inferred that his hand fully gripped and tore his garment.

Finally, the initial tear must be made by a stranger so that the mourner will feel the grief all the more inasmuch as there is a certain degree of humiliation when a stranger performs the *keri'ah.*[17]

It is mandatory to perform the burial as soon as possible, preferably on the day of death. This ruling is derived from the Scriptures where the Torah speaks of the criminal executed by hanging: "His body shall not remain all night on the tree, but you shall surely bury him on that day" (Deuteronomy 21:23).[18] When one dies in Jerusalem during the day, he is buried the same night. Another source for the prohibition of *halanat ha-met*, postponement of burial, is in Numbers 10:1: "And Miriam died there, and was buried there." The proximity of the words "died" and "buried" indicates that the burial took place immediately after death.[19]

The Zohar offers two mystical reasons why burial should not be delayed.

(a) The soul which dwelt in the body for so many years is grief-stricken at the departure and this grief lasts as long as the body is not buried.

(b) By not burying our dead immediately, we may be interfering with God's plan. Possibly when the soul left the body, God intended to transfer that soul into another body. However, this transmigration of a soul to a *living* body cannot occur while the *dead* body lies unburied.[20]

After all the preparations are completed, the burial takes place. The basic rule that the dead must be buried has its origin in the Torah: "For dust you are and unto dust you shall return" (Genesis 3:19). The human body is not to be disposed of in any other manner. In view of this, even the severed limb of a living person must be buried in the ground. Even a stillborn infant or a miscarried foetus must be buried according to Jewish law.[21]

There is a pronounced difference in custom concerning the interring of the body. In Jerusalem and among Oriental communities elsewhere, it is customary to place the body directly into the grave with only the sides lined with stones and planks. All this is based on, "From dust you come; unto dust you shall return." In other communities, the body is placed in a wooden casket, and so lowered into the grave. To comply with the requirement, "From dust you come and unto dust you return," holes are bored in several places in the casket so that the soil can penetrate. The wood of the casket will eventually disintegrate into dust; a metal casket is forbidden. In fact, even the use of metal nails in the casket is frowned upon.[22]

Before the person is buried, any jewelry he was wearing must be removed. This practice has its basis in the incident involving the Golden Calf in the desert. There the people removed their jewelry and contributed it towards the making of a Golden Calf which they worshipped. Now when the deceased must face his Maker, we invoke the maxim *En kategor na'aseh sanegor*, "the accuser cannot serve as a defender." In other words, it was gold jewelry that brought down retribution upon the Jew; Let him not wear jewelry when he has to appear before the Heavenly Court. If one was inadvertently buried wearing his jewelry, the grave would be reopened in the case of a man but not in the case of a woman, since the women refused to part with their ornaments for the sake of the Golden Calf.[23]

As the body is escorted to its grave, the entourage makes seven stops to correspond to the seven times that Solomon employes the word "vanity" in describing man's life on earth (Ecclesiastes 1:2). At each station, Psalm 91 is recited. The moral to be learned is that most of our pursuits during our lifetime are vanities. In some communities the same procedure of stopping seven times is observed upon returning from the grave.[24]

The body is lowered into the grave with the head facing towards the west and the feet towards the east. This demonstrates our belief in the Resurrection of the dead, because the resurrected will rise facing east, the direction to which we address our prayers.[25]

It is customary for those attending the funeral to participate in filling in the grave. The implication is: "From dust you came to us. Now that you are departed we return you to your origin." The shovel, however, is not passed from hand to hand. As each person stops, he lays the shovel down and only then does the next person pick it up. This conveys the lesson that death teaches namely, that in life nothing can really be claimed as one's own. Were one to hand the spade directly to another, it may appear that he is handing over an object that belongs to him.[26]

Those not given the opportunity to use the spade should put a handful of soil or some stones into the grave as their participation in the burial.[27]

In many communities, before the body was lowered into the grave, those in attendance would approach and place the palms of their hands upon the casket. This custom is explained in terms of the similarity between the broken tablets and the dead. When Moses descended from Mt. Sinai to find the people worshipping the Golden Calf, he smashed the two tablets. The broken tablets were gathered up and placed into the Ark which accompanied the Children of Israel during their journey through the desert. The remains of the deceased have also been placed in a box. By placing our ten fingers which symbolize the Ten Commandments, we indicate as it were, "The deceased was a righteous man who in his lifetime observed all the Ten Commandments."[28]

The *Shurah.* As long as the dead lies unburied, the grief of the bereaved is so intense that he is in no condition to accept any words of consolation. As the Rabbis put it: "And do not comfort him in the hour when his dead lies before him" (Avot 4:18). Once the grave is covered, the men attending the funeral form two lines—called *Shurah* (lit. "line" or "row"). The bereaved then passes between the lines as the men say to him: "May the Omnipresent comfort you among the rest of the mourners of Zion and Jerusalem." This marks the end of the *Aninut* and the beginning of his *Avelut.* (See below.)[29]

It is a universal custom to tear up grass and throw it over the shoulder before leaving the cemetery. Several reasons have been suggested:

(a) To demonstrate the grief that we experience at the sudden demise of a beloved one who was uprooted from our family. This is symbolized by tearing up the grass.

(b) Just as the grass which was torn up grows back, so will it be with the deceased. At the time of the Resurrection, he will return to life again.[30]

(c) Jewish laws forbid having any material benefit from the grounds of a cemetery such as eating the fruit of a tree growing there or using its wood. Tearing a few blades of grass and throwing it over our shoulders serves as a reminder of this prohibition.[31]

(d) Vegetation is the basic food of the animal kingdom. Even man, the most exalted of all creatures feeds on the fruit of the earth. By uprooting a handful of grass we say to the deceased: "Until now you sustained yourself from the plants of the earth; henceforth you will benefit from the spiritual sustenance provided in Heaven."[32]

(e) According to Kabbalah the soul of the departed escorts the body together with the funeral cortege until the burial is completed. The soul may not depart to its Heavenly rest until permitted to do so by the living. By throwing a handful of grass over our shoulder after the interment, we signal to the soul that it may now take its final leave of the body.[33]

Before leaving the cemetery we are required to wash our hands but not to dry them with towelling. The following explanations have been propounded:

(a) The Torah (Numbers 19:1-13), prescribes a procedure for the purification of one who had become defiled by coming in contact with the dead. There we are told that a red heifer was slaughtered and burned to ashes which were then mixed in water. A twig of a hyssop plant was dipped in the water, which was then sprinkled upon the defiled person. A vestige of this ritual was carried over to our present funeral practice of taking earth (resembling ashes) and throwing it over our shoulders together with the grass which symbolizes the hyssop twigs. The water of the mixture is represented by the water with which we wash our hands.

(b) By washing our hands, we demonstrate that we are not guilty of the death of this person. Neither by word nor deed did we cause his death.[34]

(c) We wash our hands without drying them because we do not wish to leave the impression that we are wiping away all memories of the deceased.[35]

In Jerusalem, the sons of a deceased father are not permitted to follow the bier to the cemetery. This peculiar custom is based on the kabbalistic notion that from the semen which the deceased may have unintentionally emitted during his lifetime demon-like spirits were born. At the funeral, these quasi-sons would join the legitimate offspring and by their presence would cause distress to the departed soul. To keep them away, the legitimate progeny refrains from accompanying their father to the cemetery.[36]

An interesting problem arises in the rare event when the

father of the groom or the mother of the bride dies on the wedding day. Do we cancel the wedding because of the bereavement of the bride or groom, or should the wedding be held as scheduled and the funeral postponed? The Sages of the Talmud ruled that the wedding takes priority. The funeral is held immediately after the ceremony, but the mourning period does not commence until after the seven days of nuptial rejoicing. This sequence was instituted because in ancient times the father was the only one who attended to the arrangements of the wedding of a son and the mother was the only one who looked after the needs of her daughter's marriage. By postponing the wedding to a later date, there would be no one to make the necessary arrangements. In more recent times, when wedding arrangements are attended to by relatives and friends, as well as caterers, we first bury the dead, observe the period of mourning and then have the wedding take place.[37]

Upon returning from the cemetery, the first meal, the *Se'udat Havra'ah*, of the mourner is brought in by neighbors; he may not eat his own food. The source for this custom as for many other mourning customs is in Ezekiel (24:17): "And eat not the bread of other men." The Prophet was enjoined from following the general mourning practice. Ordinary people do not partake of their own meal following the funeral; the Prophet, however, was ordered to eat his own bread. It is customary to bring eggs because they are round in shape. Life, too, goes in cycles: one generation dies and a new generation is born.[38]

Four separate and distinct periods of mourning are prescribed by Jewish Law and in each phase the intensity of the mourning diminishes. It is not that the pain is expected to recede as a matter of course with the passage of time. Rather, it is the Jewish outlook upon life and death that is translated into personalized action. This means that the Jew is expected to face reality and make the proper adjustment to a situation which is beyond his control. It may be difficult for one who has sustained a great loss to reconcile himself to reality but he must make every effort to return to normal activity.

A. The first phase, *Aninut* (the person is called an *onen*), is the period between death and burial. During this time, the bereaved is excused from performing any and all religious commandments, even from reciting the *Shema*. The immediate family, the children, for instance, are expected to attend to the funeral arrangements and thus would be unable to concentrate on prayer. The *onen* may not don his *tefillin* as the Talmud (Berakhot 11a) deduces from the instructions that God gave the Prophet Ezekiel (24:17) after the death of his wife: "Your *pe'er* (lit. "glory") bind around your head." The Rabbis take the word *pe'er* to mean *tefillin*. If God gave specific instructions to the prophet to don his *tefillin*, an every day obligation, then all other mourners must be exempt.[39]

The source for this period of *aninut* is the verse in the Torah (Leviticus 10:19) relating that Aaron, who had lost two sons on that day, said to Moses: "'And if I had eaten the sin-offering *today*, would it have been pleasing in the eyes of the Lord?' And when Moses heard this, it was pleasing in his eyes." Not even the High Priest, Aaron, was to lead a normal life on the day that death had occurred in his family. Another source: The Torah relates that when a Jew brought his tithes to the Temple, his confession included: "I have not eaten thereof *be-oni*, (in my mourning)" (Deuteronomy 26:14). This would imply that the person making the confession did not indulge on the day of his *aninut* in any other pleasureable activity as well.[40]

To sum it up: The *onen* is exempt from all religious practices and is forbidden to eat and drink at a festive table, cut his hair, wash his clothes, bathe himself and have conjugal relations.

B. The second period is called *Shiv'ah* which means "seven." This interval begins with *setimat ha-golel*—the closing of the grave.[41] After the burial, when the original shock begins to wear off and man begins to think with some measure of lucidity, the Sages expected him to give full vent to his shattered emotions during the next seven days of *Shiv'ah*.[42] He gives expression to his grief in the following ways:

1. He is not allowed to wear shoes. The same reasoning follows as above. God told the Prophet to wear shoes after the death of his wife. It follows that all others are barred from doing so. Later authorities ruled that only leather shoes are prohibited because these are worn for pleasure. Also, new garments or freshly laundered or ironed garments may not be worn.

2. He is forbidden to wash himself. Scripture (II Samuel 14:2) relates that at the time when David was grieving over Absalom, a woman was summoned and she was told, "Feign, I pray you as though you mourn, and do not anoint yourself with oil." Bathing is equivalent to anointing with oil.

3. Conjugal relations are forbidden based on the Scriptural verse which tells of David comforting his wife Bathsheba, "And he went unto her and lay with her" (II Samuel 12:24). First came the period of comforting and *Shiv'ah* and only then did he have intimate relations with her.

4. He must refrain from work. The basis for this ruling too, is Scriptural: "And I will change your feasts into mourning" (Amos 8:10). The Prophet compares the feast to days of mourning and the Sages, therefore, deduce that just as work is prohibited during the feast days, so must it be during the period of mourning.

5. Haircuts are forbidden. Here again, if God commanded Aaron to cut his hair during his period of mourning because he was the High Priest (Leviticus 10:6), it follows that all others may not.

6. The mourner is not allowed to greet people. Again the law is derived from Ezekiel (24:17) where God instructs the Prophet who is mourning for his wife: "Sigh in silence."

7. The mourner must not be sitting on a chair. The basis of this custom again is in Scriptures: "Then arose the King and rent his garments and laid himself on the earth" (II Samuel 13:31).

8. A mourner may not participate, not even as a passive spectator, in any happy or joyous events, such as weddings. However, although confined to his home during the week of *Shiv'ah*, he is

permitted to dress, wear shoes and leave the house to attend services in the synagogue on Friday evening and Saturday morning. The sanctity and serenity of the Sabbath override personal grief.[43]

9. During the *Shiv'ah*, a mourner is forbidden to engage in learning Torah since, in the words of the Psalmist "The precepts of the Lord (i.e. the Torah) are right, *gladdening the heart*" (19:9). For the same reason, he is not to be called up to the Torah, not even on Shabbat. He is allowed, however, to study the laws of mourning and those parts of Scriptures which are apt to induce grief, such as the book of Job.[44]

One of the most conspicuous customs of the *Shiv'ah* is the covering all the mirrors in the house of the mourners. There is no known source for this custom in the early Rabbinic literature. The earliest reference to it is from the Middle Ages. The following reasons are given for this quaint practice:

(a). A mirror is used for personal grooming and for cosmetic purposes. Thus it is instrumental in creating a measure of frivolity contrary to the feeling of grief which behooves the mourner.

(b). Observing someone of the opposite sex making her/himself up in front of a mirror is apt to arouse prurient interests in the mourner.

(c). During the *Shiv'ah* it is customary to hold daily prayer services in the house of the mourner. It is forbidden to pray in front of one's own image reflected in the mirror.[45]

It is customary to change one's seat in the synagogue during the mourning period. To be removed from one's accustomed place and neighbors adds to the feeling of loss and grief.[46]

C. The third period is known as *Sheloshim*, the "thirty days." During this period the mourner moves away even further from his original depression. After a week of intensive mourning and meditation, he must face reality and resume a normal life although he may still feel the pain of his loss. He goes to earn his living. He may bathe for cleanliness, but not for pleasure. All other prohibitions of the *Shiv'ah* still remain in effect. Technically speaking we should not refer to this period as "thirty days," because the seven days of *Shiv'ah* are deducted from it. However, since most prohibitions of the *Shiv'ah* also extend into the next twenty-three days, we refer to the entire period as *Sheloshim.*

Sheloshim has no explicit basis in the Torah; it is a Rabbinic enactment. An allusion to it, however, is found in the Torah concerning a woman captured as the spoils of war: "And she shall remain in your house and weep for her father and mother *a full month*" (Deuteronomy 21:13).[47]

Major holidays occurring at the time affect both *Shiv'ah* and *Sheloshim.* The Talmud (Mo'ed Katan 19b) teaches that if a major holiday falls during the *Shiv'ah*, the rest of the *Shiv'ah* is abrogated. For example, if *Shiv'ah* commenced on a Monday and a major holiday such as Passover, Shavuot, or Sukkot began that same evening, the mourner celebrates the Festival like everyone else and rules governing the period of *Shiv'ah* are abrogated. It is even conceivable that the entire *sheloshim* be nullified. This may occur on Sukkot since the last day, *Shemini Atzeret*, is identified as a holiday in its own right. Hence, if one began his *Shiv'ah* on the day before Sukkot, the advent of the holiday would terminate the *Shiv'ah*, and the eighth day, *Shemini Atzeret*, would cancel the next stage of the mourning, the *Sheloshim.* Apparently, and this is mere conjecture, the Sages required us to forgo our personal emotions in favor of the national observances of all the people.[48]

D. Whereas mourning ends for all other relatives after thirty days, it continues for an additional eleven months for parents. Happy events, festive occasions and amusements should be avoided by those who are mourning for a mother or a father. Other prohibitions concerning the person of the mourner for the first thirty days are lifted. He may now bathe, cut his hair, wash and iron his clothes and engage in conjugal relations. The Rabbis also permitted a bachelor to marry during these eleven months, in a simple wedding ceremony. The Biblical commandment of "Be fruitful and multiply" overrides the laws of mourning. On the other hand, they counselled a man bereaved of his wife not to remarry for a full year. In the first place, a husband should not forget his first wife so soon. Secondly, he should not enter into a second marriage while still retaining a sentimental attachment to his first wife. A wife who lost a husband, on the other hand, was permitted to remarry after she had waited three months. This waiting period is to ascertain that she had not become pregnant by her first husband. Apparently, the Rabbis felt that it is much more difficult for a woman to live alone than for a man.[49]

The rules concerning the twelve month period of mourning, i.e. the *Sheloshim* plus the following eleven months, remain in effect during the entire period. There is one exception: Beginning with the burial, the son recites the *Kaddish*, the mourner's prayer, for only eleven months. The reason why he is not required to continue for the entire year is to demonstrate that his father was not an unmitigated sinner. The history of the *Kaddish* dates back to the ancient days of the Talmud. We are told (Tanna de-be Eliyahu Zutah, Chap. 17) that the son's reciting the *Kaddish* raises the soul of the parent from purgatory to paradise. No man, born of woman, is entirely free of sin, and every deceased will spend some time in purgatory to atone for his misdeeds. God takes note when the deceased man's son walks in the paths of righteousness and recites the *Kaddish* which is an affirmation of His Omnipotence and Omnipresence, and He credits this merit to the soul of the departed, elevating it to a higher spiritual level. The story is told in the Midrash that Rabbi Johanan ben Zakkai encountered a man on the street, gathering twigs. The Rabbi knew that this man had died and inquired why he was not in his Heavenly abode. The man, or was it the shadow of a man, replied, "I have no one to deliver me from purgatory and I was given the humiliating chore of picking up twigs in the street. Please, Rabbi, take my son and teach him to read so that he may recite the *Kaddish* and deliver me from purgatory." If a son would recite *Kaddish* for the full year he would seem to assume that his father was a sinner. By saying *Kaddish* only eleven months, the son demonstrates his belief that his parent must have done some good deeds and is to be given credit for them.[50]

The *Kaddish* is recited in the Aramaic language only because of tradition. In the days of the Talmud, Aramaic, not Hebrew, was the vernacular. To make sure that the ordinary layman could comprehend the meaning and significance of the *Kaddish*, in which God is extolled even during a period of grief and despair, the Rabbis instituted having this prayer said in Aramaic, the language of the people.[51]

In Oriental communities, during his twelve months of mourning, the son moves about the synagogue and distributes flower petals and perfume among the congregants. This custom was intended to demonstrate the son's firm belief that his father was enjoying the pleasant fragrance of Paradise.[52]

To erect a monument on a grave is a custom dating back to ancient times. Ezekiel says: "And those that thus travel will pass through the land and when anyone sees a human bone he will set up a sign by it" (39:15). Thus, the monument is to serve as the visible sign indicating where a human being lies buried. The custom prevailing in Jerusalem requires that the monument be erected immediately after thirty days, so that the grave shall not be left unmarked for any lengthy time. The general custom is to wait until the year of mourning is over for which the following two reasons have been suggested:

(a) During the first twelve months following the death of a relative, while the grief is still acute, there is no need to add to the pain by requiring the children to attend to the tombstone.

(b) A basic reason for the monument is to keep the memory of the departed alive. During the first twelve months, it is unlikely that anyone would forget his departed relative. Hence, there is no need for any stone to serve as a reminder.[53]

The anniversary of the death, popularly known as *Yahrzeit*, is observed in two different ways.

(a) By fasting on the anniversary of the death of parents the pain of the loss is revived and the shattering experience relived. Unless one is physically unable to endure the fast, he should refrain from eating on that day as a sign of his grief.

(b) In Hasidic circles the opposite position is taken. The knowledge that the deceased is ascending, step by step, year after year, to even higher levels in the spiritual realm of Paradise is cause for celebration. In the Hasidic world the *Yahrzeit* constitutes a day of *Hillula*—the joyful adoration of God.[54] This is also the reason for the *Hillula* for Rabbi Shimon ben Yohai, the reputed author of the Zohar. On *Lag ba-Omer*, the thirty-third day between Passover and Shavuot, tens of thousands of people gather in Meron, Israel, the gravesite of this sainted sage, to rejoice in prayer and seek his intercession on behalf of the living. Candles and bonfires are lit in memory of this spiritual giant. Particularly is this tomb sacred to the Sephardi Jews and the Ashkenazi Jews who observe the Sephardi ritual.[55]

A candle is lit to burn during the day of the *Yahrzeit*. As already noted, the soul of man is likened to the light of God.[56]

Yizkor. Memorial prayers are recited in the synagogue on the concluding day of all major holidays. By reciting *Yizkor* the children demonstrate before the congregation that the parent who instilled in them a religious commitment lives on as evidenced through their coming to the synagogue to worship God and memorialize their loved ones.

During *Yizkor* those whose parents are living leave the synagogue for two reasons. First, if one remains, upon hearing the congregants memorializing their parents he may inadvertently join them in doing likewise for his own living parents. Secondly, even if he remained silent, he would be out of place and seem disrespectful by not participating.

In Sephardi congregations the individual does not memorialize his beloved ones. Instead, the cantor recites the prayer and the congregants merely mention the name of the deceased. Consequently, even those whose parents are living are permitted to remain in the synagogue during *Yizkor*.[57]

We have discussed only those rituals and customs of burial and mourning which are fairly universally observed by Jewish communities the world over. In addition to these, virtually every *Ḥevra Kadisha* in the old country had its own time honored traditions concerning the details of preparing the body and the funeral.

Whatever the minute differences and regional variations, all the rites and practices of funeral and mourning have their basis in two fundamental tenets of Judaism: the immortality of the soul and the resurrection of the dead, the latter inseparably fused with our belief in the ultimate redemption of Israel.

As an eloquent expression of these beliefs, the eulogy (*hesped*) delivered at the funeral is customarily concluded with the words of the Prophet Isaiah (25:8) comforting the People of Israel:

> He will swallow up death for ever, and the Lord God will wipe away tears from all faces, and the disgrace of His people will He take away from all the earth. . .

SOURCES

1. *Ḥayye Avraham* p. 54a.
2. *Minhage Yeshurun* p. 309.
3. *Ḥayye Avraham* p. 54a.
4. *Sefer ha-Mat'amim* p. 14.
5. *Ta'ame ha-Minhagim* p. 429.
6. *Sefer ha-Mat'amim*, Part 2 p. 10.
7. *Halikhot Teman* 248.
8. *Sefer ha-Mat'amim* p. 15.
9. *Arukh ha-Shulḥan*, Yoreh De'ah 339 par. 9.
10. *Sefer ha-Mat'amim* p. 91.
11. *Tur Yoreh De'ah, Perishah* 352 (l).
12. *Sefer ha-Mat'amim*, Part 2 p. 9.
13. *Arukh ha-Shulḥan*, 351 pars. 2, 3; *Ta'ame ha-Minhagim* p. 433.
14. *Arukh ha-Shulḥan*, 340 par. 3.
15. *Ḥayye Avraham* p. 54b.
16. *Arukh ha-Shulḥan*, 340 pars. 8, 9 13, 14, 16.
17. *Minhage Yeshurun* p. 333.
18. *Arukh ha-Shulḥan*, 357 par. 1.

19. *Minhage Yeshurun* pp. 315, 316.
20. *Ḥayye Avraham* p. 54b.
21. *Ta'ame ha-Minhagim* p. 447-448.
22. *Minhage Yeshurun* p. 314.
23. *Ta'ame ha-Minhagim* p. 449.
24. *Ḥayye Avraham* p. 55a; *Ta'ame ha-Minhagim* p. 436.
25. *Sefer ha-Mat'amim* p. 16.
26. *Ta'ame ha-Minhagim* p. 439.
27. *Hayye Avraham* p. 55a.
28. *Minhage Yeshurun* p. 315.
29. *Tur Yoreh De'ah* 376.
30. *Arukh ha-Shulḥan* 376 par. 10.
31. *Otzar Yisrael* Vol. 9 p. 92.
32. *Minhage Yeshurun* p. 318.
33. *Ḥayye Avraham* p. 55a.
34. *Sefer ha-Mat'amim* p. 16.
35. *Ḥayye Avraham* p.55b.
36. *Minhage Yeshurun* 317.
37. *Tur Yoreh De'ah* 342; *Arukh ha-Shulḥan* 342 par. 8.
38. *Minhage Yeshurun* p. 301.
39. *Ḥayye Avraham* p. 56a.
40. *Arukh ha-Shulḥan*, 341 par. 3.
41. *Arukh ha-Shulḥan*, 375 par. 1.
42. *Arukh ha-Shulḥan*, 380 par. 1.
43. *Arukh ha-Shulḥan*, 400 par. 5.
44. Ibid. 384 pars. 1, 4, 8.
45. *Kol Bo Al Avelut* I, p. 262.
46. *Arukh ha-Shulḥan*, 393 par. 12.
47. *Minhage Yeshurun* p. 334.
48. *Arukh ha-Shulḥan*, 399 pars. 1, 12, 19.
49. Ibid. 392 pars. 1, 3, 4, 5.
50. *Bet Yoseph*, Yoreh De'ah, 376; *Minhage Yeshurun* p. 324; *Ta'ame ha-Minhagim* p. 458.
51. *Ta'ame ha-Minhagim* p. 459.
52. *Ben Ish Ḥai* p. 176.
53. *Sefer ha-Mat'amim* p. 91.
54. *Arukh ha-Shulḥan*, 376 par. 13; *Ta'ame ha-Minhagim* pp. 477-478; *Minhage Yeshurun* p. 326.
55. *Minhage Yeshurun* p. 87.
56. *Minhage Yeshurun* p. 327.
57. *Sefer ha-Toda'ah* Vol. I p. 56.

day. "It's still early, of course, but he's bringing in an army of people who appear sympathetic to our point of view."

For Trump's national security adviser: General Michael Flynn, who once shared a tweet that read, "Not anymore, Jews. Not anymore."

For attorney general: Jeff Sessions, who once said immigrants "create culture problems."

For senior policy adviser: Stephen Miller, who had organized anti-Islam events with the help of his classmate Richard Spencer when they were both at Duke University.

For adviser to Customs and Border Patrol: Julie Kirchner, who had previously worked at an anti-immigration group founded by a white nationalist.

For chief strategist: Steve Bannon, the co-founder of Breitbart News, which he described as "the platform for the alt-right."

Don had always thought of Washington as "exclusively enemy territory," he said, but now he wanted to go there. Richard Spencer was hosting a white nationalist conference two weeks after the election in the Ronald Reagan Building, and he invited Don to come. Spencer expected three hundred attendees, and he had promoted the conference during interviews on NPR, CNN, and NBC. Don and Chloe looked at last-minute plane tickets to Washington before deciding to stay home. Stormfront was still experiencing a surge of new traffic in the wake of

Trump's election—and also a series of cyber attacks from hackers and antifascists. Don didn't want to risk leaving his computer.

So instead he watched a video feed of Spencer's introductory press conference, in which Spencer looked out at a jam-packed room of national journalists and told them, "The alt-right is obviously real, and it's obviously growing." Don watched as his white nationalist friends Sam Dickson and Jared Taylor hit the same talking points they had been reciting for thirty years, only now to triple the crowd. He watched as protesters disrupted the conference with chants of "Nazi! Nazi! Nazi!" Then he watched as Spencer stepped to the lectern for the day's final speech, one that would solidify him as the new face of white nationalism, the new heir. "I don't think I'm alone in thinking how surreal all of this is," Spencer began. "We willed Donald Trump into office. We made this dream our reality."

What Don admired most about Spencer was his polish. If white nationalism was going to transition into a viable political movement, it needed leaders with mainstream credentials, and Spencer checked every box. A bachelor's degree from the University of Virginia. A master's from the University of Chicago. A wardrobe of fancy watches and Brooks Brothers suits. He had grown up in a wealthy Republican family in Dallas, the son of an artist and a doctor, and he had aspired to become a theater director until he started reading German philosopher

Friedrich Nietzsche, and his views gradually drifted further to the right. He enrolled at Duke University to get his PhD, and then during his second year on campus a black woman falsely accused three white Duke lacrosse players of rape, leading to what Spencer called an "antiwhite, racist witch trial." The ensuing months turned him into a campus activist, which led to jobs as a far-right blogger, which led to his creation of AlternativeRight.com. Like Derek, he had a gift for the language of euphemism and understatement. He was not a white supremacist but a "racial identitarian," he said. His white power think tank was innocuously named the National Policy Institute. As a political activist, he made good use of his theatrical flair, releasing well-produced videos on Twitter and timing his alt-right demonstrations to calm moments in the national news cycle. "In some ways, I'm still directing a massive theatrical production," he said. "But now I'm also starring in it."

During his speech at the conference, Spencer hammered his fist against the lectern and stared at the television cameras in the back of the room.

"America was, until this past generation, a white country, designed for us and for our posterity," he said. "It is our creation, it is our inheritance, and it belongs to us. To be white is to be a striver, a crusader, an explorer, and a conqueror. We build. We go upward. We do, and other groups don't. We don't gain anything from their presence. They need us, and not the other way around. For us, it is conquer or die. Hail Trump! Hail our people! Hail victory!"

Don watched on his screen as Spencer's crowd erupted in applause. Several dozen people in the crowd stood and held their right arms high in the air, signaling Spencer with the Nazi salute. It would become one of the symbolic moments of the 2016 election, replayed on TV as America's public introduction to the so-called alt-right. But in the moment, Spencer simply nodded at his saluting crowd and smiled.

"This is just the beginning," he told them.

A few days later, there was an opinion piece printed in **The New York Times** under the byline R. Derek Black.

Derek had warned Don that he was going to write about Trump, but Don didn't know exactly what Derek planned to say, or when, or for whom. Derek drafted the article the morning after Trump's election, edited it with Allison, and later submitted it to the **Times,** and now a few weeks later there was a headline at the front of the opinion section: "Why I Left White Nationalism." Already the piece was one of the most highly read stories on the website, and it was being shared on Stormfront and other white supremacist message boards. "Jesus, Derek," Don thought. "What did you do now?"

During the 2008 and 2012 presidential campaigns, Don and Derek had spent hundreds of hours dissecting every bit of electoral minutiae on the radio. The main weakness of their show, friends sometimes told them, was that their opinions were too much the same. It didn't make good radio to have two hosts in constant agreement, echoing each other's points and completing each other's sentences. But now Don had no idea what Derek thought, or even whether he'd voted in the election. They had seen each other only once in the last few years, for dinner near the Miami airport while Derek was on a layover on his way back to Michigan from a trip to the Caribbean. They rarely spoke on the phone. Derek was slow to respond to Don's text message provocations about politics. "There's a lot more distance now," Don said. "What is there to talk about?" In November 2016, he thought the best way to understand his son's viewpoint was through **The New York Times,** so he clicked the link and started to read:

> I could easily have spent the night of Nov. 8 elated, surrounded by friends and family, thinking: "We did it . . ."
>
> I'd be planning with other white nationalists what comes next, and assessing just how much influence our ideology would have on this administration. That's who I was a few years ago.
>
> Things look very different for me now . . .
>
> I was born into a white nationalist family . . .

and I was once considered the bright future of the movement . . .

Several years ago, I began attending a liberal college where my presence prompted huge controversy. Through many talks with devoted and diverse people there—people who chose to invite me into their dorms and conversations rather than ostracize me—I began to realize the damage I had done. Ever since, I have been trying to make up for it . . .

I never would have begun my own conversations without first experiencing clear and passionate outrage to what I believed from those I interacted with. Now is the time for me to pass on that outrage by clearly and unremittingly denouncing the people who used a wave of white anger to take the White House.

Mr. Trump's comments during the campaign echoed how I also tapped into less-than-explicit white nationalist ideology to reach relatively moderate white Americans. I went door-to-door in 2008 talking about how Hispanic immigration was overwhelming "American" culture, how black neighborhoods were hotbeds of crime, and how P.C. culture didn't let us talk about any of it. I won that small election with 60 percent of the vote.

A substantial portion of the American public has made clear that it feels betrayed by the establishment, and so it elected a president who denounces all Muslims as potential conspirators in terrorism; who sees black communities as crime-ridden; who taps into white American mistrust of foreigners, particularly of Hispanics; and who promises the harshest form of immigration control. If we thought Mr. Trump himself might backtrack on some of this, we are now watching him fill a cabinet with people able to make that campaign rhetoric into real policy . . .

The wave of violence and vile language that has risen since the election is only one immediate piece of evidence that this campaign's reckless assertion of white identity comes at a huge cost. More and more people are being forced to recognize now what I learned early: Our country is susceptible to some of our worst instincts when the message is packaged correctly.

No checks and balances can redeem what we've unleashed. The reality is that half of the voters chose white supremacy . . .

It's now our job to argue constantly that what voters did in elevating this man to the White House constitutes the greatest assault on our own people in a generation, and to offer another option . . .

Those of us on the other side need to be clear that Mr. Trump's callous disregard for people outside his demographic is intolerable, and will be destructive to the entire nation.

Don finished reading and clicked over to the conversation on Stormfront. "Treasonous," one poster had written. "Typical liberal dribble," commented another, and Don felt a familiar wave of grief rush over him. After more than two years, he had finally acclimated himself to the idea that he would continue to lead Stormfront and the white nationalist movement alone, without Derek. It was lonely. It was sometimes joyless. "The Derek situation still haunts me every single day," Don said. "But it's over, and the show goes on." Now, for the first time, Don began to wonder if in fact it wasn't over. Maybe, instead of merely abandoning his family's ideology, Derek would actively oppose it.

"What are you doing, Derek?" Don asked him later that month. "Is this what you are going to be now? Some kind of antiwhite activist?"

The truth was Derek didn't exactly know. Probably not. Maybe. He still valued his privacy, but Allison had helped convince him that by spending a decade at the forefront of white nationalism, he had built up a massive public debt to society and particularly to people of color, and he wanted to pay some of it back. He occasionally thought about giving speeches at universities, or writing a book, or appearing on television, or becoming more actively involved in political organizing against white nationalism. He liked his quiet life at the University of Chicago, but lately he was finding it harder to lose himself in ninth-century texts when the current moment felt so urgent. He decided to speak about the dangers of white nationalism at Georgetown University and Harvard and give occasional interviews about his transformation. Don still had his Google alert set for Derek, and he began to monitor it with an increasing sense of dread.

"I don't understand why he's doing this," Don said. "This is the exact opposite of the life he could be leading."

The life that could have been Derek's was in Alexandria, Virginia, six miles from the White House in an apartment located above a chocolate shop, where a locked gate, security cameras, and occasionally a bodyguard stood watch over the new tenant. Richard Spencer had just moved to Virginia a few days earlier on a short-term lease, leaving his wife and young daughter in the ski town of Whitefish, Montana. He had come to the Washington suburbs with two boxes of white nationalist books and a duffel bag filled with wrinkled suits. There had been no time to move his car or any furniture from Montana, and his new kitchen was empty except for a box of granola bars and a few scattered red plastic cups. Trump's inauguration was two days away, and Spencer had rushed his cross-country move so he would be in place before the official change of power. He hoped the Alexandria apartment would function not just as a living space but also as a new headquarters for the alt-right. The alleyway entrance allowed for privacy, the roof deck was designed for hosting parties, and he'd already invited media to one press conference in the spacious living room. "We're basically becoming a part of the establishment, so it only makes sense that we start to have a presence here in Washington," Spencer said.

He poured some red wine into a plastic cup, took his laptop into the living room, and sat down on the hardwood floor to check his email. "I'm getting about forty media requests per day," he said, and his immediate answer to each one was always yes. He had spent seven years as a far-right blogger migrating from one fledgling publication to the next, trying to build up an audience for his ideas. Now the Trump phenomenon had delivered that audience to his feet, and Spencer could hardly believe his good luck. The video of his controversial speech in the wake of Trump's election—"Hail-gate," Spencer called it—had been viewed on the internet more than a million times. Now Spencer was talking to publishers about writing a book. He was "seriously" considering a run for the U.S. House of Representatives out of Montana. He was interviewing zealous college students who were competing to become his personal assistant. He was recording videos for a burgeoning YouTube channel, launching a new website for the alt-right, and planning a speaking tour at colleges across America.

Most of all, he was answering a phone that rarely

stopped ringing, repeating old white nationalist talking points to a national audience that was suddenly rapt.

"Have you heard about white genocide?" he asked a documentarian for Netflix.

"Race is real. Look at the IQ data," he told a reporter from the Associated Press.

"We don't hate anyone. We just want to preserve our own people," he told an alt-right blogger.

"Yes, I can absolutely be available later today," he told a reporter from the **Los Angeles Times** as he got up to refill his cup with more wine.

"What time do you want me?" he asked a booker for CNN.

By early afternoon, Spencer had already done six interviews. He stood up from his computer, surveyed the granola bars in his kitchen, and decided to walk out into the neighborhood to find lunch. There were pride flags painted on the sidewalk and peace signs taped to the window of the chocolate shop downstairs. It was the weekend of Martin Luther King Day, and Spencer could hear choir music playing at a holiday church service down the street. "Why do we pay tribute each year to a fraud and a degenerate?" he asked. He liked Alexandria for what he called the "historic southern charm," with its Jefferson Davis statue and cobblestoned sidewalks, but he didn't expect to fit in with his new neighbors. The city was diverse and liberal, and already Spencer had been recognized and flipped off a few times outside his apartment on King Street. He had started wearing a hat to help shadow his face.

He took a seat in back of a lunch counter and studied the menu. A few tables away, a Hispanic woman stared in his direction, and Spencer fidgeted in his seat. The waiter seemed to glance at him for an extra second, and Spencer kept his head down and rushed into his lunch order. "I'm always waiting for things to turn ugly, because I'm radioactive," he said, once the waiter walked away. Many of his former friends in Washington refused to go to Spencer's apartment out of fear of being spotted. Some of his college classmates had edited their Facebook pictures with Spencer, replacing his face with a cartoon image of the devil. In his hometown of Whitefish, an anti-hate group had mailed flyers about his "racist lies" to each resident, including Spencer's parents, who had publicly condemned his beliefs.

Spencer wanted to inoculate himself by building a headquarters for the alt-right with a full-time media staff and more security guards, but to do that, he needed about five million or ten million dollars in donations, he said. His National Policy Institute had been able to raise only about half a million dollars in total funds, most of which came from either Spencer's profits from a family inheritance of land in Louisiana or from the Charles Martel Society, a white nationalist fund-raising group run by publishing heir William Regnery II. Spencer said he had traveled around the country to meet with potential funders, but so far he had been able to raise only several thousand dollars. "The money must be out there, but people are cautious, and I don't have time to go find it," Spencer said. He had decided to outsource some of his work by hiring a personal assistant—"a smart, good-looking Richard Spencer type," he said—who could help with fundraising and also schedule his interviews.

Spencer finished his lunch and walked back onto King Street, where now on the sidewalk with the peace signs and the rainbow flags he noticed a new flyer attached to the light pole in front of his apartment. "MISSING DOG," it read, and underneath that bold type was a large picture of Spencer. "I can't believe this is starting already," Spencer said, and then he stepped closer to the flyer to read the small type.

"Racist, sexist, homophobic, and xenophobic neo-Nazi has made Old Town Alexandria his hub to recruit," the flyer read. "Must be shunned and humiliated."

Spencer pulled down the flyer, folded it in half, and tucked it into his pocket. He looked down the street and saw a copy of the same flyer attached to the next light pole, and then the next, and then the next. There were dozens of flyers posted on lampposts and business windows up and down the block, stretching as far as Spencer could see.

"It's going to be all-out mayhem," he said. He pulled his hat lower onto his head and hurried back into his apartment.

A few months later, in the spring of 2017, Don flew into Washington and went with Spencer to dinner. They were both attending a private, two-day meeting of white nationalist funders in nearby Baltimore, but Don was eager to spend time with Spencer outside the official schedule. He sensed Spencer was approaching what Don called "a strategic tipping point"—one Don recognized from his own life—and he hoped to offer a little subtle advice. "He's walking right up to that edge between pushing for our ideas from the inside and shocking people a little too hard," Don said.

The all-out mayhem Spencer had expected to instigate in Alexandria and beyond had escalated during the last several months. A different kind of flyer had been posted to the lampposts in liberal suburban Virginia early that spring. "Around Blacks Never Relax," read one; and "Stop the Islamization of America"; and "You're Losing Your Country White Man!!!" Spencer said he hadn't created the posters, but they were the product of a racist movement he continued to inspire through his work at the National Policy Institute, and a crowd of protesters had begun to picket outside Spencer's apartment each weekend morning. "Racist, sexist, antigay!

NPI is KKK!" they chanted. Spencer retaliated by organizing nighttime torch marches and "heritage rallies" at local Confederate monuments all across Virginia and the Deep South. Most of his public appearances sparked riots between white nationalists and protesting groups of antifascists, necessitating the presence of police in riot gear. Spencer had twice been punched in the face by antifascists, including once while he was in the middle of giving a television interview during Trump's inaugural parade. Sometimes, when Spencer was recognized in public, he said he had started to pretend he was not Richard Spencer—that in fact he thought Richard Spencer was an idiot. "It's something I do for self-defense," he said.

At their dinner together, Spencer told Don he wasn't sure how to feel about the last several months of his life. Sometimes he worried he'd gone too far with his "Hail-gate" speech. He wondered: Had his Hitler impersonation catapulted his mainstream political career, or effectively ended it?

It was similar to an argument Don often had with Duke, who tended to blame every failure in his political career on what he called his "youthful exuberance" as head of the Klan. Duke often said that if not for the archival pictures of him in Nazi uniforms and hooded robes, he could have become governor of Louisiana or maybe even president. But Don believed it was Duke's Klan connection that in many ways enabled his career. It fueled the undercurrent of anger in his crowds, enticed the national media, and turned his campaigns into spectacles. "There's something to be said for maintaining some edge, as long as you're still in control," Don said.

He thought Spencer was disciplined and smart, with a good sense for the history of the white nationalist movement. Don liked him, and as the night went on, he decided to bring up the subject that was always on his mind. He told Spencer about Derek, and Spencer said he remembered meeting him once at a conference. Don mentioned Derek was working toward his PhD at the University of Chicago; Spencer, a University of Chicago graduate, said he still respected the school as a place of "true intellectualism." Don was pleased, and he sent Derek a text message to share Spencer's endorsement.

Derek was always happy to hear from his father, but this text message also reminded him of the estrangement that now defined so much about their relationship. His parents had never visited him since he left Florida, at least in part because of Don's health. In their eyes, Chicago was an unsafe place held hostage by gangs and minorities. Ever since the beginning of the presidential election, it had seemed to Derek that the United States was always in the process of dividing, and in so many ways he felt increasingly apart from his own parents. They were southerners, and he was now a northerner. They were suspicious of liberal academia, and he was a PhD student. They were white nationalists, and he was an antiwhite activist. What Derek wanted was to build some kind of a bridge—a way to communicate with his father that didn't have to involve politics or Richard Spencer.

Derek's spring break was coming up later that month. For the first time in more than a year, he found a cheap flight and booked a ticket home.

14. "We Were Wrong"

Derek spent his first morning in Florida at an independent coffee shop, where a poster of Martin Luther King was framed behind the register and a sign on the front door read, "Unite Against Racism." His mother was at work and his father was busy hosting Stormfront radio, so Derek had time to catch up on schoolwork. He wanted to finish his application for a six-week summer Arabic-language class in Amman, Jordan. He also needed to finish his first major assignment at the University of Chicago, a fifty-page research paper on a subject he had been drawn to in part because it contained so many parallels to his own life.

He had chosen to write about a ninth-century religious leader named Bodo, a royal deacon who had been a rising star in the Carolingian Empire and the Christian church. Historians thought Bodo was destined to become a powerful Frankish politician, but then, in 836, he abandoned his life with little public warning. He converted to Judaism, grew out his beard, changed his name to Eleazar, and then moved to the multicultural kingdom of Al-Andalus, where he married a Jewish woman and began trying to convert other Christians. His former Frankish allies came to consider him a traitor and an enemy. It was one of the starkest individual transformations in medieval history, and the focus of Derek's research was all that remained unknown. Historians were able to recover only a few official accounts of Bodo's life and two of his original letters. No one had recorded Bodo's internal deliberations, his self-doubt, or his emotional reckoning as relationships were made and then destroyed. In the official record, his transformation was clean and absolute: Bodo to Eleazar. A Christian and then a Jew. History had preserved none of the messiness.

Now Don texted Derek's cell phone. "I'm done with YOUR radio show," he said, so Derek drove to his parents' house and picked up his father to take him to lunch. Derek's goal was to avoid discussing politics during the trip. That was their old common language, he thought, and now their relationship needed a new foundation. They drove through downtown Lake Worth toward a restaurant as Derek tried to steer the conversation toward music, exercise, and science.

"What are your thoughts on planetary exploration?" Derek asked at one point. "I was reading a book about the possibility of starting colonies for people in outer space."

"I hope it happens soon," Don said. "It's already too late for America. We're becoming a third-world country."

Derek winced and tried again. "Where should we go for lunch?"

"Someplace where you won't get recognized," Don said. "You're probably famous with the liberals now, after your big speech at Georgetown."

And on it went—Don teasing Derek with little jabs; Derek nodding, smiling, and then changing the subject—until they were done with lunch and back at the house. Everything was just as Derek remembered it from when he first left his parents' house for New College almost seven years earlier: His water bed perched in the hallway. His fish tank in the living room. His political campaign flyers from 2008 tucked into his desk. The take-out burgers for dinner that night were still from Flanigan's, their favorite restaurant, and the TV was still blaring the news. "A hate box," was how Derek now thought of that TV, but he settled into the couch between his parents and tried to ignore it.

"Can we turn it off?" Derek asked after a while, but he was told that they couldn't, or at least not yet. What if something important happened and they missed it? Lately, to Don's great delight, he thought multicultural America was unraveling one news story at a time, and on this night one of those stories was about an army veteran who spent time on Stormfront. James Jackson, twenty-eight, had watched YouTube videos posted by Richard Spencer and David Duke and eventually concluded, he would later explain, "that the white race is being eroded." He boarded a bus from Baltimore to New York with an eighteen-inch sword and two knives packed in his suitcase, and then he spent two nights stalking black men around Times Square. One of those men was a sixty-six-year-old trash collector named Timothy Caughman, and Jackson followed him into a dark alleyway and stabbed him several times. "Hate Killing," the CNN News alert read, and Don said the whole thing was unfortunate. He flipped the TV over to Fox News as one show rolled into the next.

Now it was Tucker Carlson, Don and Chloe's favorite and a new hero among the alt-right. Carlson had become a master at repackaging white nationalist talking points on what he called "alien immigrants" and "cultural erosion." The SPLC had named Carlson's show the most racist news program on cable TV, and in the America of 2017 it was also the most popular show on cable TV, with a nightly audience of over three million. On this night, Carlson was leading his broadcast with a story about an alleged rape at a Maryland high school in which a ninth grader claimed to have been attacked in the bathroom by two recent Central American immigrants. The allegation would later be proven false, and the charges against both immigrants would eventually be dropped, but for now Carlson was using the hoax as proof of the threat he believed immigrants posed to "real Americans."

"This is insanity of course. It's the sign of a sick

civilization at war with itself," Carlson said as Derek tried to ignore the TV and focus on his burger.

"Does it make a school better when people move in who don't speak English?" Carlson asked, as Derek got up to go look at his fish tank.

"Why would we want to be a bilingual country?" Carlson said.

"Diversity is our strength," Carlson said, mocking his critics. "Move along. You're racist. Shut up."

Finally the hour ended, and Derek reached for the remote. He switched the TV to Discovery Channel, his old favorite, but a few minutes later his parents took the remote and changed it back to cable news. They wanted to watch the replay of Carlson's show, just as they often did, and rather than start a fight, Derek gave back the remote. He sat on the couch with them, tuned out the show, and text-messaged with Allison until he was ready to go to sleep. He was staying nearby at his grandmother's house, and his parents offered to drive him back even as Tucker's show continued to replay in their heads. They told Derek in the car that America was turning into a third-world country. They said Derek was an antiwhite activist. They said he was accelerating the decline of the European race. They said he had many enemies who wanted to hurt him and that he needed to be careful. He sat in his seat and waited for the storm to pass, until finally his mother began to tell him about their plumbing problems at the house, and how much handiwork they still had to do, and how much they missed Derek and still loved him.

By the time they got to his grandmother's, it was after midnight. Derek said good night, and then he went inside to a bedroom that was dark and quiet and closed the door.

The next morning, Don was trying again.

"You should come back on the air with me, co-host the show again," he said, when Derek picked him up at the house.

"Richard thinks the genocide idea is part of what did it," Don said as Derek turned up the music and drove across Lake Worth toward Palm Beach.

"You should come see your old friends this year at your conference," Don said as Derek parked the car at the edge of the Atlantic Ocean, near the bench where they had gone together to watch the first sunrise of each New Year. Maybe they could establish some sort of new connection here, in a place where they had already marked so many fresh starts. Derek helped Don out of the car, and they sat together in the sun. The beach was empty and the water was calm. Derek listened to the waves, and Don closed his eyes to enjoy the sun. Derek mentioned that he had been experimenting with a basic virtual reality headset, and Don said he had already bought the same one. Derek said he was trying to play guitar more regularly, and Don said he wanted to take up keyboard. Derek said the worst part about living in the Midwest was how much he missed the ocean, and Don suggested they begin a new tradition of going together to the beach every day whenever Derek was in town.

They got back into the car and drove past Trump's Mar-a-Lago, with its gigantic American flag and its new Secret Service tower, before continuing down to the coast to a lime-green restaurant with a thatched roof. They found a table outside next to the water, where the air smelled of salt. The tide was rising against the dock, and gentle waves were rocking the sailboats in the harbor from side to side. Derek picked up his menu. Maybe a crab cake, he said, and something about the moment felt so pleasant and normal that it reminded Don of all the lunches he'd shared with Derek over the years, and Don couldn't help himself.

"I catch myself thinking sometimes that you're still one of us," he said.

Derek ignored him.

"You say things now that are so over the top," Don said. "Like race doesn't exist, or we need more immigration."

Derek raised his eyebrows and then looked up from his menu. Maybe there was no avoiding this.

"More immigration, more diversity—I think those are very good things," he said.

"That's the opposite of what you always believed."

"I was wrong." Derek stopped to correct himself. "**We** were wrong."

The waiter came by, and Derek told her they needed a few minutes. The sun had dropped behind a cloud, and the wind was picking up across the water. The waves were coming harder now, rocking boats in the harbor and slapping against the dock of the restaurant. Derek raised his voice over the noise.

"Even if you were somehow right—even if it was super important to keep races apart for preservation—the only way to do that is to put people on trains by busting into their houses and breaking up their families, which is a huge human rights violation."

Don raised his palms up above the table. "So?" he said. "History is filled with human rights violations. They could be forced to leave."

"Forcing people out?" Derek stared at his father and grimaced. "That's a horrible thing to hope for. It would be awful and inhumane."

"It's going to be horrible either way, Derek. This country is on the verge of a reckoning."

During the coming months, Don and Derek would watch as white nationalism continued to explode into mainstream politics. There would be fights over the destruction of Confederate monuments, followed by a succession of marches and rallies led by white nationalists throughout the South. One of those marches would arrive in downtown Charlottesville, Virginia, in August 2017, where Richard Spencer, David Duke, and hundreds of neo-Nazis would carry guns and torches into downtown, threatening counterprotesters with chants of "White lives matter" and "You will not replace us," until one neo-Nazi rammed his car into a crowd, killing one counterprotester and injuring nineteen others. Trump would go on national TV to explain away the violence by blaming "both sides"—what he called the "alt-left" and also "the good people" on the "alt-right"—creating a moral equivalency between racists and antiracists. Don would call Trump's comments "the high point" of white nationalism during his lifetime. Derek would write another opinion piece for **The New York Times** to say that Trump's "frightening statement" had "legitimized" a racist ideology. Don would watch Stormfront's traffic triple overnight, spiking to 300,000 daily page views, signifying what he called the "full awakening of our people." Derek and Don would both become more certain of their beliefs and more public in their advocacy, rising in opposition to each other, until the divide between father and son sometimes felt unbridgeable.

But now, at the restaurant, Don stared across the table at Derek and tried one final time. "How did this happen?" he said. "I still don't understand any of this."

"Then maybe you won't," Derek said.

"Everything you advocated for is finally beginning to catch on," Don said. "Don't you see that?"

"Of course," Derek said, because it was the one point on which they still agreed. "We're coming up to the critical moment. That's why I'm trying to warn people."

Author's Note

The reporting in this book comes mostly from my interviews with Derek and dozens of others involved in his transformation out of white nationalism. I spent hundreds of hours with Derek in the last few years, and this project was made so much better thanks to his full cooperation. He made it clear from the very beginning that his interest was in sharing an honest story, even if that often meant discussing parts of his life that he considered ugly or painful. More than giving generously of his time, Derek also helped excavate parts of his own past. He offered reading suggestions that improved my understanding of the white nationalist movement and suggested historians for me to interview. He shared hundreds of his private emails and online chats, many of which helped illuminate his transformation. Excerpts from Derek's private conversations are quoted in the book with his permission. In some cases, those excerpts are lightly edited for concision and for clarity.

Derek also made introductions on my behalf to some of his friends and family members, none of whom were more essential to this book than Allison. She not only shared her own story during our conversations but also patiently helped me to better understand concepts about racial science, psychology, and civil justice. When she didn't have the answers, she guided me to people and places that did. Like Derek, she shared her emails and chats and gave me permission to publish them. In both the writing of this book and during our time together, I relied on her empathy and her insight.

I spoke with more than fifty of Derek's former classmates and professors at New College, sometimes interviewing people over the phone and other times meeting with them in person. Some of those sources never appear in the book, but their recollections helped me better understand the politics of New College and Derek's life there. Collectively, New College alumni helped provide me with several essential documents, including copies of forum emails, photographs, student thesis papers, and notes from planning meetings before the New College student shutdown. I am particularly indebted to Matthew Stevenson, Moshe Ash, Juan Elias, James Birmingham, Destiny Lyals, Julie Gornik, Michael Stevenson, Bárbara Suárez Galeano, Blair Sapp, Bennet Bastian, Maynard Hiss, Mike Long, Sivens Glaude, Tom McKay, Kathleen McQueeney, Kotu Bajaj, Patrick Tonissen, Susan Marks, Felix Acuña, Glenn Cuomo, Dorothea Trotter, Jim Dickey, and Daniela Rizzo.

Don Black spent dozens of hours talking to me about Derek and about his own life within white nationalism. I made three trips to interview Don in Florida, and each time he freed up his schedule to sit with me for recorded conversations that regularly lasted most of the day. He was open and candid, and he mined his own archives to provide me with book recommendations and historical notes about white nationalism. When Derek traveled to Florida to see his family shortly after Donald Trump's election, Don and Derek let me tag along for the visit. I took notes and sometimes recorded their conversations with each other, one of which appears as direct dialogue in the final scene of the book.

My research into white nationalism included spending time with Richard Spencer in Virginia and speaking with David Duke and Sam Dickson. Duke's podcasts, radio shows, and autobiographies provided useful background about his life, as did Michael Zatarain's biography, **David Duke: Evolution of a Klansman.** Many other books anchored me in the history of white supremacy, but I particularly relied on **Dark Soul of the South,** by Mel Ayton; **Terror in the Night,** by Jack Nelson; **Bayou of Pigs,** by Stewart Bell; and the expertly researched **Blood and Politics,** by Leonard Zeskind.

I am grateful to **The New York Times** and **The Washington Post** for their daily coverage of the 2016 presidential election, which helped inform my framing of the current political moment. I also relied heavily on the Southern Poverty Law Center and on the archives of Stormfront. My greatest historical resource in reporting this book was Derek's own radio show, which is at least partially archived from 2009 to 2012 in various places online. Rather than simply relying on Don's and Derek's memories of his time as a leading white nationalist, I could listen to their radio show and track his transformation in real time.

The Washington Post supported and nurtured this project, as it has done with every aspect of my journalistic career. I am proud to work there. Thanks to Marty Baron, Scott Wilson, Cameron Barr, and especially David Finkel, a tremendous friend and editor. I also benefited from the close reading of Rachel Saslow, Craig Saslow, Alec Saslow, Chico Harlan, Paul Kix, Adam Kilgore, Louis Goldstein, Taylor Clark, Ellen Barry, and my parents, among many others.

Esther Newberg and Ron Bernstein at ICM encouraged me to pursue this project, and then Esther made it possible. Bill Thomas at Doubleday helped clarify my initial vision for the book and elevated the first draft with a tremendous edit. I am grateful to the entire team at Doubleday for their expertise and support, including Margo Shickmanter, Dan Novack, Michael Goldsmith, Ingrid Sterner, and many others.

Thanks to Reed College for the quiet place to write; to Soup Spoon for the nourishment; to Bloom for the coffee; and to Rachel for just about everything else.

ABOUT THE AUTHOR

Eli Saslow is a **Washington Post** staff writer and author of **Ten Letters: The Stories Americans Tell Their President.** He won the Pulitzer Prize for Explanatory Reporting in 2014 for a series of stories on food stamp recipients. He was a Pulitzer Prize finalist for Feature Writing in 2013, 2016, and 2017. He is the winner of the James Beard Award for Food Writing, the George Polk Award, and the PEN Center USA Award, among others. He lives in Portland, Oregon, with his wife and three children.